Headquarters for MGM Offices at Worthing,
West Sussex © Wells-Thorpe and Suppel

BEHIND THE FAÇADE

An Architect at Large

John Wells-Thorpe

Book Guild Publishing

Sussex, England

First published in Great Britain in 2009 by
The Book Guild Ltd
Pavilion View
19 New Road
Brighton, BN1 1UF

Typeset in Garamond by Ellipsis Books Limited, Glasgow

Printed in Great Britain by
Athenaeum Press Ltd, Gateshead

A catalogue record for this book is available from The British Library.

ISBN 978 1 84624 375 2

For Meta,
without whose encouragement — and persistence —
this book would not have been written

Contents

Acknowledgements

I would like to thank Kerrith Etkin Bell for invaluable help in giving coherent form to my writing; Carol Biss, Joanna Bentley and Janet Wrench at Book Guild Publishing for their unfailing helpful and informed advice; Mandy Woods, whose incisive role as copy editor brought clarity and accuracy to my script and finally Celia Morley who spent what must have seemed like years faithfully turning my manuscript into readable form.

I wish also to acknowledge the authorship of photographs by David Bennett, Duncan McNeill, Buckland House Photography and the *Daily Telegraph*.

Author's Note

The narrative of *Behind the Façade* spans the period from the end of World War II until the deep recession of the early 1990s.

Chapter 1

In the Beginning

If my father hadn't committed suicide I might not have become an architect. A few months after the tragedy in 1944 my mother, already tubercular but trying not to show it, found herself having to be two parents at once and was struggling with things that previously had been left to my father. Meeting my headmaster was one of them. This was to discuss my discontinuing Latin, to everyone's relief, and taking another subject in its place.

My parents had met when my father, recently repatriated from the trenches on the Somme where he had been seriously wounded, was recuperating in a requisitioned Regency house in Chichester Terrace, Brighton. He very slowly recovered, although in one sense he was never to recover. He was visited by a pretty, shy local girl who, with others, had volunteered to distribute library books, serve teas and undertake local shopping. Her home life had been harsh and at an early age she had learned to stand firmly on her own two feet. She was to become my mother. Aware of being very pretty, she was nonetheless quite unprepared for the banter of a room full of commissioned officers whose sense of relief at being 'out of it' produced the nervous cheekiness that greeted any female visitor. My father was the quiet one and, although he had a Micawberish outlook on life and readily smiled, he didn't feel comfortable with the barrack-room humour when aimed at the fairer sex. His Haileybury housemaster would not have approved either.

Having been waylaid by the more colourful occupants in the convalescent ward when she first arrived, it was only later, in an attempt to be fair to everyone, that she tried to speak to all the men and began visiting my father. He was quiet, with a boyish innocence, irrepressible optimism and sense of fun, and it would take her many years to discover that the light-hearted façade masked huge insecurity and self-doubt.

I was equally shy and, years later, when I realised I wasn't going to make

1

a Classical scholar, it took me some time to decide to tell my mother. Obviously, with my father only recently having committed suicide, it was the worst possible time to ask her to do anything while she struggled to restore some semblance of normality at home. But if I hadn't acted when I did, the school timetable wouldn't offer another opportunity for a further twelve months. Choosing a quiet moment, I asked her to intercede with my headmaster and, surprisingly, she agreed at once – probably because it was a relief to think of something else, but also because she welcomed the prospect of doing something for me, after shapeless days and nights when she seemed to find it necessary to apologise for what had happened to us and repeatedly asked if I was 'all right'. She had knitted me a pullover I really didn't need and made treacle puddings and jam tarts because she knew they were my favourites. She also let me buy a kitten and a pet rabbit, probably knowing full well that she would end up looking after them.

'John would like to do extra art instead,' she explained.

'But why art if he is already very good at it?' came the headmasterly response.

'It's because he's good at it that he wants to become even better.'

'But you must understand that any new arrangement like this is intended to give more time to a *weaker* subject,' he replied gravely.

I'm not sure why I was included in the meeting. No one spoke to me or even looked at me, my mother concentrating on saying the right thing and the headmaster considering any reference to me entirely superfluous. I was seated in a very large stick-back chair and felt overawed by the setting. The air was thick with the smoke of pipe tobacco and on the walls were row upon row of sepia photographs of First XI cricket teams going back before the Great War. And there in the dark corner was the umbrella stand containing a selection of canes, which could only be used by the headmaster, and one of which I recognised from my last visit. Then, all too suddenly, I realised the chair I was sitting on was the one you had to bend over before the chastisement commenced. My palms became sticky and I tried to think of something else – outside perhaps – like guessing the number of the bus that was pulling away from the stop and which way it was going. When that didn't work, I tried something which demanded more concentration – the study windows, divided into panes, had been protected with sticky tape in a cruciform pattern to prevent splintering from any bomb blast; after all, we had an anti-aircraft battery entrenched on the school playing field which could well have attracted the attention of the Luftwaffe. I began a mental game of noughts and crosses with adjacent window panes and thought it might be a good augury if I won.

My mother was sitting there in her Sunday best and, in the end, attempted a small smile. I'd never seen her having to do this sort of thing before and wondered whether she could handle it and get the point across with conviction. My headmaster shifted nervously in his chair, relighting his pipe for the third time as he mused on how to strike a balance between the requirements of academic organisation and pastoral support. Gauging the difficulty of the situation, and presumably having heard something of my family's predicament, he finally conceded to her irrational request and ushered us out politely to get on with something he felt more comfortable with. So 'extra art' it was to be, but I felt far too bemused by the whole episode to think where this might lead.

Organisationally, this new arrangement was something of a nuisance for the school and the only way to fit me in was for me to work in a small art-materials store next to the studio, with sporadic attention from a teaching assistant called Miss Wilde. She was very plump and had a mop of uncontrollable hair. She didn't really know what to do with me and no one had given her any guidance. After a while I realised that the extra tuition was going nowhere, so I went to the library and borrowed a book on modern Finnish architecture, and started redesigning our school with its existing ground plan, but looking elevationally as much like Helsinki railway terminal as I could make it. Any book on architecture would have been a revelation, and I had no idea whether the selected volume was the appropriate one to start with or whether the influences of Finland were any more relevant than those of America or China. I felt the first thrill of foreign place names and gazed at the sometimes avuncular, sometimes wildly romantic photographs of foreign architects with glamorous names like Alvar Aalto and Eero Saarinen. No one seemed to mind what I did as long as I kept quiet, and this was all right by me as long as Miss Wilde, who smelled strongly of sweat and turpentine, kept out of my little room as much as possible.

One of the additional thrills of wartime school life sprang from the way in which the war kept intruding in the most unexpected manner. Gas masks would be inspected, air-raid shelters dug, and after the school boarding house had been requisitioned by the Royal Artillery, we shared the playground with a fleet of camouflaged trucks driven by female personnel upon whom sixth formers would practise their pimply charms, although I was too young to really catch on what was happening.

Once my new-found independence began to pall, it was to my delight that one day Miss Wilde burst in – she seemed to burst everywhere, I decided – and announced that I had to drop what I was doing and by lunchtime the next day handpaint an emergency sign that the Auxiliary Fire Service had ordered the school to display outside the building.

On a white background had to be written in red block capitals: FIRE HYDRANT 4'6". A crash course on lettering followed and Miss Wilde felt it her duty to explain how Gill Sans was the font to be used and how the great Eric Gill lived nearby in Ditchling and how privileged I was to be permitted to use his typeface in response to a national emergency. I rather blankly accepted her word for it, knowing only that a gill was the mechanism through which a fish breathed, but I had been given my first design commission; a light had been switched on.

The extra art appeared to work because, upon leaving school, I was offered a place in the architectural department of the local art school. The Municipal School of Art, demolished long ago, at that time stood on a prominent corner in Grand Parade, Brighton. It comprised a soot-stained, brick edifice relieved by three terracotta panels beneath the classical eaves depicting improving scenes from classical mythology. More encouragingly, the school was enlivened by a galaxy of pretty, middle-class girls determined to look bohemian and shock their suburban mothers. The Department of Architecture was run by a prematurely aged Claude Miller, who had yellowing grey hair, bulbous eyes and a pendulous lower lip like a stranded cod. He wore a shiny three-piece suit to distinguish himself from his subordinates and a thick flannel shirt, summer or winter, on which was attached a shiny starched collar for a small knotted tie.

Being overweight, he seldom moved around the studio, but when he did he noisily fondled his key chain with one hand and carried a cracked tea mug with the other. His singular accomplishment was lecturing from the epidiascope, a heavy metal and brass contraption which projected a book illustration onto a screen, but was more associated with displaying lantern slides of scenes recorded by Victorian explorers and botanists. The machine usually overheated five minutes into his delivery and brought out beads of sweat on his pink forehead. His passion was the Golden Age of the French Renaissance and, if he had had his way, we would have been subjected to an Ecole des Beaux Arts curriculum of a hundred years ago. As newly arrived first-year students, we had encountered nothing like this before and accepted every word he uttered, simply because we had no one to compare him with.

Into this quaint setting were introduced six American GIs. The war had just ended and half a million combatants were waiting their turn to be transported home in the remaining mercantile fleet that hadn't been sunk by U-boats. They would be stuck in Britain for months on end, so a government scheme was hastily devised to permit interested participants to register at whatever local centre of higher education they could find.

Proud of the recently-coined epithet 'Overpaid, oversexed and over here' and fresh from combat, the Americans were even more perplexed than we were by their new environment in general, and by Claude Miller ('the Prof', as he was inevitably called) in particular. They blinked in disbelief as he introduced them to architrave, frieze and cornice and made them memorise the distinguishing characteristics of the Doric, Ionic and Corinthian orders. Their breast pockets bulged with Sweet Caporal cigarettes and they competed in winning favours from the girls who permitted themselves to be bohemian beyond their own imagining in exchange for a pair of real silk stockings.

We boys were transfixed by all that was going on around us and, coming straight from an old-fashioned grammar school, assumed that this was the norm, as presumably did the GIs, regarding Brighton as a bit of the 'old country' to tell Mom and Pop about. Claude seemed oblivious to the various needs and expectations of his eclectic charges and went on and on about the Sun King's patronage and the sublime proportions of Le Petit Trianon at Versailles, unaware that a battle-scarred stockman's son from Illinois and a fresh-faced youth still in a school blazer were probably approaching life from very different directions.

Another unexpected arrival to our year was Pilot Officer Zbigniew Adam Suppel, recently discharged from the Polish Air Force, some of whose personnel were stationed in a rundown requisitioned hotel facing Brighton's West Pier. Unnecessarily good-looking, technically astute, and speaking remarkable English with a matinee idol's accent, he soon became a new centre of attention although, to his everlasting credit, he never seemed aware of it. He was good – very good – and I was pleased when I was paired with him to measure and draw the Saxon church at Poynings, to improve our draughtsmanship and develop dimensional awareness. Having never done this before, let alone with a Polish fighter ace, I thought the best way to begin was to buy a copy of the church guide and work from the small plan drawn on the back. A pre-war, low-budget publication had survived in faded form, and we found one of these at the back of the church under an old hassock.

Quietly, each of us read the text, some of it containing technical terms of abstruse archaeological origin, and after a few minutes I paused to ask if there was any English word he didn't understand – after all, his new language had been picked up through fuzzy intercom messages transmitted between an operations commander and his individual Spitfire, but he smiled and explained that the only one he didn't fully understand was 'facsimile'. We then spent a long day equipped with a five-foot rod, a pencil and endless sheets of cheap paper to try and record the building – which didn't appear to have any right angles in it at all – with sufficient accuracy to withstand the scrutiny of our tutor. Our record had to comprise plan, external eleva-tions, a cross-section and its longitudinal counterpart. We had received no lessons in how to go about this, such as deciding who measured what, who recorded the results and how to gain access to the higher parts of the nave without a ladder. A 100-foot tape measure would have helped, but as there was only one to go round the entire year's intake, we had to measure every-thing in increments of five feet. Adam, as he asked to be called (Zbigniew was unpronounceable), had, I learned, been accustomed to making rapid calculations concerning fuel capacity and flying distances for his Spitfire and, by comparison, dimensional coordination within a very static Saxon church was a piece of cake. I was fascinated to be learning alongside someone so quietly pragmatic and confident, completely unaware that decades later I would invite him into partnership with the same admiration.

Sketching outdoors was actively encouraged, and in a town as rich in archi-tectural history as Brighton, I didn't have far to walk to find an attractive subject. One day it would be a delicately proportioned stucco-coated vicarage; on another, part of a grander terrace – I would often choose one of the most impressive and unique in the town, Royal Crescent. It comprises a grand sweep of houses directly facing the sea and is clad in black mathematical tile, a material found in various parts of Sussex and which distinguishes itself immediately from the main body of cream-coloured Regency squares and terraces elsewhere in the town. Royal Crescent was shortly to become the home of a generation of theatrical luminaries, including Sir Laurence Olivier and Joan Plowright and, nearby, Sir John Clements and Kay Hammond.

One of the stranger rituals a first-year student had to learn was how to 'stretch a sheet'. Everything in the design studio had to be drawn and coloured on watercolour paper so that it could receive layers of wash to portray the building materials accurately, as well as the sun's shadows cast by the model-ling of a façade. If you merely pinned down the paper it cockled the moment you applied a wash, so the paper had to be tautened or stretched first. Thus armed with my imperial drawing board (all drawing paper sizes had quaint names like Half Imperial, Royal, Imperial, Double Elephant and Antiquarian), paper, a sponge and role of sticky tape, I went down to the basement and queued for my turn at a cold-water tap that was normally used for the janitor's cleaning duties. The drawing board was moistened, then both sides of the paper wetted and stuck down round the edges with tape. It then had to be carried away to dry overnight, and if you left it too near a radiator because you wanted it quickly, it would often split with a loud crack and a precious half crown's worth of material would go out of the window, as you had to start all over again. Chapped hands around the cold tap in midwinter were made worse for me by my having to cycle five miles with the drawing board strapped to my back with lengths of ex-army webbing, as I couldn't afford a separate board to keep at home to continue my work on a project there in the evenings or at weekends. Propelled through the town by a following wind, I was Icarus in a cold climate.

Chapter 2

On His Majesty's Service

Two days after my eighteenth birthday in 1946, I retrieved a brown envelope from the doormat marked OHMS. I had been expecting it as it contained the formal notice of military conscription, together with a rail warrant from Brighton to Chichester. The letter explained that I would be met by a military truck at the station and taken to Chichester barracks, where I would be issued with wrapping paper and string to send home everything I stood up in, once I had been given a set of army fatigues to see me through my preliminary training.

In the train compartment I met another conscript, who introduced himself as Solly Moses and explained how pleased he was to be released from borstal prematurely in order to undertake military service. Neither of us had met anyone remotely like one another before and we quickly became absorbed in each other's backgrounds, so the journey soon passed, although it was dark and cold all the way.

The barracks were the headquarters of the Royal Sussex regiment, an infantry unit, and they had been enlarged to house a Primary Training Centre where for six weeks, rising to a bugle each morning at 6.30 a.m., we were to move everywhere at the double on pain of punishment. This regime was only relaxed on Sundays, when we could enjoy walking to our meals, the latrines or the barrack square.

I became 19112582 Private Wells-Thorpe, J., and would be known by my 'last three' – 582 – throughout my stay. Foot drill, cleaning, arms drill, rifle proficiency, grenade throwing and bayonet practice – the last involving running, screaming at and disembowelling straw sacks in the shape of enemy infantrymen – occupied our days, whilst our evenings were spent polishing boots and brass buttons, cleaning rifles, blancoing webbing and pressing our uniforms with a flat iron heated on a coke stove. In spare moments I stencilled my army number on each piece of equipment, even my boot brush. Once a week we were marched to the bathhouse and told to strip off and, supervised by a corporal, scrubbed ourselves red with carbolic. The physical regime also included soaking our feet in a tub of alum to harden the skin and prepare our feet for wearing ammunition boots for the foreseeable future. Rather more reluctantly, we were obliged to consume large quantities of tea from a galvanised vat that had been liberally laced with bromide 'to decrease the urges'.

None of this, harsh though it was, particularly affected us, probably because it was all so novel and happened at such speed and, in any case, we knew we were all in it together. Probably, without knowing it, we were experiencing camaraderie for the first time. On one pound five shillings a week, of which five shillings was sent home to my mother and another sixpence deducted for some impenetrable reason, I soon learnt to budget. Out of the remaining nineteen shillings and six pence I had to buy boot polish, blanco, brass polish, soap and toothpaste. I spent the entire balance on bread pudding in the canteen. No one was allowed beyond the barrack walls for the whole six weeks and therefore inability to pay for the cinema (standing) or half a pint wasn't a problem.

Part of the induction in the first week involved meeting our platoon sergeant, whose job it was to knock us into shape. Once we were all assembled in a large unheated annexe in Savannah block – all blocks were named after historic regimental battle honours – he began.

'All of you, yes, you with the fat mug at the back as well, *look* at me. Look slow and 'ard because you are going to remember me for a very long time. You will do everything I want you to, because if you don't you'll wish you'd never been born. You're a pile of shit and it's my miserable job to turn you lot into soldiers, God 'elp me – so take a long, 'ard look.'

'He means it,' I muttered to Solly.

'Like 'ell he does' he replied.

Solly Moses was a kleptomaniac, and as this made itself clear within twenty-four hours, we all knew where we were. As luck would have it, his bed was next to mine and whenever anything was missing from my locker I soon learned to open his and retrieve it. He would quickly dispel my anger by owning up immediately with a wide grin and 'OK mate, no 'ard feelings?' Didn't Fagin also teach his young thieves to smile?

He had had a dreadful childhood and the entire platoon was sad to see him eventually placed under arrest for some more serious misdemeanour and locked up in the guardhouse. It didn't end there – we heard later that he had reoffended and been sent on to the Glasshouse, a tough military prison where he spent the remainder of his time before a dishonourable discharge. We missed him.

My keenest sense of loss didn't arise from homesickness or absent friends, but rather from the realisation that my newly found architectural life had been snatched from me and was going to be withheld indefinitely. Just as I was experiencing the exhilaration of an endlessly wonderful new world, some unseen and all-powerful agency had put a stop to it. As we toughened up, I was very concerned that the sensitivity in my hand necessary to draw finely would be extinguished by some mishap with explosives, so I made myself draw something, anything, for a few minutes every day between potato peeling in the cookhouse and polishing my equipment for next morning's kit inspection. Chichester Cathedral could be seen clearly over the barrack walls and, as the watery sun set, it briefly illuminated the open Gothic arches of the tower just below the spire, and for some reason I found this beautiful sight very upsetting.

All the same, there was always laughter, both nervous and raucous. Following the first heavy snowfall and after lights-out in the barrack room, we competed by peeing our initials into the snow from the first-floor windows, with the most legible winning a small bar of black chocolate which had been issued earlier as part of our emergency survival ration. My calligraphy was good, but I had too many initials and found it impossible to stop and start to get the hyphen of my surname right, so the chocolate went elsewhere.

Having learnt to shoot, bayonet, blow people up, and never have fewer than thirteen studs on each boot, we were then tested for our next posting. For me the Royal Engineers was a natural home, in so far as anything in these surreal circumstances could be regarded as natural. I was therefore mystified to be told I would be posted to the Royal Artillery at Barnard Castle and upon asking why was told, 'Engineers is full up this week son.' The slender reconnection with architecture that the Royal Engineers could have provided was once again severed.

Having been intensively trained as a 'Tech Ack' (technical assistant) on 25-pounder field guns, I was given an overseas posting to South East Asia Command and in the summer of 1947 found myself en route for Singapore.

At 5 a.m. in early-winter drizzle, muffled in greatcoats against the cold, we lined the rail of the troopship *Worcestershire* and watched the blitzed remnants of Liverpool's Albert Dock slide slowly past. Nobody knew anyone else and the only thing we had in common was that we had all been posted to the Far East from various regiments. Infantry, members of the armoured corps, engineers, gunners, signallers and others rubbed shoulders with each other. We were to spend the next twenty-nine days in very close quarters at sea being transported to a world we only knew from a school atlas.

11

A sallow-faced youth on my left, Private Coffin ('and just as beautifully polished,' he insisted through broken teeth) pulled a mouth organ from his greatcoat pocket to cheer us up, he said, but managed to sink us into even deeper gloom by playing 'There's No Place Like Home'. If only he had played it badly we could have managed, but he played it quite beautifully and it was more than most of us could bear.

None of us had been to sea before, and my group had been allocated a troop deck three levels down, near the waterline, where we were issued with hammocks and told that this was where we would eat, sleep, and spend most of the day other than for short periods when we were allowed on deck for exercise. We crossed the Bay of Biscay, notorious for rough seas even in ideal cruise conditions, where living and sleeping with the smell of yesterday's soused herrings and everybody's feet made me realise how easy it is to feel seasick.

I worked in the kitchen and was allowed access to whatever I found to satisfy my appetite in between timetabled meals, and on one occasion I tucked into some raw carrots washed down with strong cocoa in an enamel mug. This was enough to upset me immediately and, running down the companionway to get to the ship's side in time, I jumped over a bulkhead and split my forehead on the steel door casing above. It hit me for the first time that this was not going to be a particularly enjoyable trip – and it wasn't, until we entered the Mediterranean.

Visiting there had only ever been a dream for us. Once we entered the Strait of Gibraltar the sea became calm, porpoises appeared and the sun began to feel warm. This vivid first impression reminded me of E. V. Rieu's description of the 'wine-dark sea' in his translation of the *Odyssey*. It was indeed a deep, dark blue I had never seen and only half imagined in books devoted to winters of content from a more leisurely age. I quickly forgot Biscay.

The journey proceeded at a pace that would be regarded as leisurely were it not for the fact that we were aboard a troopship with, presumably, a mission and a strategic destination. Passing through the Suez Canal Zone at a snail's pace, we stopped from time to time to take on water and provisions. Any military personnel stationed in the Middle East wore khaki drill uniform and regarded their base as an 'overseas' posting, with all the supposed glamour that that entailed. This was enough to spark heated if good-natured exchanges between those on the canal banks, who appeared to be only a few yards away, and those of us on deck, whose destination was twice as far away from home in the Far East and who could be recognised instantly in their olive green drill uniforms designed for jungle combat. Our appearance conferred upon us a huge and entirely unwarranted sense of superiority over those lining the canal.

'Get some service in,' yelled one of our South Wales Borderers to a gnarled-looking corporal on the bank. An indignant pause followed, and then the ultimate put-down: 'Service in? I've been 'ere since the Dead Sea first reported sick, sonny, so piss off and feed the monkeys.'

Port Said, Port Suez, Port Sudan, Massawa and Berbera passed slowly, with increasing heat and humidity, and, finally clear of the Red Sea, it was a great relief to pass Socotra and be heading east across the Indian Ocean to Colombo, where we disembarked for a few weeks before boarding another troop ship for Singapore. Ceylon was hot but not humid and I was introduced to an island that was, in the following half-century to descend into economic chaos and a brutal civil war, made all the sadder because its people, its climate and its sheer beauty should have made it one of the loveliest places on earth. I could never have guessed that, forty years on, I would invite its Prime Minister Ranasinghe Premadasa to give a keynote speech at a Commonwealth Conference I was organising in Britain, or that, within a few years after then becoming president, he would be assassinated by a Tamil Tiger suicide bomber.

Crossing the Bay of Bengal, now aboard SS *Navasa*, we were endlessly diverted by flying fish, sea turtles and, at night the phosphorescence that illuminated the bow of the ship as it ploughed its way towards the Strait of Malacca destined for Singapore, just eighty miles north of the equator where we arrived late at night. Pulau Blakang Mati was a small island, about two miles long and half a mile wide that sat a quarter of an hour's sampan ride from Singapore island itself and formed part of a sprawling archipelago that stretched as far as the eye could see. This was to be my home for the foreseeable future, having been posted to the 1st Malay Coast Battery, Royal Artillery as one of a small group of British personnel attached to a unit comprising Malays and Eurasians.

In a sense, the schoolboy venture just continued. I was still only eighteen and assumed that the life that was unfolding would go on being as full of surprises as it had been hitherto. Everything and everyone was novel: the smell of rotting vegetation, the sounds of the jungle, the sight of my young charges in sarongs – I had been put in charge of a squad of young artillery men – the feel of predatory insects on your skin and the taste of curry and fried rice. The sensory transition was complete and I had entered another world and did not find it wanting.

All my waking hours were spent trying to come to terms with a gun-drill manual for a 3.7-inch anti-aircraft gun and then, with the help of a Malay interpreter, explain to these eager brown faces how to bring the gun into action. Staying one page of the manual ahead of the training programme meant reading it up at night by the light of a kerosene lamp while enveloped in a mosquito net to exclude nocturnal invaders attracted by the light. Windows had no glazing but only metal security bars sufficient to exclude the colony of orang-utans, and therefore useless for keeping out praying mantises, furry spiders and mosquitoes.

Only when I got half a dozen pages ahead of the game did I pause to look around me and, apart from the concrete barracks, gun emplacements and fortifications that had proved so useless in repelling the Japanese in 1942, all other structures were erected by the indigenous population from natural materials obtained direct from the jungle.

In England, I was accustomed to brick upon brick and tile upon tile, all obtained by a construction company from a reliable builders' merchant down the road. But here self-help was not just an economic necessity, but also the traditional way of building which had stood the test of time and was fully understood by the head of every family for whom provision of shelter was necessary. I understood what all this meant, but felt that a couple of years as a Boy Scout learning to light fires without matches and cook 'twists' over their burning embers had done nothing to prepare me for entering a world where house building was accomplished without the benefit of an architect, construction company, estate agent or planning authority.

My fascination was increased by realising that the indigenous building form was ideally suited to the climate and Malay culture, and that more recent attempts at 'improving' the techniques by adopting western building practices were often doomed to failure.

I discovered that the traditional Malay house was a timber dwelling raised on stilts. Its framework and fittings were formed from local hardwood or bamboo and its roof was thatched with *attap,* – layered strips of thin palm leaf tied to bamboo lathes and fixed to the roof. In a constant, year-round climate of 30°C and an annual rainfall of about 250 centimetres, the forest vegetation grew in abundance and natural materials used for construction soon replenished themselves. The houses were without glazing, natural cross ventilation was easily obtained and the generous eaves overhang shielded the occupants from the sun's glare and threw the abundant rainwater clear of the house. By being raised on stilts, the dwelling was clear of snakes and other predators and the risk of floodwater from adjacent mangrove swamps was minimised. I noticed that the undercroft so formed was also a good place to keep chickens, old bikes and accumulated junk.

Houses were built in small groups in jungle clearings known as *kampongs,* but always with sufficient trees retained to give shade and coolness. The compound so formed was well kept and planted with coconut and banana, as well as guava, papaya and pineapple. There was no vehicular traffic and all the children played together spontaneously. In addition, the human scale was beautifully preserved by the simple expedient of basing linear measurements on dimensions of the human body; thus, the length of the forearm (*hasta*), the length of the outstretched palm (*jengkal*), and the length of the arms outstretched (*depa*) were all used as measurements.

Apparently the needs of the climate and culture were perfectly met without an architect or anthropologist in sight. This was a revelation, spoilt only by awareness of the increasing perversity of a colonial power which encouraged the traditional house builders to replace the *attap* with a zinc roof to reduce maintenance, and in the process make the house unbearably hot during the day, very cold at night and intolerably noisy when it rained.

In years to come I was to see and personally experience the very necessary reappraisal of traditional building techniques in the developing world when one or two western thinkers from an otherwise patronising developed world drew attention to the constructional wonders of *adobe* (sun-baked clay) in Mali, giant reed houses in the lower Tigris, goatskin tents in the Arabian desert, or log cabins in the frozen north. We were all to have our vision refocused by books such as *Architecture for the Poor* by Hassan Fathy and (rather more depressingly for me), *Architecture Without Architects* by Bernard Rudofsky.

Chapter 3

Singapore

Guard duty was both predictable and monotonous. It involved protecting the barracks and its installations from 6 p.m. at night until the following morning. The guard comprised three personnel and a guard commander, usually a lance bombardier. Based in the regimental guardroom, each member, armed with a heavy Lee-Enfield rifle, would spend two hours patrolling and four hours off during that period, overseen by a guard commander who was nominally responsible for the security of tens of thousands of pounds' worth of military equipment, including four 3.7-inch ack-ack guns. An orderly officer accompanied by a duty sergeant could make a surprise visit at any time of the night to ensure the guard was fully alert, but no one fully comprehended how a solitary eighteen-year-old patrolling outside and being bitten to death by mosquitoes and scared out of his mind by the alarming screeches and sounds of the surrounding jungle was going to prevent an armed posse of trained insurgents from taking anything they wanted. Fortunately it never happened . . . but if only they had known.

Before the guard was mounted, an inspection by the orderly officer took place on the barrack square to ensure 'you are a credit to your regiment' – not that that would have figured very highly in an intruder's list of priorities. A surprising feature of army life is that your clothes are laundered for you. In our case, this was done by a group of Indian *dhobi-wallahs*, the like of whom seemed to be installed in every part of the Empire garrisoned by the British Army. Their washing technique was to twist wet, soapy clothing and slap it noisily on an area of smooth stone adjacent to a natural stream. Whilst this cleaned it, it played havoc with metal buttons on uniform trousers, which quickly rusted through the attaching thread. This meant that we often received heavily starched and pressed drill trousers back with half the buttons missing.

17

It could have happened to any one of us, but one day, hurrying so as not to be late for parade, Nobby Clark climbed into his freshly pressed trousers and realised that two out of the four fly buttons were still somewhere on the laundry floor. As the missing ones were at the bottom, he could at least secure the trousers and cover the top with his webbing belt, trusting that the starched drill would hold everything else together. Guard mounting involved an inspection of rifles, and this was accompanied by the order 'Present arms', whereupon in three quick, synchronised movements the rifle was moved from the shoulder and held obliquely in front of the orderly officer for him to inspect the barrel. Rapid foot stamping, lifting the leg high and planting it with maximum force on the ground accompanied the last movement. This Nobby did well enough, but as he presented his rifle, out flopped his flaccid member for simultaneous inspection. The young orderly officer was completely flummoxed, and it was the well-seasoned sergeant who pretended not to notice until the officer had walked past and then hissed: 'Bring that thing on parade again Clark and you're dead!'

Twelve hours on guard is a long time to kill, and between 2 and 4 a.m. I found myself wondering whether I could build a simple structure based upon what I had seen in the *kampong*. We were not short of military buildings, so it was difficult to know what I could do usefully. I hit on the idea of providing a shelter for the troop of guns, and the next day suggested it to my second lieutenant. He didn't seem to care one way or the other, but fed the idea up the line and surprisingly quickly I received approval. The idea was to suspend tarpaulins over the parked guns to protect them from the worst of the monsoon, and that needed a light structure to support them. Unfortunately bamboo was not long enough, so eventually we used some metal scaffold poles retrieved from the shoreline where, a few years earlier, they had been used as a deterrent to enemy landing craft. I copied the configuration of the bamboo structures I had seen, added some wind bracing, and, aided by a sullen faced squad ordered to do this at the end of a sweltering day, managed to erect it. I had designed and erected my very first structure.

I temporarily glowed with satisfaction, but it took me, and fortunately all the others, a long time to realise that the strong winds blew rain horizontally *under* the tarpaulin at most times, and in Singapore's high humidity the guns' component parts would rust just as quickly whatever form of shelter was provided.

Singapore had a profoundly different climate to that of England in so many ways. Being so near the equator, it got dark at roughly the same time all the year round and, added to the fact that the temperature and humidity were also similar for twelve months at the time, the 'seasons' I was used to ceased to exist. This led to a certain monotony, and the months and years seemed to have little shape, so that guessing how long it might be before repatriation occurred was often disheartening.

There was, however, one big saving grace for anyone with eyes to see and a mind to wonder: cloud formations. For explicable meteorological reasons, tropical clouds have a clearly edged dramatic presence in the sky and come straight out of Renaissance figurative painting. Many a classical dome is adorned with celestial scenes showing resurrected saints lauded by angels, or heavenly female forms attended by mischievous cherubs, all appearing from behind cumulus of Wagnerian proportions. For the first time I witnessed this artifice brought to life and realised that no wonder English poets and French composers had been moved to create work from such compelling images and no wonder the conservative art world lost touch with Turner when he painted skies of unfathomable beauty and torment. And neither did it all stop there, because the clouds were still there at the dead of night, banked up ready for admiration when illuminated by sheet lightning, like some errant *son et lumière* that had fled a French chateau.

Although I was aware that the climate was hotter and more humid, I hadn't appreciated its effects, and experience was often hard won. Blakang Mati in general, and the 1st Malay Coast Battery in particular, were beginning to adapt to a peacetime regime, and hitherto unheard-of activities like 'recreation' were being spoken about openly. One of these was a rudimentary music club that I ran: 'Bach for Blacks', as my bone-headed battery sergeant major insisted on calling it. The arrangement was simple. Once a month I would hire a sampan to Singapore and borrow half a dozen 78 rpm records from the command record library. Until then I had no idea that such a unit existed. The records had probably been donated by the Red Cross and were in quite good condition, so I had to sign for them (with all the disciplinary overtones that that entailed) and carry them away carefully, ensuring they didn't get scratched in the truck or crossing the fast tidal race separating Blakang Mati from the mainland. On my return to barracks I put them on the edge of my small crowded table, leaving room for a drawing pad on which to print the invitation and programme. To do this properly I had to open the window shutters wide to see what I was doing. It all took longer than I thought and, after a while, I left for a drink in the canteen half a mile away, as the sun was particularly hot.

On my eventual return I was appalled to see that the sun had moved round the room while I was away and was now shining directly onto the records. Those parts of the discs overhanging the tabletop had slowly and irrevocably sagged in the heat and now hung dejectedly towards the floor. Even the obedient white dog on the 'His Master's Voice' label had faded. The whole scene spelled doom for me, for the concert and for the future of our little enterprise. I was aware that Salvador Dali's surrealist paintings had been inspired by Sigmund Freud's theories of the unconscious, and had always assumed that his well-known portrayal of a melting watch-face in a desert landscape fell safely into that category, and so would any other surrealist happening – but no, this was a very *conscious* moment, and I was responsible for it.

There was only one possible remedy, crude though it seemed. I just had to turn the records over with the bent side upwards and continue to expose them to the sun's rays until gravity had exercised its natural influence. For the experiment to work timing was vital, so I stood on the bed to hold the shutters through the security bars for just long enough, praying that the daily monsoon clouds would delay their appearance until the 'cooking' was complete. To my intense relief it worked, and I slammed the shutters closed and leapt across the room to place a couple of heavy gunnery manuals and a spare hand grenade on top of the records to keep them flat.

Extraordinarily, when played the following evening, they sounded just like any other old records that had survived the war and no one noticed a thing. Haydn's Symphony 96 in D (the Miracle) would, for me, for ever be associated with this surreal event and could not have been more aptly dedicated.

Much of pre-war Singapore had survived the Japanese invasion and the impressive neo-classical buildings surrounding the *padang* were a reminder of grander imperial times. Nearby was St Andrews' Cathedral, a competent essay in thinned-down Gothic Revival and the gathering place of the expatriate community on a Sunday. It was built with conviction and I was pleased to see it once more being used as it would have been in happier times before the invasion. Inside, apart from the overhead fans, it looked like any other prosperous shire church at home and was peopled with a freshly washed, energetic congregation eager for tennis and bridge at the club later in the day. It was difficult to reconcile the equatorial sounds and smells outside with the glories of European High Gothic inside, and although reassuring in one way, the reminder of England and a vulnerable, tubercular mother made me homesick.

It had never occurred to me that one of the effects of having an established church in England was to ensure that, wherever the Empire extended, the Anglican community would be represented. The flag and the Church went together, at best bringing healthcare, education and biblical enlightenment, but at worst asserting always that 'God is on our side'. In years to come I was to see Gothic Revival in Africa, the Caribbean, Pakistan and

20

Australasia, all executed to a rigid, and 'correct', liturgical plan with conspicuous provision for the laying-up of regimental colours whenever they were built in garrison towns. *Hymns Ancient and Modern*, the *Book of Common Prayer*, cassocks and surplices were all intended to convey reassurance, which they did convincingly, albeit trapped in a time warp.

On one occasion, I was sent by overnight steam train from Singapore to the capital, Kuala Lumpur where, upon arrival, I was greeted by an architectural confection strongly reminiscent of the Royal Pavilion at Brighton, but here masquerading as a railway station. I didn't know when it was built, but I mused on the thinking of the colonial architect who had clearly decided to give the locals something he thought would please them for a change; or was it just a post-Raj manifestation to reassure the colonial administrators transferred from the Indian Civil Service? Perhaps it didn't matter any more, because independence could not be far away.

On returning to my unit on Blakang Mati I soon became aware that, having to teach gun drill in English and have it translated, was becoming cumbersome, so I decided that I would try and learn Malay. I bought a book called *Bazaar Malay* which explained that it was the lingua franca of Europeans, Chinese and Indians, who together outnumbered the Malay population in the peninsula. It pointed out that among themselves the Malays speak a purer language called Raja Malay, but when conversing with other races, they drop easily into Bazaar Malay, so I seemed to be doing the right thing.

The compilers of phrase books are a strange breed, and in years to come I was to experience endless puzzlement over the phrases they offered. But, as this was my first attempt at translation, I accepted the book as being authoritative and, in any case, it was either that or nothing. Having mastered numbers, the days of the week, food and drink and the rudiments of health and sickness, I turned to the 'helpful exercises' printed in the last chapter.

Lesson One contained: 'Good morning, Hassan, come here. Good morning, Sir, are you well? Fine, Hassan, thank you. My wife is not well, she is not here. How is Miss Smith? Well. Where is Meriam? Meriam is well, she is over there. That news is good. Never mind, Hassan, I want to take away my baggage.'

The nuances of the social hierarchy assumed by this went clean over my head: as I was in an organisation with a clear chain of command it did not seem in the least strange that the master-and-servant relationship should prevail just as vividly in the civilian world.

The last lesson gave me rather more trouble, not so much in translation as in comprehension. It contained:

'Your hands, Miss, are pink. Chinese are light yellow, Malays dark brown.

21

They wear green skirts which are very beautiful. We use mosquito nets. At 5 o'clock I lost my temper and hit a Chinese. He is revengeful. I am afraid and worried, Sir. Red, Yellow and Green, Yellow is most beautiful. A motor car is faster than a bicycle and in a week's time I shall want to go again.'

Learning phrases like this seemed a difficult way of teaching good gunnery practice in battle conditions, so I rapidly abandoned my language lessons and relied once more on my interpreter, who guessed what had been going on the moment my instructions began owing more to Noël Coward than to a master gunner.

As Blakang Mati lay only half a mile offshore from Singapore and already possessed a military installation, the army tended to use it as a spare room and dump things there that either they hadn't got space for or which didn't conveniently fit into existing military planning. It was no surprise, therefore, to find two self-contained but peripheral units stationed on the island. The first was the Far East School of Religious Education, run by a tattooed chaplain with the rank of major who had seen active service in Burma. The officers' mess disapproved of his frequenting the lower ranks' canteen and mixing with off-duty troops, who didn't accept him either and felt uncomfortable with a senior officer in their midst when they were letting their hair down. Apparently he had persuaded the Chaplain General's office that pastoral activities in the Far East needed coordinating and this entailed the provision of a small establishment from which to work. He was allocated an old fortified emplacement on the top of Mount Serapong at the eastern end of the island, and arranged a number of recreational events for local personnel, as well as Sunday services.

The other unit to arrive was the Far East School of Hygiene, whose principal responsibility was anti-malarial operations. This involved training locally enlisted personnel how to squirt DDT into monsoon puddles and drains to inhibit the breeding of mosquitoes. Each operator carried on his back a Heath Robinson device comprising a metal canister of insecticide, the cap of which was fixed to a lavatory chain and wooden handle which was rhythmically pulled with one hand, while the other pointed the hose nozzle at still waters. Groups of bored, plodding Eurasians would set out across the island, chain-pulling morosely until they had emptied their canisters, after which no one would come anywhere near them because they stank for days afterwards. It could have been a task found in one of Dante's outer circles of Hell, but then the great Florentine didn't have access to DDT.

Both units shared a precious telephone line to the mainland and on one occasion, a Saturday evening, I was passing through the battery clerk's office when an epic signal arrived from HQ addressed to the 'Officer Commanding:

Far East School of Religious Hygiene' and demanding an immediate response. The duty bombardier asked for my advice. I was aware that on a Saturday night many of the lads would have been involved in unhygienic activities off the narrow streets of Singapore, whilst religious activities would not commence until eleven hundred hours the next morning, when the chaplain would arrive to distribute mouldy-smelling copies of *Hymns Ancient and Modern*. To my everlasting regret I couldn't think of an appropriate reply that wouldn't involve immediate dismissal, and I felt that I had let myself down by missing one of life's golden opportunities.

One still, leaden Sunday I had just rolled up my mosquito net when an orderly came in and told me that 78 Group was next for shipment home and demobilisation. *My* group! Although it was late September I hoped I might just be allowed back into the School of Architecture, although term had already started and the journey home was going to take at least four weeks. The news was hard to take in because, although the previous months had seen the departure of earlier groups, we never knew how long a gap there would be before the next one was called.

For some time I had been responsible for a troop of about twenty, all locally enlisted personnel from Singapore island, as well as my Malay-speaking interpreter. Upon hearing of my impending departure he arranged for a farewell supper in the *kampong* to be prepared by his wife, and even though this was to be given the night before embarkation I was happy to accept. It was a small party. It was a small house, in fact, with only primitive cooking facilities, but this didn't prevent Zadek's wife from preparing a mountainous rice dish full of local delicacies and tastefully flavoured with spices, some of which I'd never come across before. Australian gin at one shilling and nine pence a bottle was plentiful and had been poured into glass jugs, so that it looked like water. The evening was merry and everyone was entirely themselves, neither overdoing the leave-taking nor letting me feel that the long time together hadn't been worth it. After the last farewells, Zadek walked me through the small compound behind his living quarters and stopped me before the gate in front of a washing line where, in the dim light, I could just make out something festooned from it with wooden pegs.

'We thought you'd like to take this as a souvenir,' he said, and began unfastening the pegs.

'What is it?' I enquired.

'The python skin, of course.'

'Well, yes, how nice, but why a python skin?' I asked, totally mystified.

'Because you've just had it for supper,' came the matter-of-fact reply.

He carefully rolled it up in a page of the previous day's *Singapore Free Press* and secured it with string, assuring me that it would be a lasting reminder of our time together. Trying to question my palate retrospectively, I remembered the firm white meat, cod-like in texture, being served with the rice mountain, but hard as I tried, I couldn't recall a taste that was in any way repulsive; although I had to admit that if Zadek's invitation had included details of the menu, I might just have found my last-minute packing taking priority. I stuck the package in my kitbag and closed the top with a brass security ring and padlock and forgot about it, as I was unlikely to need any of its contents until my disembarkation four weeks hence.

I left Singapore with mixed feelings. Despite her chronic illness, my mother had always sent a weekly airmail letter, and after a while it became easier to read between the lines and realise the strain under which she had been living: her husband in an unmarked grave (such were the Church's strictures); her daughter in the Royal Navy, married and living elsewhere; and her son 8,000 miles away in Singapore. She was desperately short of money and the TB was getting worse. I had to get home. On the brighter side, the School of Architecture beckoned and the old enthusiasms were being rekindled. If only it could all be accomplished without a four-week, sick-making sea journey all over again.

My life at the time being so full of direct, tangible experiences meant that the subconscious never reached the surface, and I was quite oblivious of the effect that the last couple of years in Singapore had had on me, little thinking that fifty years later the itchy feet that first tingled on Blakang Mati would return.

The troopship pulled away from the quayside to the strains of a military band adventurously playing numbers from the musical *Oklahoma!*, and we were soon passing the northern end of Sumatra. We shortly changed course for Colombo and in the days crossing the Bay of Bengal the seas became very turbulent. The *Devonshire* pitched and corkscrewed much like her sister ship the *Worcestershire* had done on the way out and it was not long before the demob-happy contingent first went quiet, and then very quiet before we all secured a personal place at the ship's rail – and not facing the wind this time! The inevitable happened – and went on happening as we became unquestioning candidates for death. After five wearying days we docked in Colombo to take on more contingents and supplies before going further, and were given shore leave while the ship was hosed down.

One of the unexpected characteristics of prolonged seasickness is just how quickly one recovers in calmer waters. As we disembarked, we became aware of how empty we really were and decided to find somewhere to eat. A small group of us hailed four rickshaws and set off for the centre of town.

It was quite late and the roads were empty. The only sound was the flip-flop of the rickshaw-wallah's feet on the smooth asphalt. It was beautifully warm under a waxing moon and we felt our dented spirits reviving every step of the way. Finding the Peiping Chinese Restaurant, we discharged our driver, trooped in and fell on the grubby menu, faded with use and greasy hands, but wondrous to behold. We were quite ravenous and the ride had restored our long-forgotten appetites, so we ordered fried shark fin and chicken soup, followed by Fuyang hai crab with fried vegetable rice and egg noodles. They served us speedily and it didn't take long to devour. After we had finished our green tea, we found ourselves looking at each other and wondering what to do next.

'I'm still hungry,' I admitted finally.

There was a pause and then two others agreed, joined quickly by the rest.

'Shall we have some more?' one said.

'What about having it *all* again?' I suggested.

And so we did. With grave formality each of us stood up and moved one chair to the right with military precision, then sat down again and asked for the menu from a bemused and delighted proprietor. At the end, and barely able to stand, each of us signed a menu as a memento of a ridiculous occasion.

Back on board, we headed for Aden across the Arabian Sea and temperatures began to rise even further. This made life on the troop deck very unpleasant, and living, eating and sleeping on a deck well down in the hull with very few portholes challenged everyone's patience. Grumbling always passed the time, but all too often it petered out for want of something new to grumble about, until one day something really different focused our attention, not least because it was an entirely new phenomenon.

Smells in crowded troop decks emanate from various sources. There is always the usual mix of diesel, imperfect sanitation, sweaty feet and yesterday's soused mackerel, but this was a smell that was exotically different. Very soon anyone who wasn't a heavy smoker had enlisted in the hunt for the offending presence. After a confusing half hour and having complained the loudest, I was mortified to be told that the stink had been traced to my belongings which had been stowed in a metal rack above my hammock. Reluctantly I got them all down and began to unpack them piece by piece. Nearly overcome by the stench, I came across a greasy newspaper package and realised that the python had had the last word. Frogmarched to the ship's deck, I threw it overboard unceremoniously just off the coast of Socotra, recalling Zadek's last words that it would be a lasting reminder of our farewell supper.

Chapter 4

The Feeling that Anything is Possible

Mercifully, I had been reaccepted for the architecture course, even though I was six weeks late. Adam Suppel was two or three years ahead and was now teaching building construction while still studying in his last year. Things felt very different this time. I was no longer the callow schoolboy among ex-servicemen, but an ex-serviceman among callow schoolboys. Over half of the year's intake had been in the armed forces and had very different experiences to relate. Some had had very dull UK postings with very little happening to them, while others came back with stories that made your hair stand on end. I was probably somewhere in the middle.

It turned out to be a good intake and contained just the right mixture of rebels and idealists to give it colour. We believed that in post-war Britain we could perhaps make a difference and had a missionary zeal (if seldom as critical as it should have been) to promote, and often copy badly, the work of the great names in architecture filling the world stage: Le Corbusier, Mies van der Rohe and Frank Lloyd Wright. We argued fiercely and took sides – *organic* versus *inorganic* architecture; integrating with nature versus the machine aesthetic. It was the red corner against the blue corner, or Celtic versus Rangers. It didn't matter particularly which side you were on as long as you supported someone or something, and did so with passion. I became very interested in Frank Lloyd Wright, the most brilliant American of his time. Although born in 1869 he was still influential both in the United States and in Europe, and every building he designed had iconic significance.

We were taught to absorb and understand the work of great architects past and present by preparing measured drawings of their designs from published plans and photographs, or, better still, visiting the buildings and measuring them with a five-foot rod. We recorded their internal and external dimensions on sheets of graph paper and then transferred this to sheets of watercolour paper. Drawing was first done accurately in pencil and then gone over with waterproof Indian ink and, last of all, the entire set of plans, elevations and sections had watercolour washes applied to replicate specific building materials and included cast shadows to heighten the three-dimensional effect.

Frank Lloyd Wright believed that the local environment should determine a building's form, and I therefore selected the Robie House in Hyde Park, Chicago, built in 1909, which illustrated his design theory. He had for some years experimented with what was known as his Prairie style. In the flat heartland of America, he had evolved this style, characterised by sleek horizontal lines constructed with materials selected for their natural colours and textures. His interiors had a sense of spaciousness, flowing from one room to another, fifty years before open-plan designs were popularised in post-war Britain. Obviously I could not go to America to measure the house first hand, so I gathered together as much documentary evidence as I could – from textbooks, press articles and travel guides – to do the next best thing. I drew the house on a large Imperial sheet of paper and then painstakingly coloured the brickwork, stone, timber and surrounding foliage, adding cast shadows to emphasise the dramatic roof overhang and the rich modelling of the façades. It took me over three weeks and I therefore missed the handing-in date for marking and scored nil. Lesson Number One had been learnt, and there hadn't even been the compensation of *seeing* the Robie House.

Time just flew past. We were all anxious to catch up on the 'lost' years, and with boundless energy, very little money and an unstoppable appetite for life we worked and played hard with little regard for eating or sleeping. It was all thrilling, demanding and endlessly fascinating and I never wanted it to stop. Everything and everyone made an impression and the progress towards our first major exam was crammed with first-time experiences, technical, aesthetic and personal. I could have lived on air.

History of architecture lectures were enlivened by the occasional visits of a tutor who had served as a naval sub-lieutenant during the Second World War. Following the successful Allied landings on the Italian mainland at Salerno and Anzio, his destroyer had been dispatched to Greek waters where, after liberation, Athens had become the vessel's base.

Now demobilised and back in the UK, and once more teaching fine art and sporting an impressive mariner's beard, he relished speaking to architectural students because it gave him the opportunity of exhibiting his spoils of war. This he did with a sense of cheeky daring. In his student days he would have been the first to climb the nearby statue of Queen Victoria on college Rag Day and crown it with a chamber pot.

With well-rehearsed nonchalance he concluded one talk by describing how the Acropolis temples had been constructed, and identified the various marbles used in the process. To emphasise the veracity of his geological conclusions he plunged deep into his baggy jacket pocket and pulled out a piece of marble he had 'won' from the Temple of Nike Apteros, and immediately contrasted it with a large fragment taken from another pocket which he had apparently excised from the nearby Erechtheion. Carefully measuring our wonderment, he paused before revealing his pièce de résistance when, after a dramatic pause, he withdrew from his old service knapsack an even larger lump wrapped in old newspaper. He held it aloft for his goggle-eyed audience to admire. It was a piece of the Parthenon itself: no less than a fragment of Pentelic marble selected originally in 447 BC by architects Ictinus and Callicrates working with the sculptor Pheidias. In our tutor's more serious moments he probably rationalised his actions by maintaining that, over the centuries, invading Greeks and Turks had inflicted wholesale damage on the Acropolis and, much later, Lord Elgin had 'saved' portions of the frieze for presentation to the British Museum 'for the edification of all', so a few extra bits to show us were of no great moment. Having been nurtured on the adventure stories of Rider Haggard and John Buchan, I imagine he thought it was the obvious thing to do and, in any case, doubtless his initiative would be of equal interest to another post-Elgin generation.

Every year details of scholarships to travel and study abroad were published by the Royal Institute of British Architects, which I had joined as a probationer member after my first year. Such studentships were competed for nationally, and one of the most sought-after gave an opportunity for a total of five UK students to study at the British School at Rome in the late spring. With thirty-eight schools of architecture throughout the country, the odds of winning were pretty slim. Shortlisted candidates were selected from each school for further scrutiny and I was lucky enough to be one of them. Brimming with excitement, I found it hard not to share the news with my mother who had, once more, retired to her bed with tuberculosis in our near-empty house. I didn't want to raise her hopes unnecessarily, and the weeks spent waiting for the announcement of the winners seemed interminable. But it was worth it. I was selected to go, my co-contestants took the news gracefully and I hurried back to my mother's bedside with hot tinned chicken soup and the good news. She didn't say a great deal, but smiled a smile I hadn't seen for ages and said how pleased she was.

I arrived at Victoria Station one bright morning to collect instructions and tickets for the journey. I hadn't met any of the others before and I assumed that, as we had all been competing for a spell in the Eternal City, they were likely to be scholarly and would have done rather well in history of architecture. I would not have been surprised to see a copy of Banister Fletcher's *A History of Architecture on the Comparative Method* (12th edition) appear, because we had probably all spent the last three years poring over it and consigned to memory for exam purposes plan forms of the world's most significant buildings from 5000 BC Egyptian to the present day.

But no Banister Fletcher appeared, and by the time we had changed trains in Paris, emerged from the Mont Cenis Tunnel and had a few beers, the banter was not so much about the merits of the Circus Maximum as of coitus interruptus, even if such second-hand wisdom owed more to theory than to practice and had been largely culled from under-counter copies of *Men Only*, the raciest monthly we could afford between us.

We arrived at the British School in Rome, a relic of Grand Tour aspirations and a time when it was thought that without exposure to the Classical tradition, subsequent distinction in the profession would be impossible. It turned out that no one was expecting us. The place had the faded air of an institution that had rested too long on its laurels and whose loyal retainers had escaped permanently from the harsh realities of post-war Europe. They had found some slender justification, often on pitifully small stipends, to stay on endlessly for further study of some sort. As we were not staying for the full academic year, the Director found us a nuisance and quickly passed us on to his two associates so that he could continue unimpeded his archaeological excavations beneath St Peter's Basilica, which had been going on for years. His first acolyte had a thick Yorkshire accent and wore a ragged Fair Isle pullover on which was embroidered the Roman lighthouse at Ostia, and he claimed he could date any excavated Roman brick to within five years through his encyclopaedic knowledge of successful harvests and the resulting quality of the straw which had been used in the brick-making process. His other colleague, a lean and shadowy man who barely said a word, was apparently spending two years on a detailed study of the development of the egg-and-dart motif in Classical decoration. He seldom appeared and, in any case, we avoided him because he smelled.

In a haze of disbelief I reminded myself that I was really here – in Rome; but where to begin? There wasn't a moment to lose and the warmth of the sun was inviting. Ten years earlier I could have been introduced by some benevolent uncle to Hamleys toyshop in London and felt just the same. I was spoilt for choice and in danger of frittering away my prize through indecision.

Until recently I had given little thought to modern design in Italy, because anything worth seeing had been in Sweden or Switzerland, the two neutral countries who were alone in continuing to build between 1939 and 1948.

Their output was neat, clean, well mannered and rather boring because it lacked the creative spark and the big gesture, But in recent months international Italian companies such as Pirelli and Olivetti had commissioned top-class designers and architects who produced quite beautiful and sensuous work both in product design – cars, furniture, typewriters – and in architecture.

An elegant and bold design for a new railway station for Rome had just been published to critical acclaim from a profession starved for a decade of anything other than the utilitarian, and it was within walking distance on my first Monday morning in the city. The Stazione Termini on the Piazza dei Cinquecento was both sleek and monumental and imposed a very Roman authority on its setting without any of the heavy, Fascist overtones beloved of Mussolini's architects. It broke so much new ground, paving the way for design approaches which in later years we were to take for granted. It was generous in space, beautiful to use, quintessentially Italian and, out of respect to the antiquity of the site, incorporated a section of the ancient fourth-century BC Servian Wall, which was skilfully integrated into, and acted as a foil to, the refreshingly new design. The spirit of the baroque was still powerful in post-war Rome.

Competitions like that used to select the architects of the Stazione Termini were being held for major new projects in a effort to find a new voice worthy of the aspirations of post-war Italy and sometimes mindful of the epic events of recent conflict and suffering. In memory of a recent massacre of 335 Italian civilians by German troops during their retreat northwards, such a competition was held to find architects who understood the difference between metaphor and symbolism and were also capable of producing a memorial that was more than a beautifully proportioned building or piece of sculpture. It had to speak of cruelty and barbarity without the need for explanation or nationalistic assertion. The Fosse Ardeatine just outside Rome, on the Via Appia Antica, is a brilliant solution to such an emotion-laden design problem. The sarcophagi of the victims are laid in identical rows at ground level and protected, or threatened – whichever way you choose to interpret it – by a colossal slab or concrete about six metres high and fifty metres long which 'hovers' above the graves just sufficiently to admit light but, at the same time, creates a low enough ceiling to express oppression and the weight of the jackboot. Two generations later the Polish-Jewish architect Daniel Libeskind was to be equally expressive in the design of his world-famous Jewish Museum in Berlin. The Fosse Ardeatine was an entirely new experience for me: architecture which spoke for itself and was a world away from the contrived elegance obtained only by beautifully proportioned façades and adherence to the received Classical tradition which had so dominated my curriculum.

These excursions into modernity were not at the expense of history, but merely showed it reinterpreted. There was a lot still to see and experience and I was much exercised by the possibility of finding some architectural absolutes in the two thousand years of history that surrounded me to act as a guide in a career of design decision-making.

Every day was packed with visits to buildings which our small group had all studied or read about and, mindful of the monumental volumes dedicated to the architecture of Rome, we soon realised that in the time available we had to be arbitrarily selective. The Baroque churches, Renaissance palaces and remnants of antique Rome could all have held our attention for months on end, but if we were to record *lasting* impressions, we would have to have specific experiences and therefore our group divided into ones and twos to choose our own particular destinations. In any case, we had by now conscientiously visited the 'great' places and were going to seek new impressions to feed our hungry eyes.

I approached the Pantheon in the heart of the old city early in the morning. The shopkeepers were lowering their blinds, the Lambrettas and Vespas were taking the fashionable young to work (all looking like Audrey Hepburn and Gregory Peck in *Roman Holiday*) and the white-gloved traffic police were rehearsing their balletic display of extravagant gestures persuading drivers to control their individualistic behaviour, but expecting little response and receiving less. As I crossed the Piazza della Rotunda my nostrils were aware of stale urine and soon I glimpsed the great relic of Roman triumphalism, colonised by countless feral cats who had made this area their home. Emaciated, infirm and often disease-ridden, they fought and snarled over scraps in the gutter in front of local inhabitants who appeared to be entirely oblivious of their existence and condition.

Walking through the Pantheon's classical portico, I paused at the door. In his description of St Mark's in Venice, Ruskin once said that visitors were best advised to enter, sit down and close their eyes before attempting to fully appreciate the interior. I followed the advice in the Pantheon and the effect was profound. A dictionary defines a circle as 'a planet's orbit' or as 'a figure in magic', although its compilers may never have had their description corroborated by experiencing personally the inside of a majestic circular building as I did then. A circle is finite, sublime and authoritative. It was employed in the service of Emperor Hadrian, when he ordered the construction of the new temple in AD 120.

The circle has been employed from the time of Stonehenge through to the new Metropolitan Cathedral in Liverpool as the ultimate expression of religious evocation. It was used in the same way in the Pantheon. It had a great coffered dome and the entire interior was lit only by a huge circular opening – the oculus – in the crown of the dome, through which a brilliant shaft of sunlight entered, casting myriad shadows on the walls and throwing the elaborate decoration into dramatic relief. As if on cue, the hitherto-unseen organ began playing Schubert's *Ave Maria*. I found the simultaneous impression on eye and ear more moving than I had ever thought possible. But here was an old building and a hackneyed tune combining to produce ethereal beauty. How does this happen? No obvious answer suggested itself.

At the other end of the scale, a small building capable of evoking equal wonder stood almost concealed on the top of a hill overlooking the river Tiber and the old city. San Pietro in Montorio has hidden within its cloisters a small, perfect architectural gem, the Tempietto. It was designed by Bramante, the first Roman Renaissance architect of note. Like the Pantheon, it was circular in plan, but in this case barely fifteen feet in diameter. It is surrounded by a Doric peristyle behind which rises the drum, pierced alternately with windows and shell-headed niches, and crowned by a dome. I had come across an exquisite jewel languishing in an old cupboard and no one could tell me how it got there.

Post-war Italy was beginning to take on a semblance of normality. Families had been reunited and were audibly arguing in the street again; black-market Biros and neckties were being sold off the back of bicycles parked in front of the Vittorio Emmanuele Monument; Americans were discovering Rome to rediscover themselves once more and a succession of Communist governments struggled with the awesome problems of reconstruction. Rome's public transport system, consisting largely of trams, was engagingly simple for a stranger to use. The two inner-city routes were circular, one going clockwise and the other anti-clockwise – *circolare sinistra* and *circolare dextra*. Everyone pushed to get on, continued pushing during the journey and pushed to alight, seeking their neighbours' indulgence with cries of *'permesso, permesso'* as body encountered body. This was the accepted way of doing things and upset nobody.

Sometimes, when the city became unbearably hot, I would escape to the surrounding pine-scented hills and take with me a stick of charcoal and a sketchbook. The Via Appia Antica was a favourite place because it was scattered with countless relics from the past, most of them attractive ruins and a joy to draw. Through age, wars or vandalism they had deteriorated badly, although some were still partially occupied. I was attracted to them by what has often been called 'a sense of deceased actuality', and on one occasion I sat down to sketch a crumbling farmhouse that looked as if it had been abandoned long ago. I thought there was nothing significant about the stray chicken scratching on the lower step of the entrance and continued with my drawing, gradually becoming aware of a stocky, aproned figure in faded head-scarf emerging from a broken doorway carrying what looked like a bowl of pasta. Wearing a maternal, understanding smile, she limped across to where I was squatting and presented it to me, either because I looked more like the impoverished student than I cared to admit or just out of curiosity about what I was doing – after all, the sudden appearance from nowhere of a fair-haired, blue-eyed artist intent on recording a broken farmstead would have surprised anyone; but not everyone would have been so spontaneously caring.

I could have stayed in Rome for ever. I think we all could, and, following the suggestion of an expert in Renaissance sculpture at the British School, we decided to visit the Church of San Pietro in Vincoli on our last day. It is near the Coliseum and we went to see Michelangelo's *Moses*. The Church itself is not especially remarkable, but we had come to find *Moses*. Recalling that most sculpture is either mounted on a handsome plinth or stands in a specially formed niche in the wall, we began looking in all the wrong places, because in this instance the Old Testament prophet is seated to the right in the sanctuary and not immediately visible. We had been standing at the back of the church and admiring the altar when we slowly became aware of a magisterial marble figure leaning slightly forward with head turned towards us at the door. None of us spoke as we imagined our own dialogue with Moses. We felt naturally deferential and half expected him to reply, standing motionless, waiting for him to look straight ahead once more (which he looked quite capable of doing). Perhaps we were expecting some timeless utterance to mark our last day; but was he saying the same thing to each one of us? Instinctively I knew I would come back, though I wasn't to know it would not be for at least another generation; but that didn't matter if I was, for a moment, part of such timelessness.

My third year at the Brighton school included the writing of a thesis on a chosen topic and, probably because I had elected to do nineteenth- and twentieth-century architecture for my specialised history paper, I thought I'd tackle a twentieth-century topic.

When I was a schoolboy in the early days of the Second World War, my closest friend, Basil, had been billeted on our local vicar as his family lived in Southampton, and children in such places considered strategic by the Luftwaffe were evacuated to areas remote from targets. We got on well together and the vast, overgrown garden of the Victorian vicarage was an ideal place to climb trees, play Cowboys and Indians in, or see birds nesting. The vicar, an earnest, evangelical bachelor whose elderly mother still ran the house for him, tried hard to make Basil feel at home but wasn't really cut out for it. So Basil and I spent a lot of time together and, to keep him company, I joined the Bible class and the church choir he already belonged to. Two services on a Sunday, choir practice on a Friday evening and singing occasionally at a wedding (for which we were paid two shillings and sixpence) or a funeral (only one shillings and ninepence because you did not have to sing so loudly) threw me into the life of the Anglican church at an impressionable age. It wasn't surprising, therefore, that I still had a residual interest in church affairs.

The country had lost many churches in the Blitz and, to add to the problem, vast new housing schemes were being planned to provide homes and jobs away from the big cities, so these communities had also to be catered for. A new church-building programme looked inevitable, but where should I go for my influences? Inevitably, it was back to the two neutral countries, Sweden and Switzerland. These countries produced attractive architecture and there were reasonable similarities with England in building materials, religious denominations and a shared European climate. Twentieth-century art and design had inevitably exercised an unmistakable influence on their architecture and, aided by equally significant theological reappraisal, combined to produce churches which were light, friendly and uncluttered, and, most important of all, which encouraged liturgical experiment.

I had to rely on articles, books and photographs for much of my material and, as all the illustrations in the thesis had to be hand-drawn by the author, the whole enterprise took longer than I expected. Fortunately, I still had time for someone to look over it before looking for a friend with a typewriter prepared to type it up at affordable cost.

Everyone had heard of George Bell, Bishop of Chichester. His work in the Nazi and post-Nazi periods to support and succour Christians in Germany was indefatigable. He was known equally for his enlightened patronage of the arts, a gift not shared with many other diocesan bishops, and his influence in this respect was, in time, to make itself felt throughout western Europe. He had already commissioned work from Hans Feibusch and T. S. Eliot, and was shortly to appoint as dean Walter Hussey, who would further develop the idea of arts in the service of God. In time, Ceri Richards would design processional copes; Leonard Bernstein would set psalms to music, John Piper would design a tapestry, Graham Sutherland would create a painting, and his eventual successor would commission a window by Marc Chagall.

To me, it followed then that my diocesan bishop would be interested in modern church architecture, which indeed he was, but through my being entirely untutored in such matters, it hadn't occurred to me that he might have other priorities, increasingly at national and international level, which would not permit him to drop everything else he was doing, to sit down quietly in a corner and provide a critique of my draft thesis. But he did. I was entirely oblivious of his support for Pastor Martin Neimöller in Nazi Germany or of his forceful representations to Winston Churchill over the blanket bombing of cities like Dresden in the last years of the war which were of such international importance. But here he was, forgiving my impetuousness and ignoring my arrogance, prepared to help an entirely unknown student in any way he could. With great generosity he undertook what I had dared to ask. A week later he returned the draft, complete with helpful and detailed margin notes and suggestions. I had, quite accidentally, glimpsed the qualities of a great man.

Chapter 5

The Festival of Britain

A five-year training course should have felt daunting or even wearisome, but it didn't. The country was recovering slowly from war and lights were coming on again in our lives, not least for architects in the fields of design and technology. The modern movement was gaining ascendancy over the endless Georgian revival and mock-Tudor styles that had surrounded us all our lives and we seized new ideas with evangelical zeal, though often uncritically. New materials such as pre-stressed concrete and laminated timber made their appearance and liberated design to permit the building of slim, elegant structures of minimum bulk and maximum grace. This often encouraged the exposure of structure, hitherto deliberately hidden, as a positive architectural feature.

With 1951 came an opportunity for architects and engineers to put such ideas into practice and introduce them to a wider public. The occasion was the Festival of Britain and the site for its exhibition was the South Bank of the Thames, adjacent to London's County Hall in a featureless area that had languished even before the Blitz.

It was felt that an event was needed to encourage the nation to look forward once more and two distinctly different personalities emerged at the right moment. Sir Gerald Barry's vision and Herbert Morrison's faith and pertinacity provided an austerity-ridden people (some food was still rationed) with an exhibition which forcibly reminded them of their traditional ability to make the big gesture. However, these were still uncertain times – the British diplomats Guy Burgess and Donald Maclean had just vanished; King Abdullah of Jordan was assassinated; and British troops had seized the Suez Canal Zone. But international crises were not going to deter a government determined to set a new, optimistic course for post-war Britain and if justification were needed, then why not celebrate the centenary of the Great

Exhibition of 1851? At that time Prince Albert had expressed great interest in science and the arts, and the engineering genius of Joseph Paxton had been employed to build the Crystal Palace; and the Great Exhibition had even concluded with a handsome surplus of £186,000, so everyone now seemed anxious to do it again and restore national pride in ourselves.

For students halfway through their course, this was a magical tutorial, practical and sabbatical all rolled into one and, as far as limited travel expenses allowed, we spent as much time as possible on the South Bank during the months of the exhibition. All new events on this scale attract innovation, both technically and, indeed, criminally, and one of the incidents which appealed to our sense of the absurd and was sufficiently anti-establishment to be attractive involved the theft of hundreds of wheelbarrows. The ruse was admirably simple. Construction debris had to be removed from the site to avoid congestion and this involved wheeling it through the site security barrier to the nearest skip outside. Once done, the operative, without the barrow, re-entered the site at an adjacent entrance, showed his security pass and resumed loading another wheelbarrow drawn fresh from the stores on the way in. He filled it and repeated the operation for weeks on end before one of the villains fell out with the others over the division of spoils and blew the whistle in time for the police to discover countless brand-new wheelbarrows stored under the seating of an East End greyhound stadium.

Talented architects, often recently qualified, were given commissions to design individual buildings at the exhibition, and most did so with sufficient panache to get themselves noticed, setting them on successful career paths thereafter. Basil Spence, who designed the Sea and Ships Pavilion, would go on to design Coventry Cathedral and Sussex University. George Grenfell-Baines, who designed the Power and Production Pavilion, would go on to found one of the largest and most successful architectural practices in Europe, whilst Hugh Casson, who was responsible for coordinating all the design work as Director of Architecture, would become a highly successful president of the Royal Academy. All three were knighted later in their careers.

The exhibition pavilions were designed in the contemporary idiom throughout. They were daring, risky and innovative. I went to wonder and admire and inevitably became over-influenced. And the creativity didn't stop at buildings. There was sculpture by Henry Moore and Barbara Hepworth, a large mural by John Piper and a strong emphasis on landscaping, both hard and soft, showing how the exhibits *and their settings* could be satisfactorily integrated. The exhibition was the first to eschew the formal axial, semi-classical layouts of earlier European Expositions, and showed how a more informal, almost picturesque plan could provide surprise and enchantment and would hopefully be used as a test bed for Britain's urban reconstruction programme. The South Bank exhibition site quickly became recognised as an example of the first modern 'townscape'.

There was excitement and delight at every turn. Projecting viewing platforms had been suspended over the Thames from the riverbank and a 'vertical feature' to locate the site of the exhibition from a distance became the Skylon, suspended on taut cables and appearing to float high above the riverside walk. This again was designed by a recently qualified architect, Philip Powell, who was go on to become a designer of great sensitivity and insight, as well as a man of touching modesty. He too was later knighted.

The smallest details were considered. Bronze handles in the Riverside Restaurant were designed in the form of the human hand, so that the push–pull action became obvious without recourse to instructional lettering. Their designer was the irrepressible American sculptor Mitzi Solomon Cunliffe, about whom I would learn much more in years to come.

The largest building and a permanent reminder of the 1951 exhibition was the Royal Festival Hall. Designed by Robert Matthew and Leslie Martin at London County Council (LCC), it was the first modern movement building in Britain to be designed on a monumental scale, as all the pre-war works were only modest in size. This called for serious interpretive skills, and much of the design was entrusted to Leslie Martin, who years later was to become the highly influential head of the University of Cambridge School of Architecture.

The Royal Festival Hall was large and impressive and represented a huge leap forward in concert-hall design. With its centrally placed auditorium surrounded by foyers and galleries to give all-round access and protect the auditorium from external noise, it was described as being 'like an egg in a box'. Its acoustics were scientifically determined for the first time – until then, acoustics had been a black art and largely intuitive – and one of the many remarkable features was that the hall's acoustic properties were the same whether the auditorium was full or empty, through the simple expedient of providing absorbent materials on the underside of the tip-up seating, equivalent to the audience's clothing. This meant that the conductor could tune the orchestra at rehearsal for performance conditions.

The whole interior, furnished in carefully selected and specially designed materials, was warm and celebratory. A fellow student, from South Africa, stopped me as we crossed the foyer to enter the great concert hall and said prophetically, 'Savour the moment, John, because you are going to have an experience in the next few moments that you will remember for the rest of your life.' I paused and I did.

Chapter 6

The Reality of Practice

Laurence Gotch, a former partner of Sir Edwin Lutyens, architect of New Delhi and a range of magnificent English country houses, decided to open a branch office in Brighton, probably because one of his leading partners already lived there. The firm took a lease on the top two floors of a gaunt Victorian property set in a terrace of late-nineteenth-century houses. To minimise the outlay, and presumably contain the cost should the enterprise fail, the absolute minimum was done to it and the practice merely occupied a house, but used it as an office. The bathroom still contained a bath and the kitchen a larder. Coconut matting covered the floor and drawing-office benches had been made by a local joiner. Second-hand gas heaters, which looked as though they could have featured in the industrial catalogue of the 1851 Great Exhibition, were installed, and the transformation was complete.

I was employed at £7. 10s. a week, to be reviewed twelve months later. Having nothing to compare this with, never having had a job before, I was happy to accept. In any case, I had been highly impressed at my interview by discovering Imperial Leather soap in the washbasin. Obviously the firm had style.

Recently qualified, I was the most junior of the five members of staff and anxious to learn. On the first day I brought along my own T-square and drawing board and was surprised to find they already had equipment for me, although it was pretty antiquated. I was taught how to light the gas radiators, which hissed alarmingly all the time and produced pints of condensation; how to rub stick colours into a small pan of water to produce a colouring medium (much cheaper than tube paint, I guessed); and how to prepare draughting linen with talcum powder before starting an ink drawing. The mystique and ritual were part of my induction, but after five years of designing theoretical projects in the School of Architecture my greatest joy was the

41

thought of designing something that was really going to be built. I luxuri-ated in the prospects offered by each new day and worked hard, less to impress my employers than to please myself. The freedom it all promised was intoxicating and the possibilities seemed limitless, so limitless in fact that one day while the boss was out I took a long and luxurious Imperial Leathered bath in office time, glowing with the satisfaction that I was being paid for every minute of my ablutions.

The office overlooked St Peter's Church Brighton, an early work by Sir Charles Barry, who would later design the Palace of Westminster, and in front of it was a memorial obelisk and horse trough which, over time, had become a road junction. As traffic gradually became heavier the junction was controlled by a point-duty policeman. Rain or shine, traffic or no traffic, he stood there and either froze or boiled throughout the seasons, waiting for approaching vehicles. One winter's day darkness fell early and it snowed heavily. Traffic ground to a halt, but the policeman still had a couple of hours to go before his shift ended. With no traffic to direct he stood motionless and, very slowly, snow built up on his helmet to a point where it doubled its height without falling off. I sat and watched him as, at this time, none of us in the office was engaged in anything particularly interesting and I was only detailing a concrete fire escape staircase for a converted building of little architectural importance.

'A half crown on the snow staying on another five minutes,' I ventured.

'You're on,' came the collective reply.

And at that very moment a brewer's dray emerged from the gloom. The driver had lost his way and beckoned the policeman, who inevitably moved, and bang went my lunch money for the rest of the week.

I was to learn that in private practice the work flow would always be uneven. The public sector had a predictable quantity of work flowing from an agreed council budget and therefore projects arrived at fairly regular inter-vals. But in private practice, you had to go out and find the work, and once it was completed, manage to get paid for it.

We had been through a patchy period when, quite suddenly, two quite large health-care projects arrived simultaneously. As the more senior staff were engaged on existing jobs which, by their nature, took longer to complete, the only available manpower comprised the two most junior architects, of whom I was one. I couldn't believe my luck. The project also had a fasci-nating provisional title: *Neurosis Unit at Hellingly Hospital* (in whose grounds it would be built). The existing building was one of those huge nineteenth-century asylums for the 'insane' located in the depth of the countryside, and few people even knew of its existence.

The clinical proposal was novel for its time and was intended for patients who had, for instance, suffered a moderate nervous breakdown but were far from 'certifiable'. The intention was to design a building more resembling a country club than a hospital where patients could spend a few weeks receiving treatment in as non-institutional a setting as possible. The site selected was a long way from the old asylum, with splendid views over the South Downs that would have warmed the hearts of Rudyard Kipling and Hilaire Belloc, both of whom had lived in Sussex. With its own access road, the new centre would be seen to be quite independent and, hopefully, its patients would be free of any of the stigma attached to those being treated in the adjacent hospital, many of whom had been there for the greater part of their lives. Hellingly Hospital was typical of nineteenth-century asylums in being situated far from the population and almost totally self-sufficient, with its own cattle, and dairy and arable acreage. We were to build on a remote barley field, so eventual construction had to wait until the farm manager had safely harvested the crop.

Designing a building type for which there was no precedent was intriguing, and I was allowed to get on with it largely unhindered. The resulting design comprised a low, two-storey building which, while it was constructed in local Sussex materials of brick and tile-hanging, bore an unmistakable resemblance to much of the Scandinavian architecture I had recently seen and admired. The proposal was approved and I prepared a large, coloured perspective in ink and watercolour to illustrate its particular character and appearance. It came out well (they don't always, I was to discover), and I was persuaded to enter it for the Royal Academy Summer Exhibition at Burlington House. I was told that the odds of acceptance are about 10 to 1 against, but I completed the forms and handed in the framed perspective nonetheless. There followed an inordinate delay and, not knowing how long these things took, I got on with my next design. Then one day a notice of acceptance arrived, together with a preview ticket and an archaically worded invitation for me to attend before the formal opening, on what was termed 'Varnishing Day'. This oddly titled event was presumably intended for those submitting unglazed oil paintings, and I visualised a day where countless artists descended on the capital with a thermos flask of tea (or something stronger), fish-paste sandwiches and a can of old varnish to finish their work for public viewing.

Flushed with success, I decided that one way to get on quickly was to win an architectural competition, and I agreed with my other new colleague, Ronald Guy, that we should enter the very next one that came along, irrespective of what it was. To my surprise and consternation, a competition announcement appeared in the technical press immediately – for a new crematorium in

Kirkcaldy, Scotland. We didn't hesitate, but sent away for the conditions straight away. Never having entered an open competition before, and knowing precious little about cremation, we sought the advice of our local crematorium super-intendent, a round, ruddy-faced Lancastrian with a music-hall laugh, who was intrigued by what he called our 'escapade' and couldn't have been more helpful. He arranged for a tour behind the scenes.

Designed in the 1930s, his crematorium was a beautifully proportioned, neo-Georgian building which, characteristically, was very pretty to look at but very poor 'below stairs'. Its working operations were overseen by a retired 16-stone chief petty officer, tattooed up both arms, who supervised the tran-sition of the coffin from the committal chamber to the furnace room and finally collected the residual ash from the pulveriser for labelling and storage. He also had the task of turning on the timed music to accompany the closing of the catafalque curtains in the chapel – roughly thirty seconds' worth of a suitable extract from *Lilac Time*, a favourite musical comedy from the inter-war years and much loved by the average mourner. Because 78 rpm shellac records were not produced with separate tracks, the beginning and end of the selected passage had been marked by two grubby pieces of adhesive paper to enable the operator to lower the needle onto the disc where the paper started and remove it before it hit the next bit half a minute later. He would put on the record with one burly hand, and with a small shovel in the other, move quickly to the pulveriser to remove another urn full of ash before returning to stop the music. It was seldom a clean move and was usually accompanied by the sound of a blunt needle being dragged across the face of the record before the turntable stopped. Of antique origin, the gramo-phone's winding mechanism had suffered at the hands of its operative over the years and it therefore played very quickly to start with and slowed to a dirge by the end of the piece. No one seemed to notice either of these frail-ties as the members of the meagre congregation were often in such a distressed state they were beyond surprise.

We asked the superintendent whether, were he starting afresh, he would have asked for the building to be designed differently. He paused long enough for his lunchtime Guinness to settle, smiled broadly and observed finally that he would prefer the clerestory windows to be openable, "cos in an 'ot summer, some of me customers 'um a bit and it upsets them still waiting their turn'. We took very deliberate note.

The weeks flew past and, having allocated too much time to the design, we were running short of days to draw up the scheme for submission, partic-ularly as we had to work out of office hours, having entered the competi-tion not in the firm's name, but in our own.

Twenty-four hours before the stated handing-in date it was clear that, unless we worked all night, we wouldn't complete and would be disqualified automatically. So, supplied with a thermos of cocoa and corned-beef sandwiches, we watched our colleagues leave at 5.30 p.m. and settled down to draw, draw, draw. As our studio was in the attic and lit by a dormer window, there was a flat gutter just outside behind the façade's cornice. During daylight hours it was frequented by pigeons, but the nocturnal scene saw the territory change hands. Shortly before midnight, after drawing a complicated longitudinal section, I looked up to rub my eyes, yawn and look blearily into the gloom outside when, from nowhere, a wild, whiskered face appeared and snarled at me through the glass. The biggest marmalade cat I had ever seen hissed, arched its back and then disappeared as quickly as it had arrived. Unnerved by this Hitchcock-like experience, I was unprepared for what happened next. We had heard various creaks on the stairs but the property being old and ill maintained, we were used to the squeaks and groans of floorboards, though such noises always sounded stranger at night. And on this occasion no wonder: the door suddenly burst open and in bounded a burly policeman, attracted by the top-floor lights of what he knew to be commercial premises.

'And what precisely are you two up to, then?' he demanded. I couldn't think of an answer – I was still recovering from the shock of his crashing entry. 'And leavin' the door ajar for a quick exit p'raps?' After what seemed a long time, I attempted to explain.

'We are designing a crematorium,' I began, then, quickly spotting his stripes, added, 'Sergeant.'

'Designing a wot? Don't give me any of that stuff, sonny.'

'A crematorium, Sergeant, and it's very difficult and takes a lot of time, particularly if you've never been cremated. Come and have a look.'

He glanced quickly at two drawing boards, piles of crumpled tracing paper on the floor, an empty thermos and two washed-out creatures in faded tweed hacking jackets. He breathed out heavily, removed his helmet and came and had a look. We became good friends in the end, particularly after I told him that I'd lost half a crown a month earlier when the snow fell off his helmet.

Three months later we received a letter from the Kirkcaldy council explaining we had won one of the competition prizes, and enclosing a cheque for £100 to be split between us. The next day I bought two easy chairs for £60 by adding one week's salary to my share; I had coveted their design ever since I saw them exhibited at the Festival of Britain in London.

Working hard and playing hard characterised our existence, although the *playing* part still carried schoolboy overtones. One summer's day our boss, a former naval reserve sub-lieutenant who dressed daily in a navy blue blazer with brass buttons, well-creased grey flannels and polished shoes, was leaving for a site visit to inspect land for a new housing development. He departed on the back of the estate agent's Vespa and the moment the ungainly pair disappeared from view, we all climbed through the dormer window out onto the open parapet and drank lemonade in the sun until it was time to go home.

The Regency period is ephemeral – pretty and paper thin – and this applies as much to its architecture as to the Prince Regent's court which started it all, but the thought of starting an office in that setting was another matter and, following the partners' decision to move to larger and better offices, Number 26 Regency Square, Brighton was acquired. Oddly enough, it wasn't until we had been there some time that we realised it had been, for a while, the home of Augustus Charles Busby of the renowned firm Wilds and Busby, responsible for designing some of the most elegant squares and terraces in both Brighton and Hove in the early 1800s.

Number 26 was at the top of the square and overlooked the lawns down to the sea, with the West Pier beyond. The property needed a good deal of repair and restoration. It had sloping floors and each window had become distorted into either a rhombus or trapezium and reminded me of my student demonstrations of solid geometry. The prevailing wind blew through generous and unsealable gaps everywhere and the windowpanes collected a fine film of salt within hours of having been cleaned. But no one minded a bit, as we had really *arrived*. The view was as enchanting as it was unreal and my window, when I wiped away the mist, held revelation after revelation. First, the sea changed colour not day by day, but hour by hour, and would alter magically from leaden grey to dappled ultramarine as the clouds, wind and tide fused their alchemy.

Directly opposite the end of the square was the West Pier, possibly the loveliest pier in Britain, and repairs had recently been completed to restore the section blown out by explosives to deter any seaborne enemy landing in the early days of the war. A confection of cast iron and wood, its filigree presence had attracted visitors in their thousands from 1866 onwards, invited to 'walk upon the water', see and be seen, and feel the day's excursion was doing them good. Silhouetted against the horizon and the setting sun, it had qualities undreamed of by its engineers and provided a setting which, many years later, was to make it known worldwide as the film location for Joan Littlewood's sharp, satirical production of *Oh, What a Lovely War!* set in the period 1914–18.

In the 1930s, paddle steamers from the Clyde with names like *Glen Gower*,

Waverley and *Brighton Queen* would ply from the pier's landing stage during the summer months and transport you to the Isle of Wight, or offer a dinner-dance cruise down the coast for 3s. 6d. The wispy smoke from the funnels, the gentle splash of the huge paddles and the distant sound of the ship's small orchestra turned everything into a sepia photograph which had neither beginning nor end in time and stayed in my mind for ever.

Only one of the steamers survived the evacuation from Dunkirk, where they had been sent in great haste to rescue the remnants of the British Expeditionary Force, but shortly after we moved into Number 26 the survivor steamed in once more as if the intervening turmoil had never occurred. I looked up from my drawing board one day and there she was, slower and a bit creakier, but freshly painted. It could have been nineteenth-century Interlaken.

There were days when you couldn't see the horizon, not because of mist, but because the sky and sea were the same colour where they met. Everything would be still, the sea leaden and without a murmur of breeze. On days such as these the square reflected the same melancholic air and everyone who ventured out appeared listless. On one occasion, I was puzzled by what sounded like the voice of a woman singing from somewhere in the street below. There was certainly nothing noticeable to sing about, but the Edith Piaf voice hadn't chosen a happy song. Laden with remorse, it pleaded with the empty square, and when I got up to look outside there was a woman, probably in her early fifties, in what looked like widow's weeds from a Victorian melodrama, standing outside each house in turn, hoping for some response. None came, and I knew none would, and that made the song even sadder. She must have been in the empty square for a full half hour until, very slowly, a sea mist rolled in and she simply disappeared. On leaving the office I asked the others if they had heard her, but nobody had.

In the years following the war, national newspapers were getting larger again, but with the prevailing austerity, advertising income was still scarce. Inevitably, circulation wars began and one notable title, the *News Chronicle*, began to woo popularity with the invention of a fictional figure called Lobby Lud, who would visit a particular town on a well-publicised day and, if you recognised and stopped him, you were awarded with a big cash prize and national publicity. Only a vague description was given so as not to make the challenge too easy and you had to be carrying a copy of that day's *News Chronicle*. The street that led into Regency Square was lined with shops, each with a decorative awning over the fascia. One shop specialised in pipe tobacco and walking sticks and was run by a tall, spare proprietor who had thin hair with a central parting and always seemed to be smoking a Sherlock Holmes pipe which, quite deliberately, filled his shop with a distinctive aroma. I was walking down the street one summer's day when a sudden cloudburst sent everyone scuttling for shelter. I turned up my jacket collar and ran for the protective awning, only to find a number of others already there. We were all pressed together, smelling of summer dampness, as it was difficult to stand apart, when, quite suddenly, my unknown neighbour grasped me firmly by the lapels, stared into my eyes and shouted, 'You're Lobby Lud and I claim the *News Chronicle* prize!' (the advertised wording had to be right). I remember the sadness in his eyes when, startled and apologetic, I explained that I wasn't. It could have been the only (sadly misdirected) brush with fortune in his lifetime.

One of the few incentives for arriving at the office early was to witness a daily metamorphosis which never lost its appeal. It could have been lifted straight from an Italian neo-realist film of the time and was poetic in its brevity. It featured a small, rotund man in a faded brown overcoat who, punctually at 8.55 every morning, would arrive at the corner of the street leading into the square. He carried an old, well-polished attaché case and, a few paces into his transition, he would pause, rest the case on a convenient windowsill – always the same one – take out a peaked cap with the words 'Car Park Attendant' on it, rub his toecaps on the back of his trouser leg and, after pressing down his waxed moustache with the side of his thumb, make his entrance into Regency Square. In the space of a hundred yards, the suburban nobody at the breakfast table turned himself into a figure of authority, emphasised by the silver ticket-punching machine hung majestically across his chest. Fellini or Bergman would have made this brief sequence last half an hour, with an audience yearning for more. As each day passed I too noticed more – whether he'd had a haircut, limped more than usual, or cut himself shaving. The generalist in me had always resisted the temptation of knowing more and more about less and less, but because of my current fascination I began to feel guilty at having been so dismissive of the Roman scholar becoming immersed in the development of the egg and dart decorative motif.

My firm worked a five-and-a-half-day week and on Saturday mornings the senior partner, weekending with his family in Brighton, would appear and run through the previous week's work and the following week's agenda with the Brighton partner. Whilst we used to brew our own tea during the remainder of the week, on Saturdays one of us, usually me because I was still new, would be sent across the road to collect a tin tray of coffee from a genteel, lace-curtained tea shop called Mary Stuart, but known as Bloody Mary's by all of us for a number of reasons, including the awfulness of the lukewarm beverage and the condescending superiority of the manageress, who resented having to serve the takeaway trade I represented.

Eventually we grew to love these individuals in the village community of the square and I was well aware that our sudden appearance must have taken them by surprise, but for one neighbour our arrival had proved more difficult to accept. He was the elderly head of a solicitor's practice next door, which he had founded in the 1920s and which was now being run by his son and a junior partner. Father, as was common in small firms at that time, had no intention of retiring. Notwithstanding his 73 years, and much to his son's and probably the firm's clients' chagrin, he insisted on making a daily appearance and monopolising the largest south-facing room in the building. His arrival was heralded by the well-lubricated *clunk, clunk* of the elderly engine of a highly polished Morris saloon in which he continued to drive himself, albeit at the speed of a hearse, but with just as much dignity. At 10 a.m. promptly he would alight in black jacket, pinstriped trousers, wing collar, fresh red carnation and black homburg hat. Due to faltering eyesight, he found reversing difficult and had become accustomed to using the space outside our new office for part of the manoeuvre, but by now we sported one car which, obviously, we left outside. This was thoroughly disapproved of and any opportunity for hostility was quickly seized upon by a face which went shrimp-pink with anger. On one occasion our car was taking another architect to a remote building site miles away so I thought I'd park my bicycle there instead. When I later reviewed my neighbour's spluttered indignation, I realised that it hadn't been the loss of his manoeuvring space that had induced apoplexy, but the appalling realisation that the appearance of a bicycle let down the tone of the entire neighbourhood. I then remembered how he went to the trouble of wearing a fresh carnation every day of his ordered life, and wondered if perhaps he was right.

Chapter 7

'My' Job

The boundaries of English parishes were set so long ago that few can recall accurately how they came about. Based on an arbitrary mix of land ownership and patronage, such boundaries became more and more irrelevant as time passed. The parish of All Saints, Patcham extended over a very wide area, long since truncated by a nineteenth-century railway line and a twentieth-century trunk road. And then came housing estates built on the 'wrong' side. It came as no surprise to anyone to find that a large, mostly post– Second World War community had grown up cut off from the parent twelfth-century church by the London–Brighton railway line and the A23, but still falling within the old parochial boundary. It was decided, therefore, to provide it with a small place of worship of its own – a 'daughter church' to be known as the Church Hall of the Ascension – not a hall and not a church, but nearly capable of being either. I was invited to design it and, as this opportunity came only a few years after my thesis on modern church architecture, I was very ready to accept.

The site made available by the developer 'at very reasonable cost' was triangular, and adjacent roads met at its point. It sloped dramatically from one side to the other, and by the time building lines – points beyond which no structure may project – were subtracted from the total area, it wasn't much of a site. In addition, under a few inches of scrubby topsoil was rock chalk, and this would entail more expense to excavate to give a level site. Quite clearly, the builder didn't want this awkward and bitty site and that's why he sold it to the Church in an ostentatious gesture of goodwill, which the parochial church council, in their innocence, accepted as if he meant it. The construction budget was £7,500, which had to include all furnishings and professional fees. Hardly a king's ransom, but that didn't matter as I was embarking on the first commission I had been awarded personally and not through the firm for whom I worked. This gave me control of the design for the first time and it was a good feeling.

The brief was simple: the building had to accommodate 120 people and include a sanctuary which could be screened off when the hall was being used for social purposes. But it also had to allow for future expansion in the event of the congregation growing and more money becoming available. Complicated geometry costs money, so I stuck to a simple shape which, in any case, would meet my wish for a more modern design in keeping with the new neighbourhood. The parochial church council approved my proposals without dissent, probably because there was no historical precedent for this type of hybrid building anyway and also because they didn't want to discourage a newly qualified parishioner. Obviously, the design had *Scandinavia* written all over it, but no one seemed to mind.

The tenders came in and construction started. Whilst I was buoyed up by the thought that it was my design and my client, I was brought down to earth by the realisation that it was equally my responsibility and I had to get it all right first time. Living nearby, I witnessed it come out of the ground day by day which, like the watched pot, was quite the wrong thing to do; it took ages and left no room for surprise and excitement.

There is a limit to how much construction information can be conveyed in a set of working drawings and, inevitably, queries arose over how a particular detail should be executed. On the one hand I had been taught that the architect was in charge and should have the last word because, after all, it was his creation. On the other, if I were to retain any credibility and learn for the future, I found it sensible to ask the foreman what he thought before making a decision. I was fortunate in having one of the old school on this job, a dying breed even then, and *Mr* Brown, as I remembered to call him, would always come up with a suggestion, couched in tactful terms beginning with, 'I think you'd prefer it, sir, if . . . ', and I knew better than not to prefer it.

At the 'topping out' ceremony, when the roof was complete, I realised that the Church Hall of the Ascension would look better in any leafy suburb of Copenhagen rather than here, where it was surrounded by semi-detached Tudor bungalows so beloved of the English. But no one else seemed aware of the incongruity. As the date of Dedication approached, the parochial church secretary came to see me to discuss the purchase of chairs, kneelers, books and everything needed to complete the project. He generously gave me the opportunity to choose the design and textures of these, which I accepted readily. After all, no less a figure than Robert Adam had insisted on designing every detail of his grand Classical interiors and their undoubted success was no doubt attributable to the resulting unity. There was one distinct difference. Robert Adam was fluent in design and understood his materials; I wasn't and didn't yet.

I thought that I'd had a fairly smooth run until the evening before the Dedication, to be performed by the Archdeacon of Lewes. The Ascension was a hubbub of activity as preparations were made for the great day and wherever you looked, purposeful ladies of a certain age, most of whom I'd never seen before, were putting their finishing touches to the arrangements. Wishing to retain overall design control until the end, I had gone to considerable lengths to find an appropriate pair of ceramic vases for the altar flowers and, after a search taking three consecutive weekends, found a small pottery whose work was sympathetic to the communion table I had designed. The chosen vases looked absolutely right and I paid for them there and then. They would be my small gift to the parish. When I presented them to the flower ladies that evening I noticed that they were received pretty coolly. To begin with I thought that the slim elegance of the design may have been too avant-garde for them, so I was about to attribute this to suburban philistinism when one of them asked why I had chosen a narrow-necked design which precluded the insertion of more than two chrysanthemum stems. With a service to be held in less than twenty-four hours there was no question of changing them so, resourceful as one might have expected (they had, after all, been part of 'the spirit of the Blitz'), the flower ladies arranged a beautiful array of cut flowers just in front of the vases instead, carefully obscuring them.

But a more chastening experience awaited me. The curate-in-charge had only just been appointed and we hadn't met, so I was introduced to him during the evening in order to show him round. I had enjoyed designing the communion table, lectern, prayer desk and credence, all detailed in West African hardwood and finished with black lacquered tops. They were unified and looked well in the sanctuary. Eschewing ecclesiastical furnishing catalogues, whose pages filled me with despair, I had created entirely new designs and, to be absolutely certain, measured myself kneeling, sitting or standing to ensure that the top surfaces of the furniture were at the right height. Apparently, it had occurred to no one to tell me that the new curate was shorter, considerably shorter, than I was – so much so that his chin only just reached the open Bible on my lectern. Shaken by this revelation, I searched everywhere for Mr Brown who, conscientious as ever, was still on site and, without so much as a wry look, he sawed four inches off the leg of each piece of furniture, as it if were the most natural thing to do the night before a Service of Dedication. I made a mental note: *Keep the pieces – the next curate might be my height.*

Chapter 8

Surprisingly By Royal Appointment

The decade following the war had, necessarily, to concentrate on the functional and operational requirements of a country adjusting to peacetime conditions. Housing, schools and factories took priority and the practical needs of the nation left little space for environmental sensibilities. By 1957 though, outlooks were changing, principally as a result of major redevelopment threats to such well-known places as Covent Garden, Piccadilly Circus and Whitehall, where insensitive proposals were threatening priceless parts of London's heritage. Opposition built up on a national scale and the country awoke to the need for concerted action to prevent wholesale demolition in the name of much-vaunted 'comprehensive redevelopment'. Duncan Sandys, a former Cabinet minister, recognised the problem and, under his leadership, the Civic Trust was formed to help local amenity societies throughout the country resist damaging schemes and, generally, raise levels of visual awareness in towns and villages. One of the most successful ways of achieving this was to encourage street-improvement schemes in town centres which could introduce pedestrianisation and, through revival generally, give back a sense of ownership and pride to local citizens.

It was decided that George Street, Hove, a lively shopping thoroughfare, would be a suitable subject for the next Civic Trust improvement scheme. The street was long, flat and completely straight. And completely unremarkable. Of two-storey height throughout, it could have gone on for ever without attracting comment.

The improvement scheme was simple. There was first the subtractive process of removing anything that was redundant – old street signs and light fittings, cabling and overhead wires, and broken artefacts of any sort. Then followed the positive intervention: refreshing façades with paint and new fascia lettering, coordinating the treatment to give unity to the rows of near-identical frontages and, every now and then, punctuating their monotony with a selective façade picked out in bold colour or pattern to add interest. Any architectural or historic distinction in George Street was conspicuous by its absence. But occasionally I recognised traces of a former life, like the property which had been the town's first fire station where, under layers of rendering and cheap repair, there was still evidence of the borough coat of arms bearing the resplendent motto 'Floreat Hova'. This we were to restore in full heraldic colours, and it set me to looking for other traces of a former incarnation.

Work began and the old street lights, strung across the road on wires, were replaced by less obtrusive lamps bracketed to the walls of the shops. New, very 'Festival of Britain' litter bins were placed at discreet intervals and tubs of flowers appeared in between. To succeed, such a scheme was entirely dependent on the voluntary cooperation of shop owners, and although they subscribed to a traders' association that was supportive, there were those who couldn't see the purpose of it all unless it could be proved conclusively that, if it was carried out, business would improve overnight. For the first time in my life, and not the last, I was advocating a qualitative improvement to a group of people nurtured on quantitative advancement. Never talk aesthetics or the greater public good to shopkeepers.

I prepared many coloured illustrations for an open meeting at the town hall, when I would try and convince the reluctant property owners. Word had it that less than half were enthusiastic and they were determined to tell me so. In my quieter moments it had occurred to me that good luck is meanly distributed in this life but, by the law of averages, it had to appear somewhere from time to time. An unannounced visitation occurred that very evening. The town clerk told an astonished audience that the Queen and Duke of Edinburgh had that day 'graciously consented' to inaugurate the scheme upon completion. The fact that Their Majesties were already in the area for something far more important and the event was to be the last appointment in a busy day didn't emerge, so the effect on the meeting was electric. The mass conversion of doubters would have attracted the admiration of Billy Graham, the popular American evangelist visiting London at about this time, so that evening saw light abundant penetrate the dingy depths of the town hall. Some divine agency had pressed the 'release' button, and I sat down to rapturous applause.

This momentous volte-face may have solved some problems, but interestingly it attracted others, sometimes more difficult to solve diplomatically. One day while the work was being carried out, the town clerk asked if I'd go and see him to discuss progress and when I arrived he showed me a carefully worded letter from a well-known fishmonger whose premises were halfway down George Street, and in front of which the Queen and Duke of Edinburgh would walk during the royal progress. The fish-shop business had been in the family for years and apparently they had a long-standing arrangement with the skipper of a local fishing vessel plying from Shoreham harbour that, from time to time, dependent on the capacity of their refrigerators, they would buy an entire catch. That very week their catch had included a large sturgeon, a fish traditionally belonging to the Crown. Apparently, whales, dolphins and sturgeons in British waters are known as 'Fishes Royal'. Under a 1324 statute, all of them are owned by the monarch. The letter went on to request permission, since this were the case, for the proprietor to present the sturgeon personally to Her Majesty as she walked past his shop. Being well-built, the proprietor would hold all four feet of the magnificent specimen himself until she approached and then would take three paces forward, bow, and present it to the immaculately gloved monarch, as any decent, loyal subject should. Was that all right?

More Gilbert and Sullivan than real, it was nonetheless a real problem which was solved only after correspondence with the Palace, who suggested that the gift would be most acceptable on the understanding that it would be given to the several cats in the Royal Household, as it was not a fish that was commonly eaten by humans. This satisfied the proprietor who, on the day, straw-hatted and flanked by similarly attired assistants, beamed proprietorially as the Queen walked past.

The Mayor accompanied Her Majesty and led the procession, followed by me, for some reason, accompanying the Duke of Edinburgh, who was already well known for pithy comment and searching question. I was entirely unpractised in conversation with any member of the royal family and I knew it was going to be a lengthy talk, as the street contained over a hundred properties and the entourage was going to walk the entire length from one end to the other, so I hoped his questions were going to be of a practical nature, and they were. But entirely unanswerable, for instance, ' . . . and how many tons of paint did you need for this lot?' I quickly realised that the only way to survive was to ask him questions instead and, remembering that a similar Civic Trust improvement scheme had just been completed at Windsor, I enquired whether it had been a success. 'Much better, because, until recently, everyone used to throw their orange peel over the wall and now they can't.'

Chapter 9

19 Colebrook Road

I had married Ann in 1954, on the strength of £100 in the bank and having my salary raised to £8. 10s. a week. In 1956 our daughter Frances was born, followed by our son Peter the following year. We were still living in a small property, and needed more space and more tolerant neighbours; this meant a substantial mortgage and with it the unnerving prospect of retaining continuous employment for the next twenty-five years. Fortunately the practice flourished and I became Senior Architect, a fairly empty designation as it turned out, because it involved a lot more responsibility for the same pay and I remembered the feeling only too well, having been made an 'acting unpaid lance-bombardier' in my early army days in Singapore. However, it did bring with it some assurance of continuity, and this had become more important day by day.

Some time later the partners decided to open further branch offices in Bournemouth and Bristol, to be followed by another in Glasgow, and this meant inevitably a growth in numbers and further promotion of existing staff. In the same way as it is the cobbler's children who go ill-shod, a young architect in private practice finding the time, let alone the spare money, to design and build his own house is a rarity, and so it was with me. Having later become a junior partner in the firm, I was faced with a series of daunting contradictions which made my new role appear less of a clear-cut advancement than I had originally thought. On the plus side, the prospect looked superficially glamorous, with a brand-new Jaguar and arrangements for a 'top-hat' life assurance policy to mature on my retirement. On the minus side, I had to sign a thirty-six-page partnership agreement which, it was coolly explained, was more binding than a marriage and contained lengthy clauses about keeping retired partners – and their wives if their husbands predeceased them – in the style to which they had become accustomed. I also had

59

to hand over the deeds of my house as security for the firm's overdraft, which meant simply that if the firm went under during a recession, the roof over my family's head went the next day. I also had to leave a proportion of my monthly draw in the firm's bank to build up a capital account to help finance the practice's working capital, which in fact left me no better off than I had been before being invited into partnership. And finally, I could never again be reimbursed for any overtime because it was expected of every partner that they would always work overtime anyway, so that was that and I had to get on with it.

I always wanted to design my own house, but was this or was this not the right time to do so? A mortgage and by now two sets of school fees were a strong disincentive, but I recalled that history has always suggested that there is never a *right* time to make any big decision in life – get married, start a family, set up one's own practice, emigrate, start a war, or whatever – because if you do wait for one set of conditions to be right, another set of problems appears on the horizon. Procrastination isn't only the thief of time, it's the thief of opportunity.

So I decided to do it, and purchased a suitable plot of land which contained a row of mature trees along its edge that gave some privacy but still left a distant view of the English Channel. I could feel rising excitement at the prospect of making a start, and found myself doodling not only between practice meetings but often during them. As students we'd all had dreams of ourselves as ideal clients bursting with vision and creativity and freed from the mundane limitations of the day-to-day clients who commissioned us. Roofs could hang from skyhooks, a cascade of sparkling water could flow through the reception room, a Bechstein would sit on its own cantilevered mezzanine, a languorous Scandinavian au pair would tend 2.4 children, a golden retriever would sleep at my feet, and all would be illuminated by a sun which never set. As it turned out, restrictive covenants on the site stipulated the use of very traditional building materials, and worse still, the ultra-conservative building society vetoed any design that would be difficult to sell if I defaulted on repayments. Having now been through the process myself, I began to sympathise rather more understandingly with my everyday clients.

One of the many advantages of commissioning an architect to design a house is the opportunity it gives for innovation and surprise. But designing my own house obviously wouldn't provide such an opportunity. My wife was the only other 'client', and the necessary objectivity would go out of the window immediately if, against my profession's code of conduct, I found myself in the same bed as the client in question. I shared my dilemma with a friend from a nearby practice and hit upon the ideal solution – namely, that he should design my house and I would design his. This glaringly obvious solution had much to commend it and wasn't as silly as it sounded, but in the end came to nothing when he succumbed to a transatlantic offer he couldn't possibly refuse. I was dragged back to the schizophrenic problem of trying to surprise myself.

If I could no longer do this, I could at least indulge myself and have a bit of fun. The mid-1960s saw the end of coal-burning fireplaces due to clean-air legislation, and this in itself posed an interesting design problem – namely, what becomes the visual focus of a family room without a fireplace? Some alternative had to be found and it certainly wasn't going to be a television set, tropical fish tank or priceless French Impressionist painting, so I just left a big question mark, literally, on the otherwise developing plans and, Micawber-like, hoped that something would turn up. Quite undeservedly, it did.

Some years earlier, the practice had been asked to design a new radiotherapy building at the nearby district hospital and this involved the demolition of an eclectic nineteenth-century building designed in the style John Ruskin had popularised in *The Stones of Venice* of 1853, which became known as Venetian Gothic and was taken up briefly, if somewhat arbitrarily, by one or two mid-Victorian architects in Britain. Venetian palaces of the Middle Ages were built on the water's edge and shared a characteristic feature in their façades – namely, traceried arcading which, along with other lesser features, gave them their distinctive and unique appearance.

The Venetian Gothic building to be demolished in Brighton had been unused for some years and was now empty and semi-derelict, having previously served as the Brighton School for Partially Sighted Boys. Visiting the site to take measurements one day, I saw that the demolition had almost been completed and much of the old timber was being burned on a huge bonfire on the forecourt. With so much heat and smoke about, I had to return the following day and found, among the still-glowing embers, traces of stonework arcading which had previously embellished the façade. Although they were in fragments and caked with soot, I recognised them immediately and something made me collect a box full of them and take them away in the boot of my car. On returning home I then didn't know what to do with them, and inevitably they were consigned to the garage in a number of old shoeboxes where they remained for the next five years, only narrowly avoiding being jettisoned every time we had a clear-out.

As the design of the new house developed, the penny suddenly dropped and one weekend, armed with a plastic scrubbing brush and detergent, I set about cleaning the stones before attempting their reassembly. They came up well, and mercifully the missing sections were not too numerous and could probably be re-pieced by a good mason. What if I re-erected them in the long wall of the principal room in the new house, illuminated with concealed lighting, and set the whole ensemble against a background of Venetian red? Easy, but where would I find a stonemason interested in repairing bits of broken nineteenth-century arcading? I approached a number of firms I knew, who told me politely that they were 'too busy'. I was determined not to give up the idea and someone suggested I might try the Co-op, which had a monumental mason's yard for what were evidently budget memorials. Rather hesitatingly, I paid them an unannounced visit and met the sole occupant of a corrugated iron shed which served as the mason's workshop. I explained what I had in mind to the dust-capped, bespectacled figure who was hunched over a piece of the cheapest marble, carving 'sadly missed' for the hundredth time in his life but still doing it quite beautifully. He sat and listened impassively for a while and then, for the first time, looked up at me. He was older than I thought and, as a younger man, could well have harboured ambitions of being a sculptor one day and making a name for himself, but it was not to be and a war had left him crippled in one leg. I eventually persuaded him to come and see the stone fragments for himself before making up his mind. It was a revelation for us both. He beamed with pleasure at the thought of exercising his dormant skills and said immediately that he would be very, very happy to try and do it. Concerned at what all this might cost, I asked him for an estimate. He paused for a few moments and, unable to contain his enthusiasm any longer, said, 'Would thirty shillings be too much?'

The new house would contain four bedrooms, a couple of bathrooms, and a very large reception room with adjacent kitchen and utility room. There would also be a study. Of brick construction, the first floor was to be clad externally in Sussex clay tile-hanging and finished with a low-pitched roof. The reception room stretched the whole width of the house and was completely glazed on the garden side. This left a deliberately blank wall adjacent, where a fireplace would traditionally have been positioned, and in its absence a Venetian Gothic ruin would now take its place.

The new house was going to sit fairly near the road, which would give a generous-sized garden at the back occupying the former vegetable garden of the large house nearby, whose owner had died and which trustees had decided to sell. I was often reminded of this location when, after laying a turf lawn rather too hastily, I found myself cutting fresh asparagus with the lawnmower later in the year.

But the end of the garden needed some sort of design intervention, as our wooden fence had seen better days and the 1920s bungalow beyond looked terrible and needed to be hidden. Here again fire played a part in events. I had for some weeks been involved simultaneously in the restoration of a fire-damaged church in Hampshire. I was told that an aggrieved choirboy who resented being kept late at choir practice had returned later one night and set light to the sheet music of Stainer's *The Crucifixion*, which was stored under the hinged lid of the organist's bench seat. Having watched the offending organ score burning satisfactorily, the choirboy closed the lid and left the church, feeling much better for his initiative, and promptly shared every detail of the escapade with his admiring friends outside the fish-and-chip shop. Enjoying the sound sleep of the smugly satisfied, he was surprised to be woken in the middle of the night by a passing fire engine and, like any schoolboy anxious to find out where it was going, leapt to the window only to see the entire church roof alight.

By the time I was appointed no one seemed anxious to tell me any more about the unfortunate incident but, as the insurance company paid up, the remaining furnishings of the church were stripped out ready for the reconstruction. These included the oak pulpit, which I first set eyes on in the back of a contractor's skip. It hadn't been badly damaged, but because the church was going to be completely refurnished, it was decided to dispose of it along with the damaged items. I decided immediately that I wanted it, complete with the carved stone base on which it stood, so I offered the truck driver a fiver to drop it off at my house.

When re-erected on a solid new base and adorned with a decorative iron double-curved canopy I had designed, and up which I trained honeysuckle and Russian vine, it became the 'vista-stopper' I had wanted at the end of the garden. It also satisfied a suppressed urge to have a 'folly' at a fraction of the cost expended by nineteenth-century landowners who engaged in such frivolities on a monumental scale.

The move into the new house in Colebrook Road was planned, and the day before removal vans arrived I took one or two precious possessions ahead because I didn't want the removal men handling them and I couldn't leave them unguarded. They included a large bracket clock which had been in the family for three generations and had a chiming mechanism that could be changed from a Westminster peal, like Big Ben, to a Cambridge peal, which was more musical and which we preferred. I put it on its specially constructed shelf. It was the sound of my childhood and my children's childhood and, as I set up my camp bed on the empty sitting-room floor the night before the move, it reassured me of the continuity of events. With a torch, a thermos flask and a ticking clock for company, I was happy to fall asleep, intoxicated by the smell of new everything and bathed in moonlight which shone through the uncurtained windows onto the Venetian Gothic arcade which now looked as unreal as a stage set for *Romeo and Juliet*.

At about this time, the practice had become successful and we had grown in numbers; some of the new intake were allocated to my group. Perhaps I wasn't yet used to guiding, let alone controlling, equally creative spirits in the office, but I found my relationship with one of them, Paul, quite difficult. Conversations were sparing. We never drank together and neither was I sure whether the problem was that he resented working for anyone at all or whether he just found me too remote. Anyway, when the new house was ready, we invited the entire staff with their wives and girlfriends for a celebration supper.

Obviously I didn't leave Paul out, but I wasn't altogether surprised when, long after all the other guests had arrived, Paul still hadn't shown up. We were all dressed informally and I was sporting an old blue pullover on which had recently been sewn a badge depicting the smiling face of Mickey Mouse, which had been given me by my daughter as my birth date coincides with Walt Disney's best-known creation in 1928. The evening was well under way when, above the din, I heard the doorbell. When I opened it, there was Paul, looking distinctly the worse for wear, and with a totally unknown young woman who could not possibly have been mistaken for his wife. Swaying slightly, he mentioned something about getting lost on the way, which in his condition wasn't surprising, and he then noticed my Mickey Mouse badge. Straightening up, he looked at me very steadily for a moment and said, 'God, he's human after all.'

Chapter 10

The Postgraduate Medical Centre

Brighton General Hospital, the town's former Poor Law Institution (known as the workhouse), sat on the top of a steep hill on what would have been, in the mid-nineteenth century, the edge of the town. Like lunatic asylums, they were kept as far from sight as possible, despite the conspicuous benevolence of the Victorian city fathers intent on good works. Love thy neighbours, but first choose your neighbourhood.

The hospital was the poor relation of the grander, better endowed and certainly better designed (by Sir Charles Barry, of Palace of Westminster fame) Royal Sussex County Hospital a mile away. Inevitably the old hospital held the less glamorous services of the NHS and catered mostly for geriatric patients and those suffering from chronic medical conditions. However, it had one big advantage: spare land, which the other hospital did not possess.

A group of young consultants comprising a pathologist, a paediatrician and a specialist in general medicine thought that the standard of medical care and the prestige of the area might both be enhanced if a postgraduate medical centre was built for the use of both hospitals and of general practitioners. Under the leadership of Lord Cohen, a self-confessed local-boy-made-good, money was raised for its construction, the Regional Hospital Board having made the land available and the Hospital Management Committee having undertaken to meet running costs.

The centre was to contain a lecture theatre, a library, seminar rooms and a catering area and, given the openness of the site some way away from the old buildings, it was a pleasure to design. Doctors are no better and no worse than other clients when it comes to changing their mind halfway through the design process, but my group was made up of an amiable trio, and as we got on well, I didn't mind too much some spells of abortive work. When they finally agreed on what they wanted, the priority was to prepare a coloured perspective to convey what the finished centre would look like, both for the press and, more urgently, for the appeal brochure, which was just going to print. Such perspectives have to be set up accurately before being inked-in and coloured, and as it would be reproduced on the cover of the leaflet, this one took more time than usual. This meant delaying the start of the working drawings which provide all the technical information for the quantity surveyor to cost from and the building contractor to build from. I had set aside six weeks for this process, assuming I would have the help of another associate.

Before we could even begin, an unexpected political event took place which threw everything into disarray. Earlier in the year, Labour had won the 1964 General Election, and when, in the late autumn, the Labour party held its annual conference in Brighton, Lord Cohen decided to host a celebratory cocktail party at his home nearby for the members of the new Cabinet. This would include the new Minister of Health, the Rt. Hon. Kenneth Robinson, and what better opportunity would there be to cement his new political friendships than invite him to lay the foundation stone of the Postgraduate Medical Centre while he was here?

'Wells-Thorpe, I want the Minister to lay the foundation stone on the last day of the conference the week after next. I'd like you to make the necessary arrangements. Do you understand?'

'I understand, Lord Cohen, but you know we haven't yet completed the design and are several months away from going to tender and appointing a contractor?'

'I don't think you caught what I said. I need the stone laid in ten days' time,' he insisted. I paused to draw breath.

'This may be difficult, sir, because it hasn't been finally resolved where the building is going on the site and until then we can't position any foundation stone.'

'What do you think we hire an architect for? Ring me back at five o'clock this evening and tell me what arrangements you have made.'

Any building, however simple, has to sit within a cat's cradle of building lines, visibility splays, height restrictions, appropriate contours, drainage runs, and electricity, gas, telephone and water lines before it can be finally positioned, and this part of our work was still some weeks away. We hadn't even at that stage, obtained bye-law and town-planning permission. I shared the dilemma with my superiors who, with calculated indifference, said it was all good experience. But worse was to follow. I learned that the closing-afternoon session of the party conference was always prolonged as no one left until, arms linked, the entire assembly had sung 'The Red Flag'. British Summer Time had also ended the previous weekend and it became obvious that by

66

the time everyone had left the conference venue and arrived on site, it would be completely dark. I considered asking if the timing could be adjusted slightly but decided not to, because I knew what the answer would be. The jaws of death beckoned.

As I tried to make sense of it all, I remembered what an old school friend, tubercular and constantly in and out of sanatoriums, had once observed: 'You'll only survive in this life if you can turn disadvantage to advantage.' Which in his case he did, as his enforced detachment had given him a thirst for reading and he later became a very successful editor. Perhaps I should try and follow his example.

A light flickered in my mind and I could just see a ridiculous way out that might work. The carving of the foundation stone was easy and, having checked the initials and dates of the VIPs, I placed an immediate order with the stonemasons. The problem lay in what to rest it on if none of the building yet existed. In the end, after I had spent a sleepless night worrying, the ruse became simple: construct a token length of simulated wall out of softwood framing and plasterboard on which would be stuck brickwork-patterned wallpaper – all the rage at the time – and rely on the gloaming to do the rest. The contractor was nervous about the whole idea as he would have to control the hoist, whose chains were holding the stone, and stop it short of actually bearing on the softwood framework, which would immediately have splintered under the weight if he went too far. We practised it a couple of times and fortunately it seemed to work, but what if someone blew the gaff?

By now we'd come too far to chicken out, so, invoking the help of any sympathetic deity that may have been looking, we all assembled on the appointed day as the street lights were going on, to await the arrival of the ministerial motorcade. As it got progressively darker we moved a lorry onto the site and aimed its headlights at the foundation stone, which was swaying about dangerously in a Force 5 wind which hadn't been forecast. I had to steady it with my arm, and as a result was blinded by the lorry's headlights for the entire ceremony. At last the ministerial car swept up the drive, and Kenneth Robinson stepped out, pulled up his coat collar, and read a short dedication note handed to him by an equally uncomfortable aide, whereupon the stone was gently lowered into its 'final' resting place, but stopped imperceptively one inch above the wallpaper and no longer blowing about because I was holding it without looking too conspicuous. A ripple of polite applause and an indistinct loudspeaker announcement followed explaining that the Minister's full speech would now take place over tea and cakes in the nearby Nurses' Home, which everyone made for as fast as they could as the bad weather closed in.

The contractor and I couldn't encourage them to leave fast enough, as I'd got cramp steadying the swaying stone and couldn't move until we were sure everyone was out of sight. Only then, in darkness and consumed with guilt, did we gently raise the foundation stone, detach the chains and, between us, carry the stone into the builders' hut where we concealed it in sacking under a trestle table, where it would remain for a couple of months while we made up our minds where the building was going to go. None of this was a moment too soon, as the 'brickwork' was beginning to peel off in the rain and the wind, but we were very proud of the following day's press photographs which reinforced in our minds the fact that photographs, like statistics, can be made to prove anything.

Chapter 11

An Ecclesiastical Contradiction

'Mr Chairman, I feel obliged to say that I disagree profoundly with every word of the first twenty-nine pages of the report before us today.' Whereupon the Archdeacon of Chichester, still trembling with irritation, sat down with the rest of the committee considering this item on the agenda. It was *my* report, the first I'd ever been asked to prepare for the Church, and I was seated in the comer of the splendid Regency boardroom of the diocesan headquarters quietly awaiting my turn to speak.

There were three archdeacons present and I knew and got on well with two of them, but the third, who had just spoken, was rather different. He was the only one still to wear frock coat, breeches and gaiters, and previously had been the chaplain to the diocesan bishop and lived his bachelor life in the Cathedral Close. A traditionalist by nature, he was averse to any proposal that ran counter to his interpretation of church building design which, as far as I could see, was firmly enshrined between the hard covers of Anthony Trollope. My proposal had been far from traditional and was, understandably, anathema to him.

Sensing the procedural difficulties ahead, the chairman, a born diplomat, intervened to say that at this stage the committee would only be invited to *receive* the report rather than *approve* it. This took the heat out of the discussion and allowed me to describe what I had intended without being distracted by the fixed stare of the archdeacon.

The background to events was simple. Years of under-investment in the maintenance of Chichester Cathedral during the war, combined with the arrival of a large new population in Crawley New Town which needed a Church of England school, meant that action by the diocese could be delayed no longer. It all involved money, a large amount of money, estimated at about £1.5 million, which had to be raised through a public appeal.

Sir Kenneth Blackburne, recently retired from his post as High Commissioner in Jamaica, had undertaken to lead a fundraising initiative called The Chichester Campaign, and this gave the opportunity of looking afresh at the location and form of new church buildings across the county of Sussex. I had suggested that a small diocesan buildings study group be formed to offer guidance on the type of buildings appropriate for the rapidly-growing communities springing up around us. This had been agreed and I was asked to chair it and was allocated a budget.

Mindful of the fact that similar problems were being faced abroad and that some interesting, if revolutionary, solutions were being found, I decided that we should look at these first before taking any action ourselves. I asked a colleague in the group with whom I had trained, but who had since entered the priesthood, to first visit Vienna, where the diocese was experimenting with a 'demountable' church made of standardised components to be erected in the Siemensstrasse by volunteer student labour. In the meantime I visited the east coast of the United States, where prefabricated timber-framed churches were being erected to cater for their growing communities. My enthusiasm for such successful initiatives was only slightly dampened by receiving an American manufacturer's catalogue for some crudely constructed wooden sheds with crosses on them, which stated boldly on the cover, 'We want to share with you a method God has revealed to us for overcoming some of the obstacles faced by mission congregations.'

Encouraged by what had been accomplished elsewhere, our study group suggested that the Chichester diocese should now launch its own 'relocatable' church programme to meet pressing short-term needs. The typical proposal was that an embryo parish would be supplied (for a peppercorn rent) with a timber-framed kit which could easily be erected on a prepared base and made available to the locality for five years. This would allow time to test whether the new community would attract sufficient support in terms of congregation and money to justify building a permanent, more expensive church later. If that were the case, the 'relocatable' would be dismantled, given a '10,000-mile service', and then transported to another pilot site elsewhere in the diocese to repeat the procedure. It could have four such 'lives', after which it would be given away or demolished.

The project, which quickly became known as the 'hot-cross hut', attracted a lot of attention, culminating in a *Daily Telegraph* cartoon of a double decker bus with stained-glass windows being manoeuvred by a driver wearing a dog collar. This was all too much for the Archdeacon of Chichester. But encouragingly, despite his protestations, it was agreed to construct two of the prototypes that I had designed, one on the outskirts of Brighton and the other near Hastings. Excitedly, I finalised plans, built a model and launched the programme on television. This was another new experience and I had to travel with my hand-built model to the TV studio in Southampton. I was supplied with endless instant coffee in polystyrene cups too hot to hold and then quietly succumbed to a haircut which I assumed was mandatory. I protested that my parting was on the left, but it was pointed out in the sweetest of terms that I shouldn't be politically biased and it looked better on the right as it suited the studio lighting. I was then moved to 'make-up', from which I emerged as a jaundiced Gold Coast expatriate with eyelashes so caked I found it difficult to blink when exposed to the strong lights. But who was a novice to complain? Perhaps this was show business. My slot lasted all of three minutes, and the moment it was over all eyes turned on the next interviewee and I had to recover my possessions and make my departure unaided, disconcerted that the heat of the lights had buckled the cardboard roof of the model, which now looked more like a Shinto temple, and, worse still, my brand-new shirt (bought for the occasion) had a thick scum line of make-up right round the collar and on both cuffs.

As my design proposals developed I also paid a quick visit to Aalborg in Jutland, as I had seen illustrated another timber church with an A-shaped profile designed by a radical young architect, Jacob Blegvad, rapidly making a name for himself in Denmark. He didn't know me from Adam, but was enthusiastic and welcoming. And more than that, disarmingly generous. I located his office in downtown Aalborg, and after briefly saying hello and explaining that he was in the middle of a busy day and could we talk later that afternoon, he threw me his car keys and suggested I explore the area and enjoy myself in the meantime. The fact that he didn't know me, and that I didn't know the area and wasn't conversant with his car and seldom drove on the right, didn't seem to trouble him and, with an engaging smile, he closed the door behind me and told me how to find the best drinks in town. As I drove away gingerly I found myself immediately liking and admiring the man. He was decisive, assessed risks quickly and wasn't above testing a visiting British architect in a tongue-in-check way. I wondered how he would have handled the Archdeacon of Chichester. He would, I am sure, have been more cheerfully assertive than I was and would have feigned utter disbelief if tradition was seen to be getting in the way of progress. I was obviously far too deferential towards the church hierarchy, and eventually it was only with the support of others that my path was eased and I obtained approval for the project.

History will be ambivalent about the 'relocatable church' programme. It succeeded and everyone in the community loved it, but – here's the rub – forty years later it would still be there.

Chapter 12

Flowers from Covent Garden

Covent Garden Market had become impossibly congested, and heavy potato lorries from Lincolnshire would compete with flower deliveries from Holland for somewhere to park, having spent an inordinate amount of time challenging London's traffic. The fruit and vegetable section of the market, by far the largest, had already decided to relocate shortly to new premises south of the river at Nine Elms, and eyes were now turned on the flower market.

The Covent Garden Market Authority, in overall charge, expected the flower market to relocate as well but, once rid of the heavier and dirtier end that was fruit and veg, their association decided they would like to stay, not least because many of their customers were the big hotels and restaurants of the adjacent West End and it would be perverse to go elsewhere only to bring large quantities of flowers back to the centre of London.

We had been asked by the market authority to prepare development proposals for the entire site once it had been cleared, and this we had done. But the flower growers, a very different breed from the vegetable growers, now made a very good case for staying permanently and it then became necessary for us to prepare another study retaining the flower growers' market.

I knew little about how any London markets operated, regardless of whether they were meat, fish, flowers or anything else, so it was decided that I'd better find out. I asked my secretary if she would book me and an associate into the hotel nearest to Covent Garden so that we could study its activities over a twelve-hour hour cycle in order to better understand how it operated. As I was preoccupied with other work until the last moment, it was only when we were about to leave for London that I asked her where she had booked us in. 'The Savoy, of course,' Denise said brightly. 'It was the nearest one of the lot.' My colleague and I looked at each other and swallowed hard. She had done just what was asked of her, but whether our

73

clients were going to stand the bill was quite another matter. It was too late to change.

My colleague, John, and I had arranged between us to watch the way night-time activities took place from nine in the evening until the same time next morning, and we planned to leave the hotel every couple of hours, clipboard in hand, to record what we saw. As we didn't want to attract too much attention at the market, we both donned cloth caps and turned our coat collars up, but neither did we wish to arouse curiosity at the Savoy, as we realised we were more suitably dressed for the service entrance. We had some difficulty in persuading the patronising commissionaire of our honest intentions, not least because of our extraordinary comings and goings throughout the night, and took the disdainful shrug of his epauletted shoulders as sufficient authority to behave eccentrically. John was far and away the more extrovert of the two of us – he mountaineered, held strong, uninvited opinions, and wore garish neckties – but neither of us was really prepared for our Jekyll and Hyde comings and goings. We were too giggly, prone to send each other up, and feared we would lack conviction among the market traders.

We had booked into the Savoy earlier in the day and entered a wonder-land we had only seen in films and plays. On being shown our room, we explored every nook and cranny and couldn't contain ourselves when we found a water closet with a sprung and heated seat. I sat there transfixed as I contemplated the way the other half lived, and this revelation was height-ened further by discovering an inset telephone receiver next to the toilet roll. Did all the guests feel the need to telephone their stockbroker while opening their bowels before breakfast? Images of opulence and corpulence fed my imagination and I felt more and more like an intruder who might be discov-ered any moment and quietly escorted to the back door.

Our first foray into the market where the fruit-and-vegetable activities were still being conducted for a few weeks more was immediately revealing. As London's working-day traffic began to thin out, so market deliveries from far away began to arrive. Produce looked as fresh and wholesome as that at a parish Harvest Festival, but the language was a good deal pithier. Trying to engage the attention of one cockney wholesaler, I remarked how generously sized the King Edward potatoes were. He immediately picked up two of the biggest and declared, 'And these would keep the Duchess of Argyll going all night' – a reference to the alleged extramarital exploits of the Duke of Argyll's wife that had been well documented in the Sunday press. Costermongers' banter was quick and sharp and this was the way they traded. They made sales as quickly as an on-course bookmaker and words were never wasted. They would shift hundredweights of vegetables in an hour and then retire to one of many surrounding pubs for Guinness and a pie, only to return with energy restored and wits sharpened for however much of the night it took to clear the entire stock.

We were both so fascinated that we didn't feel at all tired, but by the time we had finished our inspection at about 4 a.m., we thought we had seen enough to picture how the whole place operated and decided to return to the Savoy. We were beginning to feel cold and were having some difficulty in translating the traders' pungent responses to language suitable for our questionnaire.

On reaching our room we removed our cloth caps and coats, sat down heavily and tried to think of anyone we disliked sufficiently to telephone in the middle of the night. After a drink, John brightened up and said that he had read somewhere that room service at the Savoy was legendary and that, on one occasion, Noël Coward, unable to sleep, rang down and asked for a grand piano to be sent up to his suite. We wondered if the establishment still worked like that but we couldn't decide what to ask for. We considered real tests of the system like an elephant's-foot doorstop, but realised that, to be taken seriously, our request would have to be realistic. I suggested a back collar stud, and this was agreed, so at 4.22 precisely I phoned the night porter saying a back collar stud was needed straight away in room 104. I received a courteous acknowledgement of my request and I replaced the phone. John set the second hand of his watch, and 3 minutes and 40 seconds later there was a gentle knock on the door and in walked the floor valet carrying in gloved hands a silver salver upon which, on a starched linen coaster, stood one back collar stud. 'I believe this is what you wanted, sir, and should there be anything else at all that you may require please be sure to let me know.' The system still worked.

Sadly, after months of protracted negotiations the flower growers were obliged to leave, and by about that time attitudes towards old, disused buildings were beginning to change. As a student I had been taught that most Victorian architecture was beyond the pale, a view echoed some years later when Sir Kenneth Clark, who achieved national fame through his television series *Civilisation*, observed that a man of taste could be defined as a man 'whose taste stopped in 1810'. But along came John Betjeman, Hugh Casson and others to remind us how wrong we were, so that attitudes and later policies towards our built heritage altered, and in the case of Covent Garden Market, just in time. The Greater London Council (GLC) decided to keep the iron-and-glass market buildings and converted them into retail, craft and tourist facilities. This needed a sensitive hand and highlighted an interesting problem of interpretation.

Old buildings scheduled to be restored have seldom been constructed all at one time, but are usually the result of decades, if not centuries, of adaptation by succeeding users. If it is decided to retain an existing structure, this gives rise to lengthy debate over which date to take it back to and which features can be safely described as authentically original. None of this is very widely understood, but the GLC architects' department showed the wider world how difficult it is to arrive at the indisputably right answer. Years after we had left, it produced an excellent scheme which at the same time revitalised an entire area that had languished for far too long.

Chapter 13

The American Dream

Looking through architectural journals, I became aware that part of the research necessary for the diocesan study of new building sites involved a trip to the United States. As I'd never been to America I was happy to have the opportunity to see for myself a country which, until then, I'd only visualised from the cheap seats of my local cinema. Apparently, the Episcopal diocese in Massachusetts had been experimenting with timber-framed churches and community buildings which quickly met local needs and inexpensive so, if they could do it, why not us?

It would have been foolish to go all that way only to look at a couple of wooden buildings, however interesting they were, so I decided to take some holiday I was owed and see as much as possible of Boston, where I would stay, and its surroundings. One of the city's main institutions is the Massachusetts Institute of Technology (known as MIT), where I had been given an introduction to György Kepes, a Hungarian-born abstract painter who was involved in a pioneering study linking art and science. This had nothing whatever to do with prefabricated churches, but I wasn't going to miss the opportunity of meeting him. As an easel artist working in oils, Kepes had come to realise that his work would have further impact and interest by adding the dimension of time. In MIT's technological environment electrical engineers abounded and he had found it easy to select a small team to interpret the surfaces and colours of his paintings and replicate them in coloured light on a large background screen. After some early experimental work the team produced a major design depicting the approach by air to a city at night. A sequence of endlessly differing coloured lights was programmed to repeat every five minutes, and the resulting work consisted of a rapid succession of abstract patterns depicting the night-time metropolitan panorama which, because of its time sequence, could never have been captured on a single canvas. Kepes had artists and scientists not only talking to each other, but understanding each other's work and wanting to collaborate more closely as they experienced the buzz of it all. The continuing absence elsewhere of real understanding between the disciplines forty years later makes me realise how ahead of his time Kepes was.

At that time MIT was full of excitement. The necessary mathematical modelling for the American moon-shot had been developed and refined there, and it had the stimulating atmosphere of 'a place to be'. With Harvard only down the road, the senses were sizzling and, mercifully, not always without humour. A satirical faculty review contained an imaginary conversation between two opposing scientists locked in earnest debate, and ended with the closing line 'Sure Prometheus discovered fire, but what's he done since?'

While I was there Le Corbusier, the post-war giant of western architecture, died suddenly while swimming in the Mediterranean and it was decided to mark the event by arranging a number of tributes at a specially arranged gathering in the Fogg Memorial Building. Walter Gropius, that other towering figure of twentieth-century architectural modernism, was directing the School of Architecture at that time. The world knew him as the founder of the Bauhaus, the highly innovative and influential school of design and architecture that was to influence a whole generation until it was closed down by the Nazis, who thought it doctrinally seditious. After first fleeing to England, Gropius had made his way to the States before the outbreak of war and was by now in a position of eminence he thoroughly deserved. For me he had only ever been a name in a book on architectural theory, and now here was I merely passing through Boston and meant to be doing something entirely different listening to a funeral oration by this giant I never thought I'd set eyes on. All the great names were present, including Jean Louis Sert, Luis Kahn and Paul Rudolf and there was I with a free seat in the stalls.

To coincide with the event, Kodak had mounted an impressive exhibition in the neighbouring Carpenter Center for the Visual Arts which had, in fact, been designed by Le Corbusier, although it was his only work in North America. Beautifully displayed illustrations of his work in Rio de Janeiro, Paris, Marseille, Ronchamp and Chandigarh held a rapt audience captive and it was only many years later that I learned that Le Corbusier had never visited the site before designing the Carpenter Center nor supervised its construction. I was also to learn that his impressive range of buildings for the capital of the Punjab at Chandigarh were extremely impractical and uncomfortable to use as a result of scant dialogue with representative users and only superficial knowledge of the local climate. Perhaps it is necessary for gods to have feet of clay to make them credible. I should have remembered the effect that Ovid's *Metamorphoses* had had on the European imagination ever since Chaucer.

As it was my first visit to the States I didn't fully realise how untypical of America the New England seaboard was and just how much wealth had settled in Boston. Serious inherited money from the construction of the railroad, mining, lumber and the newspaper empires found its way to cities like Boston, whose third and fourth generations were diligently conserving their wealth and enjoying a lifestyle that would remain unknown in many other parts of the country. Wealth in such a city doesn't feel the need to be conspicuous as it might in, say, Texas, but you can feel its unstrained presence just the same. When the Boston Symphony Orchestra arranged a concert for the city's patrons and well-breeched cognoscenti, it was careful to put it on at three o'clock on a Friday afternoon to distinguish it, no doubt, from venues elsewhere in the country that could only attract audiences by holding their concerts at 7.30 p.m. on a Saturday, when no one was having to work. When I asked my Bostonian hosts why the concerts were held at such an unusual time, they explained matter-of-factly that members of the audience flying in from Chicago perhaps would still like to get home in time for dinner.

Ed Bullerjahn came from Scandinavian stock and, after wartime service flying for the US Navy, married into a wealthy family and began practising as an architect, and latterly a yacht designer, in Boston. We met by chance when I walked into the office of the English-Speaking Union and, while I was waiting at Reception, overheard a pained voice say, 'I know you've got a degree, but can't you type?' Ed was remonstrating with a hapless young secretary struggling to change the ribbon on her typewriter, and my unscheduled arrival was apparently just in time to avoid tears. She left noisily for lunch without looking at me, and Ed and I introduced ourselves.

Ed and his wife Julianna were active socialites on the Boston dinner circuit and on one occasion they were guests at the table of a particularly wealthy matriarch whose unstoppable flow of conversation tended to blunt even the healthiest appetite. A resigned table had been listening to their hostess for a full twenty minutes when Ed felt obliged to do something to preserve everyone's sanity, not least because he was sitting directly opposite her. He very slowly and inconspicuously slid off his patent leather Boston pumps and drew them up onto his lap. Holding a shoe in each hand, be poked the toes just sufficiently above the table for everyone to see. Choosing his moment carefully, he waited for his hostess's eventual pause for breath, when he exclaimed, 'If you don't take your feet off my lap, Mrs Rosenberg, I shall get very upset.' He was never invited again, of course, but went straight to the top of the A list of everyone else round the table.

Ed and Julianna lived in one of a pair of splendid penthouse apartments in Beacon Hill, the other being occupied by the eccentric and extremely wealthy Miss Morse, a surviving descendent of Samuel Finley Breese Morse, who invented the Morse Code in the mid-nineteenth century. Among her many fascinating diversions, she had a passion for fur coats, which she stored on rails in a separate refrigerated room in her apartment. She had a close affinity with her furry apparel and, over the years, she developed a very close bond with all of them, widely differing though they were. As she could scarcely bear being parted from them when she left on one of her many journeys far and wide, she had come to an arrangement with Ed that he would enter the cool store at appropriate intervals and talk to them, offering reassurances that she was still thinking of them despite being hundreds of miles away and that gladness filled her heart at the prospect of being reunited with them shortly.

No one other than Ed could have carried this off with such aplomb and he relished the thought of communing with them whenever he had the opportunity, displaying a soliloquising skill that convinced me that he really believed in this charade and wanted it to go on for ever.

Ed was also a brilliant raconteur and one of the many true accounts he enjoyed sharing with friends concerned the meteoric rise to fame of a young, struggling architect with whom he had been friendly in the early days of their careers. Edward Durell Stone was eventually to become one of the most successful architects in the USA, because of his groundbreaking design in 1939 for the New York Museum of Modern Art on West 53rd Street. It was a building of startling modernity amid the brownstone and *beaux-arts* town-houses. He was later known also for his equally impressive, if showy, US embassies in many parts of the world.

But when recently qualified and penniless all those years before, he once asked Ed to help him net his first really big commercial client, involving a ruse of startling audacity. The plan, he explained, was simple. Ed knew the Italian owner of a small downtown restaurant that had vacant space on an upper floor and he persuaded him to let Edward Stone use it for twenty-four hours. Stone had himself in the meantime approached a firm of luxury soft furnishing and lighting suppliers to let him borrow a display exhibition for what he described as a very important and wealthy client about to spend countless millions upon a commercial project where their products would be specified, which he then promptly installed on the restaurant's upper floor, Ed was then to ask the Italian to provide chilled Chablis and canapés on the understanding that he would be paid without fail by the end of the month. Finally, and by far the trickiest conceit, he asked the director of the small but very prestigious twentieth-century art gallery if, just conceivably, he might with the utmost care borrow a couple of European twentieth-century masters after they closed at 5 p.m. and have them returned before opening time the next morning. Of course, they would be fully insured and he would take personal responsibility for their security, with his life if necessary. Doubt and misgiving crossed the director's face despite their long friendship, so Edward Stone hastily made reference to 'an appropriate consideration' for all the trouble.

Thus it all gradually came together, whereupon Edward Stone telephoned the young hotel entrepreneur of whose arrival in town he'd heard on the grapevine and expressed interest in designing his next hotel in the Bahamas for him. The response was cool and abrupt, and it was explained that he had never heard of him and in any case he'd fixed appointments with three other established architects on his shortlist. Fired by indignation and brimming self-interest, Edward Stone pleaded earnestly with him to spare just half an hour the next evening to at least meet him in his new atelier a couple of streets away. A rather resigned agreement followed and a rendezvous was arranged.

At 6.30 p.m. promptly a well-groomed head waiter opened the freshly washed side door of the restaurant and led his visitors upstairs to a deep-pile-carpeted reception area lit by the loveliest Czech glass chandelier anyone had ever seen. Drinks and canapés were served, after which the developer was led along a corridor to the front room that was just narrow enough to compel the intended client and his glamorous female appendage to see an original Cézanne and a real Matisse en route.

Young, pushy developers with trophy girlfriends cannot easily disguise wonder at the unexpected, and all this made Edward Stone's task easier. Deliberately avoiding any reference to his prestige atelier surroundings, he asked demurely whether he could be told a little about the developer's intentions in the Bahamas. These were outlined in some detail and at the end Stone paused thoughtfully and then, after a well-rehearsed moment of silence, said, 'OK, I'll take on the commission,' fully knowing that he hadn't even remotely been offered it. The pair looked at him blankly and he quickly added, 'But only on one condition.' They looked even more dumbfounded, so he added further, 'So long as you remember you're only the goddam client.' After a moment the girlfriend exploded with joy and threw her arms around her consort who, probably for the first and perhaps the last time in his bucca-neering career, had been wrong-footed. 'Oh, that's just *too* wonderful!' she squealed. 'He's just *got* to do it.' And with the mercurial speed of a successful punter, he took Ed on there and then and thereafter they worked together, albeit with a glittering succession of different young women on the devel-oper's arm, for many years to come.

Chapter 14

Phoenix Joins the Team

Hove had always been proud to disassociate itself from its larger and more vulgar neighbour Brighton, and although the two towns were contiguous, there was a great deal of 'keeping themselves to themselves' in the smaller town. Hove's town hall, built in 1882 and designed by Sir Alfred Waterhouse, who also designed Brighton's Hotel Metropole, was a Victorian joy to behold, brimming with solid self-assurance, and a monument to civic pride and municipal taste. Its Great Hall had been furnished with a large pipe organ costing the huge sum of £1,820 at the time, and in the tower was housed a carillon of bells which played well-known airs, including 'Home Sweet Home,' 'Bluebells of Scotland' and 'God Bless the Prince of Wales'. On Saturdays it went the full hog with rousing renditions of 'Rule Britannia' and 'God Save the King'.

The edifice was constructed in terracotta and red brick and built to last for ever. Sir Nicholas Pevsner, the eminent architectural historian, had described it as 'so red, so hard, so imperishable', but notwithstanding that, one winter's night, it burnt to the ground.

To raise income it had often been let for outside events such as dinner dances, concerts and boxing, and on that fateful occasion it had been hired for a festive event which included a reception, followed by a four-course dinner, after which the tables were cleared away for a gala ball. To achieve this turnaround in a building which hadn't been designed for such activities, the remnants from the dining tables were cleared and temporarily thrown into wet and dry bins at the foot of the staircase – food scraps in one, paper hats, crackers and crêpe paper decorations in the other. After the ball finished at one o'clock in the morning the side tables were cleared once more and their contents, including recently used ashtrays, were thrown into the dry waste bins. One cigarette end had not been properly extinguished. With textbook conditions for a fire – burning paper and the updraught of the staircase – the frames took hold very quickly. What Pevsner had described as 'imperishable' burned like a torch, made worse by the fact that in the early hours of a winter Sunday morning no one was about to notice it. Eventually a passing croupier returning home from a Brighton casino saw the fire and raised the alarm, but all to no avail as much of the building was gutted by then. The fire brigade's first task was to ensure no lives were at risk – they were particularly concerned about the resident caretaker – before trying to save the adjacent houses.

The day before, the borough had possessed a fully functioning town hall; now it didn't. The town clerk, John Stevens, had to leave his sickbed where he was recovering from influenza and, muffled in scarf, hat and gloves, he requisitioned the nearby Hove Museum. He retrieved any records and artefacts that hadn't been damaged by fire or water and established a new temporary administrative base, encouraged and supported by an energetic and persuasive solicitor, Donald Edmonds, who was mayor at the time.

The staff having camped in almost impossible conditions at the museum for a couple of weeks, it became clear that decisions had to be taken about the longer-term future if local administration was to be effectively maintained, so an option appraisal and feasibility study was quickly called for.

Although my involvement with Hove Council up until then had only been slight, involving the George Street Civic Trust Improvement Scheme and a later set of proposals for a project which didn't materialise, mine was a familiar face when something architectural was wanted in a hurry, so I was summoned to the temporary Mayor's Parlour which, it turned out, was a lot more interesting than the old one, as much of the museum's porcelain, glass and miniatures were still in place. I wasn't sure what was going to be asked of me. Was I a stand-in until a well-known London architect was appointed, or was this the real thing? After a short conversation it became clear that not only was I to prepare a feasibility study, but there was every likelihood that the full commission would follow. I left the building walking on air and in a daze, and spent an absurd amount of time trying to find my parked car.

The ruined town-hall building smouldered for days and made it impossible to ascertain how much, if any, of the existing structure could be used. The heat from the blaze had been so intense that even the phosphor-bronze mountings to the tower bells had melted and run down the inside of the tower like so much candle wax.

Following my appointment I introduced a structural engineer to the appraisal and our joint opinion was that the remnants of the old building were unsafe and would have to be demolished and an entirely fresh start made on a new building. This recommendation was accepted by the council. A generation later attitudes would change dramatically and the fact that a small part of the west wing had survived would have been encouragement enough for the preservationists, both on the council and elsewhere, to press for a period-piece replacement. Hove could well have got a Tesco pastiche which would, no doubt, have delighted the planning committee and satisfied baying ratepayers.

Hove Council then delegated detailed responsibility to a specially formed Civic Buildings Committee, the members of which, understandably, had never commissioned designs for a town hall or civic offices before, and neither had I ever designed such a building. All of this seemed to deter no one, and I was asked to produce a feasibility study so that the project could be roughly costed before the mayor, town clerk and I went cap in hand, to see the appropriate minister in Whitehall. Our case was compellingly simple. We once had a town hall, and the following day it was gone, and there was an obvious limit to the length of time the town could be properly administered by a staff hidden among the eclectic artefacts of a small provincial museum. In the circumstances, financial authority to proceed was given and we all made a prompt start before anyone in Whitehall changed their mind.

I suggested that it would be foolish to proceed with the design without learning lessons from recently completed town halls and civic centres elsewhere. Few, if any, had been built in Britain, as the post-war emphasis had been on housing, schools and factories, so I looked elsewhere and was not surprised to find interesting examples in the Netherlands, where their post-war emphasis was different from ours. The best schemes I identified were scattered about Holland and varied considerably in size and appearance, but I thought that each one had something to commend it. I drew up a tentative itinerary to include Zwolle, near the Zuider Zee; Hengelo, near the German border to the east; Arnhem to the south; and lastly Hilversum, which I had deliberately left until the end as it was the most important. Although the other three dated from after the war, Hilversum's internationally renowned town hall of 1934 had been designed by W. M. Dudok and had become one of the most definitive and well-regarded designs of its time.

It was decided to form a representative group of members drawn from the Civic Buildings Committee to go and visit these. It included previous mayors, a couple of elderly aldermen, and a woman councillor who had been included to 'advise on the ladies lavatories and kitchen'. The group flew to Amsterdam, where we picked up three Ford hire cars, the mayor driving one, the town clerk another and me the third. Our little convoy made its way tentatively to our first night's destination, a small but comfortable hotel located between the railway and the main street. I was not in the least conversant with the internal dynamics of a mixed group like this, all of its members being my clients in a sense, and I was even less aware of its real or assumed pecking order. The aldermen pulled rank as they were senior to the councillors, until the woman councillor made it clear that she should have the first choice of room ahead of any of them. The current mayor thought he should deserve some priority, which didn't go down too well with the former mayors, who were keenly aware of their seniority on the council. So the town clerk, who was clearly of greater value to the town than anyone else and the only permanent post-holder, did his best to organise everything fairly, with just the right degree of deference in each case. Obviously as the architect, I didn't figure in this process at all, for which I was deeply grateful and was happy to accept whatever came my way. As it turned out I was thoughtfully treated by all the others throughout the trip, I imagine because they had never before travelled overseas with a professional adviser and weren't quite sure how to regard one.

The oldest and most Pickwickian alderman didn't want a room at the front because he thought it would be noisy, so demanded one at the back, only to discover after he had unpacked (and after everyone else had settled in their rooms and unpacked as well) that it overlooked a railway goods yard where a shunting engine worked continuously uncoupling and recoupling goods wagons for departure from the nearby station. The town clerk, who by then was in the bath, was summoned to hear his complaint and 'do something about it'. By the time he had dried himself and reached the room the situation had deteriorated further because the alderman had snapped the pull switch off the bedside light under the weight of his flabby hand, made even less steady by its having gripped a travelling whisky flask until that moment. He could not now turn off the light. The bulb had become too hot to touch, so he had removed a sock and wrapped it round the bulb, only to find that it burned a hole in the sock. The town clerk arrived to find him stumbling around in the dark clutching his burned fingers. We were all off to a bad start.

I had for some time been wondering how I might introduce twentieth-century design thinking into a quintessentially nineteenth-century borough. The former town hall had been hard, symmetrical and inconvenient to use, so here was an opportunity to give Hove a building that eschewed municipal pomp and aldermanic pride and produce a town hall that was informal, asymmetrical and easy to use. But a glance round the Civic Buildings Committee didn't persuade me that they were ready to embrace the spirit of the time (it was the Sixties by then). The only way to win them over, I thought, was to highlight the functional shortcomings of the old building they were familiar with and show them how these had been overcome in more recent buildings – in other words, stress a convenient working environment that they could enjoy, rather than embark on a stylist hard sell which would probably encounter aldermanic resistance.

I was not sure that I was completely honest with myself or the group in solving the problem this way, as I found myself choosing the four foreign locations because they all possessed features I wanted to include in my own design which was forming all too rapidly in my mind. I didn't regard this as sleight of hand, and certainly no one seemed to take exception to the process when, a couple of months later, I presented my initial design proposals to the committee and it proved easy to garner their acceptance as I was able to explain, as we went along, that a particular feature was like the one they had admired in, say, Arnhem or Hilversum.

Of all the locations it was Hilversum that left the most lasting impression, not just because it had been beautifully designed or because the design hadn't dated. Miraculously, despite being requisitioned during the war by the Gestapo, who had shrouded the clock tower in camouflage netting supported by rusty scaffold poles punched into the beautiful cream brickwork, it had been immaculately restored so that not a trace of those evil days remained and everything looked as new as paint. In addition, the Dutch national temperament is not unlike the British and it was easy for my visitors to warm to the whole experience.

My design brief drawn up was quite enlightened and left latitude for fairly broad interpretation. This enabled me to 'democratise' the new building and gain popular approval necessary for a design many would think too avant-garde. I wasn't seeking to be 'modern' for superficially stylistic reasons, but it would have been impossible to meet the operational demands and social expectations of the day if the layout had to be shoehorned into a period stage set. I was determined that there would be no ceremonial steps to the front entrance, no uniformed functionary behind a mahogany desk to check your bona fides, no tokenistic seating on the edge of the council chamber for any member of the public brave enough to enter. Instead there would be openness, easy access on the level (long before legislation was to demand this), abundant light and informality. The new building would have to be enjoyable to be in rather than make the occupants feel intimidated by the overbearing formality of an old order.

The double-height foyer we designed was lit naturally by a 'glass cascade' with specially designed platforms to carry an abundance of luxuriant plants which looked magnificent at night, whilst the Great Hall itself (to accommodate everything from banquets to exhibitions, concerts, political meetings and dances) was acoustically tuned by a hundred hollow pyramids made of wych elm which appeared to float above the high containing walls. Stefan Grappelli, the virtuoso jazz violinist, loved it when he gave one of the opening concerts.

A semi-enclosed Japanese garden at the north end was provided to give clerical staff a pleasing view from their desks, and in the front of the town hall where it overlooked Church Road, a covered undercroft was designed as a meeting place where you could buy a newspaper or admire the impressive 'phoenix' mosaic set into the floor depicting the spot where the great fire started.

The municipal mind at its most warped has seen to it that, in the thirty years since completion, the Japanese garden and the undercroft space have been requisitioned for more office accommodation and all the plants in the glass cascade removed to cut maintenance costs, thus stripping the building of some of its most imaginative and admired features. What troubled me was not that I was never asked for my views, even informally, but that the council's actions demonstrated a total lack of understanding of what these features had been provided for in the first place.

This could never have happened in Hilversum.

Chapter 15

Culture Shock

At about this time one of the many economic recessions to hit the construction and development industry was upon us and predictably it affected all the associated professions, including architecture. Although it took some time to sink in, it became alarmingly clear that if we were going to retain key staff in the absence of UK commissions, I must find work abroad. Saudi Arabia was just beginning to flex its financial muscles as its government discovered the ability to write out bigger cheques than anybody else, and what better way of asserting national supremacy and improving life for the Saudis than developing its inadequate infrastructure? Through the absence of any higher education facilities in the kingdom, the marketplace for foreign consultants opened up just at the right time and a number of large engineering consultancies were among the first to take advantage of this situation. British consulting engineers enjoyed a justifiable reputation for high standards, set as long ago as the 1930s, and such firms were trusted for their integrity and reliability.

I knew that most civil and mechanical engineering practices, however large and prestigious, did not carry their own architectural departments and I therefore presented myself at their door rather promptly and offered to enhance their overall capability and thereby make them more competitive in what was becoming a very competitive market. Thus I became involved in what would turn out to be one of the most illuminating and fascinating periods of my career so far and that would introduce me to a Middle East I barely knew.

Ahmed bin Akib came from Oman and I had once met his father, a wealthy and influential merchant and close friend of the local emir. He had received me on the roof terrace of his expansive villa where we sat on rugs and silk cushions to enjoy the first cool breeze of the evening. I can't remember what we talked about, but I do recall that throughout our conversation he conscientiously picked his toes and never looked up.

British telecommunications consultants with whom I was working in the Middle East had asked me if I'd keep an eye on Ahmed. He was coming to Brighton to attend an English language school and they were worried that he wouldn't know anybody. After a preliminary meeting to help him get his bearings I arranged that he should spend the day with us at home. The following weekend, at an agreed time, I called at his lodgings in a not-too-salubrious part of the town. I rang the doorbell twice and eventually a harassed-looking, middle-aged woman answered wearing a plastic apron over an old housecoat. She explained in a rather pained voice that her new arrival was still settling in, but I could wait – on the doorstep. After a few minutes a disheveled Ahmed arrived at the bottom of the stairs apologising for his appearance. He was in vest and trousers and still had shaving cream on half of his face, the other half decorated with small strips of toilet paper to cover shaving cuts. He rather sheepishly explained that, at home, a barber came in each morning to shave him and his father and he was not yet used to handling the equipment on his own.

I waited another ten minutes or so on the doorstep, shifting my weight from one leg to the other and discouraging a mangy-looking dog that had decided to join me from somewhere. Ahmed eventually arrived with more apologies, reeking of musk-deer aftershave. This was certainly impressive, but lost its intended impact when mixed with TCP.

Jumping into the car, we took a short diversion around the town which, on a Sunday, was easier than usual and he asked continuous questions about my wife and family – who else would be at home and how would they be dressed? I explained that everything would be very informal and that, other than my wife, he would only meet my children and a dog. I tried to bring his attention back to the history of Brighton, but he only half listened and just as I was searching for a sensible explanation of how the Royal Pavilion came to look as it does, he suddenly put his hand on my arm and asked me to stop the car. Surely he wasn't as nauseated as I was by his aftershave, I thought – but no, he had just glanced at his hands and announced that he must have a manicure before meeting my wife. I explained that the likelihood of finding a manicurist in a rundown part of London Road on a Sunday afternoon was remote and, in any case, it didn't matter in the least because it just wasn't going to be one of those occasions. He looked at me distrustfully for a while as we drove along but said no more until we arrived home.

I gained the impression that he was the only son of elderly parents and probably found it hard to mix, even in Oman, but in a foreign country it must have been doubly difficult. He was obviously a few years older than his new classmates at the school of English, and the young women would have found it difficult to be attracted to someone of his age and demeanour. Armani-suited and heavily pomaded, finding himself surrounded by jeans and sweatshirts advertising the attractions of anarchy, he must have looked an oddball and indeed, must have felt like one.

As I knew nothing about his diet, afternoon tea seemed a safe option, so we served it, much to the amusement of the younger members of my family who were accustomed to a DIY snack at this hour. I kept the conversation going, ranging broadly and somewhat airily over the English way of life (not that ours was remotely typical) and our family structures. Dwelling on the last, and probably as a result of an ill-timed reference that may have hinted at elderly parents, he loudly interrupted to assure us all that his mother was very energetic and still had periods. It takes a lot to dissuade hungry children from finishing their favourite Victoria sponge, but on that occasion an astonished dog was left wondering why, suddenly, he had been given the supper of his life.

Such experiences were to become more frequent as my work took on a different complexion, and these educated me, as the host, as much as they did my visitors. Knowing how unfamiliar and daunting it would be for a stranger arriving in London for the first time, I agreed some weeks later to meet another client's contact, an Arabian high-flyer, at the BOAC terminal in Buckingham Palace Road. As he had had a long flight from the Saudi capital Riyadh, I thought that we might send his luggage on by taxi and give him the opportunity of stretching his legs and at the same time of seeing Westminster Abbey and the Palace of Westminster on the way to the hotel. He had telexed to say he would like to do this.

The BOAC terminal, a 1930s piece of art-deco triumphalism, was comfortable enough to wait in when it became clear his flight would be delayed. As I hadn't met him before I had no idea what he looked like, and when eventually the Saudi Arabian Airlines' passengers entered the arrivals hall I realised it wasn't going to be easy to spot him. Without exception, everyone seemed to have black hair, brown eyes, and swarthy skin, and most wore flowing white robes with a red-and-white chequered headscarf. I hastily adapted a piece of white card taken from an adjacent counter and wrote my name on it in large black letters with the title of his company in Arabic script beneath, copied from his letterhead.

Saudi Arabia had reached the stage when bright young sons of wealthy merchants were being sent to Cairo for a first degree and perhaps on to an American university for a masters, whereupon, using family and tribal connections to the full, there was every chance that a favoured son could be appointed junior minister in the fledgling administration at quite a tender age.

In negotiating business deals with Saudis there was one remarkable difference from western custom that impressed me. I was used to dealing with British and American companies that were anxious to win a construction contract and would be all over you with oily charm and excessive hospitality up to the point where the contract was signed, but thereafter relations would revert to arm's length as their claims surveyors went into action seeking extras to inflate what had been a dangerously low tender submitted to win the job in the first place. But dealing with the Saudis was different. They would be quite distant and seemingly detached during the negotiating stage, but once they had entered into a contract they would treat you warmly as a friend. So it was with Abdullah Khan, who was to work closely with us in Britain as the client representative.

He eventually appeared in the arrivals hall and didn't take long to identify me. He looked as bewildered as most first-timers are, but as we entered Buckingham Palace Road together an hour later than originally planned, he looked distinctly apprehensive at the teeming rush-hour masses and the level of noise everywhere. We walked closely together as far as Victoria Station, and when we entered Victoria Street the tide of commuters became even pushier and louder. Quite suddenly he grasped my hand and held on to it firmly thereafter. Not unexpectedly, one or two of my Brighton-based neighbours and friends happened to pass us on their way home and, after encountering a few raised eyebrows which were beginning to annoy me, it struck me that none of them would be remotely aware that in Jeddah and Riyadh, say, it is quite common for male colleagues to walk hand in hand without the slightest cause for comment. Aware that *qui s'excuse, s'accuse* would make things worse, I responded with a neighbourly greeting or some fatuous comment about the weather, knowing fully that the cocktail circuit in Brighton would grasp the incident gleefully and studiously embroider it for weeks to come. As it transpired it did, but for months rather than weeks, providing limitless amusement.

Chapter 16

Visiting Mecca

The Hippodrome, Brighton was one of the last surviving music halls in the south and I had warm memories of being taken there by my father in the 1930s to watch ten or more variety acts that made up an evening's entertainment. Funny men, vocalists, ventriloquists and contortionists held the stage in turn, supported by a live, if rather moth-eaten, orchestra for whom, even my tender age, I always felt sorry. Max Miller, Brighton's 'cheeky chappie', often performed and it had become a proving ground for many a stand-up entertainer. My sister, who had her first job nearby, was attracted, as were most of her teenage friends, to the glamour of the greasepaint, and was befriended by one of the troupe to the consternation of our father and the fascination of her much younger brother. It was he who, in his more sober moments, introduced the family to the timeless aphorism 'Be nice to them on the way up because you are going to meet them again on the way down', and all this was a generation before Laurence Olivier acquainted us with Archie Rice on the way down in *The Entertainer*.

The Hippodrome survived World War II, but only just, and after a change of ownership it was decided to convert it into a bingo hall for the entertainment giant Mecca, and my firm was asked to provide architectural services. A regional director in a shiny, wide-lapelled bird's-eye suit met two of us at the Hippodrome and showed us round, accompanied by the very deferential local manager. When confident that the manager was within earshot, he embarked on what, for him, must have been a well-worn mantra. He said that Mecca had three simple objectives, which were, first, to look after their loyal staff – 'and what a privilege that is'; second, to provide the public with the popular entertainment 'they deserved'; and third, dropping his voice: 'to make a little money' .

If I'd been brave (and solvent) enough to walk away at that point I would have done so, but as I wasn't, the next stage of my induction was put in place. I was asked to attend the vast converted picture palace in Streatham High Road and see how a large-scale bingo session was organised. Equipped with a programme, I was to attend the three o'clock session the following Thursday afternoon. I was told that this arrangement could not in any circumstances be postponed as the whole project was on a very tight timetable, not to say tight budget. I quickly agreed to the arrangement if only to end the meeting, but on returning to my office realised that the date clashed with a lunch invitation at the Athenaeum I had accepted from Sir Kenneth Blackburne, who was determined to thank me properly for the work undertaken on the relocatable church project despite, or perhaps because of, the fact that my ears were still ringing from the archdeacon's admonition. Sir Kenneth had invited me for 12.15 p.m., which was a help, and as I knew he had to get away promptly afterwards, it looked as if I could probably still make it to Streatham on time.

I had never entered the Athenaeum before but knew that the club was designed by Decimus Burton (who also worked at Hove) and was opened in 1830. I was vaguely aware that its membership comprised for the most part retired admirals, diocesan bishops and former diplomats and I had therefore to dress appropriately, but I reminded myself that later that afternoon I didn't want to stand out like a sore thumb in the queue outside the Streatham picture house. I couldn't have it both ways, so I settled for looking as though I was lunching at the Athenaeum. Its interior of faded glory, with its sense of curious displacement and slow revelation, was yet to benefit from an overdue post-war refurbishment. The turkey carpet was worn and wrinkled at the edges, the curtains carried a fine festoon of dust, and all the brass handles were dented and loose on their spindles. My host was, as ever, charming and apt and made me feel as though I was a guest who really mattered – so much so, that after he had ordered boiled eel for us both, having asked if I liked 'fish', when the waiter soon arrived with a covered silver dish to seek our approval, Sir Kenneth nodded in my direction and the waiter lifted the lid solemnly for my approbation. There sat a long, muscular eel decorously coiled by the chef on a bed of parsley and I had not the slightest idea of what was expected of me. The fish looked fearsome and unappetising and I was keenly aware that I wouldn't know an overcooked specimen when I saw one. Bearing in mind that this was a shared order, was I meant to indicate how many inches of the coil I would like for my portion? In the end I smiled at the waiter and said that it was a long time since I'd seen such a fine eel and hoped he'd take that as sufficient response to go away and serve it. Obviously he had seen the untutored before, and with a set face removed the fish for dissection elsewhere.

Sir Kenneth Blackburne was encouraging and thoughtful and showed genuine interest in my developing career, recalling the many pitfalls he'd had to encounter, not always successfully, in his early diplomatic career. True to his word, he had to depart quite promptly after lunch, which enabled me to call a cab and scamper to Streatham with all speed. The roads were surprisingly clear at that time of day, and with a quarter of an hour in hand I arrived at my destination, or more accurately at the street corner just beyond it, as the last thing I wanted was to be dropped at the head of the queue opposite the main entrance, looking as if I'd just left the Athenaeum.

The queue hadn't begun to move, so I had just enough time to hastily modify my appearance. Keeping my coat buttoned up, I tore off my rarely worn regimental tie and pulled out an elderly cloth cap I had stuffed into my coat pocket at the last moment. I found myself at the end of a very animated queue surrounded, it appeared, by the entire female workforce of a local laundry who'd finished their morning shift and were coming to gossip and have a flutter on tomorrow's pay packet. My unorthodox appearance among them caused some good-natured consternation, and when I admitted that I'd never played bingo before and had been sent along to learn, I found myself immediately adopted by a group of turbaned, hair-rollered peroxide blondes whose feet were giving them hell and who insisted that I join them once we got inside.

The auditorium was huge and had been built in the expansionist days of the great picture palaces. It soon filled to capacity, and everyone chatted noisily as they awaited the arrival of the host and caller. His dramatic appearance on stage amid coloured spotlights and deafening canned music brought forth gasps from an adoring audience as they feasted their eyes on his all-too-tight sequinned suit. He also wore patent shoes, no doubt equally too tight to help facilitate the mincing trademark walk. I suppose he could have been anything between twenty and fifty, but with bobbing blond hair attractively highlighted in psychedelic pink, he couldn't go wrong and nobody minded his age. As I was probably the only member of the audience for whom he didn't do anything, I felt out of it all.

'Eyes down!' he shrieked.

'Dirty Gertie thirty!' (a roar of approval).

'One more time seventy-nine!' (even more deafening).

'Between the sticks eighty-six!' (helpless laughter).

'Half way there, forty-five!' ('Get it in lover boy!' came the auditorium's rapturous response), and on and on it went.

When they found out I came from Brighton, they called me 'fifty-nine' for a reason which only became apparent when he called 'Brighton line fifty-nine!, whereupon I was overwhelmed with podgy hugs from the laundry ladies, who felt that my initiation was working a treat. In the end I gave up trying to absorb the gutsy art-deco interior and concentrate instead on my almost unblemished card, lest my jolly minders felt that their boisterous efforts to make me feel at home had been in vain.

I glanced at my watch. It was hard to believe that only three hours earlier I'd been face to face with an eel in the Athenaeum.

Chapter 17

Designing for the Numinous

In common with friends in other professions, I found that an architect in a private practice could seldom determine the future course of his work. For the most part, our clients appeared because they'd had a personal recommendation, they'd fallen out with one of our competitors or they'd liked the last job that we did for them. Where clients came from and in what order remained unpredictable – and to an extent still does. You think you've made a good impression with *A* only to discover that he goes elsewhere, whilst the unknown *B* arrives at your door unannounced.

I also began to realise that it was all too easy to become typecast, and I suspected this had happened to me when a totally different archdeacon from the one who had given me such a hard time over the relocatable church project asked if I would be interested in designing a new church at Burgess Hill in West Sussex. The Venerable Peter Booth, Archdeacon of Lewes, could not have been more different from his erstwhile colleague. He was a former naval officer who had landed at Salerno during the invasion of Italy, and he had a refreshingly direct, pragmatic and enthusiastic approach to any project, which I liked.

At about that time (the late 1960s) a number of influential books appeared which explored the theological and liturgical reasoning behind the more exciting church designs in mainland Europe, particularly in western Germany, Switzerland and the Netherlands. Following the Second Vatican Council, a fresh approach was encouraged. The idea of *corporate* worship became a reality so that, with the celebrant now facing the people and speaking in the vernacular, the entire congregation could feel involved and be able to gather round an altar which was now located in the body of the church. The days of a distant priest mumbling Latin with his back to the congregation were gone; the people now participated. This meant designing a radically different ground plan, more centralised and far removed from the long, thin naves of medieval origin. If the plan shape was to be different, then the natural lighting, circulation, and architectural emphasis had to be rethought as well. This made it an engaging concept.

The topic of my student dissertation was still at the back of my mind but the opportunity to develop further its tentative thinking hadn't presented itself while I was still employed in a largely commercial practice. I was attracted to the pioneering work of the New Churches Research Group, but wasn't sure whether this was only due to the inclusion of 'new' in the title. My generation was, after all, charged with an almost missionary zeal to promote the aims of the modern movement or, more accurately, we thought we were, and tended to rally around any passing cause that caught the eye.

Meanwhile, Birmingham University was setting up the Institute for the Study of Worship and Religious Architecture, whose deputy director, the felicitously named Gilbert Cope, became a firm friend and a serious influence on my architectural thinking. Up until then church design, as far as I could see, had been the preserve of the architectural profession's grey eminences, well mannered, scholarly, but dogmatic. And then, out of nowhere, Le Corbusier's pilgrimage chapel at Ronchamp arrived and Mies van der Rohe's very different, minimalist design for the new chapel at the Illinois Institute of Technology in Chicago appeared. Taken together, these two architectural giants had shown the world not only that it was time to break the established neo-historical mould, but that there was more than one way of doing it. The scales fell from my eyes.

In our academic training we had been nurtured on Le Corbusier, Mies van der Rohe and Frank Lloyd Wright and anything they offered the world from Mount Olympus compelled immediate and serious attention. I had to visit Ronchamp to see Le Corbusier's Chapel of Notre Dame du Haut for myself and I really had no idea what to expect.

I was told that from time immemorial pilgrims have climbed the winding road to the summit of Haut Lieu which had always been regarded as a hallowed place in the foothills of the Vosges. Over the years the chapel at the top had been destroyed, the last time during World War II, but always rebuilt by the loyal parishioners of the small town of Ronchamp below. It is a place of pilgrimage and is approached up a long, winding track the last section of which is barred to traffic and you have to walk. I imagined that the toil up the hill, the exertion, the breathlessness are all part of a spiritual preparation for the pilgrims and by the time the summit is reached and the first glimpse obtained of what has been aptly described as 'the greatest piece of twentieth-century sculpture' one is altogether humbled and submissive. It has been said that the building is not susceptible to systematic analysis with respect either to the work of Le Corbusier or to other religious building. This being so, the visit was not going to add to my growing knowledge of European church design, but that was immaterial, I was looking once more at the great oculus of the Roman Pantheon.

A huge, billowing roof over-sailed slanting walls each of which were punctuated by deep-cut windows arranged randomly. One side of the chapel contained a projecting outdoor pulpit for open air masses, while another framed the huge pivoted door embellished in bright enamel colours. The interior was sublime in the proper sense of that word - 'set aloft; lifted on high; exalted'. There was little seating; this was not a parish church after all but a place of pilgrimage and it would be expected that any supplicant would stand or kneel. Jewel-light coloured glass painted the deep window reveals in myriad shapes, moving minute by minute with the sun. No one seemed able or willing to utter a word and all I could hear was the slow shuffle of feet and whispered prayers.

In 1960 Peter Hammond, the respected author of the influential book *Liturgy and Architecture*, felt it was 'probably the most completely satisfying modern church which had been built in any country – though its effect on the work of lesser architects promises to be catastrophic; a rash of random windows already extends from Berlin to Tokyo'. This was chillingly prophetic. When Le Corbusier spoke at the consecration of the building he told his audience that some things are sacred and others are not sacred – whether they are 'religious' or not! This caused Peter Hammond to observe that 'in France, as in other countries, the Church has been compelled to recognise that there is no art or architecture *less* sacred than what commonly passes as religious art and architecture', an uncomfortable fact that was hard for England's church establishment at that time to comprehend or accept.

I'd thought about Ronchamp for days afterwards and it began to dawn on me that there are such things as absolutes in the world of architecture, if only because having experienced them, your perception is extended and the designing process thereafter takes a different course. This is nothing to do with anything as superficial as appearance, but everything to do with sensory and spiritual perception. In subsequent years my awareness of form and light became foremost in my mind, and this may not have been so but for the vision of Ronchamp.

Chapter 18

History in Comfort

The prospect of restoring a fourteenth-century Kentish yeoman's house for a wealthy American client seemed too good to be true. So often in any new project there is a critical ingredient, such as preoccupation with money, which prevents it becoming anything more than the next job in the office. But occasionally, very occasionally, the prospect of a marriage made in heaven becomes a reality and lifts the careworn spirit. Harrods Estates had acquired this listed house of great antiquity for an American purchaser of considerable means, and he was an existing client of Ed Bullerjahn, my friend who had been involved in the fake-office escapade on the US east coast. He had accumulated sufficient wealth in industry to allow himself to indulge his tastes in the Old Country, and in so doing, to embrace, during his short stays in Britain, a lifestyle given only to the leisured classes.

The house, not unexpectedly, needed a lot doing to it, but working on it I was sure would be a revelation. Until then I had, when not building afresh, only worked on nineteenth-century properties, which were interesting enough, but as this one was dated five hundred years earlier and involved the challenge of revitalising a historic property for a modern owner, it promised real excitement. Ideas for restoration and enhancement filled my mind, but I had yet to meet the client.

When I did, I quickly realised that my relished challenge was going to be of an entirely different order. The new owner, wanted to entertain on an impressive scale and, among other things, arrange days out hunting for the enjoyment of his carefully selected guests. This meant – and he was very specific about this – that when the party returned from the field and had dropped their muddy tack in the boot room, they would all repair to their rooms and simultaneously require hot tubs of lavish proportions.

'Big faucets you can turn on with your feet; volcanically hot water; water closets which flush completely first time' (he'd obviously visited England before) 'and a rapid response from the air-conditioning system.'

'The *air-conditioning* system?' I spluttered.

'Haven't you guys heard of air conditioning?'

'Well, of course, but not inserted into a fourteenth-century Kentish yeoman's house of incalculable historic importance,' I explained.

'Look, I own the house and I hire you. If you can't do it, fine, and I'll ask you to find someone who can.'

I paused for a moment. He came from a country where mountains weren't allowed to get in anyone's way. His pioneer forebears would have moved them and this was how he saw things. In England I reflected that we'd probably have a six-month public enquiry about moving the smallest hillock and, irrespective of the outcome, eventually find that the enterprise was too expensive in any case. I acquiesced.

Very old houses have low ceilings, very small windows and often priceless wood panelling. How could I successfully conceal yards and yards of galvanised metal trunking and outlet grilles in such a setting without vandalising the place? Not to mention work out the size of the cold-water supply and hot-water tanks to provide the mandatory six simultaneous Las Vegas–style hot plunges? Even if the crooked and creaking oak roof could carry the load, the space required would far exceed the volume that existed. Before he could say 'and that's what we pay architects for' I gave in and, with a weak smile, reached for my slide rule, hoping I could dispel my forebodings and find some way of doing it.

The problems were manifest though. How could I detail the fascia for the concealed lighting he had ordered without ripping off the top section of beautifully made oak panelling all round each room? And if the air-conditioning ducts could only be hidden above a suspended ceiling in the passageways, how could they be accommodated behind ceilings which were too low in any case?

The new owner was Ed Bullerjahn's client and as Ed and I had never collaborated professionally before I invited him to stay with us in Brighton while we got the job started. He was, too, my conduit to a mercurial client who could never be relied upon to be in any one place, let alone any one country, when you needed to consult him.

Eventually, I did find some way of doing the near-impossible, but not before a degree of disappointment had set in, never to be completely dispelled. The owner thought that the builder was not only slow, but was taking advantage of a conspicuously wealthy employer. On one occasion I spotted him sitting artfully behind the leaded window panes counting bags of cement being delivered to compare the total with the amount listed in the bill of quantities the contractor had tendered against. Ed felt himself torn between the client and me, his architectural colleague, and I felt we were only *just* accomplishing what we had set out to do through a series of dubious compromises which impaired the integrity of the building and edged us nearer to Disneyland.

But despite everything, Ed was a delight. He was larger than life and, although totally impossible, you always forgave him. Ed radiated confidence and drew beautifully with a pencil in a style no longer taught. It never occurred to him that he shouldn't dominate every conversation or monopolise the (quickly identified) most important people in the room, all of whom were instantly fascinated by him. During the course of an evening at home he could empty a whisky decanter single-handed and remain sober, the only sign of its effect being an increasing flow of beautifully embroidered anecdotes that would keep us up until the early hours. So much so that on the third night after his arrival my wife remonstrated that she'd never get up in time later that morning to prepare our breakfasts if she didn't go to bed straight away. Ed would hear none of it. 'We'll all go out to breakfast, on me. There's a lovely old hotel in Lewes that looks just dandy.'

He was referring to the White Hart, one of the old Trust Houses, formerly coaching inns, that every county town seemed to have, and that in this instance provided lodging for the itinerant judges appointed to the assize court immediately opposite. The hotel's regime was predictable, ordered, courteous and hidebound, and the prospect of non-residents who were complete strangers arriving unannounced off the street and demanding breakfast was unthinkable. Without wishing to offend Ed, I joined Ann in protesting, and explained that his generous offer couldn't realistically be accepted.

'Of course we're going – your husband is a slob, Ann, and I really don't know how you cope,' he said, throwing me a big fat wink. So, after a very short night, I drove the three of us to Lewes and rather glumly parked the car at the hotel entrance. Before I'd locked the car Ed had leapt out and proceeded to stride up to the duty manager, at whom he beamed and offered a reassuring hand.

'I'd like a breakfast table for three with a beautiful view down the river straight away,' he announced.

'Of course sir, I've got just the very table and it's a pleasure to welcome you to the White Hart.' Ed turned to Ann with an extravagant gesture and in a stage whisper announced to the entire dining room, 'I told you your husband was a slob.'

Ed was an accomplished host in any setting and had a wide circle of friends. When, in turn, I made a visit to the States some time later, he invited me down to Virginia where he and Julianna were spending the weekend with friends. Our hosts, a comfortably-off, late-middle-aged couple who had known them for a long time, lived in a huge, white clapboarded house on a generous, heavily treed site. It had a free-standing guest suite at the end of the long garden which came complete with an equally generously built black housekeeper. After an evening which included beautifully prepared wildfowl served on inherited porcelain and with fastidiously chosen wines, Ed was once again in full flow. Virginia was new to me, and only that morning I had read in the newspaper of an event which was not uncommon in these parts – a death caused by a rattlesnake bite. Had it not been the death of a well-known senator it might not even have figured in the press, but I was anxious to introduce my own meagre offering to the conversation. No one else thought it was worth dwelling on, though – there were bigger things happening in the stock market, and no one had yet been introduced to the new owner next door who was reputed to be one of the undeclared lovers of Cary Grant.

Despite the fascination of endless speculation, we eventually decided to call it a day and find our way to bed. Ed gallantly escorted me to the wide veranda at the back, down whose wooden steps I would go to cross the garden to the guest suite. He equipped me with a large torch to light my path, as it was by now velvety black and I couldn't see a thing, and into my other hand thrust a heavy walking stick.

'I haven't had *that* much, Ed, but thank you for the thought.'

'I know you haven't, John, but you need it if you meet a rattlesnake between here and the guesthouse, as they often come out at this time of night.' He was quite serious.

The following day he asked me casually over breakfast if I had brought my basseting boots with me. Not wishing to display my ignorance about basseting, I enquired, 'Why do you ask?'

'We've been invited to follow the hounds at the hunt on the estate over the way. I thought you'd love to go.' I agreed, not quite understanding how a hunt could be successfully held with splay-footed, floppy-eared basset hounds, but was curious to find out.

Later that morning we assembled in front of a great house, even grander than last night's, set in acres of rolling landscape, and were immediately entertained to a welcoming drink before setting out. We were predominantly male and I found myself surrounded by a genial group of relaxed, wealthy neighbours, whose Burberry Englishness had nonetheless been very carefully considered before setting out – an East Coast accomplishment lightly carried.

When being told that all was ready, we gathered by the classical portico in time to see a couple of low-loaders discharge their cargo of basset hounds who, for all the world, could have walked straight out of a cartoon film. Their ears dragged on the ground and they looked far too well fed to be remotely interested in anything more than a stroll. I recalled once, long ago, hearing how dachshunds were originally used for hunting in certain countries, and as recently as World War II could be seen responding to the call of the hunting horn in Indian gymkhanas during the dying days of the British Raj. Absurd though that was, at least their ears didn't drag on the ground when pursuing their quarry.

Eventually the hounds moved off in something resembling a trot and we all followed on foot in groups of three or four. Most people seemed to know each other, and those who didn't were soon introduced. It soon became clear that, apart from strolling quickly enough to keep up with the dogs, no one was really interested in the hunt but far more preoccupied in talking about their neighbours, berating corrupt politicians or, in one fascinating case, attempting to predict tomorrow's Dow Jones Index. It was a gentleman's club smoking room on the move in sepia-tinted picture-postcard surroundings.

I kept an eye on the dogs, more out of curiosity than anything else, and they seemed happy enough, chasing smells and irrelevant trails at regular intervals. After a couple of hours, the cry went up and the dogs, feigning ferocity by baring their teeth, dropped into top gear and even the Dow Jones Index conversation fell quiet. But no, it came to nothing and we discovered eventually that the hounds had done nothing more than terrorise a chicken that had strayed from home territory. Conversation quickly resumed and the hunt continued until the Master looked at his watch and, seeing it was nearly four in the afternoon, suggested we repair to the house, which we were all happy to do, and there we were served with the largest 'hunt breakfast' I have ever set eyes on. A groaning board of Cecil B. DeMille proportions was set out for as far as the eye could see down the pillared hall. We happily pretended to be tired and hungry after the day's exertions and agreed that the hunt had been its customary success and needed to be celebrated by eating and drinking to excess. The date of the next hunt was enthusiastically announced and the dogs, who by then were quite hungry, having caught nothing, were coaxed onto the trucks to be taken back for a square meal.

A year or so later a rather sober Ed wrote, telling me that his client had sold the house in Kent on which we had both laboured for so long. The novelty had worn off, I imagine, and it had gone back on the market.

Chapter 19

Greek Street and Yoga

London, like many other blitzed cities recovering from the war, contained many properties that had been seriously neglected, either as a result of peripheral damage during air raids or because the owners had been difficult to trace at the end of hostilities. This situation provided a happy hunting ground for young entrepreneurs anxious to make their way as budding property developers, and one of them asked me if I would advise on the potential of a pair of such properties that had come onto the market.

The two I was asked to look at were far apart in London and we had to decide how best they could be restored and converted for 'beneficial use'. The first was in Cable Street in the East End, and the second in Greek Street, Soho. The visit to Cable Street made me realise just how badly this part of London's dockland had been hit and the extent to which comprehensive redevelopment was still necessary.

Soho had not fully recovered from the war, although, on the plus side, its colourful cosmopolitanism had, if anything, been enhanced by the service personnel from many nations who had passed through the capital before D-Day or who had returned to London at the end of hostilities, awaiting repatriation. Non-rationed goods from liberated countries had begun to arrive and the traditional trades extinguished by the war effort were reappearing, like the maker of ballet shoes, the harpsichord builder and the purveyor of exotic food. The area had not yet been cleaned up by the Metropolitan Police and the place contained thrills and menace in equal proportions.

I found Number 4 Greek Street easily enough and, from the outside, it looked no worse than its occupied neighbours. After fumbling with a handful of assorted keys, it became clear to me that the house had been subdivided for a number of unrelated uses, so I began in the basement and planned to make my way up the building to the top. Apart from the top flat, the property was entirely empty. Knowing how scarce accommodation was in central London, I couldn't imagine why this was so, but it soon became clear when I eased open the door to the basement front room and found there, hastily stacked from floor to ceiling, hundreds of tins of powdered milk which were obviously on their way to somewhere, having earlier 'fallen off the back of a lorry'. I closed the door quickly in case someone had seen me and went upstairs. It appeared that the ground and first floor had been used as an unlicenced private club for out-of-hours drinking, illegal gambling and sufficient 'leisure activities' to attract and retain the punters. The inside door was half off its hinges and revealed a large room where its occupants must have been surprised by a recent police raid. An untouched gin and tonic was growing mould around the floating lemon slice; a telephone directory lay open on the floor with two bookies' adverts outlined clumsily in lipstick; two chairs lay overturned evidently in the rush to the fire-escape exit at the back; and blowflies were noisily breeding in an unflushed WC. I seemed to register the colourful chaos in black and white. Because of its Graham Greene-like seediness, the frozen moment resembled an abandoned still from the cutting-room floor. I paused and hoped for something less discouraging upstairs.

As I approached the top floor I believed I could hear something, indistinct and muffled. Continuing more cautiously, I was alarmed to hear what sounded like a breathless gasp from time to time, and I stopped dead in my tracks. The door to the top flat was firmly locked, which added to the mystery, and I began to feel distinctly uncomfortable. Moments later I remembered that the adjacent house was of an identical layout and I decided that I could obtain all the measurement information I needed by requesting access there instead, so I quietly made my way back down to the front door. On my way out I glanced at the array of bell pushes on the outside door frame. All but one of these had been taped over or had names scratched out. The one that remained in use belonged to the top flat and carried a handwritten card announcing quite simply 'Model: press hard'.

Nowadays architecture is not alone in providing unexpected glimpses of other people's lives; it's the same in medicine, law and countless other occupations, but the main difference is that, in architecture, you always see the other person in their own particular setting – a house, a workshop, a church or whatever, and this tells you something more about them, often revealing aspects of their lives they are unaware of or, in some cases, would prefer you not to see.

Nigel Green, the actor, had an established reputation for playing the stern, resolute, good-looking individual who led from the front and behaved unswervingly like a gentleman unless, as sometimes happened, he was cast just as successfully as the polished, suave character who only pretended to behave like a gentleman. It appeared that his life had become worryingly eventful and very complicated, and upon the advice of a close friend he had taken up yoga. So impressed was he by this experience that he took the lead in establishing a new yoga centre in Brighton, devoted to the teaching and spiritual discipline of B. K. S. Iyengar, whose reputation had earlier been enhanced by acting as guru to the finest international violinist of his time, Yehudi Menuhin. Under Iyengar's tutelage, Menuhin had adopted an ascetic regime which enabled him, for instance, to attend a full concert rehearsal in London in the morning and be equally accomplished performing a different work to a large audience in Madrid later the same day. It was easy to understand how anyone would have been attracted to such an ordered and productive lifestyle.

Nigel Green and his close friend had acquired a small mews property in part of Regency Kemp Town and asked me – I had recently taken up yoga following a gastric ulcer – to act for them in converting the premises into a yoga centre. It was suggested that I should first attend a lecture and demonstration by Iyengar, to be held in the local Quaker meeting house, and acquaint myself with his theories and practice. I was aware that the Western world is generally ill equipped to fully understand traditional philosophies from the East, but erroneously thought that my recent acquaintance with the work of the brilliant Bengali thinker, poet and sometime mystic Rabindranath Tagore might help. It didn't, gifted though he was, so I realised that if I was going to do anything more than scratch the surface I would have to abandon superficial comparisons and concentrate on learning with a completely open and receptive mind.

Iyengar was late middle-aged, of superb physique, and able to control his physical and spiritual responses with a discipline that could only have sprung from a well-ordered inner authority. We were told that, when young, he had been among hundreds of victims of famine in the remote region of India where his family lived, and that he had been taught, presumably by a parent or elder, to survive for what amounted to some weeks by adopting a pose of complete physical and mental equilibrium. This reduced his respiration and pulse rate, so that only the most minimal demands were made on his system as he set about surviving solely on small amounts of water in the absence of any morsel of food.

We use glib expressions like 'mind over matter' in the West to explain this unique ability to deal with severe adversity in this particular way, but none of us can fully appreciate not only what it must feel like in such circumstances, but also the extent to which it equips one for life's unexpected rigours thereafter.

How could any architectural interpretation adequately reflect such a self-controlled state of being? Eventually I decided to use natural light as a defining element, or, more precisely, reflected natural light. Ever since experiencing Le Corbusier's chapel at Ronchamp, I had been looking for an opportunity to use natural light as a design determinant. As long ago as 1650 the English antiquarian and divine Thomas Fuller had observed that 'Light, God's eldest daughter, is a principal beauty in a building', and I'd never fully understood why this had been overlooked by so many architects in succeeding centuries. In order to achieve a convincing break with the outside world and its noise and superficiality, I decided that one should neither be able to see out from nor see into the centre. This was achieved by designing canopied, horizontal 'shelves' on the façade which reflected light from the sky up onto the interior's ceiling, thereby producing a timeless and ethereal setting for contemplation. This solution had the merits of achieving its design objective and of being inexpensive, and B. K. S. Iyengar was happy to accept an invitation to perform the opening ceremony.

Alas, the new enterprise, intended to instil equilibrium and inner peace, lasted only a short time, as Nigel Green lost the battle with his demons and one day in 1972, died by his own hand. Within weeks the centre closed and shortly afterwards the property was put onto the market and sold.

The first thing the new owners did was to dismantle the delicate light reflectors and punch new holes in the outside wall to form mock-Regency windows onto the street. It was, after all, to be a 'des res'.

Chapter 20

Green-field Ecumenism

I always found it revealing when, on being told that I was an architect, acquaintances would invariably ask, 'And what sort of houses do you design?' When I explained that I seldom designed houses, they would look surprised and disappointed and the conversation would move on to something more promising. The plain fact, which is as true today as it was then, is that on our congested island that sensibly protects its green spaces, plots of land suitable for an individual house rarely come onto the market in the first place.

Moreover, many architects turn down commissions to design one-off houses in any case because the process can be fraught with difficulty, as I found when planning my own house in Colebrook Road. Many clients have totally unrealistic ideas of what their cherished wishes will really cost or, sometimes, families are completely unable to agree among themselves what they want, with one party waving an illustration torn from an American magazine found at the hairdresser's that very morning, and the other acting out the 'informed patron' and asserting that 'if you keep a dog you don't have to bark yourself', thus giving carte blanche. There was even one architect practising nearby, a bluff, recently retired Royal Navy officer, who advised me over the largest pink gin I had ever seen, 'Never design a house for a woman, and never, ever for one going through the "change".

Having effectively been dissuaded from designing houses for private clients, I began accepting strategic planning work, which was broader in scope and, in many ways, broke interesting new ground. One such project was centred on Milton Keynes.

Following the First World War the government of the day had come up with appealing, if often empty, slogans like 'homes fit for heroes' to signal the development of decent, affordable housing for 'Tommy, back from the front'. In reality, such homes were conspicuous by their absence, but it wasn't surprising to find the same ideals being expressed towards the end of World War II, only in this case the results were to be a lot more tangible. Development corporations were to be set up to plan and build Crawley, Stevenage, Basildon, Harlow and other New Towns in Britain, to provide new housing, factories, shops and schools for existing city communities fragmented by the Blitz. Over the next generation, such townships were constructed with varying degrees of success, but they often produced socially monochrome neighbourhoods because the adjacent factory estates invariably required a large blue-collar workforce.

In 1967, the government announced a larger and bolder enterprise – namely, the creation of an entirely new *city*. It was to be called Milton Keynes – for reasons no one fully understood at the time. Looking for clues in the separate names, I remembered having to study John Milton's *Paradise Lost* of 1667, but couldn't believe anyone today would want to be quite so cynical. As for John Maynard Keynes, his most influential book on twentieth-century economics had been published in 1936 under the title *General Theory of Employment, Interest and Money*, which again left me none the wiser.

Over twenty square miles of north Buckinghamshire countryside was identified as the 'designated area' and the intention was to build a new habitat for a quarter of a million people over the following twenty-five years. The chosen site would be near the M1 and the main railway line linking London to the north, and the Grand Union Canal would run through it. We were told it was roughly equidistant between Oxford and Cambridge, which (although it had no real bearing on the decision to site the Open University there) obviously gave a sheen of cultural respectability to a brave new venture. The designated area included the existing town of Bletchley in the south and extended northwards to the small railway town of Wolverton. The remainder of the entire area comprised a handful of small villages and hamlets and a wide swathe of agricultural countryside.

The proposal for the new city contained some innovative features notably missing from the first New Towns, such as integrating managerial houses with blue-collar housing and also encouraging a far wider spread of age groups. Both of these moves were intended to make the place feel more like an ordinary town that had grown and mutated over the ages. By comparison, when Crawley was first built it had numerous shops selling prams and baby wear, but not a single funeral director.

The Milton Keynes master plan had been prepared by well-known planning consultants Llewellyn-Davies, Weeks, Forestier-Walker and Bor, who produced radical proposals for segregating vehicular and pedestrian traffic in a way not seen before and proposed an informal grid of roads about one kilometre apart which would give structure to the new housing areas.

To their credit, the senior echelons of the diocese of Oxford, within whose boundary Milton Keynes fell, saw not only that they needed to become involved before all the strategic planning was done around them, but also that an unparalleled ecumenical opportunity presented itself, one that was too important to be ignored. Diocesan boundaries in England and Wales are quite archaic and bear little or no relation to present-day demography. In addition, there are cathedrals whose siting is the result of an accident of history, so all in all, diocesan offices were not always expected to produce as apt and timely a response as they did here. But the diocese of Oxford acted, and, under the chairmanship of the Suffragan Bishop of Buckingham – a lean, lively man who looked every inch a tennis blue and who managed to cherish ideals and exercise common' sense with equal ability – the decision was taken to put the diocese firmly into the Milton Keynes picture at an early stage.

They had got a long way before I was asked to help, and had already set up a Church's Provisional Sponsoring Body which, despite its dispiriting non-committal title (which was probably a device for getting round the existing set-in-stone diocesan committee structure), had made great strides and brought together Anglican, Baptist, Congregational, Methodist, Roman Catholic and Salvation Army interests with the common purpose of deciding how to respond to the published proposals for the new city.

Broadly speaking, I was asked to look at the entire building stock of about twenty-five separate church buildings and advise on their future usefulness within the master plan. This, until I learned more, sounded deceptively simple. Only after accepting the commission was I told that I was *persona grata* to all of the denominations but one – the Roman Catholics wished to appoint their own architect, Desmond Williams. This could have spelled disaster, but when we were introduced we hit it off immediately. Through sheer energy and enthusiasm, Desmond was braver than I was at pushing at established boundaries and, in the process, shared the risk with me and doubled the 'what if' excitement of it all.

All of this gave me a glimpse of the Church in action: it was quite capable of packaging good intentions in a hermetically sealed bag rather than risk the terrifying prospect of change, and I found myself meeting clergy and laymen equally capable of demonstrating enthusiasm or doubt over the whole enterprise. There wasn't time or skill available to embrace all the theological and legal niceties which could have held us up, so Desmond Williams and I concentrated on capturing the vitality of the occasion and getting first ideas down on paper, which we knew could do no long-term damage as they would only amount to recommendations.

At a time when management skills were being taken up by the professions, it was sobering to see how easily one or two of the clergy remained inefficient for touchingly laudable reasons. One canon in particular, a balding, spectacled figure in a shiny black suit whose task it was to minute our meetings, was impossibly slow in circulating them before we met again, and as a consequence, any action agreed upon at the time had seldom been taken by the date of the next meeting. I decided to go and see him. He lived alone, and upon being admitted to his small house, I glimpsed a spartan way of life borne not out of meanness (although his stipend would have been modest) but out of a mistaken interpretation of humility. No one minded his frayed cuffs or the odd soup stain on his lapel, but he insisted on typing the minutes on a pre-war Remington with one finger and, through diminished acuity, seldom got round to changing the ribbon or the carbon paper, so that everything other than the top copy was almost unreadable. I knew we had money in the budget for part-time secretarial assistance, but when I suggested it, it was met with unequivocal refusal and a gentle reminder that his was a life of service and, notwithstanding his seniority as a canon, he needed to demonstrate to his flock that he would never ask others to do for him what he could quite well do for himself. He explained that this was the true nature of humility and I was about to tell him that in this instance it was a sure recipe for inefficiency which effectively prevented us from doing what we were commissioned to do, thereby delaying our work and adding to cost and frustration all round, when just in time I had spotted an oval, mahogany frame over the upright piano in the small parlour where we sat, containing a faded sampler embroidered with the prayer of St Francis of Assisi:

> O Divine Master,
> Grant that I may not so much seek
> To be consoled, as to console;
> To be understood, as to understand;
> To be loved, as to love;
> For it is in giving that we receive,
> It is in pardoning that we are pardoned,
> And it is in dying that we are born
> To eternal life.

He was older than I was, he was lonelier than I was, he was more serious than I would ever be, and he'd made up his mind on certain matters long ago, so how could I tell him he'd got it all wrong?

The next day Desmond Williams and I pored over a large-scale map of the area and saw how the new development proposals were superimposed on the sparse rural landscape. Existing churches, some of medieval origin, lay scattered about like so much historical confetti, bearing little or no relation to present need and still less to future need. Originally, the churches would have been the focus of the village, but some had been declared redundant even before the new city was dreamed of. It was obvious from the new housing areas proposed in the master plan that residential areas were to be sited near to roads, factories, shops, schools, and health and leisure facilities, and any relationship to the existing rural churches was largely accidental. It was clear that pastoral relevance was to become an important criterion for assessing the usefulness of any one church in years to come, alongside historic and architectural significance and the general state of repair. These criteria were often in conflict, especially when you had a beautiful church, rich in history, in a location where it was destined to remain in splendid isolation for ever or, even more annoyingly, an ideally situated church of unspeakable ugliness which, through years of neglect, was in such a poor state it merited demolition.

And then there were the ecumenical considerations. A recent attempt at Anglican–Methodist union had failed and this left some clergy either embarrassed or bruised and a shade more hesitant about arrangements for active collaboration, although an encouraging number had turned the other cheek and showed great willingness to listen.

As time went on it became clear that churches *per se* were not the only consideration. Modern theological thinking suggested that in places like Milton Keynes we might consider 'pastoral centres' and even 'house churches' that could be provided less expensively, that would be easier to share legally, and that would go some way to encouraging the involvement of those who didn't like anything that looked too 'churchy'. Church schools, particularly for the Roman Catholics, also had to be considered, and then, of course, clergy housing, and what about a crematorium and, if they had one, what could be agreed upon as the most appropriate form of liturgy? And had anyone seriously considered the liturgical reordering of the older churches to be retained? Problems bred like rabbits and Desmond Williams and I seemed to spend an inordinate amount of time rescuing our clerical colleagues from doctrinal cul-de-sacs. But this was still a lot more fun than designing a five-bedroomed house for a Jaguar distributor, or so I thought.

I discovered it was surprisingly easy to fall into your own elephant trap by being too helpful and, on one occasion, I attracted the opprobrium of my practice partners. I was in discussion with one enthusiastic community about to build a church they couldn't possibly afford. Although I pointed this out, they persisted with an evangelising zeal that brushed reason aside and left me powerless to object until, in desperation, I came up with the suggestion that instead of trying to raise countless thousands it might be simpler to buy a minibus and transport members once a week to a remaining large church two miles away. This was divine revelation indeed and came with an attractive serving of humility which they found irresistible. They agreed with alacrity and thanked me profusely, leaving me with a glowing satisfaction that was only too quickly dispelled by my partners who, when they heard of it, said that they had never seen anyone throw away such an attractive commission so thoughtlessly without the slightest regard for the welfare of the practice. So much for humility.

One of the churches in the new city area was at Willen, a small village near the north-east boundary. It was built by one Robert Hooke in 1680 and was by far the most distinguished church in the whole area. A small number of local parishioners had restored the exterior and installed a new heating system over the years, but much repair and redecoration work needed to be undertaken internally, which hadn't been done due to lack of funds. This became part of an all-too-familiar picture and added to my growing feeling of despair now that the full extent of the condition of most churches was beginning to emerge. Obviously, most of them we couldn't restore, even if they were in the right place. But in this case something happened to save the day. The celebrated jazz duo Johnny Dankworth and Cleo Laine had just moved into a large house not far away, having sensibly escaped the big smoke but still needing to be near the M1 to reach London for performances. They came up with a novel suggestion. 'Why not have a Willen Festival?' Had anyone locally suggested this they would have been laughed out of court, as it was all too easy to visualise members of the church choir doing extracts from *Oklahoma!* alongside hula-hoop contests and home-made jam stalls on the lawn. But when the Dankworths said it, and promised to appear in it *and* to ask lots of their friends to help, the effect was magical and everyone threw themselves wholeheartedly into planning the event.

Due to pressure of other commitments, there were to be two evening performances only, but it would be a ticketed, long-skirt and interval-wine affair. It sold out within hours of being announced and in the end provided more money for Willen church repairs than could have been raised in a year. It was the upside of the new city, full of energy, free of precedent and full of hope, and it was a moment to savour, because we all knew that developing a city over the next twenty-five years would involve pitfalls, disappointments and delays, and the memory of something good like this could still encourage people in years to come, long after I had left.

Despite all the difficulties, I found this commission a lot more fulfilling than designing private houses, and where would I have discovered humility in working for the new rich?

Chapter 21

From Hove to Northern Rock

Our firm's senior partner had a war-related injury which was still bothering him, and he decided to retire prematurely. This was quickly followed by the unexpected death of the next partner in line, so it seemed as good a time as any to leave and start my own practice. During previous years I had gathered a sufficient number of personal clients whom I knew would be supportive if I ventured out, so the decision was an easy one. It wasn't something I had been seriously considering, but events had moved quickly and, having made the decision, I felt as exhilarated as I did apprehensive. I wasn't sure whether there would be sufficient work for the number of staff who chose to work for me rather than stay with the old firm, but I could at least select those who were prepared to take the plunge and share with them some of the excitement of starting afresh.

One of my first sizeable commissions was a new headquarters for the Sussex Mutual Building Society, a well-established local organisation loyally supported, if sometimes too unquestioningly, by its stakeholders.

In the nineteenth century, when communications were less advanced than they are now, every town in the country was a lot more self-sufficient. Each had its own brewery, its own clockmaker and its own omnibus company, for instance. The late nineteenth century had seen the emergence of mutual societies of one sort or another, and the laudable paternalism of the time responded to the need to help those who worked hard buy their own property. In the twentieth century, although regional development saw a broader rationalisation of manufacturing and services, local building societies still continued to flourish. They had often been established by a group of local businessmen involving, perhaps, a well-known estate agent, a solicitor, an accountant and a handful of trusted colleagues in the town. As it transpired, the 1970s were to witness the last flowering of such local societies because, as the years went

119

on, it became clear that they would no longer be able to compete with the emerging national giants who had infinitely greater reserves, more effective management and formidable advertising power. Undeterred, a number of smaller building societies still decided to modernise and rebuild during the 1970s, and the Sussex Mutual was to be the first of two to ask me to design their new headquarters.

As with Hove Town Hall, I suggested that, before we started, the president, the chairman, the managing director, the office manager and I should see what others had done in this field and learn from their successes and failures. Two sprang to mind – the Bristol and West Building Society in the West Country and, in the far north-east, the Northern Rock Building Society, both of which had moved into purpose-designed premises. It was decided by the board that a small group of us should visit them and see for ourselves what had been achieved. In later years such friendly cooperation would never take place, as the large building societies were now competing for the same customers nationally, and jealously guarded their operational and management systems. But in our case, Sussex, Bristol and Newcastle were far away from each other's territorial ambitions and our hosts were quietly flattered that their achievements had been noticed so far afield.

When these visits were discussed it became clear that, if we were going to keep to our timetable, agreement on dates between the participants was going to be difficult to achieve, as the journey would involve no less than three nights away and no one could manage to free themselves for this length of time on the same dates. The answer lay in visiting both destinations in one day by using a chartered air-taxi and, after a deep intake of breath by the finance director, arrangements were made with a firm operating out of the small airport at Shoreham which, after wartime use, still only had a grass runway and was subject to periodic flooding from the nearby river Adur.

We were given an itinerary and told to report at the airport early one Tuesday morning. None of us was particularly conversant with private flight hire so we did what we believed was expected of us and arrived at the recently redecorated art-deco terminal a full hour before departure. Documentation was simple and didn't take long, so we sat down on a bench in an orderly row awaiting our call, looking more like the occupants of a suburban railway waiting room destined for a day in the City. Two of the older members of the party did well to conceal their reservations about the whole enterprise and chatted unconvincingly about the latest cricket scores by way of diversion. After half an hour we were still sitting there, so the office manager who had made all the arrangements was despatched to find out what, if anything, was happening. On his return he told us that the air-taxi was based elsewhere overnight, but there was nothing to worry about and our departure time would still be met. A further twenty-five minutes elapsed and the president, who had never waited for anything in his comfortable career, began to get tetchy and fiddled with his gloves and his snuffbox, demanding hard information and prompt reassurance. While the managing director, who was his son, attempted the doubly difficult task of calming the situation, the glass swing doors from the airfield opened and through them strolled a figure in tweed hacking jacket, baggy cavalry-twill trousers and a pair of battered brown brogues.

'You chaps ready then? We mustn't hang about as the wind is just fine at the moment, but may veer later.' He beamed confidently at us all, concealing any amusement he might have felt at seeing this briefcased, earnest little party who were his responsibility for the rest of the day.

We stood up and the president led the way, leaning heavily on his embossed cane. In a dutiful crocodile, we followed in order of perceived importance until we reached the plane, when I got in last and squeezed into the back.

'Can't swing a cat in here,' muttered the president, buckling himself into the front seat, to which the pilot responded gaily, 'Don't worry sir, you won't have to try, it's against regulations.' This appeared to go over the president's head as he deliberated whether, after all, he wanted to sit so near the nose. 'Let Wells-Thorpe sit there,' he finally decided. 'He's got long legs and I'll sit quietly in the back.' No one was going to disagree – the pecking order was too well understood for that – so we all had to get out of the plane again in order to rearrange ourselves. The pilot didn't turn a hair; he'd seen it all before, and since he'd been paid up front for the full day's work, he didn't worry terribly about how the time was going to be spent.

'Everyone happy?' he asked, and, before waiting for a reply, began taxiing across the bumpy, wet grass to the windsock at the far end of the landing strip. He put the aircraft through all the necessary preflight procedures and exchanged a few friendly words over the radio before we took off in a burst of smelly noise. As, to our collective relief, we left the ground and began to turn, I saw the magnificent minster chapel of Lancing College to our left; we were clearly flying north up the Adur valley. The pilot suddenly turned to me and said, 'Which way would you like to go?' Completely unaware that passengers ever entered into the equation on such occasions, I replied, 'The pretty way, of course,' and he twitched his voluminous moustache and nodded.

Once we were north of the South Downs we made a steep left turn and followed the line of the hills westward. I could see the Isle of Wight and, just beneath it, the complex geography of Portsmouth harbour, principal base of the Royal Navy from time immemorial.

One of the advantages of a light aircraft is its ability to fly relatively low and allow its passengers to witness a lot more than would be possible in a commercial jet. Our pilot was an easy-going type who enjoyed chatting while we travelled. After I noticed the spire of Chichester Cathedral and saw that we were going to fly right over Portsmouth harbour before turning inland towards Bristol, I said casually, 'I wonder if that carrier is the *Ark Royal*?' 'Dunno, let's find out,' he replied, and before we could catch our breath, we peeled off in the manner made famous by German Stuka dive-bombers during the war and made an unnervingly low pass over the quayside where the vessel was berthed. To make sure of its identity, we flew right past the ship's gold lettering on the bow before climbing sharply and heading inland. The other passengers went quiet and, not having overheard my conversation with the pilot, were mystified at the manoeuvre, but kept their mouths shut in case this was a perfectly normal thing to do on a private flight on which, possibly, part of the pilot's remit was to give his passengers an interesting time.

Later that morning, once we had inspected the Bristol and West Building Society's new head office and made admiring noises about the beautifully polished brass marine telescope in the managing director's office ('I can even read the city clerk's confidential minutes on his desk in the building opposite,' he maintained), we were entertained to a convivial lunch.

As we were now situated in the West Country, it quickly occurred to the managing director that, flight-wise, we couldn't be far from Swansea, near which there was a factory assembling Canadian cedar prefabricated bungalows. The building society was currently being approached by one or two adventurous borrowers who had seen these advertised, and Sussex Mutual would need to make a policy decision on whether to lend on forms of construction other than traditional bricks and mortar. It was decided there and then that as we had the air-taxi, we should make a quick detour to see for ourselves whether such an unconventional form of construction would make a good risk. Arrangements were made over the phone, the pilot ('just call me George') was as easy as ever, and shortly afterwards we departed to our extra destination, heading for Swansea's embryo airport about five miles outside the city.

The runway, although surfaced, seemed to follow the contours of the field, and it was necessary for George to select part of its length that was flatter than any other part before landing. Apparently he had flown artillery spotter planes during the war and could land on a cricket pitch, so for him this was no more than par for the course. He called up 'Dai' on the radio, received a muffled 'OK' and landed perfectly. 'You'll like Dai,' George announced to whoever was listening. 'The place wouldn't work without him.' We were soon to meet him face to face and witness his legendary resourcefulness.

Dai welcomed us at the door of the wooden hut which served as the terminal, control tower and passenger hall all in one. It had one first-floor room, from which he could see approaching aircraft and talk them down; having done so, he'd take off his earphones and run down the wooden staircase to open the door. Once the arrivals were safely inside and had been informed of Llanelli's amazing rugby win last Saturday, he'd disappear behind the counter, don a striped apron and dispense coffee in unmatching cups and saucers. Look as we might, we couldn't see anyone else about at all – Dai seemed to do it all and do it with genial efficiency. We'd all begun talking when suddenly he left the counter, ran outside and cupped his ear to pick up the sound of a distant engine. Once satisfied that he recognised it, Dai the Radar, as he was inevitably called, ran inside and up the stairs, and donned his headphones for the whole cycle to begin once again. He loved it, we loved it, it probably broke every rule in the book, but it all seemed to work and we beamed at him with admiration when we finally made our departure for Newcastle.

By now the weather was poorer and the cloud lower, and George became conspicuously more professional as we landed in very poor light. 'I *think* this is Newcastle,' he announced, hoping that we'd all be quietly disconcerted. 'If it is, I'll be in the Mermaid, and if it isn't, I'll be in the first pub on the way into town.' This didn't work either, but I was glad he gave it a try.

The Northern Rock team were equally pleased to see us, equally hospitable and very generous in their advice. From my point of view this single day had knocked a couple of weeks off the design programme, helped the clients understand what they wanted and why they wanted it, and enabled me to understand how, architecturally, I could deliver it. As a young firm we were buzzing with energy and enthusiasm, but I was very aware that, in all the excitement, little practical necessities would get overlooked and impair our progress. In a perfect world, Dai would have become our general factotum.

Designing several thousand square feet of air-conditioned office space was easy, but less easy was the task of giving the new building, and particularly the banking hall used by customers, an identity which reflected the history and nature of the business. If I wasn't careful the design could all too easily become like any other contemporary commercial building and say nothing about its purpose, or where the society saw itself in the life of Sussex. I thought the most effective way of portraying these things was graphically; it usually was, and had been since biblical narratives were explained to a medieval community through the medium of stained glass. I had recently seen illustrated the work of a young ceramicist, Philippa Threlfall. She was combining the use of natural materials with fired clay to great effect, and I was attracted to her work.

Unlike the remainder of the headquarters building, the banking hall was double height to accommodate a mezzanine floor which overhung the long cashier's counter. The upper level provided a semi-private meeting place for customers, where they could converse with staff before agreeing to what was probably the biggest single financial transaction in their lives. The mezzanine overlooked the banking hall and had a long, plain balcony front. I decided that this would be an ideal place for a ceramic mural whose theme could be the varying architectural vernacular of Sussex, whose ninety-mile seaboard provided a rich and varied panorama of nearly every building type, domestic, industrial, commercial and ecclesiastical. All of these would have been financed in one way or another and could be seen as being symbolic of the building society's role in the county.

I invited Philippa down to see the half-completed site and she immediately saw the potential for extending still further her newly developed design technique. The work would be called the Sussex Mural and would be fabricated in a number of separate panels extending some forty feet from one end of the banking hall to the other. The board was very happy with the suggestion, and she was promptly commissioned to prepare her design. Fortunately, I had a substantial number of illustrative references for her to work from and we readily agreed on the key buildings I wanted to include. These extended from Chichester Cathedral and the Market Cross in the west to the fishermen's net drying sheds in Rye to the east, via Arundel Castle, Brighton's Royal Pavilion, Anne of Cleves House in Lewes, and the oast houses on the border with Kent. Philippa used fired terracotta and glazed tile for part of the composition, together with natural materials such as slate and pebble to give depth, warmth and textural emphasis.

As she was working single-handedly and had an infant son by the time the commission was half completed, the whole work took longer than expected, but as we had started early enough it looked as though we would still just make the opening date. This was only accomplished towards the end by her making day visits from her home in London, driving down complete with the infant's playpen which she erected in the banking hall where she supervised the hanging of the panels, made good the almost inconspicuous jointing, and undertook any minor repairs that were needed before the panels were hoisted into position. By now the plate-glass windows of the banking hall overlooking the pavement were already in place and a small group of bystanders used to gather every day to watch a gurgling infant test the strength of the playpen while his mother was perched precariously on a trestle high above the floor, epoxy resin in hand, and mouthing soothing reassurances over her shoulder while fixing a loose piece of mosaic. It struck me how very different our lifestyles were, and probably how very ordered and dull she regarded mine by comparison with hers.

Chapter 22

The Quinquennial

As I had shown an interest in church design over the years, it wasn't surprising that I was sometimes asked to survey existing churches and advise on their state of repair, or lack of it. Back in 1955, the Inspection of Churches Measure had been introduced, laying down that every consecrated church building should have an inspection by a qualified architect every five years to decide what repairs were necessary. This procedure involved making arrangements with the incumbent or his churchwarden and having a local builder in attendance with ladders, implements for lifting manhole covers and a bit of friendly advice.

The inspection took in the entire fabric and fixed furnishings of the building, from the lightning conductor on the spire down to the foundations, and was usually a dirty and dispiriting job – dirty because the 'good lady cleaners' could not be expected to clean anything above head height in the interior, and dispiriting because, through neglect or the parochial church council's sheer inability to pay for maintenance, rot, decay and erosion would usually have set in and further weakened an already fragile structure.

When I was first approached to do this sort of work I sought the advice of a more experienced practitioner in a nearby architectural practice. Bearing in mind that, as well as the inspection, the task also involved writing up the report and then costing its recommendations and, as likely as not, discussing the contents with the parochial church council at their next meeting, the 'customary fee' set down in the diocesan handbook was hardly generous. When my old friend heard of my intention to undertake quinquennials he dryly observed, 'Fifteen guineas for three days' work and jackdaw shit down your neck? You must be mad.'

Nevertheless, I took it on and over the years looked after a couple of dozen churches, some in towns and others deep in the countryside, some well-heeled, others desperately poor, but all, in their own way, worthwhile, if only for the people I met.

I had a glimpse of clerical, and, indeed, architectural life that I thought had been left behind in the time of Trollope when I read a report written by an earlier architect, who had inspected the church I was about to visit. Although it had been only fifteen years earlier, it opened with the paragraph: 'I was blessed with fair weather for the morning inspection and was received respectfully by the local builder and undertaker. All appeared sound. I repaired to the vicarage for lunch where the parson and I enjoyed game pie served with cranberry and I asked that my thanks be conveyed to the cook.'

Two of my charges, Kingston Buci at Shoreham and the church at Bishopstone, near Seaford, were of pre-Conquest origin and therefore of great significance. I found myself looking at stone which had lain there for an entire millennium and had been maintained through plague, pestilence, fire and civil disturbance. Although I couldn't let awe get in the way of objectivity, I had to think really hard lest some cavalier intervention on my part imperilled this remarkable work. In the end you can only adopt the most appropriate form of conservation you know and get on with it; after all, that is what all my predecessors had done and it had worked. A surgeon mends a broken bone of a king and a pauper in the same way; I had to mend broken stone, whether it was relatively new or of sacred age, with the same practicality, despite the weight of history, although after I'd done it I often went on worrying about whether I'd done the 'right' thing.

After a few quinquennial inspections, and following an experience that bordered on the surreal, I learned to be wary of evangelising enthusiasm among my clerical clients. I could cope with the evangelism; after all, that was the way I had been brought up – not that anyone would have noticed – but the unstoppable enthusiasm was another matter. One particular rector not only thought he understood the condition of every inch of the building, he believed he knew the remedy for each defect, to the extent that he shadowed me everywhere, up and down ladders, deep into the crypt, along parapet gutters, all the while being 'extremely helpful' and, worse still, jolly. I suppose I should have expected this when he received me earlier in the day with a crushing handshake and a 'Welcome on board, old chap.'

I had just opened the trapdoor above the bell-ringing platform of the tower, and, after pushing aside some old sacking and other debris, had climbed awkwardly into the dim interior above. I knew immediately from the stench that the belfry had been colonised by bats and, as it was late in the summer afternoon, they were beginning to stir before leaving through a narrow broken window for their twilight foray for gnats, which hung in wobbling clusters between the trees outside, lit by falling shafts of late sunlight.

Steadying myself against the timber framing, I switched on my torch to find the walls encrusted with bats, and they began to stir at the sight of the lamp. I needed to inspect the tower wall for cracks and look at the bell frame for death-watch beetle, but in these circumstances it was going to be impossible, particularly as the bats had now started to flutter around me in the gloom.

'Don't worry, old boy, I've got just the thing. I'll be back in a jiff, so just hang on a mo,' came the reassuring voice shadowing me. By the time I looked round he had disappeared to the vicarage nearby, only to reappear minutes later with an old tennis racquet, a plastic bucket and a brush and dustpan. I blinked at him as he emerged through the trapdoor with his armoury of equipment and rather feebly asked what he had in mind. He was now standing clutching the racquet, with his shirtsleeves rolled up, and I caught the glint in his eye as he explained that I was to hold the torch beam steady to attract the bats and he would bring them down, one by one, with a smash shot worthy of Centre Court; and then, between us, we would sweep them up, put them in the bucket and dispose of them later. Rather shyly, he told me that he had captained his university tennis team and could be relied upon 'not to make a mess of it', although it was perfectly obvious to me that a revolting mess was exactly what we were about to make of it.

Although this was long before bats were declared a protected species, I had to think of some way of getting out of this ridiculous situation and, after a moment's reflection, fell back rather weakly on the only excuse that came readily to mind – namely, that my, and probably his, insurance policy didn't cover this sort of activity and it would be unfair if something went wrong and the parochial church council were saddled with a claim (God knows from whom, I hadn't thought it that far) that would put them in the red for years to come. His theological training hadn't covered such contingencies so, to my intense relief, he concluded that perhaps, after all, we shouldn't do it.

So, from past experience, I guessed that a tower of that age would have *some* cracks, not least because the ivy outside was probably the only thing holding it up, and that timber of that antiquity would very likely be affected by some rot. I then drafted one or two general observations for my report in the dim light and called it a day. As I never heard anything more, I concluded that my guesses were about right.

I had a good head for heights, so when I was once called upon to examine a metal cross that topped the spire of the Church of St John the Baptist in Palmeira Square, Hove, which had suffered recent storm damage, I arranged for scaffolding to be erected so that I could discuss with the mason what should be done on the spot. When the scaffolding was ready, on what turned out to be an extremely windy afternoon, I arranged my rendezvous at the top of the structure with one of the best stonemasons in the business, whose depth of knowledge I had always respected. I kept a scruffy and by now almost buttonless old coat for this sort of work and, as it was cold, donned it before climbing the first set of ladders. I was so preoccupied with keeping a firm grip during my ascent that I barely noticed the double-decker red buses going round Palmeira Square under my feet. The scaffold poles were rusty and jagged, and in the wind my loose coat periodically wrapped itself around me, slowing my progress. During one sudden gust, when I stood motionless and just hung on, the last remaining button ripped off and my coat flew out horizontally from my shoulders like a billowing sail in a force 8 gale, pulling me away from the spire. From the ground I must have resembled a grotesque medieval gargoyle – the type that has spiked wings and a grimace, both of which I was now fully equipped with.

The mason, who did this sort of thing every day of the week and was not so foolish as to wear a long coat, reached the top long before I did. After a couple of deep breaths I slowly climbed the last twenty feet to meet him. By the time I arrived the wind was screeching so loudly that we were both inaudible, despite being locked in a near embrace, him hugging one side of the spire top and me the other, with our arms overlapping in the middle. We muttered at each other and all I could see was his mouth, complete with loose dentures, opening and shutting at regular intervals without a single syllable reaching my ears as the wind howled around us. We looked at the fractured metal cross and the split stone beneath it and then at each other, finally accepting, by a series of semaphore messages with our eyebrows, that the only sane thing to do was reunite ourselves with the ground and discuss the whole thing over a mug of tea. I should never have insisted on meeting him *in situ* in the first place, and never did so again.

The dead may be dead, but they are still capable of having the last laugh and upsetting the best-laid plans of the living. It happened to me twice. On the first occasion I was designing what was to become known as the Brighthelm

Centre, a new multi-purpose building for the United Reformed Church in North Road, Brighton. For numerous reasons it had taken many years to resolve the preliminary stages of the project – so many, in fact (nineteen from my first appointment to physical completion), that, to my astonishment, I was re-interviewed for the job in year eleven upon the appointment of yet another new minister who wanted to start the entire project all over again. I survived that and slowly, as the necessary finance became available, we began the detailed design which was to include a substantial amount of 'social' space for weekday and evening use. Such accommodation was to be let to the NHS, the Chinese community, gay groups and other diverse organisations which proliferated in Brighton. A building which is intended for multiple use usually ends up being barely suitable for any *single* use, but eventually, after sometimes anguished struggle, we obtained agreement for the designs from the client and the planning authority and commenced construction. At last, after all these years, we were putting one brick upon another, although this came too late for many of the original founders, who had either retired from the scene, moved away or died.

The contractor worked with a real sense of purpose and we were congratulating ourselves on the early progress when a mechanical excavator working on the foundations excavated first one and then two human skeletons. Work stopped immediately for a closer look and before long archaeologists, forensic pathologists and ecclesiastical lawyers arrived to make their inspection. The ongoing and, by now, more delicate digging finally recovered seventy or eighty sets of human remains, but no one was able to throw much light on the dreadful event which had resulted in such a hastily prepared and unmarked mass burial. Local historians put it down to some unrecorded outbreak of typhoid or cholera a couple of hundred years earlier perhaps, but no compelling evidence emerged to satisfy a hungry media who, in the end, only ever got half a story. Construction had to stop completely while formal notices were placed in the local newspapers, stating that twenty-one days would elapse before construction restarted, during which time any known relative was entitled to claim the earthly remains of their ancestor for re-interment at the client's expense. Not surprisingly, there were no takers, but the first substantial extra on the contract was recorded because of the delay and ate up immediately most of the contingency sum set aside for such unexpected events, which would leave us sadly exposed should anything else untoward happen during the remainder of the programme.

The second occasion when death cast an equally expensive shadow was at the church in South Malling, Lewes, where a modest vestry extension containing a lavatory for clergy use had been planned. This involved laying a new drain across the churchyard to the nearest public connection. We meticulously surveyed each grave in the immediate vicinity and wound the line of the new drain around them all except one, where the presence of a large tree denied us an alternative route. Permission to re-inter the contents of this particular grave was sought and granted and the headstone lifted prior to digging. After we had removed the moss and lichen from the gravestone, we came across barely legible lettering at the base, hitherto obscured by weeds, stating that the deceased had contracted anthrax, a deadly bacillus, most common in sheep and cattle, but communicable to man. Because its spores are so resistant to destruction and can cause such serious effects even generations later, the project was closed down, the earth backfilled and the constabulary informed within the hour. As the police cordon went up, journalists and television crews arrived from nowhere and I had the strange experience of seeing the smallest job I had ever undertaken given the widest national media coverage and, as everyone else had fled, talking to camera about a subject I knew absolutely nothing about.

Doctors and the clergy are trained to handle bad news; architects aren't, but over the years I found myself having to learn a few rudimentary skills when reporting the result of quinquennial inspections. All too often time was spent happily, if highly uneconomically, inspecting a little Romanesque gem of a church hidden in the corner of the county, lovingly tended by a handful of loyal folk who were unable to contribute anything near what was required to keep the aging fabric in good order.

John Betjeman's church poem 'Septuagesima' evokes such a scene:

> . . . But most of all let's praise the few
> Who are seen in their accustomed pew
> Throughout the year, whate'er the weather,
> That they may worship God together.
> These, like a fire of glowing coals,
> Strike warmth into each other's souls,
> And though they be but two or three
> They keep the Church for you and me.

How did I find a way of telling them that dealing urgently with the subsidence, dry rot, perished plaster, eroded stonework and rusty ironwork would cost at least £30,000, a sum I knew they could never raise? I soon became adept at adopting the demeanour of a village doctor faced, yet again, with a friendly octogenarian in his waiting room suffering from multiple chronic

132

conditions. I listened, I euphemised, I talked about 'wear and tear' and I finally observed how grateful they must all be to have in their midst a building of such charm and antiquity – so what about raising £75 at next summer's garden fete to fix that loose finial on the chancel roof, as that was *really* urgent?

Chapter 23

The Arabian Experience

Buildings erected in times of plenty are a conspicuous manifestation of confidence and prosperity, but in the long post-war era, economic recovery came in fits and starts as all European nations slowly adjusted themselves to half-forgotten normality. Boom was followed by bust, with the effects felt immediately in the development and construction industries. A bad Budget could knock millions off previously announced spending plans for hospitals, schools, housing and roads, and the effect on all the construction professions – architecture, structural and civil engineering, quantity surveying and the like – was immediate. Commercial and political life at that time was still volatile; the unthinkable happened when Rolls-Royce went bankrupt in the early 1970s; the prolonged miners' strike led to the 'Three-Day Week' and unemployment figures passed the one million mark. In architecture no one tells you when the workload is about to fall away; it just happens. Politicians, when cornered, reluctantly admitted to 'a blip on the screen', and my professional competitors were unlikely to share their similar worries in case they might be the only practice going through a thin time and none of us wanted to lose face. I didn't know what the true position was or, more importantly, how long my own difficulties were going to last.

More depressingly, when the recessions did begin to bite and we had begun to weather them, it didn't occur to any of us that they were going to get worse in the future. After all, new buildings are eminently deferrable and money can be 'saved' overnight by cautious clients and governments alike. Rather than 'release' staff (a cruel phrase), we all had to look elsewhere to sustain a workload if we wanted to keep good design teams intact, and for this task most of us were ill prepared.

At about that time, and in common with many large, London-based organisations forced to relocate elsewhere due to high office rents and unaffordable

135

housing, two well-known firms of consulting engineers arrived in Brighton. The town has excellent rail links to the capital, a pleasing environment in which to work and raise a family, and is only half an hour from Gatwick Airport, so it was an obvious choice.

Preece, Cardew & Rider (PCR) was the first company to arrive. It was long established and originally one of its founding partners had been the Postmaster General in the early days of telegraphy. In fact, one of its later claims to distinction was that it had employed a talented young man recently arrived from Italy called Guglielmo Marconi, who went on to develop commercial wireless telegraphy. His invention, together with the development of radio valves, led to the birth of the modern wireless and, in 1909, long after he had left PCR, he was awarded the Nobel Prize.

It so happened that I had been looking for some reliable mechanical and electrical consulting engineers for some time and, shortly after this company arrived, I invited them to design the air-conditioning system for the Sussex Mutual Building Society project nearing completion on the drawing board. They were pleasant people to work with and I was pleased when they reciprocated by asking me to come and see them about some possible work in the Middle East. Although they were a large multi-disciplinary practice which included civil engineering, they had no in-house architectural capacity. I was happy to be asked to fill that gap and even more pleased that the work was in an area untouched by western recession – namely, Saudi Arabia.

PCR had an enviable reputation in telecommunications design and had been invited by the Ministry of Information to prepare proposals for the Saudi kingdom's first television service. Whilst this was largely an electrical engineering project involving, among other things, the choice of optimum routes for a signal, it also required the design of television studios and related transmission stations, and this was the work they wanted me to do.

I was inexperienced in studio or station design, but this seemed to deter nobody and in the end didn't deter me either. Early in my career I had come to the fairly obvious conclusion that a lifetime in square one awaited me if I wasn't prepared to take a risk. Arrangements were made speedily for me to join a group of their engineers who had gone out a week or so earlier and were based in Abha in the Asir province of Saudi Arabia, just north of the Yemen border.

Being attached to a group of highly experienced engineers as an architectural sub-consultant had to be thought through. Most engineers are very focused individuals who relish the practical, hands-on aspect of any technical challenge. However, they tend to regard architecture as a fringe activity peopled by practitioners whose feet are seldom grounded and who speak largely of aesthetic considerations in terms the engineers find not only foreign, but completely unnecessary. I was going to be nearer the road to Damascus than I would ever be in Brighton and I began adjusting my persona accordingly, realising that it was going to take time to gain their confidence. I therefore talked to the engineers more enthusiastically about concrete foundation design and the state of English football than I would normally have done.

The national airline Saudia, on which we were obliged to travel, flew out of London and, because it was fairly new, came under the wing of an American airline who provided the flight-deck crews and undertook technical maintenance. Whilst the air hostesses were female, as they all were in those days, they did not include Saudi women, who were forbidden to do such work. On my flight a Lebanese woman worked beside a Glaswegian, which was probably easier than might be imagined as no alcoholic drinks were permitted and the lukewarm cans of peach juice had large pictures on the label, so their understanding of the written word was less important. The spoken word should have been easier, but I soon found I could only communicate in English with the Lebanese flight attendant, as the Glaswegian had me completely defeated.

In the early 1970s not a great deal was known about Saudi Arabia in Britain. My schoolboy atlas told me its land mass was equivalent to over half of Europe and it only had about six million inhabitants, mostly concentrated in a handful of large towns, with some of the remainder still nomadic. I read Wilfred Thesiger's *Arabian Sands* and *The Marsh Arabs* not just for the information they imparted but also because they were written by someone who was literate. So often books by seasoned travellers who can't write fight for shelf space with books by writers who are not genuine travellers, so it was refreshing to find a genuine traveller, probably the last of the great explorers, able to express himself with easy elegance based on first-hand experience.

It was the first time I had worked overseas and certainly my first experience of a land which had no connection whatever with English culture or language: we were going to be something of a novelty to each other, and this made it all the more fascinating.

King Faisal, a son of the great ruler Abdul Aziz Ibn Sa'ud who had originally brought the great kingdom together, was faced with the most challenging of tasks in his reign – namely, how to hold together a land in which the basic way of life had altered little in the previous thousand years but which through recently acquired oil wealth, was now attracting western ideas and attitudes that were complete anathema to a country that, first and foremost, regarded itself as the cradle of Islam.

And here were we, admittedly by invitation, happily delivering television with scant regard for its long-term influence on this fragile situation. On one occasion before we left, I obliquely, and very gently, touched on this with one of our microwave specialists, who looked up from his calculations and dryly observed, 'We're engineers, not anthro-bloody-pologists, so can we get on?'

The Saudia flight left Heathrow on time and followed a route over the Alps and later over Egypt and the Aswan Dam, yielding views I had only ever seen on the coloured pages of the *National Geographic Magazine*. We landed at Jeddah, the point of entry to the kingdom. Here, customs formalities took place. These involved a bureaucratic examination of passports, vaccination certificates, visas, boarding cards, transit slips and entry forms, and only after all this was complete were we permitted to re-board and fly on to the capital, Riyadh.

Only in recent history did Riyadh become the seat of government, as the Red Sea port of Jeddah had been the capital for as long as people could remember, and maybe for this reason, Riyadh contains little of historic importance. I found it big and sprawling and entirely lacking in cohesion, with new and old buildings jostling for space.

For foreigners working in Saudi Arabia a sponsor was necessary to act as intermediary, local partner and, more likely than not, 'fixer', so my first day involved going to the old quarter to meet Mohamed Kaki. The journey to his office came straight from the pages of Graham Greene. I was conducted through an area of decrepit properties awaiting redevelopment and along a narrow, unsurfaced and undrained street until we found the solid, heavily bolted door which served as his office entrance. A bare staircase led to a large first-floor room lit by a single harsh light and there, attended by two mute, shuffling employees in headscarves, sat Mohamed Kaki, trader, entrepreneur, arranger and company director. Shrewdness was etched in his face and it was perfectly clear that he had no need of reading *Parkinson's Law: The Pursuit of Progress*, which was a current success in Britain and dealt in a commonsense way with successful management long before business schools developed it into a major industry. In it, Cyril Northcote Parkinson described the Chinese coolie who, owning nothing more than the ragged shorts and T-shirt he stands up in together with an old bicycle, works laboriously year after year until he gradually accumulates some money. Significantly, as he prospers he continues to wear the same old clothes and ride the same elderly bicycle and, by minimising his overheads, is able, by continuing to work hard, to accumulate wealth more quickly than his western counterparts who would usually increase their personal expenditure in line with their enhanced income.

Finally, some years later, when the coolie is rich enough, he transforms himself *overnight* by buying a large house, a Mercedes and a sharkskin suit to match, all the while free of debt. Mohamed Kaki understood all this and could well have written the book first.

He received us courteously, his silent servants poured us coffee, and he asked us in what way he could help, assuming we were new to Riyadh and would need a number of useful contacts if we were to make progress. As well as owning an automobile concession, he distributed a non-alcoholic drink called, unattractively, Kaki Kola (whose signs were all over the place), and he traded in every commodity and knew everyone. He also knew how valuable he was to the English visitors, and I only hoped that PCR had included a necessary disbursment, and more, in the final fee they had negotiated with the ministry.

At the conclusion of the meeting he assured us that if there was anything further we wanted, all we had to do was telephone, which turned out to be less helpful than it sounded, as the following day I needed urgent help arranging some internal flights, only to be told by one of his lackeys, not once but twice, that 'the Chief Engineer is not in the office today and is very busy in any case'.

The next day it began to sink in that time meant absolutely nothing in what was still essentially a desert culture, and, in the crippling heat, there was no good reason why it should. It slowly became clear that everything was going to take much longer than we had planned and the carefully coordinated programme we had prepared in the UK was going to drift badly. With hindsight, we might perhaps have anticipated one of the delays, but could never have envisaged the particular combination of circumstances that caused it.

The first occasion resulting in a delay was typical of what was to follow. Our clients, the Ministry of Information, had arranged previously to pay for three transceivers to be used by the PCR team for the microwave survey. This equipment had been despatched from the UK in good time, but upon arrival in Riyadh, had been impounded by the customs department who, because it was classified as radio equipment, needed clearance from the Ministry of Communications, with whom we had no dealings and who therefore didn't know us. This ministry needed a formal letter describing the specification and purpose of these sets, for consideration by the appropriate committee when it next met and it would not authorise customs clearance until this had been completed. Despite my protestation, it became evident that a direct approach to the Ministry of Information was going to be fruitless as they had no powers to tell another ministry what to do, so all we could do was wait.

The second occasion had the makings of a Molière farce. I had been joined by a new colleague, Colin Lancaster, a key microwave engineer. As his work needed to continue when the local driver was unavailable (at certain times during Ramadan, on Fridays [the Muslim holy day], and on other rest days), he needed to obtain a local driving licence, so he presented himself at the appropriate office with his passport, UK driving licence and extra photos, and expressed a willingness to submit to any further checks and tests that may be thought necessary. Having had to wait twenty-four hours to receive his passport back from registration, he didn't reach the driving-licence office until 9.30 the next morning. The formalities lasted until 11.50 a.m. and there only remained a cursory eyesight test. This was merely a formality, but the Ministry of Health official to whom he had been sent said that as the office closed at 12 noon for prayers, he couldn't deal with him. The advertised office hours indicated that the department would reopen at 12.30 until 2.00 p.m., and absolutely nothing could be done to dissuade the official who, even though he didn't even join the others for prayers, insisted Colin could only be dealt with by revisiting the office at 9.30 the following morning.

We immediately cancelled our carefully made arrangements to travel to Abha together, as I had already been delayed and couldn't wait yet another day before joining the team, who were waiting to start work and were dependent on my involvement. So Colin and I split up and I now had to arrange a flight back to Jeddah and hopefully catch a plane on to Abha as, on this particular day, there were no direct flights from Riyadh. Neither was there any way of contacting the Abha team as there were no reliable telephone or telex links, though I knew they would be sending a truck across forty kilometres of particularly rocky desert to meet me off a flight I wasn't going to be on and, worse still, I couldn't even let them know which plane I would eventually catch. I wished Colin good luck, joined a long queue in the Saudia booking office and eventually caught a delayed flight back to Jeddah.

My intention was to take the early-morning flight next day to Abha so, after leaving my overnight hotel, I presented myself at the check-in as early as I could. This meant leaving the hotel in pitch darkness with an ill-tempered taxi driver who, upon arrival at the airport, picked an argument with a porter he obviously knew and hated, over who should be entrusted with my luggage or, more to the point, who should collect the tip. The departure hall was full and, amid the kissing, weeping, yawning and general clamour, I elbowed my way forward only to be told, 'Very sorry, flight full, come back tomorrow. Next please.' My despair was compounded by realising that I now had to trace my route backwards. Every airport in the world is planned sequentially, with one clear route for departures and another for arrivals, so having to leave the airport from the departures section had never been visualised. Doors, if they opened at all, swung against you, there were no porters and, worst of all, there were no taxis outside as they had left to pick up recent arrivals. The sun had risen, it was hot and humid and I was already sweating. I began dragging my luggage back in the direction of the hotel before I realised I didn't know where it was, as I'd arrived and left in darkness and never saw any street names, and even if I had, couldn't read Arabic. There was nothing for it but to sacrifice a ridiculous amount of local currency and seek immediate help from anyone interested in folding money. As if by magic, men and boys anxious to help appeared from nowhere and got me back, in a variety of ways, to the hotel I had left a couple of hours earlier. My old room hadn't been reallocated but had already been stripped so, on reaching my floor, I rummaged through a pile of dirty sheets and a heap of grubby towels in the corridor, and, watched by an appalled cleaner, chose a couple that looked the least disgusting, entered my room, drew the curtains and, flinging myself onto the bed without undressing, fell into a heavy sleep.

The following morning I checked out once more, feeling a lot more confident about the geography that had so confused me the day before. Again it was very early and dawn was only just breaking, but I wanted to be at the airport first and was determined to be through the doors before anyone else. I found my way completely barred, not by a secured entrance, but by thirteen white-robed bottoms of airport support staff whose heads were deeply bowed towards Mecca for the first of the day's mandatory observances. I couldn't get past them, over them or through them, so I sat on my luggage behind them, ignored the unedifying view, and tried to look calm and reverent until prayers were finished.

The flight from Jeddah was short and bumpy but full of visual wonder. I was transported into yet another issue of *National Geographic*. We flew south along a range of dusty mountains which ran parallel to the Red Sea until we turned inland, where the geology became almost surreal. Huge, overlapping slices of toast spilled from the table of some giant's feast, stretching as far as the eye could see, and then, quite suddenly, disappeared to give way to primeval thumbprints as big as a town, which, after a few minutes, merged into the cultivated terraces of Asir, the southernmost state of the kingdom. For the first time greenery appeared and I realised that Abha, its principal town, must be relatively high above the scorching desert of the Empty Quarter it abutted to the east.

Khamis Mushayt, a small military airstrip in the desert, served as the 'airport' for Abha, our final destination. Its runway was unmetalled and had been roughly flattened, with only the bigger rocks removed before the sand was compacted. Our aircraft made a dusty landing and it was impossible to see outside until the sand had settled sufficiently to reveal a simple hutment and a windsock. A handful of passengers disembarked and were met by an assortment of local people who had arrived in trucks and battered automobiles.

As no one knew I was there and I didn't know how to reach Abha across a roadless desert, it took me some time to decide what to do. For some obscure reason I remembered being recently shown the cockpit of a training aircraft where, above the instrument panel, there was a Dymo-taped exhortation saying, 'Before you do anything, do nothing.' So I stood there long after the other arrivals had vanished and did nothing. The departing aircraft threw up another cloud of dust, and after it settled I became aware of a solitary figure in a brown tobe and chequered headscarf looking vaguely in my direction. He stood motionless and was presumably waiting for me to move, which I was reluctant to do as I had heavy luggage and the sun was at its height. Slowly he walked towards me and I noticed that his deeply lined face was totally expressionless. One hand carried something behind his back and he stopped once more and jangled some car keys and prayer beads in his free hand. As there was no one else to be seen, he was my only hope of reaching my destination, so I walked slowly towards him. I said something in English, he replied in Arabic, and a long silence followed, like a scene from *Waiting for Godot*. He moved closer and suddenly produced from behind his back a piece of cardboard which he thrust within inches of my nose. On it was scrawled 'PCR', and to my great relief I realised I was being met by the PCR reception committee. I smiled broadly but he remained expressionless, though he beckoned me to follow him to the truck. It was a Toyota four-wheel drive and was closely modelled on the UK Land Rover. In fact, we would probably have been travelling in a Land Rover but for the fact that its makers had been blacklisted by various Arab states for trading with Israel, thus providing Japan with a gift from heaven.

Contrary to common perception, a desert does not comprise endless miles of undulating sand, but more resembles the surface of the moon, bleak, dusty, plantless, full of strewn rocks and featureless, so the lack of intelligible speech between the driver and myself didn't matter: there was nothing interesting to remark upon.

When we reached the Aseer Hotel, Abha, the PCR base, their team leader happened to be outside unloading some equipment from another vehicle. 'You must be the architect we've been expecting. I'm Frank Reynolds. By the way, what kept you?' I searched my mind for a snappy riposte, and in retrospect only wish this incident had taken place a few years later, when I could have used the timeless reply of Prime Minister Harold Macmillan who, when once asked what had caused his proposals to be altered, said simply, 'Events, dear boy, events.' Frank had a rich Cornish accent, reddish hair and bright blue eyes, and looked particularly impressive in an Afrika Korps hat with a neck protector. He not only looked the part but enjoyed looking the part, and in the following days proved to be every bit a leader.

The Aseer Hotel was something of a misnomer. It resembled a Clacton-on-Sea boarding house out of season, except it wasn't damp but bone dry, with every surface warm to the touch. Through no fault of its proprietor, it suffered frequent power cuts and a fluctuating water supply, but so did everywhere else in Abha, so no one felt the need to grumble or apologise. It took me some time to work out why every meal was lukewarm when it arrived; I eventually discovered that the cooking and serving was done in an annexe right at the back of the building and by the time someone was found to carry the plates filled with hot food into the dining room (never easy because they were probably doing laundry elsewhere when needed), the food had cooled. By the same token, if the kitchen served a cold dish, it hung about long enough to absorb heat, so it was tepid by the time it reached the table. I gave up trying to determine the origin of any meal.

We slept three to a room – Ben Bolt, a former BBC engineer; Colin Lancaster, who had arrived on the following plane; and me. It was all very informal and comradely and took me back to life in the barrack room, sharing ointment for chapped lips, checking dhobi, calling out log-table and slide-rule readings, and sharing the day's gossip.

Our first day together was taken up selecting a suitable site for the TV studios and, before I had arrived, two had been shortlisted which were roughly opposite each other on the road to Jizan, about a quarter of an hour outside Abha. Technically, either would have done, but one of them possessed a sandstone outcrop of distinctive shape that gave it an immediate identity, whereas the other site was featureless. In profile the sandstone feature, some twenty feet higher than the surrounding hill formed by centuries of erosion by wind and sand, looked uncommonly like the head of a giant turtle protruding from its carapace. Buildings should never look as if they had been plonked down arbitrarily, and my intention was that the new studios and the rocky outcrop should form a complementary composition and remind the spectator that the building belonged to that place and that place alone. The genesis of any design depends on its context. If a particular feature pre-exists, it can and should have an influence on its new neighbour.

Having inspected and drawn site plans of both candidates, I had to clearly identify each one for subsequent reference and discussion. For clarity, I provisionally annotated my favoured site 'Turtle Hill', and in all subsequent conversations with the team everyone knew which one it was. Despite some bleak looks from my engineers and a conspicuous lack of interest by the Saudis, I was allowed my choice of site as it met all the other important criteria. Over the next few days I developed the design and entitled my drawings 'Proposed TV Studios at Turtle Hill, Abha for the Ministry of Information, Kingdom of Saudi Arabia'.

It was only some years later when I returned to the region for another project that I was supplied with a newly printed town map by the local authority and saw that on it, to my amusement and slight embarrassment, was printed *Turtle Hill* to identify the new suburban area. I hadn't given the origin of place names much thought since my school days, when I recall instances of a Roman name for a place where a river could be forded or a French title for a hilltop dominated by a Norman fort and assumed that the whole process was a lot more formal and hallowed by history. But perhaps not – some of them could have been just as accidental as mine, and I felt quietly pleased.

Choosing the transmitter sites was more difficult. For obvious reasons they had to be on or near a mountain top so that the signal could be bounced straight down the valleys as well as across open terrain. The first was at Therah, the site of a derelict Turkish fortification, situated on a clear-cut promontory and approached by a winding dirt road that got progressively steeper as we ascended. The fort had originally comprised central quarters overlooking a compound, with the spectacular views from all sides so necessary for defence at the time. The site had the advantage of being the nearer one to Abha.

The alternative, more distant transmitter site was at Jebel Nahran. It looked out onto cultivated terraces to the west and was high enough to permit green scrub near the summit. The views from the top were alpine, but were crueller and looked much more like the foothills of the Himalayas. Swirls of tortured rock buttressed the steep slopes, punctuated by acacias of such delicacy they could have been spirited from a traditional Japanese watercolour. I spent a lot of time photographing the stupendous views from the site until reminded by the team that they'd brought me all this way, and at great expense, to photograph and measure the site itself. To make the point, I was invited to unload the survey equipment and carry it up the last three hundred feet of rock that were inaccessible to the truck. The theodolite was in a large hardwood case held by thick leather straps and the tripod on which it sat was made of equally dense hardwood with brass hinges. On arrival at the summit, suitably chastened and sweaty, I decided it would be easier to do what was expected of me in future.

Meetings, whether with clients or with senior functionaries, took a form we were unfamiliar with. The arrangements were clearly time-honoured and everyone understood the process and its origin except us. I needed to photograph some of the older buildings in the town to try and get a feel for the local vernacular and how it might influence the appearance of my new designs, and I was told that this needed permission from the local prince, who was away in London. Instead I was ushered into the presence of the region's deputy governor. I was offered a seat and immediately given an Arabic coffee, clear and honey-coloured and tasting of aniseed and aromatic herb. The potion came in small cups and, not particularly liking it, I swallowed mine all in one gulp. This was immediately interpreted as approval, and before I could decline a second serving, my cup was refilled by a servant who moved among the petitioners and replenished our cups from an ornate brass pot some distance away with the utmost dexterity. Over my right shoulder I suddenly noticed a streak of what looked like camel's piss aimed straight at my cup, and before I could say anything he had moved on to the next recipient without spilling a drop.

I was surprised to be heard directly I arrived, seeing that other petitioners were already there and patiently waiting. Apparently Arab hospitality demands instant acknowledgement of a stranger's arrival, so the moment I sat down I was invited to speak. Somewhat embarrassed and concerned that I may be thought to be queue-jumping, I introduced myself and was beginning to describe our work when another petitioner arrived. The deputy governor, showing equal courtesy to the newcomer, switched his attention while I was in mid-sentence, and listened to what he had to say – in this case, about the likelihood of two missing goats having been stolen by his neighbour. This new petitioner was getting into his stride when yet another arrived and the deputy governor's attention switched again, and so the audience went on. No one looked particularly put out by all this and I began to realise that everyone who had got there before me had been cut off halfway through and they were all waiting to complete their petitions, when, predictably, the visitors for the morning finally stopped arriving.

It would be at least another generation before the Western world would have the wit and humility to learn from local traditions, and no more so than in architecture. Abha was a compact town surrounded by lightly wooded hills which gave way to inhospitable mountains beyond, and its buildings were constructed of readily available natural materials, with baked earth blocks used for the walls. They were built thick enough to provide coolness inside and had very small windows set deep into the reveals, preventing sunlight from penetrating the interior. The ground floor was often painted white to reflect the heat, while the upper storeys were faced with courses of thin stone, about a foot apart, inserted edge-on into the walls so that they projected from the face, shielding it from direct sunlight. This device not only provided a cool interior in the height of the desert summer, but also protected the earth wall from disintegrating under storm-water conditions when, very occasionally, the heavens opened and thunderous rain fell. They must have been building like this for centuries; everyone knew how to do it, everyone knew that it worked, and no one had ever heard of architects and building contractors, nor need they have done.

In the conscience-stricken West, the Green Revolution was only just beginning, but for the PCR team, and for me in particular, Abha was a revelation and, in years to come, I was going to see equally simple and effective solutions in developing countries around the world.

The particular design problem that faced me was difficult to resolve and was all the more fascinating for it. I wanted the traditional buildings of Abha to influence the layout, construction and appearance of my new designs for the television complex, but obviously, certain factors were so different they demanded different answers. For instance, no one was going to live in this building, so its daily cycle of use would vary from that of its domestic neighbours. Acoustics were of paramount importance, internally for studio sound levels and externally to eliminate the noise of a passing thunderstorm. Access for the delivery and maintenance of technical equipment had to be provided and this involved some very wide external openings and equally wide clear spans internally which could only be constructed in reinforced concrete. The more I thought about it, the wider the differences to the surrounding architecture became, to the point where, if I wasn't careful, I would be left with no legitimate references to the local vernacular I so admired.

For functional reasons, the layout and construction were bound to be different, but what of external appearance? (I avoid the word *style* because it is so often, quite wrongly, used to describe the external aesthetic only.) Was there anything that I could rescue from the local surroundings that had so impressed me? I decided that, for functional reasons, the studio building would have a horizontal emphasis that fitted in with the neighbouring buildings. It would be almost windowless, albeit for reasons of acoustics rather than solar gain, and that was another plus. Tonally, the external wall could be given a sand-coloured finish which would be both practicable and good-neighbourly, so gradually I began to find my way back to something that didn't look aggressively out of place. In the end my only arbitrary concession to the local vernacular was the inclusion at cornice level of small decorative features of no obvious functional origin. I knew I couldn't really justify their inclusion in practical terms, but I liked the look of them and hoped they'd go by on the nod.

Architects seldom agree on how to acknowledge the *genius loci* of a particular place, but I hoped I wouldn't score less than seven out of ten on this occasion. After all, it was my first try and, with a bit of luck, there would be so much talk about retaining the 'Turtle Hill' that no one would notice much else, and in the event they didn't.

The enthusiasm to get on with the design was tempered by the reality of much preparatory work on the selected sites, both of which had to be accurately measured and contoured. There are no short cuts in surveying. It has to be painstakingly accurate and, since I was thousands of miles away from the office in which the architecture and engineering design would be developed and finalised, there could be no slipping back to check a missing dimension. John Corin, a very conscientious civil engineer, operated the theodolite while I, some distance away, held the staff (a telescopic measuring post rather like a huge vertical ruler). I had to stand in one position for a long time so that John could take and plot accurate readings; the sun was merciless, and it was far more exhausting being stationary than it was carrying equipment on the move. At the end of an interminably long day, we packed up and I began carrying our equipment down the loose rock to the waiting truck below. Probably because I was tired, I missed my footing near the bottom and twisted my right ankle. After proving I could stand on it, we continued back to the Toyota and thought no more about it. It was only several hours later when we were back in our shared quarters that it began to swell badly. Until then I had regarded the barrack-room arrangements of our accommodation as merely quaint, but on seeing my problem, Ben Bolt produced an old bottle of iodine. 'I've had it since the war,' he informed me. Seeing the torn label and stained cork, I stopped myself asking, 'Which war?' Almost simultaneously, Frank produced a crepe bandage of seemingly equal antiquity and helped me apply it. It reminded me of scenes twenty-five years earlier where spontaneous and heart-warming camaraderie in the army involved looking after each other as a matter of course. Suddenly I realised how much I had missed it in the intervening years.

Very early the following day the PCR team were to leave on a three-day trip to Nazran, near the Yemen border. They spent half the night discussing transceivers, heliographs and microwave routes and, by the time I awoke, they had gone. I was going to develop the studio and transmitting station designs in their absence, but as I did not need all my waking hours to do this, I thought I'd collect my thoughts for a while and go up to the flat roof where a shaded portion remained fairly cool and captured what little breeze there was. I took the solid-state five-band radio with me and looked out onto the still-sleepy town where Ramadan had just begun, and beyond it to the panorama of geological prehistory reaching into the distance. After the hectic activities of the last few days I sat quietly for a while and tried to place myself. The muezzin's call to prayer heralding the break of day had transported me to Asia; the daily fast of Ramadan had immersed me in Arabia; and a pair of tethered camels whose owner was delivering grain next door reminded me that I was a very long way from home and in a very foreign land. After a while I turned on the radio and found the BBC World Service covering the Conservative party conference in Bournemouth. I wished I hadn't, because the sudden sound of an English voice interrupted my musing on whether Wilfred Thesiger would ever have accepted me as a bag carrier for one of his expeditions across the Empty Quarter.

The daily pattern of weather remained the same, beginning with brilliant sunshine and a cloudless sky. Shortly after the hottest period at midday, a quickening breeze heralded an overcast and cooler interlude which, by about 5 p.m., disappeared to give way to a tranquil and exquisite sunset and a cloudless, still night, full of beauty. I made a point of returning to the roof after dark every night to sit and wonder at the celestial canopy and gaze at everything I'll never completely understand. The brilliance of diamond-sharp stars in that clear atmosphere filled even a moonless sky with radiance.

During the absence of the other members of the team the hotel was empty, or if there were any other occupants, I didn't see them. There was no question of choice at mealtimes and I was served silently and deliberately by one of two very different kitchen staff. The first was a tall, handsome and serious young man wearing a jaunty, beaded pillbox hat and who, in the absence of any other customers in the dining room, would stand silently beside my chair until I'd finished. If I took exception to any suspicious morsel on my plate he would frown and show impatience until I had consumed everything, which didn't make our silent relationship any easier. I concluded that his ill humour was due to hunger and fatigue during Ramadan because, on eventually hearing the maroon fired at dusk from one of the old Turkish forts overlooking the town signalling the end of fasting, the kitchen would erupt into noise. My much-relieved servant would then immediately join the animated group of staff and visitors, most of whom I had never seen before, who had assembled for a gossip in the passageway outside. The other servant was a far more genial Sudanese with parallel scars on both cheeks who, having served me, would sit down on a comfortable chair across the room and not care whether I ate anything or not.

Being on my own, I had plenty of time to take in the hotel's interior, which had all the cheap, brittle gaiety of a fairground. The colours were garish, everything was heavily patterned and at night the public rooms were dimly lit by 40-watt bulbs, or else, in the more important areas, bare fluorescent tubes hung as you might find them in any second-hand car workshop. Plastic flowers in plastic 'pebble' pots abounded and the bare walls were decorated with faded Saudia Airline posters advertising cheap flights to Mecca. The decor was completed by pink, mauve, pea-green and orange curtains, complete with tasselled pelmets, which were draped across every door and window. Opening a door therefore involved two free hands, one to depress the handle and the other to push aside the tightly draped curtain to prevent it being split when the door opened. Little wonder the technicolor curtains had been decorated still further by innumerable food stains as kitchen staff had negotiated their way to the dining room with only one free hand.

As Ramadan wore on I began to understand why the place was so quiet. It wasn't just because my team was away elsewhere, it was because most Saudis, if they had the opportunity, would slip away and sleep for part of the day when they couldn't eat. After all, they had all been up well before dawn to consume the one large meal that had to last until dusk, and often found themselves running out of steam early on in the taxing heat.

Having achieved more than expected with my designs in the team's absence, I was beginning to feel at a loose end and was delighted when, late one evening, I heard Frank's stentorian voice supervising the unloading of our truck and simultaneously ordering large quantities of fried eggs from the kitchen. Their excursion had been a success and we were all back on schedule with our work. All that remained was to coordinate our presentations which would shortly be made in Riyadh and make arrangements to leave Abha, with this phase of our work completed.

Once back in Riyadh, we settled into our accommodation and made appointments to see our ministerial clients, from whom we would, hopefully, obtain approval for our proposals. Hope played a larger than usual role in this as, apart from getting them to agree plans and specifications, we had to obtain written authority from our clients certifying that they were *in every respect* satisfied with the delivery of our professional services. If that were not the case, an exit visa could not be obtained and an expensive and indeterminate after-school detention would ensue, which was something we couldn't bear thinking about.

Our first call was to the deputy minister. He displayed a detailed knowledge of Asir province and asked a number of pertinent questions that we were able to answer, most of which had cropped up at meetings earlier in the day when we had made similar presentations. A long period of discussion followed and by the time we had explained everything to everyone, I was reaching the stage where I was forgetting whether what I was about to say had already been said, and if so, to whom. I would never have made a vacuum-cleaner salesman. As I was finally collecting my drawings from tables, walls, chairs and the floor, the deputy minister announced that his superior, the Minister of Information, had expressed an interest in seeing the proposals and we were to wait in an anteroom until he was ready to see us. It was already 10 p.m. and, as we'd been working since dawn, I was feeling a bit jaded. Saudis, on the other hand, particularly at senior level, rest during the hottest part of the day and reopen their offices at sundown, so they had a clear head start in the wide-awake stakes.

My heart sank to see the minister's anteroom full of other people; unless Allah intervened, we were going to be in for a long night. In the event he did and, although all the others shook hands warmly with us on arrival, we were quickly ushered into the presence of the minister ahead of them.

By now I was accustomed to gauging the pecking order within a hierarchy by observing the size and degree of embellishment of a particular office; what I was unprepared for was the very human contradiction of finding that the dignitaries seemed to get smaller the more senior they were. The deputy minister was short, but the minister himself was positively diminutive. A sheikh in his own right, he was quiet-spoken, reflective and informal. When he came to sit beside me on the long couch to look at the felt-pen drawings I had spread out on the gilt-and-glass table, I noticed his feet didn't quite reach the floor. His interest was genuine and informed and, despite his modest stature, he showed all the quiet confidence of someone who had arrived and, for good measure, had started his journey by being born into the 'right' tribe. He asked about thunder and its effect on studio acoustics; about the need to try and mollify local emirs whose district might still fall within the TV signal 'shadow' from adjacent mountains; and about the political need to strengthen the signal so that it could be received well beyond the Yemen border and across the Red Sea to the Sudan.

I should have found it easy to concentrate but, apart from my exhaustion, there were numerous distractions. The air coolers were particularly noisy, and for some reason a radio was on at full volume. Added to this, a large television set dominated the room and was screening the latest episode of *Gunsmoke*, a popular American Western. Video cassette recorders were yet to become available, and the minister was clearly not going to miss the action, so with complete composure (he must have made a habit of this), he divided his time between my presentation and the snappy dialogue and noisy gunfights.

He accomplished both with a benign smile and found time to say how inter-ested he was in my proposals. All the while the fox-eyed deputy minister interspersed our conversation with sharp questions we'd answered already, clearly to impress his imperturbable superior. Next to him, a twitchy director of television kept glancing nervously at the TV set, not so much to follow the episode, but more to ensure that the line-hold was steady and that all was entirely to his master's satisfaction.

To my surprise, Frank Reynolds rounded off the meeting by showing the minister a cartoon I had drawn the night before, illustrating the arrival of television in Abha. It showed a tethered goat whose vertical horns had been joined by a horizontal rod half way up to form an 'H' aerial, connected to a television set around which a group of Bedouin were seated. My sketch was meant strictly for home consumption and, for a moment, I thought that Frank had made a tactical error and the minister would find the drawing patronising. Mercifully, he didn't and he proudly showed it round the room, each recipient being careful to show just as much enthusiasm as their boss (but no more). By now it was past midnight and, by the time we reached the Aseer Hotel, were too tired to go to sleep so, despite the absence of alcohol, we talked light-heartedly and celebrated what felt like the end of term. In a way it was as, with our work completed, we were returning home shortly. We were very animated and everyone had to contribute an anecdote, charade or barrack-room ballad of some sort. When my turn came, I tried to parody Rudyard Kipling's 'Mandalay', which has the lines:

> On the road to Mandalay,
> Where the flyin-fishes play,
> An' the dawn comes up like thunder outer
> China 'crost the Bay!

But it ended up as:

> On the road where Abha lay
> Where the wadi's dry all day
> PCR will give them pictures in a box,
> Engineers and experts all
> Short and stout, and thin and tall
> They spend their day up mountains and on rocks.
> Not for them the easy life
> Air-cooled rooms and local wife,
> This loyal band are fighting off the ticks.

When December days are duller
Think of Abha with its colour
And its squared eyed nomads tuning in at six.

It was all very silly, but we were demob-happy and it didn't matter. During our subsequent packing I handed Frank back his crepe bandage and he turned to me and said, 'You're wasted in architecture.'

Chapter 24

Local Authorities and Local Difficulties

The beginning of the 1970s saw profound political and economic change in Britain. Events took place that could never have been visualised in the immediate post-war years, and included Parliament voting to join the EEC and the introduction of decimalisation. When the first of two miners' strikes took place in 1972, power cuts were introduced and in the following year the Arab oil producers decided to cut supplies drastically. By 1974 a longer and more damaging miners' strike led to the imposition of a 50-mph speed limit on the roads to conserve fuel and the 'Three-Day Week', which affected everyone, but particularly commerce and industry.

Professional offices were as badly hit as anyone else, and as I had only been going a couple of years under my own flag, I was concerned that we maintain our momentum of work. The fact that the strike came in the middle of a cold winter didn't make things any easier, and in the days following Christmas I had to ask the staff to take work home for the remaining two days of the week. Locally there was a predictable run on camping gas, paraffin and candles, and in order for the skeleton staff to keep the office open on 'closed' days, I quickly struck a deal with my local ironmonger. We also worked through the lunch hour to take full advantage of any residual heat in the system.

But you can't draw with cold hands and inadequate light, and we were considerably disadvantaged compared, for instance, with the professional offices of solicitors and accountants, who could manage in overcoats and gloves and, by late afternoon, candlelight.

Interestingly, everyone accepted the privations cheerfully and, although we enjoyed grumbling, our productivity, so vital at this stage of the practice's development, hardly fell. Most of the staff had been through the war and, by comparison, all this was a pushover and we often enlivened the day by

153

regaling each other with reports of meetings we had attended elsewhere where innovation (hot-water bottles on the lap) or Dickensian quaintness (a paschal candle from the vestry of a disused church lit by the mittened hand of a solicitor's clerk) recalled both the spirit of the Blitz and local amateur dramatics.

There was still a newness about running my own practice that meant that novel experiences of this kind were just part of the unfolding adventure, in much the same way as taking a bath in my employer's time at 21 Richmond Place had been years before.

Eventually, when the power restrictions were lifted and life got back to normal, there were new commissions to be sought as the firm's name wasn't yet well known enough to sit back and wait for new work to come in. One day, on the strength of the Hove Town Hall project, I received a preliminary enquiry from an adjoining district council asking if I would like to be considered for a new civic centre and administrative offices in Shoreham, a small town to the west of Brighton and much more historic than its larger neighbour.

Their process of selecting an architect was fairly conventional and, after an initial meeting, we were formally commissioned to prepare sketch plans and a construction estimate for presentation to the full council which, if accepted, would enable us to proceed with full contract documentation and then supervise the construction. It was pleasing to be working in a historic setting and devising an architectural expression suitable for such a context, so, within a few weeks, we were ready to present to the council which, like all small authorities, met in the evening as all of its members had day jobs. Before local government reorganisation, communities were run by county borough, borough, urban district and rural district councils. The smaller they were, the more likely they were to have councillors drawn from the ranks of local tradesmen – hard-working, down to earth and blunt, and who understood every inch of their territory. I wasn't sure what this one was going to be like.

I arrived at the old town hall with an array of coloured drawings and construction budgets for the 6 p.m. meeting and was shown into a small retiring room to wait there until the relevant agenda item was reached. A kindly councillor had been detailed to look after me and he asked if I'd like a drink as the council had a long agenda. He searched diligently for the drinks cupboard key and eventually found one which fitted the worn lock. When, following a hearty tug, the door finally opened, he suggested a gin and tonic. He wiped a smeared glass on his cuff and dispensed the last few drops from the gin bottle. As there was no tonic in sight he searched elsewhere, eventually spotting a half-full bottle hidden behind an old inkstand, so he poured its flat contents into my glass.

'There you are – good health!' he said merrily. But the drink looked danger-ously unhealthy, a large greeny-yellow blob of mould floating on top. I hesi-tated and, seeing the offending article, he took the glass from my hand and with a used teaspoon from one of last night's coffee cups, scooped it out and handed back the glass. 'That's better,' he said, sounding like a parent rubbing a child's bruise, and added, to be on the safe side, 'Penicillin never harmed anyone, did it?' He departed with a friendly smile to rejoin the meeting, leaving me trying to guess for the next half-hour what the rest of the council members would be like.

On entering the chamber, I pinned up the drawings and arranged my notes before looking up to survey the scene. It looked a fairly amiable group and I noticed that, rather like Hove's Civic Buildings Committee, it contained one woman councillor, who placed herself between me and the chairman. I was soon to realise that this was deliberate. After a brief introduction, I was invited to present the designs upon which we had been working for much of the month. I was fairly satisfied with them at this stage and confident that they were capable of being developed within budget and built by a specific date. After half an hour I paused for questions and observations and was gratified to hear general approval from those who spoke. I thought that somehow it shouldn't be quite this easy, but as it was getting late, guessed that those who hadn't spoken were happy for my proposals to be adopted before closing time. But my nagging reservation about it going by on the nod was only too well founded. As the chairman was about to wind up, the lone woman councillor rose to her feet and, visibly indignant, addressed the meeting, seeking support for a resolution that stated that not only should my proposal be rejected outright, but that the council should appoint another architect, preferably from the public sector, and furthermore that I should not be paid any fees for my work so far. The chairman, perhaps from past experience, made no attempt to stop her and I doubted if it would have made any difference had he tried. She was burning with resentment, and as I nervously glanced round the chamber, I derived a tiny shred of comfort from the rows of faces that told me they'd heard it all before and on numerous occasions, and that, given a few more minutes, the storm would blow itself out. I felt completely bewil-dered and the chairman and members looked suitably embarrassed. To try and reassert control, the chairman eventually rose to his feet, thanked me for the presentation, asked me to leave the drawings with them, and indicated that they could conclude the meeting without detaining me any longer. I mumbled my thanks, bade them good evening and left.

Outside, I sat in the car for a while trying to work out what had happened and why, but by that time I was too tired and hungry to make any sense of it all. On reaching home, I found my appetite had vanished and settled for a long drink. Within minutes of my sitting down the phone rang; it was the leader of the council, full of profuse apologies for what had happened, deeply regretting the discourtesy and assuring me that no one else associated themselves with their female colleague's remarks. He hoped I wouldn't take it personally and think ill of them all. Almost as an afterthought, having offered his apologies yet again, he added that my proposals had been fully accepted by the council with only one dissenting vote. That was all I needed to hear, so I tried to put the penicillin and the melodrama out of my mind and go to bed. I went to bed but sleep eluded me as I lay there still attempting to make some sense of the whole episode.

My *bête noire* was a militant socialist and represented a minority group. Being so far Left, perhaps it was difficult for her to agree to any commission being given to the private sector, and particularly to someone with a double-barrelled name and (to her) a plummy accent. It just about made sense and I left it at that.

It was only some weeks later that I heard she had offered herself as a prospective parliamentary candidate for a vacant seat in the Midlands, and was told that the burghers of Shoreham were so enthusiastic about her possible removal from their midst that even Conservative members offered to travel north and canvass on her behalf. I never heard what happened but, at all events, she was not seen again.

Nearly a decade later a similar incident took place, again motivated by politics. I was asked to present a very large comprehensive redevelopment proposal designed by other architects for whom I was acting as consultant. They had telephoned to ask if I'd act on their behalf as 'the silver tongue' at the meeting. The site was on the water's edge in Portsmouth, making use of land and property which had lain derelict since the Second World War. The proposal comprised a large leisure development which also contained housing and shops. Private developers had responded to an invitation to submit proposals for this new scheme, and our team was one of two finalists addressing the full city council on this occasion. My clients were London-based and although they had a good track record they were 'outsiders' and 'developers' in the eyes of the Left, who held the balance of power on the council.

Surrounded by coloured perspectives, architectural models and all the paraphernalia for a half-hour slide show, I began my presentation, which was received courteously enough. After the illustrations the lights went up for me to read my supporting report from the lectern and I saw directly in front of me a leather-clad, miniskirted, cropped-haired woman searching noisily in her voluminous handbag. As I got into my stride I slowly became aware that she had decided to distract me sufficiently to throw me off balance and impair my presentation. She fidgeted and shuffled in her seat, which was only a yard or so in front of me, and crossed and recrossed her black-stockinged legs to expose an unnecessary amount of flesh above the stockings. Being equally determined not to be distracted, I ploughed on with a long list of statistics and costings, which caused her to redouble her efforts. I then saw her clammy hand dig deep into her bag and withdraw a packet of toothpicks whereupon, leaning back still further and exposing what little there was that I hadn't seen already, she opened her mouth and began work on her upper set, making sucking noises in between each foray into her cavernous mouth. Then, with even greater energy, she attacked the lower set, one tooth at a time, never letting her piercing black eyes off me for a moment. One gets used to anything after a while if it goes on long enough, like living next to the railway or having a wooden leg, and by now I knew, or hoped, she was running out of tricks. I wound up my presentation and, to be on the safe side, asked my assistant to place two dozen copies of my report gently in her lap with a courteous request for her to distribute them to her colleagues. This brought her chair's front legs back on the floor and, with a slightly exaggerated bow in her direction, I left the platform.

We were not awarded the commission.

Chapter 25

Unexpected Conversations

In the same way as coffee breaks are often the most professionally valuable part of a conference, so it is with unexpected conversations, where you learn more about the wider community your clients come from than you ever would talking formally over a drawing board. If I was going to attract new clients, then I had to go out of my way to know them better.

Obtaining new commissions for a relatively unknown practice involved a good deal of out-of-hours activity. This could take many forms. The golf club and the cocktail circuit were well-established hunting grounds, but as I had had to forgo golf due to two successive bouts of frozen shoulder and, being rather reserved at that time, I wasn't an obvious candidate for the cocktail circuit, I had to think of something else. Fortunately for me, architecture was not just a job but had always been something of a hobby. I enjoyed talking about it and had countless boxes of photographic slides which I had taken over the years. Invitations to speak to amenity societies, university groups or parochial church councils or to write for magazines arrived from time to time and, as a result of one such happening, I was surprised to receive a phone call from the features editor of *Homes and Gardens*, a journal anxious to stimulate interest in the new wave of design awareness originating from the Festival of Britain. The editor asked me whether I would consider interviewing the Duke of Gloucester for the magazine. As Prince Richard of Gloucester, he had read architecture at Cambridge, and after some practical work-experience in London, he had been elected a corporate member of the Royal Institute of British Architects. The editors felt that he would be bound to hold views on domestic design which would interest their readers, and there was the added influence of his young Danish wife, formerly Miss Birgitte van Deurs, whom he had met at Cambridge, and who presumably would bring a fresh Scandinavian approach to the domestic setting in which they raised their three small children.

Arrangements for the interview had to be made through a Colonel Simon Bland (ex-Scots Guards, whose recreation was listed in *Who's Who* as shooting and whose club was named as Bucks). As private secretary and equerry to the Duke, he controlled matters such as interviews and had for many years been assistant private secretary to the Duke's father. He asked to see and presumably approve the list of questions I intended to ask if granted an interview. This was disconcerting as I suspected, perhaps unfairly, that any really interesting, if edgy, questions – like why most of the royal family lacked any interest in the Arts – would be edited out by a bluff ex-colonel who had learned his craft with an earlier generation. I imagined him exerting too much influence over the Duke on which invitations to accept and which ceremonial uniform to wear on any occasion and, in this case, prompting him never to let down the 'firm' when asked a key question.

And I was right. By the time a dozen unsurprisingly bland questions were finally agreed upon, I was feeling a lot less enthusiastic about the whole enterprise, but, having said I'd do it, I finalised arrangements for the meeting. Photographs were not permitted, but I would be allowed to take a tape recorder. I found the Duke remarkably diffident but disarmingly open, never seeking to dissemble or hide behind protocol. Perhaps it was a shade easier for him talking to another architect, and obviously the agreed questions were easy enough to answer. As the tape recorder hummed on the sofa between us he would look up fleetingly, push his spectacles back and then look down thoughtfully to ponder his next answer.

I decided that the only way to save the interview from banality would be to leave the tape recorder running at the end of the set questions and then add those I had really wanted to ask all along. This worked well, restored life to the interview, and would eventually form the basis of the magazine article. Towards the end of our conversation his wife entered the drawing room with one of the children and I had a glimpse of how everyday and ordinary their domestic setting was and how difficult it must be to maintain this amid the unnatural background of tradition, formality and etiquette that encircles the entire royal family.

In the end we were able to broaden the discussion to include his views on the value of Victorian design, at this time still roundly condemned by many people, but whose virtues he quickly recognised, probably encouraged by the compelling arguments of Sir Nikolaus Pevsner, who came to lecture at Cambridge during his time there. With disarming modesty, he described being sent to the USA to speak on behalf of the Victorian Society, only to hear Alistair Cooke, in his speech of welcome, say that whilst everyone was particularly delighted to have the Duke in their presence, 'what a shame it was he'd come merely to protect those dreadful Victorian buildings!' How lethal is friendly fire.

As I knew he had another residence at Barnwell Manor near Peterborough, I asked his opinion on the New Towns which had sprung up since the war, particularly Corby nearby. He offered an opinion which any of us would have echoed in the 1980s – namely, that the council estate housing, with its pleasingly harmonious brick-and-tiled dwellings, was worthy of its prize-winning status, whereas the adjacent private development (an early example of social engineering in the town) 'comprised Spanish-style, Texan ranch house-style, everything and anything'. He went on: 'One assumed that the people on the private estate consider themselves incredibly superior to those who live next door. In my view the council tenants are getting much better value for money.'

The sharp ears of Fleet Street weren't going to ignore this gift, and a few days later the *Daily Mail*, under the strapline 'Duke's nice council houses are battered by vandals', asserted at some length that the public-sector housing had now been roundly rejected by the community and that the private estate was doing very well, thank you. By the date of this publication the Duke was abroad and it was left to Colonel Bland to explain rather limply that HRH was currently in Switzerland and probably 'hadn't seen the estates for two or three years'. All this was some years before an American wit would equip us with the timely exhortation, 'Love thy neighbour; but first choose your neighbourhood.'

In a fairer world, members of the royal family not in direct line of succession to the throne would reasonably be allowed to voice their opinion on current issues, particularly when they had expert knowledge, without remaining vulnerable to exaggerated criticism they were unable to counter because of their position.

A year or two later I found myself being invited by a captain of industry to lunch at Quaglino's to discuss design issues of equally topical importance, but on this occasion with a very different outcome.

Environmental awareness among leaders of commerce and industry was barely discernible at this time and it would be another generation before prophecies of global warming and ecological degradation would be taken seriously. Many large industrial organisations were only too aware of the prohibitive cost of cleaning offending emissions and effluents and, in any case, reliable technology wasn't yet available. It was therefore left to a few to signal the dangers ahead and encourage large companies to grasp the seemingly intractable problem of reconciling what would become known as 'sustainability' with their necessary profitability. At government level there were no votes to be gained on this topic, and at shareholder level, there was even less enthusiasm.

Sir Peter Parker, a Renaissance man if ever there was, was one of those who felt compelled to do something about it and, with his trademark combination of charm and unstoppability, gathered a small group of industrial leaders around him to thrash out a policy (interestingly, more carrot than stick) to raise awareness of the global problem and chart a practical way forward.

He became the first president of the newly formed Business and Industry Panel for the Environment, whose aim it was to persuade leaders in both the public and private sectors to re-examine their industrial processes and procedures to see whether, with minimum extra effort, they could minimise pollution in the first place and thereby render control measures unnecessary. As this approach involved a lot of imagination and lateral thinking but relatively little money, it wasn't surprising that the idea caught on. The National Coal Board, whose fuel drove most of the power stations at the time, was one of the first to show interest, and others quickly followed. In passing, it was interesting and encouraging to read that both Lord Ezra, Chairman of the National Coal Board, and Sir Peter Parker had originally read non-vocational subjects at university and probably had a broader vision and a more developed social conscience as a result. Naively, I had always thought that the tough-at-the-top brigade all had numerate or engineering backgrounds, but over the years I discovered that some of our most gifted industrial leaders turned out to be historians or philosophers.

Peter Parker, who had once played opposite Shirley Williams in a university Shakespeare production, had gone on to Cornell and Harvard on a fellowship and was quickly recognised as a born leader. Had there not been a sudden change of government he would have been appointed chairman of the National Ports Authority, and by the time I first met him, he was chairman of Mitsubishi Electric in the UK and also chairman of the Rockware Group. He would be best remembered as a chairman of British Rail when, despite an era of financial stringency, he managed to find serious money to restore some of our finest nineteenth-century railway stations and encourage us to look again at the quite splendid architectural heritage of which they formed a part.

He had an engaging smile, an ever-present twinkle in his eye and always led from the front: 'We'll share sweat and get this thing done together.' He talked incessantly, brimming with new ideas worth trying. Difficult situations were overcome by newly minted epithets. He referred to himself as 'a worn optimist'; he bemoaned the state of the great London railway stations that suffered from 'terminal disease', and professed surprise that a day of 'industrial action' always turned out to be a day of industrial *in*action.

Like many architects, I had become interested in environmental issues and was attracted by Peter's enthusiasm and foresight. I had tentatively offered a few ideas at a previous meeting of the panel he had invited me to join, and one day, as he left breathlessly for another meeting, he suggested we meet for lunch as he was anxious to hear more of my ideas in a quieter setting.

When I arrived at Quaglino's he greeted me with a beaming smile and thrust a menu into my hand because he had already decided what to eat. As I pored over this embarrassment of riches he bade me not to hurry as he began to outline new approaches to the panel's work that he thought may be worth exploring, whilst I listened attentively, ordered my meal and nodded from time to time. When the hors d'oeuvres arrived he got into full swing and by the time the main course was set before us he was developing a long-term strategy which might also involve the CBI, the Institute of Directors and local Chambers of Commerce. I ate my dessert while listening to his views on developing lines of political support and drank my coffee to the untapped potential of European industrial cooperation. Eventually he stopped for breath, looked at his watch, leapt to his feet and said how sorry he was to have to dash, but how nice it was to see me again. He ordered me a double Rémy Martin as he left and begged me not to hurry.

I hadn't spoken a word.

Chapter 26

Bringing Power to a Cinque Port

As my practice began to grow, it became clear who the major clients were, particularly those in the south east. We were becoming known for the design of regional and national head offices for organisations whose rapid development meant that they had outgrown their existing properties and needed larger, more modern facilities to accommodate latest business methods and technology.

One such client was the South East Electricity Board (Seeboard) who, in a heavily populated part of the country, had embarked on a major construction programme and, quite sensibly, used a number of local architectural practices for their work. I knew the principals of all the firms involved, and although there was friendly rivalry and keen competition between us, we were all on very good terms. We all played cricket and tennis against each other and, more importantly, drank together. Architects from one office would sometimes date secretaries from a rival office and the whole atmosphere was relaxed and good-natured.

My practice had just designed and built regional offices and a depot for Seeboard at Tunbridge Wells and now it was the turn of another practice, Hubbard Ford, to undertake a similar project in Hythe, a small and ancient town near Folkestone. The board had purchased a site containing derelict infantry barracks dating from the Napoleonic Wars, last used for small-arms training during World War II and for a short time afterwards. The essentially utilitarian buildings were of no great architectural interest, in poor condition and of only slight historical importance in my view. The intention was to demolish them and construct a new Seeboard complex on the site. To the disappointment of those living locally who hoped they might get a new job there, and to the surprise of the Seeboard, their planning application was refused, largely due to heavy lobbying orchestrated by a young local solicitor

165

who made much of the barracks' historical significance. The applicants went straight to appeal, and shortly before an inspector was appointed to conduct the hearing, I received a phone call from the firm of architects involved asking whether I would act as an 'expert witness' on their behalf. It was known that I had an interest in architectural history and they believed that I could help their cause. As we had only recently engaged in a tightly contested game of cricket with them I was happy to help.

This meant becoming acquainted with their design and planning proposals in great detail so that I could conspicuously sing their praises in public at the inquiry (not something I would have been inclined to do in any other circumstances). I therefore needed to inspect the site, look at its surroundings, learn something of its history, and hopefully gauge the depth of opposition to the proposals. After a while I became aware of Hythe's history as one of the Cinque Ports alongside Hastings, New Romney, Dover and Sandwich. The name is an ancient jurisdiction linking all five ports that were originally charged with the responsibility for the defence of the realm along our southern coast. Their responsibilities were set out by Edward I in the Great Charter of the Ports, and in return for their services the ports enjoyed extensive privileges.

It was obvious that Hythe had a long and important history. I remember reading that at Sir Winston Churchill's installation as Warden of the Cinque Ports in April 1946, the Archbishop of Canterbury said: 'From the Cinque Ports came an exemplar of English civic life, for in their history and in their charters were embodied sturdy independence and free cooperation, self-government subject always to the common weal, the active life of trade and enterprise regulated by order and justice and liberty never assured, always to be defended afresh against aggressors, and by the price paid for its defence made the more precious. Upon this confederacy of coastal towns fell for long the chief burden of guarding our shores and transferring our armies across the narrow seas: from them till Tudor times came the bulk of the King's ships. A ceremony such as this which speaks to us of the ancient virtues of our race can never be without deep significance to us.'

I realised I was going to have to take the history of Hythe more seriously than I originally thought if I was going to make any impression at all at the inquiry. After purchasing a book on Romney Marsh which included a section on Hythe, I read that although by 1634 the harbour at Hythe had gone and the town became vaguely Royalist in the Civil War, it later evolved from a port to a market town with a school of musketry and, still later, was a holiday resort for the refined.

The penny began to drop and I visualised a large number of Colonel

Blands, or their naval equivalents, making life hell for the local council when their anger was up, and an assault on the history of their chosen place of residence would have guaranteed this. It seemed that half the town wanted an economic future and the other half a quiet life free of change.

Following meetings with counsel for the appellant I thought that I should speak to those best able to explain the nuances of local politics and the extent to which the great and good could be relied upon to help, or hinder, our case. One wet evening in the depths of winter a group of us gathered in the lounge of the best-known, but at this time of the year largely deserted, hotel to discuss tactics with the mayor, who this year was a postman. Outside, the wind howled and rain lashed the rattling windows as we awaited his arrival from work. After a while, we looked out to see him park his bicycle under a flickering lamp post, turn up his collar, lean into the wind and make for the entrance. He walked into the lounge in his uniform overcoat with his cycle lamp still clipped to his wet lapel (the only sensible way to read envelopes in a semi-rural setting with infrequent street lights at the back of the town). He was young, honest, streetwise and very, very wet, and someone brought him a cup of steaming hot tea. He knew his council and his town intimately and made very practical observations about how various people could be relied upon to support us. Apparently, the vote at council to refuse planning permission had been very close and he personally was most disappointed at the outcome, as he had great hopes for the town's prosperity. Counsel had been given a list of names thought to be sympathetic to Seeboard's proposals, and when asked for his opinion on a particular person, the mayor would demonstrate detailed knowledge of their family, the state of their businesses, the behaviour of their offspring and any other titbit that came to mind. Towards the bottom of the list came the name of a distinguished rear admiral who had long ago retired to the area and who was well regarded in the town. Counsel asked the mayor directly, 'Is he going to be for us or against us? Can he be relied upon?' As the great man's house was on his postal round, the mayor answered equally directly, 'Oh, he's all right, he gave me a guinea at Christmas.'

I completed my proof of evidence and the opening day of the inquiry arrived. The venue was packed for the occasion (Hythe didn't offer a wide range of free entertainment), and for the first two days we sat through much righteous indignation, mock surprise, and back-row mutterings of 'Oh no' and 'Over my dead body' in the customary pantomime atmosphere I had grown used to in attending previous planning appeals. Townsfolk with super-market bags and National Health spectacles rubbed shoulders with faded gentry in worn cuffs, as no one could resist finding out which side of the great debate a particular neighbour supported. The planning inspector, a reserved man in his late fifties sporting a Royal Engineers tie, had seen it all before and remained courteous and calm as he took us through the proceedings at a measured pace he must have perfected over the years.

It was customary for each side to be notified in advance of the names of witnesses appearing, so that counsel could have some idea of how they would cross-examine and on what particular aspect of the topic under review. By the time the advertised witnesses had completed their submission, more often than not generating more heat than light, the inspector took the unusual but very fair step of asking whether the objectors wished anyone else to speak for them despite no previous notice having been given. Their counsel then briefly addressed the inquiry, seeking permission of his learned friend opposite for one further witness to appear. This seemed very reasonable to our counsel and, as it wasn't late, he agreed. I was aware of a slight frisson around the room but couldn't make out what was afoot. The surprise witness ('Our secret weapon,' I heard an elated objector mutter) was none other than Lord Kenneth Clark, whose international fame had been established as a result of his memorable 1969 BBC television series *Civilisation* which was subsequently shown around the world. Unable to conceal his pride at being able to effect this *coup de théâtre* at the last moment, counsel for the objectors embarked on a long-winded explanation of why Lord Clark had been invited to appear, determined to share in as much reflected glory as possible. Obviously this sort of opportunity didn't occur frequently in his provincial life.

I should have realised that Lord Clark lived at Saltwood Castle on the hill above Hythe and could justifiably be included on geographical grounds alone. From the castle's battlements, hidden among trees, you can see the sea and beyond it the old town and be reminded daily of Hythe's historic role as a Cinque Port. To my horror, counsel concluded that 'Lord Clark had been invited to question Mr Wells-Thorpe on various aspects of aesthetic judgement included in his proof of evidence'. I went cold at the thought of it and realised how foolish I had been to participate in all this in the first place. Along with millions of others, I had been completely absorbed by every eagerly awaited episode of *Civilisation*, a magisterial review of how western Europe evolved after the collapse of the Roman Empire and produced the ideas, books, buildings, works of art and great individuals that made up a civilisation. Scales had fallen from my eyes in a way that had not occurred since I was a student in Rome, and the thought of being cross-examined by a figure of such eminence on a topic for which he was world-renowned left me numb. This was like facing an Australian seam attack when batting as a tail-ender in a village cricket match. It was going to be humiliating at least and dangerous at worst, as any professional credibility I had so far attained could be demolished at a stroke and any vestige of professional self-confidence shattered for ever. In a drowning moment the names of all Kenneth Clark's noted volumes flashed before my eyes: *Leonardo da Vinci*, *The Gothic Revival*, *Landscape into Art*, *The Nude*, *Looking at Pictures*, *Ruskin Today*, *Rembrandt and the Italian Renaissance*, and *Piero della Francesca*. In a nightmarish swirl of mixed metaphors I waited for the axe to fall and, glancing up, saw this slight, balding figure rise to his feet and be introduced by counsel. There was a pause, the room fell silent and Lord Clark quietly asked his first question, which was unbelievably easy to answer. I guessed I was being deliberately lulled into a false sense of security and felt doubly tense. He asked a second question, of equally innocent intent, which I answered simply and directly. Their counsel looked a little concerned and interjected, 'And would Lord Clark like to question the appellant's expert witness in greater depth?' After a moment's reflection Lord Clark quietly replied, 'I think not, Mr Wells-Thorpe has quite satisfactorily answered what I put to him.' A couple of easy underarm balls he knew I could hit: I must be dreaming. This couldn't be the end, surely? But it was, and to this day I can only put it down to the fact that he knew only too well how easy it would be to crush me beneath the weight of his intellect and he would have thought this both unfair and unnecessary. In short, and at the risk of using an expression that would later be expunged in a world of political correctness, he 'behaved like a gentleman'. At the end of the hearing, I made my way through the throng to speak to him, but apparently he had slipped out just before the concluding submissions and returned to Saltwood Castle.

Some months later, when we learned that Seeboard's appeal against refusal had been allowed and they could go ahead and build, we heard that the villain of the piece, the person who had actively encouraged the council's rejection of planning permission in the first place, had been the young solicitor responsible for lobbying the council. He had wished to gather authentic experience as material for a dissertation in his final law examinations, and from his point of view the entire episode had been very enriching. Bearing in mind the year's delay and the considerable cost to which all parties involved had been put, it was yet another reminder that our cherished democracy often comes at a price.

Chapter 27

Artists and Others

Moses looked very hard at me all those years ago in San Pietro in Vincoli in Rome and I could never imagine the church without him. Neither could I imagine San Vitale in Ravenna without the glowing mosaics of Justinian and Theodora. The more I thought about the fusion of art and architecture, the more aware I became of successful examples in my own time, recently culminating with the new cathedral at Coventry where its architect, Basil Spence, had commissioned sculpture, tapestry, painted glass, mosaic and letter-cutting to enhance and add meaning to his design. Here was a wholesale commitment to artistic collaboration on a scale seldom seen in the twentieth century and, strangely enough, not seen much since.

The modern movement, the teaching of which dominated my professional training and influenced my thinking, found little or no place for artistic involvement. Earlier in the century Adolf Loos in Austria and later Mies van der Rohe in America abhorred any form of ornament and decoration. They rigorously excluded the arbitrary and insisted that 'less is more', and this was readily taken up by architects where high technology was their chosen means of expression. They produced entirely self-sufficient designs and wanted nothing to detract from their complete offering.

In my own mind, and not just because I was not a high-technology exponent, I felt that the divorce between art and architecture was arbitrary and not a little arrogant and that, as long as a suitable opportunity presented itself, the integration of other artistic expression was not only acceptable but could be positively advantageous. After all, much of our cultural expression was the result of collaboration – artists with authors; set designers with librettists; musicians with screenplay writers – the list was endless, and some of those artists were immensely versatile, like John Piper. He collaborated with writers as different as Osbert Sitwell and John Betjeman, was an official war artist, created sets for Benjamin Britten's operas, and designed glass for Basil Spence's Coventry Cathedral. Was he an exception, and would he have been a very easy person to work with? I asked myself these questions because many artists and architects maintained that collaboration between them was at best tricky and at worst, disastrous. Surely it must depend on who you choose, how you treat each other and the extent to which you acknowledge one another's skills? There was only one way to find out: do it.

The first opportunity came when I was designing the church of St Christopher in Southampton, which was being built to serve one of the city's post-war housing estates. It was heavily influenced by West German and Scandinavian churches I had visited, and was a brick structure comprising two simple geometrical elements of nave and chancel, each with a mono-pitch roof, but slanting in opposite directions. This deliberately left a plain wall behind the altar, relieved only by a richly coloured window in the form of a Greek cross high above the communion table. Due to financial constraints, this was to be the only coloured glass window in the entire building and therefore had to be good. Having never worked with a glass artist before, I began to look around for someone to commission. It was too small a work for the big, well-established names and, among the less well-known practitioners, I could find no one whose style would have been appropriate to that particular setting. A lot of what I saw was 'safe' or too sentimental and would have looked out of place.

The Victoria Line on the London Underground had been opened a few years before and a relatively unknown artist of South African origin, Hans Unger, had been commissioned to design glazed wall tiling for the platform walls, each depicting, in either abstract or naturalistic form, motifs peculiar to each station on the line. An abstract maze represented Warren Street, a plane-tree leaf depicted Green Park, a 'Penny Black' queen's head was used for Victoria, and so on. Here obviously was a man who enjoyed a challenge and could work equally well with representational and non-figurative subjects, so I asked him whether he would be interested in working at St Christopher's. Although he was of Jewish origin, I hoped he would have no reservations about designing for an Anglican place of worship. He didn't, and indeed I would have been surprised if he had, bearing in mind Jacob Epstein's huge commission for a figure of St Michael near the entrance to the Anglican cathedral in Coventry. Hans Unger quickly produced a design which was an immediate success. He obviously understood light and mystery and, cleverest of all, how to give an image cohesion even when broken up into the four separate arms of a Greek cross. He was pleased with his innovative work (he'd never done anything like this before), the congregation liked it, and I found I had successfully negotiated my first collaboration with an artist who would go on to acquire a national reputation.

Later, the United Reformed Church, a fairly recent amalgamation of the Congregationalists and the Presbyterians, commissioned me to design a new centre for them in North Road, Brighton. It was not a church as such, and although it included a 'drop-in' chapel and an assembly hall that could be used for Sunday worship, its 'week-day presence' was equally important. It provided for a very mixed, downtown community of the haves and have-nots, locals and itinerants, and I was asked not to make it look too 'churchy'. But in the absence of the conventional symbols of cross and spire something was needed to signify what the building was for. The notion of 'service' to the community was uppermost in my clients' minds, but they weren't clear about how this should be portrayed. We talked about it for a long time without arriving at a satisfactory answer until one day a miraculous solution suggested itself. What about loaves and fishes and feeding the five thousand? Of course – what else? This was to be a centre for the needy and poor in spirit in the town and I didn't feel it was an occasion to impose avant-garde design on them, however much it might have appealed to me. That being so, I knew exactly who I wanted and approached John Skelton (a pupil of the late Eric Gill at Ditchling), who had recently completed a new font at Chichester Cathedral.

It turned out that we had been in the Army together in Malaya, although we were unaware of it at the time. I had asked him to carve stone or slate for me before, but nothing on this scale or with such wide scope for interpretation. I gave him plenty of notice and we had a year to develop the design. After a while he prepared a small plaster maquette for the church elders to approve and they liked it immediately and gave his estimate the nod. They were enthusiastic about it being about the only eye-catching feature on the entrance façade fronting the street and felt that it would say all the right things about the purpose of the centre.

First ideas are often the best and John Skelton altered the design very little as he slowly translated it into its final form some nine feet wide. A generous hand held in its palm a cottage loaf-shaped offering, while two rudd-like fish entwined themselves over and beneath the fingers, the whole composition having occasional voids emphasising the depth of carving and relating it to the parent building. I visited John's studio frequently, not just to view progress but to marvel at his unstoppable energy and enthusiasm for the task in hand. We agreed the final position for it in the façade and I suggested we set it back about a foot so that I could include a pair of recessed uplighters to illuminate it at night. This made it appear even more three-dimensional and it was a focus of popular attention.

I revisited it two decades later. Still in the care of the same owners, the sculpture had become heavily stained through lack of washing, and large competing notices on either side had been bolted to the wall advertising current events, a threat of wheel-clamping, and the setting up of a 'women-only' group. Collectively, and because they were newer and brighter, these effectively eclipsed Loaves and Fishes, which now looked like rough, unkempt stone ripe for graffiti. To render the *coup de grâce* more effective, both recessed floodlights had been removed and the gaping holes filled with concrete. Much though we all still miss him, I'm glad John Skelton is no longer around to see it. What is it about the British?

I was standing in Liliane Lijn's London studio in semi-darkness (it was a converted garage at the end of her garden) staring at an eight-feet tall figure with a terrifying aspect. The head had long feathers in it and bulbous eyes that lit up in frightening colours, and from time to time (she was still adjusting the mechanism) a puff of steam screeched out of the side of the head and the body shook. 'You asked what I'm working on currently, and here it is,' she said enthusiastically. My vocabulary deserted me and I could only respond, 'It must have taken a very long time to – devise? – assemble? – think up? Utterly fascinating.'

It was the novelty that preoccupied me though, and the realisation that Liliane Lijn, who had a considerable reputation, had been recommended to me by Carol Waugh to design a piece of external sculpture at Poole in Dorset, where we were currently designing a new headquarters office for the National Mutual Life Association of Australasia (NMLAA), an old-established and very traditional life assurance company who had been in London as long as anyone could remember. The organisation was staffed with very nice people who, by virtue of their actuarial business, were, by instinct, risk-averse. They were overseen by a board of directors who were thoroughly good sorts and probably knew each other from early days at public school, contesting for silverware at fives, cricket or rugby football. And later perhaps there was the kinship of adjacent regiments in World War II.

It was evident that Liliane was not someone you told what to do, but when I suggested that she visited the site overlooking the old town first, before making up her mind, she seemed pleased. On her return she was bubbling with ideas, handfuls of sketches and a passion for the job. I had given her the barest background, mentioning that Poole was an ancient port with a long maritime history and that the NMLAA had been founded many years ago on trading links with the Antipodes, and both connections were rich with mercantile enterprise.

She bridged the gulf between the classically educated company board and her own exuberant creativity in a single stroke by taking as her theme the myth of *Argo*, the ship that carried the Argonauts to Colchis for the purpose of fetching the Golden Fleece, which was suspended in an oak tree in the grove of Mars and was guarded day and night by a dragon. Liliane went on to describe how she would use the idea of billowing sails as her leitmotif, and this appealed immediately to the board, who gave their agreement to the commission proceeding. The resulting sculpture, some twenty feet high, stood on high ground just outside the headquarters' offices and comprised folds of perforated metal sheet billowing from mast-like posts. It was totally abstract, quintessentially twentieth century, yet immediately expressive of its intent and a vivid example of how to win hearts and minds without compromising avant-garde creativity.

The largest and in many ways most significant art commission occurred some years later in Bristol. By that time we were designing the biggest head office to be decentralised from London that we had worked on. It was for the second-oldest life assurance company in the country, which had been founded in 1806; it was an ideal opportunity to incorporate some form of commem-orative art. The building and its information technology would be new, as would its management systems, so I decided that something should express newness built on the solid foundation of the past.

Bristol had been chosen for the location as it had good rail and road communications, was a less expensive place to live and work in and gave the company room to expand still further if they wished. It is also a fine city, rich in history, and this provided the key for the thematic content of the work of art I visualised.

Because substantial numbers of staff arrived for work at the same time, most working on upper floors, I planned a pair of escalators to reduce the congestion resulting from people waiting for lifts in the foyer. These were about 25 feet apart and this arrangement left a purposely designed plain wall in between that was a full storey high, immediately facing the main entrance. This was to be the position for a mural which would dominate the area, and whose content would underline the *genius loci* of the site.

In the past I had seen examples of commissioned art that had sometimes failed, causing understandable tension between artist and architect, because the commission had been left too late or was often a last-minute piece of 'remedial art' used to brighten up what might otherwise become a dull corner.

It was clear that if the same was not going to happen here the art concept needed to be included and integrated at the *beginning* of the architectural design process and not tacked on apologetically at the end. I had in mind two themes to give no more than a general sense of direction to the artist, and in no way were the topics to be treated as prescriptive. Bearing in mind the background of the move, they were: 'The links between the cities of London and Bristol' and 'The historical significance of the site'. The artist could choose between the two.

This process had been preceded by a more disconcerting experience when I had a couple of informal conversations about the project, first with Eduardo Paolozzi at the Royal College of Art, and then with an adviser to the Arts Council in London.

Why Paolozzi agreed to meet in the first place remains unclear, but after I described the setting in which any work of art could be sited and emphasised that final decisions on building materials, colours, finishes and lighting had been deliberately deferred to allow the artist to have the last word on the context of any work, he wanted me, as a precondition, to redesign whole sections of the building well beyond the foyer and ended by saying that only when he had finished a current job in Munich would he be prepared to tell me if he was interested in doing the job. But he had the grace to allow me to buy him two pints of beer.

The Arts Council was, at the time, a body all too frequently racked with organisational pain and internal dissension. The adviser let me look at the council's photographic slide library covering work by artists currently practising. As a result, I suggested a name to be added to my shortlist, only to be told, 'Oh, his work is far too ingratiating for what you have in mind,' which, in the cool light of day, meant that it might just be accessible to the average viewer, which would be unthinkable. And elephant dung was still twenty years away.

Finally, with the help of Alan Bowness, director of the Tate Gallery, three names were chosen to compete and they were invited, for an agreed fee, to produce a maquette based on their selected theme. Upon his advice, the board selected Patrick Caulfield for the commission. He was well on his way to becoming Britain's most admired semi-abstract artist and had studied with David Hockney and R. B. Kitaj at the Royal College of Art in the early 1960s. His work had been shown in over twenty one-man exhibitions and a retrospective of his paintings had been held at the Walker Art Gallery, Liverpool and the Tate Gallery, London. And yet, as he was to tell me later, he had never before been commissioned for any major work in Britain. I showed him our architectural proposals and a scale model to illustrate precisely where his work would be seen. He adopted the second of the suggested themes, alluding to the historical significance of the site, with enthusiasm, and we agreed that it need only form the basis of his work and should not extend to documentary verisimilitude.

The mercantile history of Bristol is particularly rich, and after some careful thought, Patrick Caulfield included symbolic representations of important colonial imports such as tobacco, cotton and timber. To this he added reference to a flourishing wine trade and glass-making tradition and, in his final maquette, included a reference also to Brunel's suspension bridge, the whole ensemble contained within a heavy, dark frame as an allusion to the slave trade. In lesser hands this abundance of subject matter would have fragmented the design, but Patrick Caulfield's powers of distillation were such that an image of compelling clarity emerged. Here was a telling example of 'site-specific art', and my clients readily agreed to his work being commissioned.

There is all the difference in the world between a two-feet-wide maquette and a four-hundred-square-feet finished work, and the practicalities to be faced soon became clear. He decided that the mural would have to be broken down into twelve panels for ease of painting, and he borrowed Howard Hodgkin's London studio in Charterhouse Square which was larger than his. We used to meet about once a month to discuss progress and I always found him quiet and reserved. Artists, by and large, unlike art critics and historians, do not have to rely on a persuasive vocabulary, and his simple descriptions were all that was necessary to support his design. It took a while to get used to the fact that he rarely finished a sentence as his words got progressively quieter and then trailed off to nothing, leaving him still looking pensive, but I soon came to admire his single-mindedness and the rigour with which he approached his work. Our conversation never strayed beyond the task in hand, and I wasn't sure whether this was shyness or merely the result of a disciplined and closely focused mind.

After a year's work the mural was completed and then had to be lifted out by crane through the studio window to begin its road journey to Bristol. There, the Arnolfini Gallery, part of a clever warehouse conversion nearby, mounted an exhibition of Patrick Caulfield's work to coincide with the formal opening of the building. The centrepiece of the show was the original maquette from which the mural had been developed, but, shamefully, it was stolen (perhaps to order, such was his reputation) within twenty-four hours of the exhibition opening. We were comforted only by the thought that at least the same could never happen to the real thing without hiring another large crane and creating a good deal of noise.

These experiences were sufficient to persuade me that, given the right choice, artists and architects *can* work together very happily.

177

Chapter 28

Europa Nostra in Extremis

I'm not sure what finally took me back to Saudi Arabia in 1976, but Preece, Cardew & Rider had offered me further projects, this time for radio stations on the Red Sea coast and also inland, and I was tempted. I could have delegated the task, but in the years since my first visit I had found my fascination for the place growing, so I accepted the invitation. I had just read Robert Lacey's *The Kingdom* where, in the opening paragraph, he describes 'a country of astonishing contrasts; where the computer print-outs open with the words *In the name of God*; where men who grew up in goat-hair tents now dominate the money markets of the world; and where murderers and adulterers are executed in the street. By its own reckoning this country is just entering the fifteenth century.'

Saudi (Sa'udi) Arabia was the only country in the world to carry the name of the family that ruled it, as it was the House of Sa'ud that established the kingdom about the time I was born. Its recent history had been dominated by the figure of the great Ibn Sa'ud, and more recently, by his austere son Faisal, who was given the impossible task of holding a kingdom together as it jumped a millennium on the back of sudden and incalculable oil wealth. Had not the land been blessed with geological treasure in such abundance, the Western world would have shown scant interest in either the territory or its people.

I relished the prospect of revisiting a strange land where a gallon of water cost more than a gallon of petrol, and was fascinated by all its apparent inconsistencies. They gave colour to my working life as I became vividly aware of history in the making. In the 1970s Western Europe was preoccupied with a much more diverse agenda which, encouragingly, included the formation of an organisation under the leadership of a former UK housing minister, Duncan Sandys, whose aim it was to raise awareness of our archi-

179

tectural heritage and the need to safeguard it. In 1957 he had founded the Civic Trust in Britain and, against that background, had seen the need for a similar initiative in mainland Europe as, in the rush of post-war construction, cherished older buildings were often endangered through ignorance or greed. *Europa Nostra* was born and 1975 was designated European Architectural Heritage Year to draw attention to the need for imaginative custodianship coupled with effective government support. The year was marked with exhibitions, publications and conferences in various capital cities and one of the more lasting and useful outcomes was the production of a 16-mm film entitled *New Life for Old Buildings* which drew on a wide range of examples to show how threatened historic buildings had been saved from demolition by devising a new role for them that was socially relevant and financially viable.

It soon became clear that even worse problems were arising in newly rich countries around the world where construction was proceeding at an unparalleled pace with blatant disregard for history. In South East Asia, Singapore and Hong Kong people seemed particularly oblivious of the problems, and it looked as though the same was beginning to happen in the Middle East.

Having always been interested in our built heritage, I was known to the Civic Trust and on a number of occasions had been an assessor for their annual awards, so it wasn't totally surprising that when they knew I was going to Saudi Arabia, it was mentioned to Duncan Sandys, who asked if I'd see him before I left. The arrangement was that I should take a copy of the film with me and show it both to city leaders in Riyadh, and possibly Jeddah, and to Riyadh's new University School of Architecture, which was still at an embryo stage and, hopefully, open to persuasion. I walked out of the Civic Trust headquarters with the large reel in its plastic container and promised to do my best.

A few days later, on my arrival at Jeddah airport, I once more encountered the crushing humidity and the disorganisation with luggage and customs. It was necessary to disembark in Jeddah as it had the only Immigration & Customs facility in the country and, irrespective of ongoing destination, all passengers and luggage still had to be processed there, even though we all knew we would be reboarding, some hours later, on our original planes. It was about 10.30 p.m. and, after a long flight, I was beginning to fray at the edges. Having opened my case, a heavyweight customs official plunged his hairy hands in and out of the contents as if kneading dough, all the while muttering, 'Any alcohol? Sure, no alcohol?' He left the carefully laundered contents of the case in a squalid pile, single socks stuffed up the arms of shirts, toothpaste in underpants, and only gave a grunt of satisfaction when he reached the blue plastic case containing the *Europa Nostra* film, which I had carefully wrapped in clothing to protect it during the journey. Without waiting to be asked, I explained as simply as I could that the film was educational, but I might have saved my breath; he wasn't interested. Foreign films were a spiritual risk to the kingdom whatever they were about, second only to alcohol, and he explained that strict regulations meant that my film would have to be inspected before I was be allowed to continue my journey to Riyadh.

I was only too aware that my ongoing flight to Riyadh departed in just over an hour, so I asked as politely as I could if the film could be cleared promptly. A more senior official was summoned, who told me flatly that the member of staff responsible for such matters had gone off duty after dusk prayers and I must present myself to the same counter again the following day. As I had no confidence in the film being forwarded to Riyadh if I went on without it, I had no choice but to wait, and although it had only been temporarily impounded, I knew it could stay there indefinitely. I demanded a receipt. The customs sergeant painstakingly wrote out a two-word description on the 'contents' form which I stuffed angrily into my pocket before going in search of a vacant space on the terminal floor (there were no seats in this section) on which to bed down for the night. Sleeping on marble has the fleeting illusion of oriental luxury, like bathing in ass's milk, but however beautiful it appears to the other senses, trying to find somewhere for your hip bone if you turn on your side is impossible. As it turned out, I couldn't have slept – I had to safeguard my hand luggage, the noise was intolerable and an assortment of churlish porters and inquisitive layabouts prodded me from time to time. In a state of resentful gloom all I could recall was T. S. Eliot's insomniac reflection which begins:

> In the uncertain hour before the morning
> Near the ending of interminable night
> At the recurrent end of the unending . . .

It went round and round in my head like a cracked 78. Eventually, so very eventually, I became aware of a chink of first sunlight glancing off the marble floor and simultaneously a surge of water against my tired loins. A Yemeni cleaner with a squeegee wasn't going to say in perfect English, 'Excuse me sir, I have to clean the floor at this hour, would you terribly mind moving?' So I slowly got to my feet and left. After a fruitless search for some breakfast I made my way back to the customs counter, which was just opening, and searched for my receipt. Bleary-eyed, I glanced at it before handing it over and saw that my property had been described in abbreviated English

181

monosyllables as 'Film (blue)'. Yes, the plastic reel cover was blue, and yes, it was a film, so the telegraphic annotation in pidgin English was logical enough, but oh, the sense of foreboding over what could ensue.

I knew the Saudis could become apoplectic if they found either porno-graphic material, a copy of the Holy Bible or any garment with a Marks & Spencer label still attached, but 'blue film' topped the list. I had a horrible feeling that the whole situation was going to run away from me, and this was soon confirmed by a superior who asked me to attend an adjacent shed where I found they had rigged up an elderly Bell & Howell projector to examine the film. Inevitably, at least one member of the staff understood what 'blue films' were and in a flash word got round the entire airport that something was about to take place that in no circumstances should be missed (only once before had I experienced a similar buzz, when it became known that a public beheading was to take place in the city square in Riyadh after Friday prayers later in the day).

The shed had a rough concrete wall covered with cracked plaster and there was one window to the outside through which the sun poured, causing the rapidly gathering throng to edge away from it and pack themselves tightly along the shadier walls. The fact that porters, sweepers and taxi drivers had pushed in didn't seem to bother the customs staff: collective curiosity masquer-aded as tribal brotherhood on so special an occasion. As they tried to fix up the equipment a boy of about fourteen climbed in through the window and shook hands with everyone. When he reached me I must have hesitated and he snapped his fingers and grinned at me until I responded, whereupon, as quickly as he had arrived, he left again but this time through the door. Above the wooden trestle, behind which a burly uniformed official with brown teeth was seated, a hand-painted notice read 'Ministry of Information Office'. For some reason this sounded slightly less intimidating than 'Immigration' and encouraged me to provide as much 'information' as possible. Slowly, and in great detail, I emphasised the words 'cultural' and 'educational', and quickly added for the avoidance of doubt 'nothing pornographic, of course', and for good measure, 'architectural'. The last word beat them completely, which made them all the more doubtful about my intentions.

Brown-teeth then read aloud my letter of authority from the Civic Trust (which I had dictated in any case) and by the time he finished it was abun-dantly clear that no one believed a word I had said, or understood a single sentence of the letter, so the only thing to do was get on with the film and let them make up their own minds. The projector light went on and, due to the smallness of the room and the multitude who now occupied it, the throw of the lamp was reduced to about six feet. This produced a lit image about

12 inches wide, and as the lamp was aimed at the nearest wall (there was no screen) it illuminated an area of cracked grey-painted surface covered with scuff marks on which the sun from the window shone brightly. This meant that the self-adhesive mass had to press round me and the projector even tighter to get a glimpse of what had been promised.

It crossed my mind that, true to my undertaking to Duncan Sandys, this was the first showing of the *Europa Nostra* film in the Kingdom of Saudi Arabia, even if it wasn't quite what my master had intended.

The projector shuddered to a start and there, sure enough, were impressive views of Gothic edifices and Renaissance masterpieces universally regarded as gems of European culture. After a few panoramic sweeps the film began to concentrate on finer detail – a colonnade here, a pediment there – and the sense of growing disappointment in the room was palpable until, that is, a close-up shot of a pair of sandstone caryatids (bare-breasted female figures used as columns) filled the screen. The effect was electric as those about to slope off turned on their heels and reclaimed their places and those who had remained there all along let out a collective gasp (whether of shock or approval I wasn't sure). Out of the corner of my eye I could see the customs supervisor bite off the cap of his old Biro and begin writing, frequently looking up to make sure he missed nothing else. It so happened that the offending bosoms came from the Marais quarter of Paris, which had recently been restored and revived by skilled craftsmen and was often used as a case study at the time. It was, though, the only contentious image. The heat was appalling, so after a further ten minutes or so following a detailed exposition of cornices and flying buttresses I sensed that their interest was flagging and, with it, the taste for blood. Eventually, a perplexed supervisor and his glum audience became restless and the latter began to leave. The supervisor eventually countersigned the customs receipt and prepared to depart, giving instructions to the 'projectionist' on the way out, which I only understood after I had been handed back my empty spool and saw him winding off the reel from their own spool which was obviously government property. I remonstrated with him as he emptied his spool onto the trestle table, leaving me with a sweatily fingered spaghetti of film to try and reassemble by hand. Clearly pleased that he couldn't understand me, he left promptly, taking the projector with him, and returned to man his rubber stamp in another department. Dripping with perspiration, I spent a full half-hour winding the film onto its original spool and eventually restoring it to its blue (*why* did it have to be blue?) protective case.

I recalled having it drummed into me in the Army that there is no such thing as bad experience, it is just experience. I suppose it was, but when I eventually arrived in Riyadh a day late with a film portraying classical façades barely discernible behind a skein of thumbprints, I was doubtful.

After such an inauspicious start in Jeddah, I approached the showing of the film *New Life for Old Buildings* in Riyadh with some caution. I harboured no illusions over its success and would probably have settled for a politely neutral reception – after all, they could reasonably have asked themselves whether they needed to listen to an infidel promoting Western cultural values. But mercifully my reservations were misplaced. The Department of Architecture in the university sent a message saying that they were looking forward to the presentation the following day and to introducing me to a number of the faculty who had expressed an interest in attending. Unfortunately, a postscript informed me that they had, for some reason, advertised the lecture as 'Urban Renewal in Europe', which meant that I had quickly to rewrite part of my commentary. New life for old buildings was part of urban fabric certainly, but only a small part. Still, I was grateful for small mercies and concocted a coda which I hoped would place the topic in a broader context without it looking like sticking plaster.

Ahmed al Kilani, a young and ambitious Saudi who had recently completed his architectural training and was now working for the ministry, collected me after breakfast and drove me to the university's engineering faculty, which housed the Department of Architecture. Here, he introduced me to his former tutor, Abdel Ismail, an Egyptian, who was now Professor of Architecture, an idealistic, if perhaps unrealistic, charming enthusiast in his thirties. He was eager to discuss every theory and counter-theory currently appearing in the international journals and pressed me hard to declare my various allegiances. He had a sharp intellect and took great pride in showing me his work on Arab vernacular architecture and the organic growth of desert towns, which had formed the centrepiece of his doctoral thesis at Karlsruhe. Other faculty members arrived, most of them Egyptians, and they greeted me courteously and enthusiastically. A great deal of handshaking followed, and before I was invited to talk, I was shown the first-year work, mostly graphic and illustrative art, followed by a final-year conservation study for the area around Deera Square in the heart of the capital prepared under the guidance of Abdel Ismail. They were both lively and relevant studies and I felt encouraged by their general air of optimism and sense of purpose.

About eighty students, together with two more professors, had assembled. Abdel Ismail told me it was good attendance for a visiting speaker, and they listened intently for the next three quarters of an hour. They liked the film and asked plenty of thoughtful questions. I deliberately slowed my English delivery, used monosyllables wherever possible, avoided technical jargon and included a number of informal asides. This was appreciated, and when I had finished Abdel observed: 'Not just academic, but social-academic; I like it much.' I was glad I had not mentioned the Jeddah airport experience in passing – it could have embarrassed them.

It is always difficult to gauge the success of one-off occasions like this. After it was over I returned immediately to my work with the engineering team to justify my existence in Riyadh in the first place. As far as the film was concerned, I forgot about it. It was some nine months later, during a subsequent visit, that I was contacted by someone from the university once more who, hearing I was back in the country for a while, asked if I would run a seminar on 'New Life for Old Buildings' and help them develop further their thoughts on the subject and how it affected the kingdom as a whole. The seminar took place in the same lecture theatre as before but was hosted by another Egyptian, Dr Mohammed Awad Raslan, who showed equal courtesy and had invited both the rector and the dean of the faculty on this occasion.

All this reinforced my conviction that it had been worth it. These were people who were seriously concerned that their built heritage was being threatened by powerful commercial interests who were quick to recognise the real-estate value of any downtown site occupied by older buildings. To add to the problem, the government was anxious to demonstrate to the rest of the world the kingdom's determination to modernise and be seen as a forward-looking nation. This wasn't just the old academe-versus-Mammon argument that goes on everywhere; it was far more critical and infinitely more important than that. As I was to find out later when speaking to the mayors of Riyadh and Jeddah, the city fathers were hell-bent on constructing high-rise, fully glazed, air-conditioned structures to announce their rightful place in League Division One and the last thing they wanted was any reminder of mud-brick tribal forts or goatskin tents. The past was rapidly becoming an embarrassment in their eyes and they were banishing it by spending inordinate amounts of money on prestigious construction projects in order to identify with nations who had already 'arrived'. They sought to replicate Manhattan wherever they could.

The response from the mayor of Jeddah was unremarkable, and that of his Riyadh counterpart positively dusty. National pride was at stake and anything that I or others might say was not going to deflect them. My intention was to persuade them to draw breath for a moment to establish, with the help of their own academics, whether a form of architectural expression could be evolved that would reconcile twentieth-century technology with Islamic culture without resorting to pastiche. They remained conspicuously unimpressed by such cultural arguments, despite my plea for retaining some historical 'depth' to inform later generations. Their new-found ability to write larger cheques than anyone else seemed to dominate their thinking throughout and this led me, in the end, to play the only decent card left in my hand. 'And think what vast savings could result from not having to expensively air-condition acres of glass façades in desert temperatures rising above 110 degrees Fahrenheit in summer,' I suggested. 'Unlike many nations, we can easily afford it,' came the flat reply. Anthropology never appealed to me particularly, but I could see the fascination of trying to understand more completely the mindset of emerging power. From tents to technology in one generation and sudden untold wealth were enough to unbalance any nation, and Saudis were quick to recognise how important many of them had become overnight. This sometimes produced an arrogance that concealed their surprise at what Allah had so generously provided. Conspicuous consumption was there to embrace and native cunning gave it an awkward twist. I could see what their academics were up against, but had little faith in their prospect of succeeding: they hadn't got the political clout.

Military service in Singapore, when I had been attached to a Malay regiment, had given me a glimpse of another way of life and a different set of values, but thirty years later all that had gone a bit rusty and I had become more Eurocentric (as my foreign colleagues would later call it) than I was prepared to admit. This made more vivid the contrast between the way I thought local people would act and the way they did act. Sometimes it was just a small incident, like the occasion when Ahmed introduced me to a director, Bruno Gravanti, working for a large Genoese construction company that had been attracted to Saudi Arabia by the prospect of supplying new health-care buildings. I went to see him at his villa. He looked something of a matinee idol, was married to an American and lived in splendid surroundings consistent with his conspicuous ambitions. He displayed boundless energy, charm and an astute business head, was obviously streetwise, and had easily assimilated the Saudi way of thinking. He asked if I was interested in designing a 100-bed hospital which he was presently giving thought to and even suggested that we might introduce Roche, the international pharmaceutical giant, into the consortium. As he wanted quick answers, I there and then shared some detailed thoughts, regularly and plentifully sustained by Italian espresso and illicit Scotch. At the very point at which it looked as though a workable solution was within reach he paused, looked at his watch, smiled and gave his apologies, explaining that he had to leave to honour an appointment to play cards. I never saw him again.

One of the most energetic people I ever encountered, Mohamed Al-

Jumaih, was well into his sixties and appeared never to stop. He must have hailed from tough, wiry, nomadic stock, and he had the bright eyes of a hawk. I had been introduced to him by Ahmed al Kilani, who told him I was an architect already working in the kingdom and was interested in expanding my local portfolio. I met him with Ahmed in his office in an old building no doubt awaiting redevelopment. Its appearance certainly gave no clue to his importance. Three telephones sat on an iron safe kept next to his desk, and a constant stream of subordinates scurried to and from an adjacent room seeking summary decisions and directions on an endless range of questions. He snapped out answers in the middle of phone calls, listening meanwhile to the supplications of two visitors who had arrived earlier trying to gain his attention. From time to time he pinned them down with quick-fire questions and pithy comments but hardly ever looked at them, keeping his gaze firmly on the procession of minor functionaries from the next room.

We had taken the precaution of telephoning ahead to confirm the time of our appointment with him, but this meant absolutely nothing. Having arrived, sweating heavily from the long walk between the car and his remote office, we waited for over an hour on a black plastic-covered settee in the corner of the room next to a fierce fan used to cool the entire office that chilled us until our teeth chattered. Eventually, after dismissing the two supplicants (I never did find out what they wanted), Mohamed Al-Jumaih obviously thought it was time to show his considerate side – maybe because he thought that a Western architect might be of help in his future business plans. He explained that he had sole concessions for Pepsi, Shell, Chrysler and a handful of other household names, which explained why he had been described to me as one of the wealthiest men in the country below the rank of prince. So that we could 'show our paces', he suggested we design and price a group of eight-bedroom villas within the next couple of weeks. He rattled off a design brief, undeterred by still further interruptions from phones and functionaries, as if he had been actively considering it for months, and then promptly bade us farewell to get on with it. Not a word was uttered about fees or whether this assignment was only an opportunity for us to prove our professional worth in his eyes. He wasn't going to elaborate and he knew we weren't going to ask him. Later that day we prepared a few sketches, but our heart wasn't really in it. We never saw him again either.

When our work in Riyadh neared completion I booked a flight home which was routed through Bahrain. Here, on one previous occasion only, I had met an older, well-respected Iraqi architect who for many years had been a professor at Baghdad University. When the Ba'ath Party came to power, he and many like him had twenty-four hours to get out, so he and his family fled to Bahrain where, at a late stage in his career, he had to re-establish himself and virtually start all over again. By the time I met him he had formed an atelier. Here, relatives and a handful of his old staff formed one big, extended family under the protection and patronage of their old master.

His name was Mohamed Makiya and, after early training locally, he had come to Cambridge for his PhD and, incidentally, met his English wife there. He loved Britain, enthused about the architecture of the Cotswolds and was anxious to know if the abstract artist, Ben Nicholson, who had influenced an entire generation of post-war architects, was still alive. We got on famously and I spent an entire day at his villa and studio talking, arguing passionately, and eating and drinking until night fell. We hoped that one day we might meet again in Britain and even do some work together.

Much later, when I remembered that I would be in transit in Bahrain, albeit at 1.00 a.m. local time, it reminded me of that day together and prompted me to telephone him saying what a pity it was that, although I would touch down on the island, I would not be able to see him on this occasion. And that, I supposed, was that. On arrival in Bahrain I found that my next flight originated in Delhi, so I stretched my legs and walked to the transit lounge assuming, rightly as it turned out, that the India flight might well be delayed. I could snatch some sleep on the plastic-covered seats. I half-dozed for a while until, looking up to check the time, I saw a welcoming beam from a bear of a man I thought I recognised. Could it possibly be Mohamed? It was, and it was not just him there, but also his wife Margaret and a young relative who worked in his office. They all embraced me warmly and explained that they had booked a table for some dinner at the adjacent Hilton and, having checked the latest flight times, we would not be rushed. He had also come to some arrangement with the airport authorities, who seemed quite content to let a transit passenger drift off, so we walked, arm in arm, into the middle of their night.

When this touching episode was over and I was safely on my way again I asked myself – unnecessarily, because I already knew the answer – whether on the basis of only one meeting I would get up in the middle of the night and drive to Heathrow to greet a transit passenger. Probably not – and would this be because 'it's not expected' in England?

By the time of my last visit to Saudi Arabia in 1976 I and my colleagues were becoming more conversant with expatriate life; we had developed a good-humoured acceptance of the privations, insularity and sillinesses such an existence involved and had become used to an alien existence with no obvious historical, cultural or linguistic links to the way of life we had temporarily left behind. Frustration, usually with the bureaucratic system, was often mingled with sheer wonder at each day's events, and on many an occasion we would enliven a dull evening at the firm's villa recounting incidents that bordered on the ridiculous.

One day we had just finished some communal laundry in the domestic bath, accomplished with the use of a huge wooden ladle we found in the kitchen and with which we stirred and pummelled the dirty shirts and socks. The result was not particularly pristine, but it worked in a Boy Scout sort of way. While we were waiting for it all to dry, one of our number, George, who had been out in the desert earlier in the day checking microwave readings, described how, in the shimmering heat, he had seen in the distance two figures who, on closer inspection, turned out to be a pair of Swedish water engineers standing forlornly at the side of the track with their equipment stacked neatly beside them. Apparently they had been out in their Toyota truck plotting a line for a new supply pipe when they were approached from nowhere by a very luxurious, high-powered pickup whose Saudi occupants breathlessly explained that they were part of the prince's party hunting with falcons and one of their vehicles had broken down. It was necessary therefore to commandeer immediately the Swedish truck – in the name of the prince whose territory it was, of course – as they couldn't risk losing the scent of the prey at this critical moment. The Saudis said they would radio back to the town and ask if another vehicle could be sent out to pick up the Swedes before nightfall and, after demanding the ignition keys, they sped off as quickly as they had arrived. It is said that you can print a full anthology of Scandinavian humour on the back of a smorgasbord, but George was unprepared for the red-eyed state they were in: offended, mystified and resentful in equal measure, straight out of an Ingmar Bergman black-and-white film. But in a kingdom which had little to offer by way of sport, such things happen, and the Saudis took their hunting very seriously. There were the camel races, of course – one of which I had been invited to attend by a generous host who thought that I might prefer it to a good seat at a public beheading arranged for the following Friday, which was also on offer. A running camel somehow looks wrong: it was created not for running, but for methodically planting one foot in front of another for days at a time across inhospitable territory. But, absurd though it looks to a Westerner, camel races are plentiful and popular, if bizarre – especially the sight of diminutive Pakistani boy jockeys being secured in their saddles by strips of Velcro sewn on the inside face of their trousers. Saudi boys were seldom used: they were not so expendable.

Hunting with falcons was far less Disneyesque since, like camel racing, it had been practised since time immemorial and was a sport beloved by tribesmen of all ranks. In the case of princes, of which there are several hundred, a marquee strewn with rugs would be set up in a remote area known for its quarry in which the hunting party would sit quietly, chatting and sipping from small cups of coffee. Outside, falcons would be perched on tasselled pommels driven into the sand like so many leather-covered mushrooms. Such birds are lean, hooded and ferocious and, from time to time, flutter impatiently. When game is spotted, the leather hoods are removed and the jesses securing their scaly legs released, and in a flash they are off in pursuit of their prey either feathered or four legged. If for any reason prey is scarce, then a few pigeons they had taken along just in case, or even a stray cat or dog, are released, so that the hunting party didn't return empty-handed. After a satisfactory day, the group would come back singing a verse or two from a victory chant handed down to them by their forebears in the desert long ago.

So popular is falconry that breeders are attracted from all over the world to supply fully trained hunting birds to those wealthy enough to indulge regularly in the sport. Once, about to board an internal flight from Riyadh to Dhahran on the Gulf coast, I took my place in the queue to check in at the airport. I found myself standing immediately behind one such breeder, a very laid-back American, who was about to deliver a superb pair of falcons to their new owner. Hooded, they sat firmly on his protected forearm while we waited and, in his free hand, he carried a pair of spiked pommels to which they would be tethered on reaching firm ground. I was curious to know how the ground staff would deal with such an unfamiliar trio, as I couldn't visualise the birds being allowed to travel uncaged; they would probably be consigned to the hold. The check-in staff looked up when his turn came and explained that he must hand over the pommels, which would need to be stowed separately during the flight, as they would be regarded as a hijacking danger and could penetrate the skin of a pressurised aircraft. The wildlife dealer accepted the procedure and handed them over for safe keeping. Apparently everyone was happy to let the birds travel on his forearm with him in the cabin. Everyone, that is, except me. He and I had got chatting while waiting in the queue and, as a result, were allotted consecutive seat numbers. Towards the tail of the aircraft the cabin narrows and on each side of the aisle there are only two seats. I found myself sitting between the fuselage on one side and the American's feathered consignment on the other. He made light of it all and chatted amiably, explaining that, when we took off, he would have to remove the birds' hoods, lest they took fright and make a disturbance. As we left the runway he whisked off their decorative hoods and they steadied themselves on his arm and flapped their huge wings once or twice to regain their balance. Huddled in the corner right next to them,

I glanced at my feathered neighbours out of the corner of my eye. What talons, what menacing beaks and what cruel, unthinking eyes. When both birds looked back at me simultaneously I quickly averted my gaze, but they hopped around to face me. I was busy wondering if the fleshy lobe of my right ear might prove to be one temptation too many, when my lunch tray suddenly appeared and was passed under their very beaks by the steward who had begun serving from the back of the aircraft. The American went on talking, as he had just eaten before catching the plane, but the birds were completely oblivious of his presence; their attraction lay elsewhere. I felt their eyes move from the ear lobe to the tastily arranged savouries on my plate. I began eating. (Should I do this quickly and beat them to it or eat in slow motion so as not to attract their attention unnecessarily?) Pressing my head hard against the bulkhead and leaning away from them at a drunken angle, I began cutting up the meat, half wondering if I should keep the fork as a defensive trident. With my elbows pinned into my sides and my head by now just above the surface of the tray, I transferred morsels to my mouth, minimising the distance between plate and palate. We suddenly hit an air pocket and both birds took off as far as their leads would let them. Mistaking this for the long-awaited attack, I slammed my paperback down on top of the food and pressed the overhead button for the stewardess to collect my tray all in one convulsed movement. The American was beyond himself with mirth. 'Oh, you English are just *so* very amusing!' he spluttered. I'm sure Bertie Wooster and Jeeves would have done it with more decorum and Woody Allen with more pathos, but life doesn't prepare you for such events.

Anecdotes apart, time hung heavily in our leisure hours as there was nowhere to go and nothing to see. Cinemas, theatres, restaurants and clubs didn't exist, so we were down to a good book and an apple again, except that fresh fruit didn't exist either and there were apparently no bookshops. However, the American community, often working in support services or suppliers to the oil giant Aramco, were more comfortably established and ran an English school for their children. Once a week a portable screen was erected in the playground and we were invited to sit on folding classroom chairs under a star-filled sky to watch the latest movie. I enjoyed the easy companionship of Westerners after the tensions of the working day, and a balmy night in the open air made it extravagantly bearable – in fact, an evening on a hard seat watching Jack Lemmon in *The Front Page* whilst clutching a lukewarm Coca-Cola and contemplating the moon on its back during the interval could be the highlight of the week. Such events attracted everyone in the community, often including those I had been trying to contact by telephone all week, and this made it doubly pleasant.

Occasionally, after the evening meal I'd take myself for a walk and felt perfectly safe, even in a poorly lit street. The kingdom's statute book contained chillingly harsh penalties for theft and assault, punishment for the first being public amputation by sword of the offending hand of a thief, and for the second an equally public flogging for any assailant. As an otherwise dour Saudi colleague once observed, 'At least they only cut your *head* off for rape.'

Deera Square was the hub of the city and contained the offices of the governor of Riyadh and the central mosque. Everything took place in the square, including, most recently, the public beheading of King Faisal's assassin. Carpet vendors spread their wares on every available space at the roadside and each doorway seemed to contain a scribe offering his services to the illiterate. The burgeoning economy had attracted migrant workers from Yemen and Pakistan to do the menial tasks, and many of them needed help in sending letters and money home to their families. One day I left the bank where I'd changed some traveller's cheques and returned to the car, where I found that a truck had pulled up alongside fitted with a padded crossbar across its open back, on which perched two quite majestic falcons, hooded and tethered, oblivious of all the noise in Deera Square and patiently awaiting their next assignment. I wondered if they were the same pair I'd encountered on the plane, but wasn't going to get close enough for them to recognise me in case they were. Fathi, from the local office, who had accompanied me, described how he had once visited the house of a prince who kept fifteen hawks and between them they devoured two sheep a day.

Having travelled all the way to Saudi Arabia it seemed sensible to see if there was any other work on offer, as none of us would have contemplated a separate speculative visit. However, such possible contracts often came to nothing, either as the result of misunderstanding somewhere down the line or because of duplicity. On one occasion, amid much excitement, one of our group thought he was onto a real winner, and a juicy one at that, when he announced that a new archives building was needed for the Ministry of Finance and a sheikh he had just met was preparing a shortlist of professional advisers for the project design. He explained that he had already directed the sheikh towards the very latest electronic systems for data storage and retrieval and gone on to suggest that while His Eminence was in the UK he should visit his head office, which had decentralised to a stately nineteenth-century pile in East Sussex set in magnificently landscaped grounds. Believing that they should do nothing by halves, and hoping to impress the sheikh to the point where the award of the commission would be only a formality, the firm hired a helicopter to whisk him from a five-star London hotel to Sussex. Detailed arrangements were made, air traffic control notified (as it was near a flight path for Gatwick Airport), liveried chauffeurs and cordon bleu cooks hired, and meteorological forecasts double-checked. The appointed moment arrived and the distinguished visitor spent three or four hours apparently satisfying himself that he was speaking to the *right* people.

Three days later, the firm learned from a separate source that the design contract for this prestigious project had been awarded three years earlier to a Saudi who had submitted his final proposals only the previous week. This hopeless news quickly reached us in Riyadh, leaving the whole camp feeling irritated and depressed. It was made worse by our inability to contact any other senior officials and pursue fresh enquiries due to them taking extended leave after the festival of Eid, which marks the end of Ramadan.

'Sod it – we've just blown ten thousand pounds – what the hell are we doing here?' We didn't care whether it was a misunderstanding or duplicity, but were so angry we preferred to think the worst.

I wasn't due to leave for a couple of days, but as I had almost completed my work, time hung heavily, particularly in the prevailing atmosphere. I couldn't even escape with a book to a shaded part of the balcony because the wind had changed and acrid smoke from piles of street garbage blew straight in. As there were no municipal collections everything was thrown into the road and burnt before the stray dogs and goats could get to it. If a fire went out an ill-tempered Yemeni servant would shuffle out and make a half-hearted attempt to reignite the stinking pile, but all that ever did was ensure the mess smouldered for twice as long. In desperation, and just to get a change of scenery, I walked to a nearby general store which, to my complete surprise, had a few elderly magazines in English, no doubt aimed at the emerging expatriate community. Thumbing through them, more to relieve boredom than out of interest, I was astonished to find a back number of the *Architect's Journal*, the UK weekly most widely read by the profession at the time. I wondered how it got there: probably left on a departure-lounge seat and rushed in by an enterprising cleaner hoping to make a riyal or two. Unbelievably, the store was asking 20 riyals for it, but as I couldn't take any currency out of the country, I bought it despite the ridiculous price. Having read it and felt temporarily reunited with sanity, I sat down and wrote to the journal's London editor, Leslie Fairweather, who all those years ago had been a first-year student with me in Brighton in 1945 and, I seemed to remember, saw things as I did.

Riyadh, Oct. 16, 1976
Dear Editor,
Thumbing my way dolefully through one of the Kingdom's dirtier bookshops (they are all covered in dust, but some are more covered

than others), I found my weekly Architect's Journal, without which the sun would not rise over the wadi or my camel give milk. But, sand in your eyes and infertility on your goats, it cost me 20 riyals, that is, in your worthless currency, £3.25. I protest at this extortion and may Allah cast stones on the Cadillacs of your avaricious distributors.

Yours, in abject wrath,
John Wells-Thorpe

By 1976, the establishment of higher education in the kingdom was becoming more evident, and a Department of Architecture had been opened in the new university at Dammam, on the Gulf coast. Presumably, word had got round that a foreign architect suggesting new approaches to familiar problems was passing through and could probably be persuaded to speak to the students. I accepted an invitation when it arrived, as I had to visit nearby Dhahran for a couple of days in any case.

There is always something attractive about a brand-new enterprise: it has idealism and energy, horizons are limitless and there is often an almost religious fervour about reaching objectives. But everyone knows that outside the groves of academe there are powerful political and economic forces that could easily distort the picture and thwart intellectual enquiry. The government wanted to catch up with not just its neighbours, but the rest of the world as well, and therefore results, and quick results, were of conspicuous importance.

The burgeoning newness was seductive. The notion of higher education was new; all the faculty were new; there was no baggage from the past; the buildings were new, as was the study of architecture, the latter made all the more fascinating by the fact that a 'language' for modern architecture in Saudi Arabia did not yet exist. All this made the thirst for international opinions even greater.

I wasn't asked what I'd like to speak about; it was by now assumed I was the Western exponent on 'new life for old buildings', so that is what they expected. I was getting rather bored with the topic by now and, had I felt more confident, I would have suggested that instead we could examine the more pressing topic of how to evolve an appropriate form of architectural expression for the new nation, one that synthesised traditional Islamic culture with twentieth-century technology. It would have been a hard nut to crack, but I would dearly have liked to make the first dent. One reason I didn't force the issue was because I knew that you can't go out one Monday morning and just invent a new style; it would have to evolve naturally over a period of time, and not be forced into existence by a whim. In the inevitably slow progress towards maturity there would be false dawns, contradictions and much argument before anything worthy of later historic record would emerge. Nonetheless, the nagging conundrum about whether new styles arrive through evolution rather than revolution was tantalising enough to make me want to be involved somehow.

But it wasn't to be, and I was to speak on the by now publicly advertised topic. A large poster, executed in careful Arabic calligraphy in various colours, announced the event at the university entrance, but as the only part I could read was 'John Wells-Thorpe' in roman capitals, I had to take their word for it all.

Once more I made a plea for the retention and use of some of the kingdom's better buildings under immediate threat from the bulldozer. After all, they were executed in locally found materials, often stone or compacted earth, in forms of construction perfected over the centuries and which reflected a culture and way of life that was going to disappear for ever. But, unfortunately, such buildings did not lend themselves easily to modern use, couldn't be air-conditioned and were thought to send out the wrong message to the outside world.

I fervently wanted the young academics to win, but knew they wouldn't – they had no status or strength yet and would be incapable of influencing anyone at this early stage of their existence, however well argued their case.

Leaving Saudi Arabia wasn't going to be a simple matter. In addition to the burdensome customs and immigration formalities, I had to be in possession of an exit visa, confirming that those to whom I was contractually obligated in the kingdom were fully satisfied with my services. I also needed to demonstrate, in writing, that my flight had been reconfirmed, although I knew that even if it had, in the event of the flight being overbooked, my name would have been removed mysteriously from the manifest by the time I reached the check-in desk. Or worse, if a senior minister or member of the royal family suddenly needed a plane to themselves, then Saudia, the state-run company I had to fly with, merely withdrew the flight altogether.

The previous day, a Friday, had been spent trying to finalise various strands of our work – architecture, telecommunications and civil engineering – so we'd started in the office very early indeed and were just beginning to get somewhere when our Saudi office boy said that the religious police were in the street checking whether there was anyone still working on the holy day. Quick as a flash, he ran outside and lowered the metal security screens so that the light over our drawing boards wouldn't be visible from the outside. Thus secured, we went on working but, alas, to no avail. One of the brighter members of the inspectorate had seen a chink of light through the shutters and the next thing we heard was the beating of rifle butts on the metal blinds which would obviously go on until we stopped. We stopped.

Preparing to depart therefore took longer than expected, so on my last night I was late turning in. My part of the work was finished, although the others still had some loose ends to tidy and were staying on for another week. I was entertained in a local hotel by two of the team, who made a valiant attempt to mark the occasion as appropriately as possible by ordering a bottle of (non-alcoholic) wine to accompany the main course. The hotel dining room was full and fairly noisy but there were not, of course, any women in sight – even Western women. Those rash enough to accompany their husbands for a stint in the kingdom had to understand that they could not go about in public unaccompanied or do ordinary things like shopping alone, and neither could they hail a taxi or rent a car on their own. Having been in the country for a while, I no longer felt that they were conspicuous by their absence, but when it came to celebrating, even something as unimportant as my departure, it seemed very artificial without their company.

The meal we ordered, served by a Sudanese waiter with an expression that indicated either contempt or clinical depression, was passable, but the wine was a totally different experience. We knew it would be sweet and would be poured from a bottle bearing a crudely pretentious label. What we were unprepared for, never having ordered it before, was its effect. So conditioned are we to expect merriment, however superficial, to flow more liberally with each glass refilled, that we felt unnerved when the opposite happened and we found ourselves facing each other feeling progressively glummer as the evening wore on. Seeing this, my generous host ordered a second bottle, and all this did was reinforce the gloom and leave us even more depressed by the time we left the table. Perhaps our Sudanese waiter had drunk the dregs from too many such bottles in his time. As we drove back to the villa the only thing to tickle our numbed sense of humour was the road sign giving directions to the Accident and Emergency unit which read, 'Beidi Hospital opposite crush factory'. Laurel and Hardy would have made much of the episode.

Because of the delays and unfinished work I thought it all the kinder of my colleagues to not only have taken me out to dinner, but to have offered to accompany me to the airport at 4.30 the following morning.

On my last night we stayed in a cheap rented apartment on the outskirts of the city to be nearer the airport. It was in a small, unprepossessing suburb that looked fairly characterless. In the fading light I could see the silhouette of a nearby minaret and could also smell next door's chicken run, but beyond that it could have been anywhere. The flat was ill maintained, dusty and hot; it was tiny, but suited us for just one night. We set the alarm clock for 4.00 a.m. and went to bed. I slept fitfully and when I woke, I was covered in sweat, so I flung open the shutters. The cheap concrete construction must have absorbed the sun's heat all day, and at night it radiated it back to its occupants like a primitive night storage heater. It was a relief, therefore, when it was finally time to get up, and I switched on the light, a bright 100-watt bulb that hung over my bed near the window. The landlord had methodically removed anything that could be stolen, like lampshades, window catches and bath plugs, so we blinked our way to the bathroom in turn. The toilet seat was missing and the last occupant had left an old bar of soap which, mysteriously, had a selection of small insects imprisoned beneath the surface slime, as if deliberately arranged by an insomniac entomologist who wanted to warn his bed companions who they were sharing with.

I was looking at them in disgust when I heard the shrill crowing of next door's cockerel, whose run was unexpectedly bathed in a shaft of bright light from our room. I began to hear noises next door as the occupants rubbed the sleep from their tired eyes and set about their ablutions; this made everyone a lot brisker. However, on hearing the cockerel, the muezzin, who lived nearby, must have shaken himself, unable to believe what a short night it had been, struggled into his thobe, kicked on his leather-thonged sandals and shuffled towards the umpteen steps of the minaret which took him to the outside balcony at the top. He switched on the loudspeaker, a cracked and wheezy affair, and, after clearing his throat a couple of times, began his gravelly, much amplified call to prayer, 'Allahu Akbar' ('God is most great'), something he was going to repeat four more times that day, and repeat the same procedure every day. A sleepy and slightly mystified suburb heard the call across the rooftops, and another day had apparently begun. It had been overcast recently, so the absence of the sun's first rays to prompt the muezzin didn't at first trouble anyone.

It wasn't until we had packed and cleared our breakfast utensils that we began to look at each other. We had never heard such activity at such an unearthly hour and couldn't make it out. Was it a special festival? Had something catastrophic happened that we were unaware of? Were all our watches wrong? My telecommunications colleague, who practically slept with a slide rule under his pillow, such was his obsession with accuracy, slowly worked the sequence back to the point where, fatefully, the finger of guilt pointed directly at me. Like the sorcerer's apprentice in Goethe's ballad, I slowly realised that by throwing open the shutters in the middle of the night I had done something quite irreversible, but unlike the apprentice, it looked as though I would get away with it. No one would notice until they reached the mosque or their workplace and discovered they had assembled two hours earlier than they needed to, and by then I would be at the airport.

Chapter 29

Reunited with the Old Order

I had decided to stop over in Rome on my journey home because I needed a break after the pressures of Saudi Arabia and, in any case, it would be a welcome opportunity to revisit a city that had made such an impression on me a generation earlier. It was late January and I would have the place to myself and could roam the Eternal City at my own pace, without obligation to any companion or the intrusion of tourists. It was only 5°C there and felt blissfully cool after the desert, so I was glad I had packed my British Warm, a military overcoat, even if it had meant carrying it around most of Arabia to the amusement of my Saudi colleagues, who insisted on examining it in great detail. The novelty of seeing, and handling, an *overcoat* attracted curious onlookers, particularly when I was checking in my luggage at a hotel or airport. I was usually asked when and how it was worn and why I had brought it to Saudi Arabia. They were fascinated by its leather-covered buttons, always asking politely where they could buy some.

It was in more than one respect that I shook the dust from my feet upon arriving in Rome. I still had grains of sand in my clothing (and in my ears, such was the high wind in Riyadh when I left), and the short, sleepless night flight had left me tired and unwashed. On reaching my Rome hotel, therefore, I showered and went straight away for a shave and shampoo in its opulent barber's shop, where I was greeted by a short, plump, balding Roman who looked like Figaro on a bad day, and who ushered me into a chair with extravagant gestures and an ingratiating line of patter he kept for foreign visitors. No sooner was I seated than the chair swung back and hot towels were slapped on my head, leaving a small gap for my nostrils. As I had sweltered in the desert for weeks on end, this was not the respite I was looking for but, lying nearly prostrate in what looked like a prohibition-era barber-shop chair, I was in no position to argue. Had I done so he would have taken

199

no notice for, by now, he was well into Verdi's *Il Trovatore* as he pummelled my scalp like a quick-fire phrenologist. Then came the shave. I don't think I'd ever had myself shaved before, and I was looking forward to the sheer luxury of it all. Highly perfumed shaving cream was applied in baroque quantities to pores opened by the hot towels, and this was the cue for some well-rehearsed choreography with the cut-throat razor, which he sharpened elaborately on a leather strop next to the mirror and then waved imperiously in front of my face with low swooping movements before making contact. I knew at once the tip would have to be enormous, not least because there wasn't another customer in sight and he had obviously made the whole performance so elaborate to impress the 'bird in the hand'. He succeeded completely, and as I left the chair I felt like a million dollars, some of which, by right, must be his. As I handed over a pile of change he said, 'Thanks guv,' in a thick cockney accent.

The impressions of buildings I had visited before as a student came flooding back as I walked out of the hotel the following morning, and I experienced again an exhilaration I thought I'd lost. At a push, I knew I could still sketch from memory the city's three great triumphal arches – one raised in honour of Titus, to commemorate the capture of Jerusalem; one for Septimius Severus, to mark the emperor's Parthian campaigns; and one for Constantine, for well-documented deeds a full century later. To prove it to myself I had had a go at drawing them on the back of the breakfast menu before I left, and they were surprisingly accurate.

In the back of my mind I knew that I wanted to look again at the temples, churches and palaces that had so captivated me originally, to see if the magic still worked and, if it did, to decide whether such works were absolutes of some kind, to which I could safely refer for the rest of my architectural career. I was also aware of having changed a bit in the intervening years and was only too conscious of tastes having altered, if not matured. In music the 'easy listening' of Tchaikovsky and Strauss had long ago given way to Bach and Britten. In writing, Kipling and Betjeman had been superseded by T.S. Eliot and Iris Murdoch, whilst in art, the work of popular illustrators had been eclipsed by Bridget Riley and David Hockney. So, presumably, the same would be true of architecture, and there was nowhere better than Rome to see if this were true, and no time better than now, a full generation later.

It didn't matter that there isn't a complete chronological sequence in Rome as there is in Florence. There is the Rome of the Caesars and the Rome of the Popes and, to a smaller extent, the Rome of Mussolini, but scant evidence of medieval Rome; however, this wasn't important for the purpose of defining absolutes.

I began a small pilgrimage on foot, alone and unhurried, and had a good hard look and an equally hard think about 'then' and 'now'. The Pantheon was still a knockout and the passing years would never detract from such epic achievement. Structural daring, dramatic effect, geometrical clarity – it had it all. The Piazza Navona, in the heart of the old city, was still utterly magnificent. The baroque façade of Borromini's Sant'Agnese in Agone faces Bernini's great fountain, the Fontana dei Fiumi, probably the sculptor's finest creation, which had been consecrated by the Pope in 1651. It consists of a group of majestic figures representing the four great rivers of the world – the Amazon, the Danube, the Nile and the Ganges – and each is immediately identifiable. The figure nearest Sant'Agnese shields its eyes from Bernini's façade, some say as a gesture of the artistic hostility between them. Whether this is true or not doesn't matter – it is civic theatre at its very best.

And then I returned to the Stazione Termini, the first significant non-Fascist piece of twentieth-century architecture, which had, by now, weathered down and lost its self-conscious newness and looked more than ever part of the confident city to which it belonged: another plus. Crossing the Tiber, I walked up the Via della Conciliazione towards St Peter's and, near the end, placed strategically in front of the cathedral, stands the great semi-circular sweep of Bernini's arcade, whose nobility, scale and simplicity could never be surpassed: an unarguable absolute. No wonder Browning wrote:

> with arms wide open to embrace
> the entry of the human race

However, on the way up the Via della Conciliazione I became more aware that the majestic appearance of St Peter's had been severely compromised by the later addition of a façade by Carlo Maderna which effectively truncated the view of Michelangelo's great dome: a big minus that I hadn't noticed originally when I had obviously allowed myself to be carried away by its great interior.

On a second viewing, the Trevi Fountain looked clumsy and vulgar, although Hollywood may have been responsible for its more recent overexposure. Looking like melting meringue, it would be more at home in Las Vegas, and I was only sorry it had attracted so much attention in Fellini's *La Dolce Vita*. Again, my revisit to Bramante's Tempietto made me feel the long climb up the hill to reach it had barely been worthwhile because its ridiculous siting, shoehorned into the courtyard of San Pietro in Montorio, meant you couldn't really take it seriously, beautiful though it would have been as a free-standing artefact.

And what of the palaces? The Palazzo Farnese, designed by Sangallo and which had impressed me, really looked rather boring when compared with the counterparts in Florence I had seen more recently, such as the Palazzo Riccardi built for the Medicis, or the Palazzo Strozzi. What was immediately striking, though – and until now the comparison had eluded me – was the similarity in spirit, though not in design, between Italian palaces and major buildings in Saudi Arabia. Both had façades to the street which were sternly formidable and implied that they could be defended against all comers. This was as important to the Medicis as it was to the merchant princes in Jeddah or Riyadh, so I suppose the similarity wasn't all that surprising. And equally, all the symbols of lavish hospitality were safe from the street, on the inside, where shaded courtyards and fountains emphasised a level of prestige and hospitality appropriate to great wealth. The external appearance was deliberately unwelcoming, as if to reassert the difference between the haves and the have-nots. The have-nots could never enter, and would go through life oblivious of the plenteous reception that awaited any invited guest.

The following day it rained heavily. There was an exhibition of self-portraits spanning several centuries being shown in one of the major galleries so, thinking I would be distracted from the pursuit of absolutes for a few hours, I went along. The opposite happened, however, as when I examined a Zoffany self-portrait of about 1776, I noticed in one corner an ambiguous Latin inscription which read: 'Art can produce a kind of immortality, yet life is too short to master its difficulties.' It was unattributed, but it was sufficient to remind me that someone had trodden the path before, and that perhaps I should try something easier – and certainly less contentious – than attempting to form timeless judgements on great works of the past.

My trip to Rome was so successful that I concluded that a space for decompression was always vital for my sanity if I was to return home in good order. Breaking my journey home from overseas therefore became a tradition. Sometime later, when returning from a different destination, I decided to revisit Aegina, a small Greek island offshore from Piraeus, and whose principal activity was the production of pistachio nuts. I'd been there before and it seemed a perfect setting for a few days incognito. I remembered the main town, Aiyina, had one or two small hotels, an open-air cinema next to the prison, a metalled road lined with eucalyptus trees which led to the fishing village of Perdika and, on an exquisite site at the top of the hill, a well-preserved temple dedicated to Aphaia. Aiyina also had a little place, I recalled, where you could hire a bicycle.

Having broken my journey in Athens, I began my holiday the moment I reached the bustling port of Piraeus where countless ferries were berthed end-on to the quay, such were their number. They served the multitude of islands that form the Cyclades and are a reminder that the easiest means of transport, even within the Greek islands, is by boat, as the mountainous terrain of the interior makes road building difficult and expensive.

At the Piraeus quayside, trays of freshly baked aromatic rolls were carried on the padded heads of vendors, who picked their way between boxes of swordfish and squid and the sellers of ferry tickets, official and unofficial, who approached me at every turn. The trip to Aegina only took an hour, on deep blue water smooth as glass, and by the time I disembarked, I knew immediately that I had done the right thing. Having deposited my belongings at the hotel, a simple affair in the centre of Aiyina, I wandered off to the harbour to watch the sunset and, spotting what might be a newsagent, went in to buy some stamps. No one was about so I looked around the dishevelled interior until I saw a small counter on which were spread haphazardly old and new newspapers, journals, catalogues (often of agricultural implements), ferry tickets and bus timetables. The shop also sold tinned food, live bait and black-and-white photographic film with all the sell-by dates crudely obscured. It reminded me of a shop on the outskirts of Leith, near Edinburgh, that I came across when, years ago in the Army, I was stationed nearby. One November day, hearing of an impending kit inspection, I found I lacked a toothbrush in reasonable condition, so set off post-haste to make good the deficiency. I found the only shop in the village and, like the one on Aegina, it sold everything – sliced bread, pencil sharpeners, hairnets, and all that was necessary to sustain life in the area. I asked the bearded proprietor if he could sell me a toothbrush, and he replied, 'Och noo sonny, the Christmas novelties haven't come in yet.'

After a while my eyes lighted on a Greek phrase book. Although yellowed with age, it was the only copy, so I bought it and it wasn't until I got back to the hotel that I opened it. As with the one from my Army days in Malaya, it was a revelation. However, this one was arranged under the customary headings 'In the restaurant', 'At the doctor's', 'Travelling', and so on. Under 'At the railway station' it included the useful phrase, 'What time is the next train to Manchester', and under the heading 'At the newsagent' was the phrase, 'Have you any epistolatory paper?', which would have proved useful to Paul of Tarsus during his Greek journeys. But perhaps the most perplexing of all was the phrase 'I need a new tie-pin', which appeared under the heading 'At the dentist'. The compiler must have been British, and I visualised a pre-war, pipe-smoking, prematurely retired Mancunian Classics master (his maiden aunt having left him a comfortable sum) who had exchanged the chill of the

Pennines for the balm of antiquity and who spent his leisure hours, when sober, compiling helpful tips for those of his countrymen who shared his tastes.

Apart from the pistachio harvest, the little island is best known for its Temple of Aphaia, which sits on a summit near the centre. Aegina was already celebrated in the Homeric period, and the subjects represented on the temple's two tympanums (the carvings over the entrances) show scenes taken from the Battle of the Iliad; its statues are now exhibited in the sculpture museum at Munich. The shrine was built of shelly limestone and several of its Doric columns still show part of the stucco surface which was applied to give it the appearance of marble.

It is magnificently set on the top of a hill and the visitor first glimpses it on the climb up through gnarled pines and olives, so that its silhouette is seen against the enamelled blue sky and, although quite small, the temple looks undeniably heroic. From the summit you can just see Salamis across the water, a vivid reminder of the glorious role of the Aegina fleet in the battle there and in whose honour the temple was raised in the first place. This view reminded me why Greece exercised such an enduring charm on the Romantic poets: Keats was fascinated by its myths; Shelley, still thought of as a 'poet of moonshine and cloud shapes', wrote prophetically of the delivery of Greece from the Turks; and Byron went as far as joining the Greek insurgents who had risen against the Turks in 1823. The sight of the Temple of Aphaia would inspire anyone, so rich was it in history, so compelling in symbolism and so sublime in appearance.

I had almost forgotten that Turner had once been commissioned by Charles Cockerell, a well-known architect of the day, to prepare a watercolour based on sketches he had made during his Grand Tour, but on learning that the artist's fee would be 35 guineas, he quickly changed his mind. An unimaginable loss.

The approach to any great piece of architecture should be on foot and should preferably involve physical exertion. As I found in years to come when approaching for the first time the Acropolis in Athens or Le Corbusier's chapel at Ronchamp, the necessary exhaustion prepares and conditions you, so that you arrive in a suitable state of submission. Only then, with your ego weakened, can the building really speak to you. The Temple of Aphaia has this effect.

There was only one bus on the island, a single-decker which everyone used for a wide variety of purposes. It linked market, school and church with habitation, and you could just as likely be seated – or, more probably, find yourself standing – next to a sack of onions or a tethered goat. On one occasion

I was seated opposite a very old man who carried an oddly shaped plastic bag on his lap. He enveloped it with large, bony hands and periodically readjusted his parcel to compensate for numerous bumps in the road and the hairpin bends. He seemed to fidget endlessly with the package and I assumed that, due to his age, he suffered from some debilitating condition. As the bus swerved around a particularly tight bend, I saw him struggle to hold the awkward parcel so I leaned forward to help. As my hand reached the bag, the head of a large chicken popped out and, temporarily released from his grip, screeched and pecked me. No one turned a hair; after all, he had just been to market and was on his way home – how else could you transport a day's purchase in this place?

The last bus of the evening left at about 4 p.m. and was always very crowded, no matter what day of the week it was. One day, having spent the afternoon exploring on foot, I decided to catch this bus back up the hill; it was exceptionally hot and I didn't feel like another challenge. A small cloud of diesel smoke heralded the bus's arrival in the square and a surge of waiting passengers who had anticipated exactly where it would stop swept past me, so that I was the last one to get on. There wasn't really room for me, but I wasn't going to tackle the hill on my own and therefore behaved like a Greek and eased and squeezed my way through the gaggle inside until I reached a handrail to clutch. Sweaty bodies breathed metaxa and garlic over each other as the ancient engine cut in and the bus ground into first gear. The Oxford Circus Tube at 5.30 on a Friday evening prepares you for an etiquette which most people seem to observe – namely, the closer you are, the more care you take not to look directly at the face in front of you. On this occasion I was aware of a middle-aged man who, as the bus lurched, inadvertently stood on my feet from time to time, but I avoided looking at him and instead concentrated on a bundle of plastic curtain rails he was holding upright in his hand and which were as tall as he was. Deliberately focusing on them, I could read the imprint of the Taiwanese manufacturer's name and the index number for reordering. Try as I might to avoid his face, I somehow felt that he wasn't a Greek. I saw a wisp of auburn hair over his ear and the beginning of a cheek that was aflame with unaccustomed sunburn. A tourist perhaps or, more probably, considering his household purchase, a second-home owner. All the while I felt he was looking hard at me, but I still kept my eyes averted. After a while I heard an English voice say, 'And how's Brighton then?'

I looked at a face I didn't know and replied rather feebly, 'OK when I left it, I think.'

'And what about Patcham?' he quickly added. I found his second question unsettling because that was the district in which I had been brought up and wasn't sure where he was leading.

'Do you know it?' I asked, trying to sound as casual as possible.

'Know it? I used to live there and you were my Sunday school teacher.'

He studied the look of complete incomprehension on my face as I struggled to recollect whatever episode he was alluding to. I couldn't recall having ever been anyone's Sunday school teacher, let alone his. The closest I had come to that was having been persuaded to join the church choir by the school friend who had been evacuated to Brighton from Southampton during the Blitz and was billeted on the local vicar. I was utterly flummoxed in the Greek bus and remained so until thirty years on, when my choir friend and I shared a reunion holiday in the Algarve, I recalled this strange conversation and asked him to try and fill in the gaps. He was as puzzled and intrigued as I was until he began to remember that he had suffered a bad bout of chickenpox which had laid him low for several weeks, and a stand-in had to be found to take the class he was responsible for. This must have been me, and I now dimly recollected acting as his hapless substitute for about a month. But how I managed to so impose my stamp on an unknown Sunday school boy through my efforts all those years ago, I couldn't begin to fathom, and I began wondering who else I may have equally marked at school, in the Army, or while studying architecture.

This encounter also demonstrated another thing: here was I, smugly incognito and enjoying the innocent elation that brings, only to discover that such an illusion can be shattered in a shrinking world where it is now almost impossible to 'disappear' completely. John Stonehouse MP, the disgraced postmaster general, once thought he had done it when he escaped the law and the media and fled from Britain. Having carefully stage-managed his 'drowning' off Miami Beach in 1974, he thought he had been successful, but through a stroke of bad luck, he had left a clue sufficient to alert the police, who promptly extradited him back to Britain to face trial in London. I don't believe that anyone, even if they wished to, can escape any longer: Lord Lucan probably drowned during his Channel crossing.

Before leaving Aegina for what was to be the last time, I spent a day enjoying the blissful simplicity of cycling along the coast on the road to Perdika. How biblical that sounded. The road followed the coastline after it left the town and wound its way through a eucalyptus grove before rising steeply to a hilltop from which I could freewheel down into Perdika and its tiny clutch of white-walled fishermen's cottages just visible on the small promontory. The overnight catch had long been brought ashore and I knew I could have red mullet for lunch for the handful of drachmas I had been given in change when I paid for my bicycle hire.

I wanted this simple, timeless, fleeting episode to last for ever, but even if it couldn't, I took comfort in the knowledge that it was already an indelible vignette that I could draw upon and savour in years to come, like looking again at a long-forgotten, favourite engraving and remembering afresh what it felt like to see it for the first time.

Chapter 30

City History

Fascinating diversions in the Middle East were one thing, but sustaining a UK practice was another. It would have been only too easy to jeopardise the firm's future if my preoccupations had remained elsewhere, so I reminded myself that we were practising at home in a very competitive market. Fortunately, at about this time, projects in London began to come our way – slowly at first, but they held promise for the future. Apart from their intrinsic importance to the practice, they also brought with them a historical perspective seldom found in overseas projects. London was the next step on the ladder and we would have been happy to design a public lavatory if it fell within the sound of Bow Bells.

Whilst buildings don't design themselves, there are occasions when external factors so strongly influence the process that the genesis of a scheme emerges of its own accord. Such a project was the new London office for the Bank of Boston to be built next to St Paul's Cathedral. The area around the cathedral had been completely demolished by the Luftwaffe during the Second World War and the peacetime planners were presented with a clean sheet. Lord Holford had been appointed as planning adviser and prepared proposals for the two new piazzas around the cathedral, the first opposite the great west front and the second on the north side flanked by substantial new commercial development. However, the entire site was still bounded by the historic street pattern, and on the east side facing Cheapside this left an irregular-shaped parcel of land facing a bend in the road. The new bank was to be built on this site, which was effectively a promontory and could be seen all the way up Cheapside, from New Change to St Martin's le Grand and along Newgate Street. Sited on a peninsula like this, any new building would be very visible and would have to be designed in such a way as to 'turn the corner' where the road bent in order to satisfy townscape objectives. To make life even more difficult, the whole structure would have to be built over the existing and very busy St Paul's underground station, so design constraints abounded. To begin with, we had the irregular-shaped site; then there was the imposition of strict visibility splays for traffic safety, and then a height restriction in relation to the cathedral; and in addition, there were hideous complications with the foundation design in relation to the Tube station underneath. All this told us a lot about what we *couldn't* do, and while we were trying to reconcile all these conflicting demands, a message was received from the GPO informing us that running beneath our site was the hotline from 10 Downing Street to the Kremlin, which had been installed at the height of the cold war. In no circumstances whatsoever could that continuity be broken during construction work on the new bank, and furthermore the line had to be accessible for instant maintenance twenty-four hours a day.

It would have been tempting to walk away from the commission at that point, pleading impossibility, but we persisted and began testing one option after another. False dawns came and went. Time and time again the resultant 'footprint' we came up with looked like a pig's ear, so our near-impossible task was to turn it into as much of a silk purse as we could. After weeks of work, during which we gradually distilled and refined its profile, a design emerged in polygonal form with a cut-back base to improve traffic sight lines at street level. In architectural terms, the design comprised a hexagonal super-structure containing the offices which was cantilevered over a recessed plinth housing shops and cafés. This gave the whole form a clearly defined, faceted appearance which we decided to repeat in the elevational treatment. It was beginning to come right at last. As a free-standing block it would catch the sun at different times of the day in a way that was impossible with the conventional, rectangular blocks that filled the remainder of the St Paul's redevelopment area.

I was particularly concerned about our scheme's proximity to the cathedral and decided it would be perverse to ignore the materials from which St Paul's had been built centuries before. I therefore selected Portland stone for the cladding, riven slate for the big soffit overhanging the shops, and lead for the roof. This choice wasn't just an attempt to avoid controversy – these materials were in any case best in terms of permanence and low maintenance and I knew they would weather gracefully over the years.

Geologists tell us that Portland stone is many millions of years old and has been quarried (and more recently mined) on the Isle of Portland in Dorset for centuries. Six million tons of it were ordered by Sir Christopher Wren to rebuild the City, including St Paul's, after the Great Fire, and its use in the twentieth century was equally prolific. The United Nations headquarters in

Manhattan is faced with it, as is the BBC building in London's Portland Place, and also Waterloo Bridge, among many other examples, and it always looks good. Records show that since AD 1200, some 32 million tons of stone have been mined and installed.

As passers-by could get close to our new bank building, I felt it should present a rather more interesting texture than the plain ashlar gives to the cathedral and I therefore journeyed down to the quarries and eventually selected stone from what is known in the trade as the Roach Bed, which has a slightly pitted surface containing remnants of small crustacean shells that give surface interest. The quarry master was generous with his advice and, following my explanation of the job and location, gave me all the encouragement I needed to specify it in the contract. He was one of a dying breed. From the age of 14 he had been trained by his father, and the job had probably been in the family for generations. He knew instinctively how to place an explosive charge: too little and you just shattered the surface, too much and a whole face would disintegrate into unusable chunks. Craftsmen of all trades spend a lifetime learning the characteristics and limitations of their chosen material, be it stone, iron, glass, hardwood, lead or brick, and I have always learned more from such people than was ever possible during my five-year professional training.

All these design considerations took place a long time before the buzz-word 'contextualism' entered the planning vocabulary, but in the end I felt that our attempt to reconcile the design of an honestly constructed twentieth-century building with its adjacent baroque masterpiece at least showed that we had thought about the context, and I hoped that future generations would not find it offensive. In succeeding years, the building would go in and out of fashion of course – all buildings do – but I somehow felt that this particular one might just stand the test of time.

Coleman Street lies in the very heart of the old city, linking London Wall with Lothbury, and is only a five-minute walk from St Paul's. The area has equally deep historical significance and every property has seen many incarnations since the land was first built on.

Number 80 was the sort of building you could walk past every day of your life but, if asked to describe it, you wouldn't be able to remember a single distinguishing feature. The country is full of such buildings, and planning permission for their design can always be relied upon from lay committees taking refuge in gutless compromise. This particular building had for some time contained the board suite for the London Life Association, the second-oldest life assurance company in the country. Its administrative head

211

office, housing all the staff and records, was situated a short distance away at King William Street, but the directors and their senior staff met at regular intervals in the lovely panelled boardroom at Coleman Street. A pair of delicate chandeliers hung over the highly polished table, and an open marble fireplace, surmounted by a mahogany-cased bracket clock, stood at the far end. The formally draped curtains smelt faintly of expensive pipe tobacco, and a richly patterned Axminster carpet completed the setting, all of which spelled establishment, reliability and trust. When the association acquired it after the war it had been 'modernised' prior to sale by the vendors, who were obviously torn between bringing it right up to date or giving it some semblance of historical flavour, with the result that it failed miserably to do either. I had been asked to redesign the façade, upgrade the interior and plan a large extension at the back. The last two tasks were easy, but the choice of architectural expression for the street frontage needed a bit more thought. The extent of Blitz damage was uncertain, but the property had probably been remodelled in the Victorian or Edwardian periods and this, in turn, would have replaced a Georgian version. I considered it was too small a façade to suddenly go avant garde and, as it was sited between two fairly conventional neighbours anyway, I opted for a classical London Georgian façade with Tuscan portico, well-proportioned first-floor windows with glazing bars, and finished with a bracketed cornice, all of which could be accomplished with a minimum amount of structural intervention and might have resembled what stood there originally. I could even include an extra mansard storey on the roof behind the existing parapet wall. Having spent thirty years designing in a twentieth-century idiom, it was fun to turn out something a bit scholarly, and I enjoyed it.

My clients and the city planners were quick to approve the design, and contract drawings were prepared without delay. I was even more pleased when the lowest tender was received from one of the oldest-established firms in the city, who I knew would give the standard of work I wanted. The builders soon erected scaffolding to begin the new facing and I visited them frequently to watch the layers of onion being peeled away. Yes, there was evidence of a robust nineteenth-century façade and, thankfully, equally good evidence of eighteenth-century work, so I guessed that I'd done the right thing. I was able to turn my attention to the back of the building, which was to house a new administrative function requiring large open space and deep foundations to carry what few columns there were. Having satisfied myself that the front could now look after itself, I was disconcerted to receive a phone call from the site foreman, Fred Clark, one day, asking if I would come down straight away.

Above: JW-T's gunnery squad on Blakang Mati, Singapore in 1947.
Below: Façade of vicarage at 87, London Road, Brighton. Watercolour by JW-T.

87, LONDON ROAD BRIGHTON

Left: House in Royal
Crescent, Brighton.
Pencil sketch by JW-T.

Above: Cartoon by Ffolkes in *Daily Telegraph*, 1969, following national launch of the 'relocatable church' project.

Below: Proposed entrance to Neurosis Unit, Hellingly. Watercolour by JW-T in Royal Academy Exhibition.

Above: Painted glass for St. Christopher's Church, Thornhill, Southampton, by Hans Unger.
Below: Hove Town Hall and Civic Centre, East Sussex © D. Bennett.

Derelict farmhouse on the Via Appia,
near Rome. Conté sketch by JW-T.

إعلان

يسر قسم العمارة دعوة جميع أعضاء هيئة التدريس والطلبة
لحضور المحاضرة التي سيلقيها
الأستاذ جون ويلز ثورب   Mr: John Wells Thorpe
موضوع المحاضرة : تجديد المنشآت والمناطق الأثرية في أوربا
URBAN RENEWAL IN EUROPE
موعد المحاضرة ، الساعة ١٠ صباح الثلاثاء ١٨ محرم ٩٦ هـ
٩ يناير ٧٩ م
المكان : صالة المحاضرات لهام بكلية الهندسة
يعرض فيلم سينمائي ٤٥ دقيقة عن تجديد المنشآت والمناطق الأثرية في أوربا تعقبه
المحاضرة ومن ثم المناقشة .
نبذة عن المحاضر : أستاذ جميعه الدارسين ﻟﻤﻌﻘﻢ مجاء معظم لو راس با قطعر ا
ممثل (RIBA) جمعية المملكة للمهندسين مع طعام سيبد لمريطا نيديم في المبانات كليهم
ممثل (RIBA) بمجلس جامعة سوسكس بانجلترا
والدعوة عامة .

Left: JW-T's driver and cook at Jebel Nahran, Abha, Saudi Arabia.

Right: University notice announcing Civic Trust lecture in Damman, Saudi Arabia.

Below: 'Loaves and Fishes' sculpture for Brighthelm Community and Church Centre by John Skelton © D. McNeill.

Above: JW-T discussing progress of the London Life mural with artist Patrick Caulfield © J. Collins.

Below: JW-T with aerial survey colleagues and helicopter crew on Malta.

Above: Offices and showroom for Porsche near Brighton © D. McNeill.

Below: JW-T's former offices on fire at Richmond Place, Brighton © The Argus.

'What's the problem? Haven't you seen enough of me already?' I asked.

'Not so much a "problem" as a "situation", sir, so we'd like to see you a bit quickish.'

'I'm not following you, Fred. What are you on about?'

'Well it's like this, sir. You said we'd restore the building to its original – Georgian – but underneath that lot we've just found an oak timber frame and we think it's a bit medieval-like.'

'It can't be, Fred – remember the Great Fire wiped that lot out.'

'Before my time, sir, but an oak frame is an oak frame and there's no mistaking.'

My heart sank. Coleman Street was in the middle of the old city which had been engulfed in fire that raged for days on end, so how could this be? Archaeological references to the Great Fire are plentiful, but understandably nothing I'd come across recorded the precise limits of the conflagration, and historians had made assumptions. So had I. I had persuaded my clients that we were restoring the building to something like its original appearance and, worse still, I had persuaded the city planners that it should be easy to recommend permission because we were proposing a historically authentic solution.

'Fred, you had a heavy night celebrating Millwall's two-nil away win and you've come over a bit funny this morning and keep seeing double. Have a couple of pints on me and forget about what you think you've just seen. Okay?'

'If you say so, sir, that's good enough for me.'

At least the vestiges of a possible former age are still intact for another generation to discover.

But the 'solution' of one problem only heralded the arrival of a more disconcerting one. Because of poor subsoil conditions, the structural engineers said we would have to pile the foundations for the new block at the back – that is, penetrate deeper to a sound substratum. This wasn't surprising, as London clay doesn't carry much concentrated weight, but I knew it would be an awkward operation and we'd have to notify the owners of neighbouring buildings, in writing, informing them about possible noise and vibration. The requisite notices were served and, in acknowledging their notification, the clerk to the company on the north side drew our attention to the existence of the cellars in their basement and sought our assurance that, should any of their very valuable wine be found to have been adversely affected by the vibration from our piling rig, we must undertake to make restitution to the full value of the spoiled wine as assessed by an independent arbitrator appointed by the Worshipful Company of Vintners.

As you can't construct a building without noise or sink piles, however carefully, without some vibration, we were put in a very awkward position. There was no question of stopping the contract while the matter was resolved, as it might have dragged on for weeks and the abortive construction costs would have been disastrous, so we had to think of an effective response. Fortunately, the association's chief surveyor, Derek Brightwell, with whom I worked closely, had been in the Royal Engineers and probably knew a thing or two about placing explosive charges under enemy bridges. I had served in the Royal Artillery and equally knew something about explosives and their behaviour, so for the one and only time in my civilian life, this experience was to prove very useful. Having guessed, correctly as it turned out, that the livery company clerk had served in neither regiment, we played our trump card and told him that we'd be very happy to compensate the company for any loss incurred, as long as he could first demonstrate conclusively that any deterioration perceived in their precious wine had not been caused by high-explosive bombs dropped nearby during the Blitz. Our reference to surprisingly accurate wartime records showing where high explosives had fallen in the neighbourhood emboldened us to take a forthright line, and it had the desired effect. From that moment on no further reply was ever received, although grudgingly Derek and I both admitted it had probably been worth a try on their part.

Chapter 31

A Sense of Occasion

Progress in the construction of a building is traditionally marked in a number of ways, all of which involve a ritual of sorts. A media-conscious client will use such occasions as public-relations exercises, whilst others will be content to let the symbolism of the event speak for itself, as in the consecration of a new church.

The initial action is 'cutting the first sod' (a term now sanitised by politically correct extremists who refer to it, feebly, as a 'ground-breaking' ceremony). Then comes the laying of the foundation stone, which customarily is set at plinth level and tapped into position by an invited worthy, such as a Lord Lieutenant, a Masonic Grand Master or, more frequently today, a current 'celebrity' who everyone will have forgotten in five years' time. When the structure nears its full height, but before any work is executed internally, there can be a topping-out ceremony, sometimes signalled by tying a small spruce tree to the highest section, often a chimney, which is a custom of Scandinavian origin. Finally, the formal opening of the building takes place, which, until recent health and safety legislation came into force, included as its centrepiece the splitting of a barrel of ale for all the construction workers, who would queue up for a generous fill; however, over the years this became impossible to control, and apprentices could be seen falling off the scaffolding like flies, so it had to stop.

There are endless variations to all these ceremonies and there is ample scope for innovation. I had once been asked to design a new Ford dealership for Tommy Sopwith, son of the aviation pioneer and yachtsman, Sir Thomas Sopwith. It was to be built on the site of an old Roman villa in Brighton. This had been excavated by archaeologists long before, but when the new foundations were being dug, further antique remnants were discovered which included a small glass vessel, a woman's comb and a handful of coins. Much of the cache had been given to the local museum, but I retained the largest and best-preserved coin for reuse in our topping-out ceremony. Ideas about how this should be undertaken were exchanged and eventually led to the spectacular, if somewhat contrived, arrangement of hoisting an original open-topped Model T Ford from road level onto the flat roof, whereupon Tommy Sopwith, a celebrated racing driver in his own right, drove it across the length of the building to where the boiler-room chimney penetrated the roof. Here he alighted and climbed the short ladder to a scaffolded platform where the last 'lift' of concrete had just been poured. I handed him the burnished coin and, with a flourish, he pressed it down into the wet mix to be hidden from view for another century or two.

Of all the events, it is the formal openings which include the most public speaking, with topics ranging from the epic to the banal, and sometimes to the quite bizarre. It seems that when an ordinary event is elevated to an occasion, we lend a more receptive ear and remember what is said. The earlier experience of the Duke of Edinburgh asking me how many tons of paint was used for the Civic Trust improvement scheme in Hove years ago was one such example.

Official openings bring a sense of occasion which not only celebrates the completion of a project, often after many years' gestation, but also induces a collective sigh of relief that it's all over and we can give thanks. For me, the experience always reminds me of the annual speech day at school when we sat in rapt attention listening to a retired major general no one had heard of going on about duty, pluck and determination, but whose oration we would receive with extravagant applause only because we knew he would, by tradition, recommend that the school receive an extra half-day holiday to mark successes in scholarships and exhibitions to Oxbridge.

Once, unexpectedly stuck with a fellow architect in a remote rural idyll for a weekend due to a rail strike, I recalled some of the more unexpected experiences and it struck us that we were lucky, compared with most professions: a successfully completed architectural project is marked much more conspicuously. Other than a bottle of Veuve Clicquot, there will be nothing much to mark a lawyer's reputation-saving advocacy in court or a surgeon's life-saving skill in theatre, whereas the near pageantry of the opening of a new building can be witnessed by an entire community, either first-hand or through press and television coverage.

In 1984 the Royal Institute of British Architects celebrated the 150th anniversary of its foundation by holding a gala evening at Hampton Court Palace. The Prince of Wales was invited to bestow personally the Royal Gold Medal, the profession's highest honour, on the distinguished Indian architect and planner Charles Correa, as a highlight to an event which also included the restaging of a Stuart masque in the style of Inigo Jones, a spectacular firework display, a concert by the Nash Ensemble and a sumptuous dinner. What the Prince of Wales chose to say on this occasion is well recorded elsewhere and he didn't endear himself to the profession as a result. A few years earlier I had witnessed royal unpredictability when HRH had been invited by the governors of Lancing College to formally open the new boarding house for girls we had designed following a decision by the school to break with tradition and open the place of learning to both sexes. To facilitate easy integration with the boys it had been decided in the first instance to introduce older girls only – namely, those at sixth-form level.

A suitable location was chosen on the edge of the campus, formerly the site of a small agricultural settlement known as Manor Farm. Although our designs were for a separate, free-standing building, it would be adjacent to a number of nineteenth-century Gothic Revival blocks and therefore they demanded some contextual consideration. We couldn't afford fake Gothic, nor would we have suggested it, so we decided instead to be good-neighbourly in terms of scale, silhouette and massing, and although I chose a silver-grey facing brick which sat happily alongside the existing flintwork, it was nonetheless a twentieth-century building, and I wasn't anxious to engage with any royal over stylistic matters.

Following lunch with the governors, the prince was escorted by the headmaster to the start of the entrance path leading to the girls' new house, where I was introduced and asked to lead him to the foyer, where he would unveil a commemorative plaque and meet some of the senior girls who had formed a welcoming party. As we walked he drew a paper from his pocket and quickly asked, 'And what is this place called?'

'Manor House, sir.'

Twelve blossomy girls in Laura Ashley dresses beamed at him.

'Manor spelt Manna, don't you think?'

I was stumped for an answer. It had been a lot easier calculating for his father how many tons of paint I had used.

A commission for a new centre for Church Army followed shortly afterwards. I knew little about the organisation, but was told by a clerical friend, perhaps tongue in cheek, that it was the Church of England's answer to the Salvation Army. At any event, it did a marvellous job caring, residentially in this case, for a number of older and more vulnerable men and women who had fallen on hard times, some with records of alcoholism, prison or vagrancy. There was a orderly but caring regime and the female residents had to undertake some of the domestic tasks. But curiously, not so the men. I once asked

217

the reason for this and was told that as there was only a small surrounding garden, 'men's work' was very limited, so for much of the day they sat lining the walls of the men's day room, dressed in collarless shirts and cloth caps, mostly smoking and watching a small television set in the corner, without ever admitting to seeing very little due to the layers of blue haze and their fading eyesight, while the women toiled away elsewhere.

When the then Minister of Education, Margaret Thatcher, was invited to visit and conduct the formal inauguration, her aides insisted that no special arrangements be made as she wanted to see the house as it was normally used, so this is what was planned. On briefly entering the men's day room, she was mystified to see them idle while their female counterparts were busy with mop and saucepan. Apparently, it was assumed that none of the male residents had any domestic skills and would quickly become a liability in the kitchen. She immediately questioned this assumption.

'Then let them shell peas,' she suggested (in a voice which two centuries earlier had, with equal determination, suggested 'Then let them eat cake'). 'It's very important for them to have something useful to do,' she added. 'My father used to help in the kitchen at home.'

The following day it was tried, but as fresh vegetables were solidly refused in any case, tinned beans were quickly reinstated and the male residents returned to a daily routine they were perfectly happy with.

By far the nicest example of savoir-faire occurred when the new Hove Town Hall was opened on Tuesday 5 March 1974 by Lord Rupert Nevill. He was a quiet man with an easy charm, about whom nobody knew very much except when the newspapers reported that the Queen and Duke of Edinburgh had gone down to his seat in East Sussex to stay the weekend.

To follow the formal opening a celebratory lunch was to be served in the Great Hall and, as I had glimpsed the toast list and menu beforehand, I knew that we would be having tomato mousse and salmon, cream of asparagus soup, boned whole quail, raspberry vacherin, petits fours and coffee, all of which was being prepared in the kitchens on the lower ground floor, immediately beneath the entrance foyer where the official ceremony was to take place.

The town clerk's department issued the usual instructions over who stood where and in what order they would be presented to Lord Nevill. Everyone seemed to be aware of the pecking order and took their places accordingly, although there did seem to be rather a lot of people wishing to get in on the act and at least two extra rows, mostly composed of minor functionaries, formed behind the presentation party. On the dot of 11 o'clock a lordly car arrived and introductions began. His lordship was rather short, but made up for it by possessing extremely good looks, with beautifully coiffed silver hair and an engaging smile to melt the hearts of all the women and disarm those councillors who thought that this was going to be yet another stuffy, awkward occasion.

When he reached the end of the presentation line I noticed him quickly glance at the hopefuls who by this time had broken rank and crowded in behind.

'Back in a moment. I must go and say hello to everyone in the kitchen,' he said, and down the stairs he went, his appointed hosts scurrying to keep up with him on this unexpected diversion. The cooks, waiters and helpers were elated by his sudden appearance, and after he had asked what was smelling so nice and stuck his finger in the pot for good measure, he thanked them in advance and returned up the stairs to greet everyone else before pulling the golden cord to reveal the commemorative plaque.

'Good breeding,' mumbled the alderman next to me; 'knows how to talk to the troops.'

An architect is usually contracted to give 'partial supervision' of a building contract, but not to provide 'constant superintendence', which means that, during the construction process, periodic site visits are made to ensure the building is being erected in general accordance with the plans. Much detailed work is discussed with specialist subcontractors, and although we always built a model and described the intent of the design to the entire team, there was still a certain amount that could safely be left to common sense, or so I thought.

Having by now designed a number of churches in several dioceses, I had a fairly clear idea of what was needed. They had to work both liturgically and functionally and, bearing in mind most churches are sited to face east, I was always at pains to avoid the glare which comes from a traditionally sited east window behind the altar. As the liturgical activity takes place here at morning service, wherever you are in the land, the early sun shines directly into the eyes of the congregation. This also means that the priest facing the congregation is usually seen in silhouette only, his or her features obscured by the wash of strong light from behind. It is rather like trying to read the front registration number of a car whilst its headlights shine into your face. The simple solution to this problem is to have a deliberately plain east wall behind the altar and admit ample light from coloured glass on the south side nearby, so that it provides visual interest, and perhaps even a sense of the numinous, as it falls on the plain surface.

It isn't always easy to get this just right: the sun's arc has to be plotted, any overhanging trees assessed and the appropriate glass colours carefully selected – but on one particular occasion at a new church in Surrey it worked out perfectly. I had visited the site a few days before the official consecration by the Bishop of Guildford and satisfied myself that the sweep of the plain, but beautifully textured, east wall looked perfect when illuminated with coloured light from the side and was an ideal foil for the richness of the altar which stood before it.

The day of the consecration arrived, and after the congregation had assembled, the doors were closed behind them. A small party of us remained outside ready to process in at the right moment. While we waited and the expectant congregation enjoyed the last part of a Bach prelude, the two church wardens, the archdeacon, the bishop and I chatted about the design and it gave me the opportunity of explaining why there wasn't a conventional east window. I wanted to prepare them for the dramatic impact of a completely plain wall, which they would see for themselves in a few moments. At 3 p.m. promptly the bishop, attired in mitre and cope, struck the oak door three times with his crook to seek entry and our procession began. I had planned seating either side of a central aisle down which we walked to take our places at the front. On cue, the sun came out to scatter shards of chromatic light over the unblemished canvas and all that I could wish for came true – except, that is, for the largest, most unimaginable worm in the rose. To my horror, there facing me on the great wall was a thermostat, fixed some twenty-four hours earlier by the electrical subcontractor, who had concluded that the sanctuary needed a device of its own and its temperature should not have to rely on the counterpart in the nave. Graffiti would have been easier to accept – I could have written that off to extremism – but a last-minute bid to make everything perfect by an honest, hardworking, conscientious electrician was too much to bear – and it wasn't even on straight.

Perhaps the last word on the subject should be devoted to a far less splendid occasion which nonetheless stays in my mind for containing a riposte that would render any subsequent conversation pointless.

The terraces forming the flat roof of the Brighton Aquarium had been leased for entertainment and leisure purposes that included the usual variety of seaside attractions – a crazy-golf course, a ghost-train ride, candyfloss stalls and the rest. The lessee, was an ebullient figure with a florid complexion who had dabbled in a wide variety of activities during his working life and had a touch of the fairground proprietor about him. He was sharp as a razor, made snap decisions and parted with money reluctantly. I had done my best on a very limited budget to improve the appearance of some of the pavil-ions and stalls and, as the season began on Easter Saturday, we had driven the contractors hard to complete on time. I had worked throughout with his manager, or, more accurately, with his fixer, Steve, a sallow-faced, poorly shaven character with receding, lank hair, who was responsible for keeping the tenants in line and extracting their rent. A modest, very modest, opening was arranged for twelve noon on the Good Friday preceding the bank holiday weekend. I arrived a quarter of an hour earlier to check that all was well but, to my surprise, encountered the proprietor, looking more florid than was good for him, at the bottom of the steps.

'Where's Steve?' I enquired.

'Doesn't work here any longer.'

'Oh,' I said.

'Thought he was indispensable, so I sacked him.'

Chapter 32

The Mangrove

Preece, Cardew & Rider, by now close working colleagues, were celebrating seventy-five years of practice and decided to mark the event with a gala dinner at the Hotel Metropole, at the time Brighton's best-known five-star venue which, when it first opened in 1890, was the largest hotel outside London. Much later it was popularised in the 1953 film *Genevieve*, starring John Gregson and featuring the RAC London to Brighton Veteran Car Run and all the conviviality which follows the successful arrival at the seaside.

PCR had invited clients from all the parts of the world where they were undertaking projects, and the top table included guests from at least three continents. When the firm first arrived in Brighton I had introduced them to one or two of my own clients and, to mark their appreciation, they invited me to join them on the top table. They also asked me to respond to the toast 'The Guests', although this was probably because they weren't too sure how many of their more important overseas guests would cope with a formal occasion in a second language. This meant that I was undeservedly well looked after and I found myself seated between the chairman of the Cyprus water board and a senior executive from the Malaysian electricity generating company. I had visited Cyprus once and liked it a lot and so spent much of the time speaking to the amiable Greek on my left. I became aware of the fact that I had more or less disregarded the guest on my right until the dessert course was served, when I hastily tried to make amends. I found myself looking at a slimly built Tamil with receding hair and slightly bloodshot eyes, an appearance that I had become familiar with in Ceylon during my Army years, and I guessed that he hailed either from that island or from South India. However, the guest list said he came from Malaysia, so my approach was tentative.

'I don't think you remember me, do you?' he said.

I really had no idea, and came out with a harmless rejoinder which sounded flat and meaningless to both of us.

'I'll give you a clue,' he said, his face softening with a hint of a smile. 'You used to bowl off the wrong foot, didn't you?'

This was about as helpful as being told that my paternal grandmother was educated at a remote convent in Belgium (which I only learned upon her death at 93, incidentally). Fortunately, my neighbour and I had had sufficient to drink by this time to see the silly side of the conversation, and obviously if I had known him he must have changed a good deal as the man seemed completely unfamiliar, whereas I flattered myself that I was still easy to spot as I was as slight, fair-haired and blue-eyed as I had been during my student days. Maybe he saw that this was an unfair contest, so he helped me out.

'I came to Brighton in the late forties to read for a BSc in electrical engineering and we played cricket for the same team on a Saturday.'

'Ram, *of course* – you haven't changed a bit!' I found myself saying rather stupidly. Ram was short for Ramanath, and he was one of the very first students from Malaya to arrive in the UK after the war. I did indeed bowl off the 'wrong' foot in cricket, but it wasn't illegal as there was nothing in the rule book to say which foot you had to bowl off, though it was considered idiosyncratic and had the helpful effect of confusing the batsman and indeed the rest of the team, of which Ram was an important member. No wonder he remembered me.

After I'd made the last speech of the evening and while we were relaxing over the port and cigars, he asked me what I was working on at this time. I told him, after which, to my surprise, he asked if I'd be interested in acting as architectural consultant on a massive new power-generation project at Port Klang, downstream from Kuala Lumpur, and whether I'd like to undertake the environmental impact study as well. He explained that I would be working with Ewbank, another large Brighton-based consultancy. I eagerly accepted and later walked home filled with thoughts about how much would still be recognisable from my days thirty years earlier with the 1st Malay Coast Battery.

The design of power stations presents formidable visual problems, and I had been intrigued by a recently published solution to the problem of visual coalescence – the tendency for large separate masses to merge into one amorphous shape when seen from a distance. Because of their size, such plants were visible for many miles and the apparent coalescence militated against any attempt to refine the design. Although I had immediately said yes to Ram, I was rather more hesitant about carrying out the Environmental Impact Assessment (EIA), a study to predict the impact on the surrounding area of any new project in terms of its infrastructure. It would involve looking at the organisation and structure of housing, roads, transport, communications, health care, education and recreation and it meant that I would have to predict the effect both of constructing and of running the power station on its locality in social, environmental, and ecological terms. I was particularly attracted to the last of these criteria because Barbara Ward, the distinguished environmentalist, had recently coined a good phrase to describe ecology – namely, 'Rules for the care and maintenance of a small planet'. This placed the topic in its political context, and therein lay its fascination. EIAs were demanded by the World Bank, which was involved with financing this scheme, but there was as yet no universally established methodology for their compilation. The whole proposal sounded intriguing, but I hadn't done an EIA before – although I reminded myself that neither had most people. I felt emboldened to accept, knowing that I'd have to mug up on the subject p.d.q. if I was going to deliver anything credible.

I felt the same buzz I had experienced when I devised the relocatable church project years before, but a hundred times stronger. I was going to have to fly by the seat of my pants, and the prospect was irresistible. I would not be alone though, as we had to assemble a team to cover all the separate disciplines involved, and that in itself would be exciting. Some of the appointments were easy to fill, particularly under the headings of engineering, architecture and planning, but I still needed a marine biologist. I had learned that a power station needs an abundant supply of cooling water and therefore, wherever possible, it is sited on the coastline so that seawater can be used. In cooler climates like that of Britain, this can be fairly straightforward, but in tropical waters like those around Port Klang on the Strait of Malacca the year-round temperature hardly varies at all, and any man-made intervention would be critical. Once it is used, cooling water is discharged back into the sea at a temperature slightly higher than normal, and if this isn't treated beforehand, it can kill local marine life unaccustomed to such variation and thus adversely affect the whole food chain – in this instance ranging from plankton to shellfish. And if, like here, fishing is the principal employment for local people and had been for generations, the whole local economy could be jeopardised, with immediate social and political consequences. We therefore appointed a leading marine biologist, Pauline Marstrand, but no sooner had we done so than we came upon an even more difficult conundrum. The electricity authority had decided to build the station at a particular coastal site before we were appointed, and the area comprised part of a large mangrove swamp, which more properly is called a mangrove *forest*. Apparently the mangrove stabilises and maintains the coastal ecosystem and is important in preventing erosion and providing a vital link in the food chains of aquatic life in the area. Such forests even supported limited employment for local indigenous groups who harvested the mangrove.

We had struck an area of the study about which none of us knew anything, and I became acutely aware that we needed expert advice. It was agreed that we would have to find and appoint someone who knew all there was to know about the ecology of a mangrove swamp. I like a challenge, but only relish it if I think I might, in the end, rise to the occasion. Where should I start? The Yellow Pages were not going to help, Google was a generation away, and I didn't think I'd get much help down the pub. I tried hard to think of ways in which the impossible challenge of finding just the right person for the job had been overcome in the past. Only one example came to mind, and true though it was, it sounded far more like a chapter opening from P. G. Wodehouse. I was in Oxford during the long vac one summer and saw a poster advertising the twelfth-century music drama entitled *The Play of Daniel* to be performed by the New York Pro Musica. W. H. Auden, whom I had never seen, was the narrator, so I bought a ticket immediately. The performance, though essentially musical, had moments of visual splendour, and one particular scene portraying Belshazzar's palace involved a professional fire-eater who, together with tumblers and court jesters, entertained the king's guests. It was so vivid and memorable that I enquired of a cast member during the interval how they came to find such performers. With difficulty, it appeared, and the show nearly had to be cut when they couldn't find what they wanted. In desperation, they had placed a classified advertisement in a well-known broadsheet which read:

Fire-eater required, preferably with ecclesiastical experience. Apply Box No. XX.

Astonishingly, they found their man. Should I do the same and seek a mangrove-swamp expert with ecological experience, or perhaps an ecologist with mangrove-swamp experience? It was too ridiculous to contemplate, so I fell back on hoping that some friend of a friend might just help. The statistical chances were remote, but such is the perversity of life that this is exactly what happened. I was introduced to an Edinburgh University-based landscape architect who had recently taken a particular interest in the mangrove, notwithstanding the fact that the Far East was totally unknown to him. Archie Young was a Scot through and through and a sheer delight to work with. We met in London so that I could describe to him the nature of the work and we could exchange notes about our respective pasts. He told me that his father had been a mole catcher. He could so easily have dressed this up with some more impressive title but he didn't, so I knew his hands-on involvement was going to be honest, thorough and entirely usable. I then asked him if he'd like to join the team for a while in Malaysia, and I had barely finished the sentence before he agreed.

Archie's Calvinistic demeanour dissolved quite rapidly when we arrived in KL, and his eyes filled with wonder at every turn. The hot, humid climate produced plants and blossoms of Byzantine opulence and our nostrils, ears and hands vied with our eyes for sensory delight. He couldn't stop talking about it, but there was one occasion quite early on when he sounded surprisingly lost.

On arrival at the hotel, we had been allocated adjacent rooms, and at the end of a long day I was showering before we met for dinner when I heard the phone ring. Thinking it might be the clients who we were due to meet the next day, I ran from the bathroom to take the call. It was Archie.

'Er, John . . . ' he started hesitantly. 'A nice girl in a sarong has arrived in my room and wants to know whether she can give me either a foam or a herbal bath. What should I say?'

'Say both,' I replied and replaced the receiver.

After having dined alone that evening, I made a point of only talking about mangroves at breakfast the next day.

If you are going to design a building, let alone prepare an EIA, you've got to know the site like the back of your hand before you start. I'd flown over it once, but there is nothing like experiencing the real thing, its contours, its substratum, its smells and the natural life it supports. I was anxious to explore most of these, but I was rather more hesitant about the natural life. Mosquitoes at low tide would be a known nuisance which we accepted, but none of us knew much about the reptilian occupants. To make full use of the occasion, I suggested that as many of the group as were free should join me and I arranged for a driver to pick us up early so that we could spend all the daylight hours there. I ordered about twenty rounds of sandwiches to be sent to my room so that I could take enough for us during what could turn out to be a long day.

Upon leaving the city, our jovial Sikh driver took us onto forest tracks which got narrower and narrower as we approached the site. By the time the Land Rover's wheels began to struggle in the mud, we were sufficiently near to walk the rest of the way. The driver knew where the site boundary was and led us to it, intending to wait only until we had entered the mangrove. Mangrove roots continued above the waterline in huge, sinuous arches reminiscent of dark Art Nouveau illustrations in a menacing Gothic tale, and these, combined with the overpowering stench of rotting vegetation, made for an uncongenial scene. We were in a forest of ribcages stripped clean by predators and deliberately left to scare the unwary. Unexplained noises added to our unease and all our senses turned to amber and stayed there. Caution was paramount.

The driver was about to leave but stopped momentarily as he watched me tentatively lead the others into the mangrove. Uncertain of what I might find or, worse still, disturb, I stepped as daintily as I could from root to root, trying to reduce any noise as I went. An incredulous Sikh voice barked at us, 'Do you want to die?' and this was followed by a peal of laughter which echoed eerily around us. 'Not particularly, driver, what's up?' I replied. Without answering, he lumbered towards us, picked up a length of branch and lurched forward into the swamp, swiping left and right as he went, bellowing like a bull and creating a huge disturbance. A miscellany of dark green things scampered or slithered out of his way and took to new hiding places until the storm abated. 'That way you won't get hurt; your way, you'll surprise them and they'll get angry. I'll collect you at 16.00 hours.' And with that he lunged his way back to the truck and drove off. It was all so blindingly obvious when we thought about it later, but it didn't stop us feeling stupid as we made manic noises in the mangrove for the rest of the day until our throats hurt.

The entire experience – both designing the power station and predicting the effect it would have on its environment – was very rewarding for the entire team and it was with some reluctance that we returned home to our decidedly less exotic jobs.

Two months later, I was puzzled why our fee account still remained unpaid, but I had clearly underestimated the contagious influence of the old Indian Civil Service procedures which for years were still used verbatim in far-flung colonies, often unchanged to suit local circumstances. These involved armies of clerks checking, double-checking and rubber-stamping every expense chit rendered, in the belief that this would root out dishonesty. One such clerk's eyes must have sparkled at the thought of promotion at finding that an expatriate professional had ordered twenty rounds of sandwiches for a room with single occupancy, and I was asked to explain why. It was obvious to him that I had eaten one round and run the rest round to the bazaar 'for pecuniary advantage', hoping no one would notice if I did this only once.

In fact, it took another six weeks of correspondence and, in the end, telephone calls to the ministerial office in Kuala Lumpar, to explain what had really happened. Seemingly, a team picnic lunch in a mangrove swamp lacked credibility.

Chapter 33

The Commonwealth

The Commonwealth is a free association of separate sovereign states, most of them brought together in the days of empire and therefore sharing much common history. Systems and procedures in politics, law, administration, education and health were progressively introduced, often using British counterparts as models in the first place. As time passed and member nations achieved independence, such systems were modified to better suit local circumstances, although a very strong cultural thread is still perceivable in many places.

It soon became clear that, despite newly independent nations going their separate ways, they were by no means self-sufficient and therefore could benefit from maintaining contact with each other; this was done in the spirit of the Commonwealth's objectives of mutual help and the moral obligations of the West to the Third World. It was particularly the case in architectural matters. Developing nations faced huge challenges in planning a proper infrastructure, providing basic housing, schools and hospitals, all within severely constrained budgets, which made mutual help and understanding very necessary. It was sensible to share expertise, and the benefits were by no means one-sided. Technology transfer from the developed to the developing nations was amply repaid by Western architects learning more of the cultural traditions of the emerging nations which widened and enriched their own perception.

The Commonwealth Association of Architects (CAA) was one of the first professional organisations to be set up under the Commonwealth Foundation whose overall task, in turn, was to 'increase interchange between Commonwealth organisations in professional fields'. With fifty-four member nations, the task was ambitious, and made more so because the countries spread across all five continents, reflecting wide differences in climate, economy and state of development.

The CAA was established at an inaugural meeting in Malta chaired by Sir Robert Matthew, a resolute and forceful Scot who had been chief architect to the London County Council at the time of the Festival of Britain before founding his own very successful private practice which, some years later, would design the highly original Commonwealth Institute headquarters in Kensington. Despite a slender funding in the following years the CAA held well-attended conferences in New Delhi, Lagos, Canberra, Ottawa and York, and by the time I came to hear of it, it was planning another in Hong Kong.

Through my recent interest in designs for power generation I had got to know the current honorary secretary of the Royal Institute of British Architects (RIBA), Gordon Graham, whose practice had undertaken a lot of work in the same field. When it became known that the current president of the institute would not be free to take part in a conference in the Far East, Gordon suggested that, as I had just been working there, I should stand in for him. Although I knew Singapore and Malaysia quite well, I had never visited Hong Kong, so I jumped at the opportunity.

I arrived in Hong Kong to a tropical downpour and the inevitable scramble for taxis outside the airport. A policeman urged everyone to form an orderly queue (such was the influence handed down by generations of British police officers as queuing doesn't come naturally to most races) and I found myself standing next to another English-speaking passenger. I had not received a delegate list beforehand so didn't know who my colleagues would be, but my neighbour turned out to be an affable Yorkshireman who was also attending the conference. I had earlier noticed him speaking to a much younger woman while we were waiting and, after introducing myself to him, I glanced at her from time to time. He ignored any inference from that that they were together and went on talking about Yorkshire's cricketing achievements that season. I became aware that she was looking particularly uncomfortable at being left out of the conversation, so I held out my hand to her. 'Oh yes, eh, and this is my *accompanying person,*' he said breezily. She obviously was torn between hitting him and crying, and I was glad that a whole string of taxis had turned up together and I was able to leap into one of them. The traffic lights were out of action because of the flooding so I was surprised to be overtaken by a couple of Rolls-Royces in identical cream and chocolate brown livery which seemed to have some form of priority because, I learned later, they transported guests to and from the colony's best-known hotel, the Peninsula, to whom everyone, including traffic police, seemed to defer. On arrival at my destination, I asked the driver how much the journey had cost and paid up in rather large notes as I had not yet been to a bank or bought anything. Jet-lagged first-timers not conversant with the local currency must stick out like sore thumbs, and it wasn't until I was in the foyer that I realised that the driver had added another nought on the end and, apart from it making his day, had satisfactorily notched up another point against the colonialists.

Hong Kong consists of more than 230 islands and a portion of the mainland known as Kowloon and the New Territories. Hong Kong Island was first occupied by Britain in 1841 and was formally ceded by the Treaty of Nanking the following year. The complete colony fell into place over the course of the next fifty years or so and it would be another hundred years before China assumed sovereignty. Hong Kong's reputation was legendary. Its seven million population worked hard and played hard and I soon found myself thinking it was the most exciting place on earth. Service industries comprised the greater part of its economy, but at the same time, gambling provided 45% of the GNP. Predictably, it attracted nearly eight million visitors a year, and it doesn't take long before you ask yourself whether anyone there ever goes to sleep. It seemed as busy at 3 a.m. as it did at three in the afternoon and it was not uncommon to find visitors who had spent the entire night being entertained, crossing by ferry to Kowloon for breakfast at dawn.

For my first visit I had been booked into the Excelsior Hotel, which overlooks the harbour's typhoon shelter and upon arrival direct from the UK was too exhausted to take in very much. Hisham Albakri, the Asia region representative, had flown in from Kuala Lumpur and we arrived simultaneously; even though he had only had a three-hour flight, he complained of jet lag. Seeing the state I was in, he said that I would only sleep properly if I indulged in some immediate physical activity, and suggested a game of tennis. He knew this part of the world better than I did so I rather weakly agreed. The tennis court was on the flat roof of the hotel with splendid views over the harbour. We hired some equipment and began our rather flat game. I seemed to be playing in slow motion, striking any ball like an automaton and planting each foot as if half anaesthetised. Somehow I managed to win; I assumed that he must have been even more tired than I was. We gazed at each other through bloodshot eyes. I finally moved to depart to my room when he (presumably because he thought he was responsible for my dishevelled state through having persuaded me to play in the first place) suggested 'a long relaxing massage; that will do us both good'. I was sufficiently awake to link the words 'Hong Kong' and 'massage' and told him that a session of nudge, nudge, wink, wink was going to be quite beyond me. But Hisham insisted it could put me back together again, and I was much too tired to argue. I trudged behind him to the lift and we got out at the seventh floor entering what was called the 'Health and Recreation Centre'. I sat down next to him in the heavily perfumed reception area and waited for something to happen.

Finally, a sleek, charming hostess enquired softly, 'Are you room 234?' I supposed I was and she told me her colleague would come to me in a moment. Nonplussed, I started fidgeting for my wallet to make sure I still had it with me, but she added in a silken tone, 'You won't need that, sir, it just goes on your bill.' I looked at her blankly as she smiled and walked away. A few moments later I heard soft approaching steps and looked up to see a balding, late-middle-aged cripple (blind since birth, I later learned) who was their senior masseur. He led me to his treatment room and, in the space of half an hour, silently reassembled me in a way I would never have thought possible. Not a word was uttered as his delicate fingertips discovered knotted muscles and strained tendons without the slightest guidance from me and he quietly applied the skill of generations to anoint me with fragrant balm to leave me in such a resurrected state that I could have got up and worked for a week without sleep. I thanked him so profusely that, for the first time, he turned his inscrutable, milky eyes towards me. They held an expression of disbelief that anyone could ever have doubted the efficacy of his administrations. There is much we still have to learn from traditional Chinese medicine that we continue to scorn in the West and by so doing deny ourselves access to unimagined healing.

The members of the Hong Kong Institute of Architects were conscientious hosts and went out of their way to persuade the visiting British delegates that they were well up to the task of conference-organising and quite capable of standing on their own feet despite, or perhaps because of, years of colonial administration. They also demonstrated their bonhomie by taking one or two of us on a breathless tour of the island's 'nitespots', lightly disguised as places where you could find a drink. Within an hour we had visited three topless bars, but they were keeping their pièce de résistance for the last call. With much whispering, they got us back into the cars and triumphantly announced that we were about to visit Hong Kong's latest attraction, a bottomless bar. I was ferried towards it in a state of trepidation, only to find on arrival that the police had closed it down two hours earlier.

Their love of novelty mixed strangely with their love of things British, such as three-piece suits, restaurant menus in French, MG sports cars, Burberry umbrellas and double-decker buses, and this, although part of the charm of the place, often led to incomprehension when something quintessentially Chinese intervened. During my stay I asked if I could visit the school of architecture at the university and my hosts immediately went one better and asked if I'd like to set a one-day design assignment for students based on a 'live' – that is non-theoretical – subject. Having only an hour's notice and no time to think of anything totally original I wrote a design program around something I had recently been involved with – namely, an old people's home.

Copies of the design brief were quickly typed and distributed to the students a few minutes before my arrival in their room. Anxious to ensure that they fully understood the wording of the programme, I asked if there were any questions before they started working. No one put their hand up, so I assumed that there weren't any and sat down in a corner of the studio to talk to their young lecturer. No one started. After a long pause a young woman left her drawing board, came up to my host and whispered in his ear. He nodded to her, and after she had returned to her seat, he leant across and, with widened eyes and open palms, explained something to me. With great diffidence he emphasised that what he was about to say should not be regarded as discourteous and he hoped that I would understand the dilemma the students faced. No one in the studio had ever heard of an old people's home and didn't know what it was for, so they would welcome an explanation before they started. This was a bit like having to explain why, in times past, we burned witches or why fox-hunting was still popular in Britain. It hit me like a thunderbolt as I realised that my very limited glimpse across the cultural divide had prevented me from seeing and understanding the revered status enjoyed by grandparents in a Chinese family, and how naturally the grandchildren regarded them as a source of wisdom to be cherished under the same roof.

At the other end of the professional spectrum I became aware of a less engaging national characteristic, and this concerned the racial pecking order within the Commonwealth and, in this instance, between conference delegates. The Hong Kong Chinese ensured that table placings put them with British, Canadian and Australian representatives, and that the next group down was for delegates from South Asia (India, Pakistan and Sri Lanka) who, it appeared, were happy to be distinguished, in turn, from the last and largest group, from Africa. Despite our privileged position in their racial pecking order, the Chinese could not resist twisting the British lion's tail at every opportunity, and although this was done and accepted in good humour, it only reinforced in my mind the impatience with which they awaited the end of colonial rule, although I had the impression that even their most fervent advocates of independence had not really thought through what might happen to them after the final handover years hence.

The CAA conference took place in the World Trade Centre adjacent to the Excelsior where we were staying which, although it sounded convenient, insulated me from the outside climate so that I didn't know what to expect if I wanted to stretch my legs in between sessions. After a lengthy opening ceremony when too many people who had had speeches written for them wearily read what was placed in front of them, there was a break for coffee. During the whole of the ceremony I had been stuck on the podium with other national representatives and got colder and colder as the fiercest air-conditioning imaginable played over us like a police water cannon. I had dressed for Hong Kong and taken careful note of all the guidebook advice on what to wear, but this particular experience left me with my teeth chattering to the extent that immediately we broke for coffee, I hastened to the lobby, hailed a taxi and drove at breakneck speed to somewhere that sold long-sleeved woollen pullovers that wouldn't look too absurd with my tropical suit. There was no question of choice – the precious minutes were ticking away and I was on next, so my audience would have to accept the conspicuous eccentricities of an Englishman abroad.

The theme of the conference was 'Shelter for Mankind' which was a good topic for an event where First and Third Worlds came together and where, for instance, a simple knowledge of structures could infuse indigenous building methods with Western expertise to enhance their effectiveness. I recalled an excellent example years ago from the Nile valley where, for centuries, the local headsman had used dried mud to build simple structures. They were adequate but the material had little tensile strength and this limited its application. A visiting industrial chemist suggested that they just add some gypsum to the mix and, upon doing so, they found they could immediately construct bigger and stronger structures. This is the West at its best: take a traditional method, enhance it and hand it back so the community can continue almost as before. 'Minimum intervention' is easy and cheap and avoids expensive high-tech and high-dependency solutions being imposed.

The Hong Kong conference theme was to be one of many well-meaning such themes that I would get used to in years to come, and although they left everyone, both haves and have-nots, feeling good at the time, failure by governments and other responsible organisations to follow up the conclusions really diminished their usefulness. There should be an enormous advantage in having a commonwealth. A close network with common means of communication should put everyone streets ahead of the world competition. It has enormous potential and offers tantalising opportunities for good, but all too often nothing much happens beyond a display of tokenism that can be mistaken for a problem solved and another box ticked. Perhaps this is down to its size or sometimes down to plain despair at contemplating the sheer scale of the problems member nations face.

One evening, after a particularly dense agenda I went to dinner with another English delegate to Aberdeen Harbour on the far side of Hong Kong Island. It is famous for its multicoloured, exotically lit floating restaurants which, despite their enormous size, serve a tantalising variety of regional dishes. Away from the air-conditioning, we had both got into T-shirts and shorts and were finally experiencing and enjoying our oriental surroundings. We both deserved a few drinks, and beer seemed the most obvious answer. It transpired that my colleague, Robert, and I shared a client, a large public utility company, whose property manager we both agreed was a pleasure to work with and who was quite open about sharing out his commissions between three or four different practices. He had a zest for life, a schoolboy sense of fun and an enviably unstuffy attitude when dealing with outside consultants like ourselves. We shared an affection for our joint client, and after what must have been five or six beers we decided we'd drop him a friendly line and tell him that we'd just met on the other side of the world. Over further drinks we decided that, just for fun, we would write on a shared, jumbo-sized picture postcard and pen alternate lines, as one might do in a party game of Consequences. We wrote very small to accommodate our various declarations of undying loyalty to his organisation and, of course, to wish he was here. We meant the latter because he would have shared with us our toyshop wonder of everyone and everything around us. We spent ages trying to write the card and on one occasion had to buy another one and start again because the first was too smudged by beer. With a shout of triumph we finally finished it, a creative offering that we were hugely proud of. Unfortunately it never arrived as, in our final stages of disorientation, we forgot to put a stamp on.

Before leaving Hong Kong I was determined to go across the border into the Communist mainland if only on a day-permit which, I found wasn't too difficult to obtain. The border post was a fairly ramshackle affair and was manned by militia who scrutinised our passports and day-permits although, quite clearly, they had no idea of what they were looking for. When they returned our documents, we were each presented with a copy of *Quotations from Chairman Mao Zedong* (the 'Little Red Book'), printed in quite good English and bound inside a bright red plastic cover embossed with political symbols. As we studied them the border guards bared their teeth in encouragement. The booklet was a mixture of quasi-Confucian exaltations and unbending political polemic and we were assured that every Chinese schoolchild carries one for daily enlightenment.

The extent of territory we were allowed to see was fairly limited, and while the area had no shops as such, our trip did include an escorted visit to a government store, not unlike the GUM stores in the Soviet Union during the Stalin era. Goods and provisions were distributed through government outlets and therefore no one had any retail experience or any knowledge of how to attend upon customers or show any interest in them. Apparently, if you needed food or items of clothing, you obtained them from a state distributor, so no one had to compete for customers, and common courtesies were both superfluous and bourgeois. You put your coins on the counter and in return your goods were pushed across. This was poetically illustrated to me when I tried to buy something; I wanted to show willing and also to have a of souvenir of my first visit to a Marxist state. I thought a shirt might be a simple choice. I looked around until I saw a sufficiently inoffensive one hanging lopsidedly against a concrete wall on a bent wire coat hanger, and indicated that I would like to buy it. The sullen face on the other side of the counter made signs to indicate that I couldn't have it. It took me some time to realise that this was the 'display' sample and had to stay there. Using a sequence of gestures and childish impressions, I enquired whether they had another one like it in the back room. He began to understand my request but nonetheless stood rooted to the floor as he wasn't there to be helpful. I persisted and fluttered one or two extra banknotes under his nose in the hope that he might feel it was worthwhile to retrieve one from the back, even if it involved moving one foot in front of the other. Without altering a muscle in his face, he slowly turned his back to me and paused just long enough to emit a tremulous fart of improbable duration before shuffling off to get my shirt. Some minutes later he returned with it, took my money without looking at me, and left the unwrapped item on the counter for me to carry away while he proceeded to deal, even more reluctantly, with another customer who had unfortunately entered.

Chapter 34

Kenya After Mau Mau

The CAA conference and General Assembly to follow Hong Kong was held in Kenya in 1981 and I was pleased to be asked to represent RIBA once more. Unlike the Far East, Africa was totally unknown to me as I had only brushed its eastern seaboard when my troopship stopped to refuel on its way to Ceylon all those years ago. Beyond the sights and smells of Port Sudan and Berbera, I knew nothing.

Nairobi is the largest East African city and it is easy to see why the British chose it as the colony's capital. Although it lies very near the equator, its altitude (a mile high, they tell you) gives it a delightfully temperate climate, so that its million and a half inhabitants move about with a bustle that would be impossible anywhere else on that latitude. The main roads are lined with jacaranda, hibiscus, frangipani and bougainvillea, which cascade colour into the streets. It seemed an ideal, if atypical, introduction to Africa. It lacked the humidity of the Far East and smelled and sounded completely different. Birdsong was exuberant and raucous and, at that time, you could still hear it above the traffic. Mangoes and coconuts mingled with fresh cabbages in the street market and everyone was colourfully dressed. Vehicles drove on the left, uniforms and newspapers had a familiar look and everywhere the structure of government and public services reminded me of the indelible British model.

Earlier generations of English settlers had enjoyed an enviable lifestyle. Colonial administrators, tea and coffee farmers and game hunters would meet at sundown on the Lord Delamere Terrace (named after the pioneer agriculturist) at the Norfolk Hotel, which still carried on its walls faded caricatures of a white ruling class for whom England, between the wars, was a poor substitute. Elspeth Huxley's *The Flame Trees of Thika* describes with great imagination and character her life as a daughter of Kenyan pioneers and her vivid childhood experiences, one of which rather appealed to me. It related to the chameleon's ability to change colour to match its immediate surroundings. After what must have been a languid, alcoholic picnic one day, the leisurely group discussed whether you can induce a nervous breakdown in a captive chameleon by placing it on a tartan travelling rug. This was still an age when a privileged class could while away a whole day with madcap, if inventive, diversions of this sort.

However, not all white activities had been frivolous and some, like the work of the Leakey family, were to take their place in the annals of world anthropology. Louis Leakey, the distinguished palaeoanthropologist, discovered two clearly distinguished groups of fossilised hominids, and over the years went on to collect further evidence to show that what is now Kenya was indeed the cradle of mankind. In 1972 his son Richard Leakey and his team made a sensational discovery of a skull which was estimated to be about 1.9 million years old. Little wonder that President Jomo Kenyatta, the country's first leader after independence, claimed that Kenya's contribution to the world had been man himself.

It had been the Mau Mau uprising of the late 1950s which had led inexorably to this independence which was fully achieved a decade later. Sadly, this didn't extinguish long-standing tribal rivalries, which were still evident beneath whatever political sheen existed. As I became better acquainted with the country, I began to sense them in my dealings with professional bodies. They even affected the conference at one point.

The CAA conference and General Assembly, bringing together architects from all five continents, many of whom had never met, let alone thought about each other, demonstrated the strengths and weaknesses of the Commonwealth. The selection of 'noble' topics for discussion – disaster housing, self-build construction, regional vernacular design – showed a positive attempt to close the gap between developed and developing countries. At the same time, some poorer countries thought such themes were patronising and they were far more interested in copying the latest in Western design, despite its irrelevance to the real needs of their country. During the General Assembly, weaknesses began to show even more clearly. Within the Africa region, for instance, the Nigerians appeared to take it for granted that they were top of the heap and some of them behaved accordingly (usually 'making an entrance' by arriving late in full national costume and making a point of leaving early to demonstrate how valuable their time was). Again, within the Asia region, there was a marked juxtaposition of the haves and have-nots, like prosperous Malaysia and impoverished Bangladesh, and this led to difficulties in making regional vice-presidential appointments to represent the shared area.

When tribal supremacies within Kenya made their appearance, they did so very forcibly. The association's president, Frederic Rounthwaite, an avuncular Canadian with a fondness for Britain and a distinguished Second World War record, was introducing a discussion and attempted to put the topic into its local historical context by alluding to Kenya's recent nationhood. In referring to 1963, he used the words 'when you were given independence . . .' and before he could complete his sentence a Kikuyu tribesman in the front row jumped up and shouted angrily, 'We weren't *given* independence, we *fought* for it.' Frederic Rounthwaite was far too nice a person to indulge in gratuitous offence and was so upset by the interruption that he abandoned his text and hastily introduced the next speaker. What was interesting was the fact that it had been a member of the Kikuyu tribe, which had been prominent during the Mau Mau uprising, who had made the noisy interruption, despite the well-documented involvement at the time of the Meru and Embu tribes as well. Everyone present seemed to accept that a Kikuyu would speak on their behalf and continue to take credit for their liberation.

At one point during the General Assembly, discussion over an election to office became very intemperate when two very different contestants were unwilling to compromise in any form whatsoever. It was to the credit of an architectural father figure from West Africa that he was able gently to defuse the situation by recalling a memory of a childhood experience at the mission school where he had been raised. The delegates, some groaning inwardly at the prospect of a lengthy paternal speech, could, nonetheless, not take their eyes off this unfolding and, as it turned out, unarguable piece of theatre. The venerable figure settled his large frame into one of the biggest chairs in the room and carefully draped his flowing robes around him so that his enormous hands rested magisterially on his ample lap. With a slow and deliberate delivery, as if he were addressing a Sunday school class in the shade of a baobab tree, he began to talk using exaggerated gestures. To demonstrate to the audience the nature of opposing points of view, he recalled his sense of wonder as he watched the inevitable movement of the pendulum in the classroom clock and saw how it slowly but surely moved from one side to the other and thereby managed to retain its balance and long-term reliability. His eyeballs followed each tick in one direction and then rolled slowly back to the tock in the other, and he soon had his audience mesmerised. His intervention probably lasted no more than five minutes, but by the time it was over, the evil spell had been broken and no one could quite recall what all the earlier fuss had been about. Patriarchal authority had come to the rescue in a way no Westerner could possibly match and I was left wondering whether his wisdom came from a long tribal tradition of storytelling or whether he was one of life's natural teachers; probably both.

Despite the tensions of the conference, or perhaps because of them, socialising in the evenings was relished, although sadly, ad hoc groups seemed to form on strictly racial lines. On the first night I was invited to dinner at the home of a British architect who was part of an expatriate partnership founded in the 1950s. Post-war London, with all its shortages and restrictions, had offered few attractions for newly qualified architects, so George and Molly Wilson, like others, had come to Kenya, a decision they were not to regret until many years later when the political atmosphere altered dramatically and one of their partners was murdered during a break-in at their bungalow. The Wilsons were generous and well-practised hosts, and they laid on a sumptuous meal, the most memorable course of which comprised luscious, creamy avocados the size of small rugby balls. Like any expatriate community, they were glad to have news and gossip from home and enjoyed the company of occasional visitors from the UK. Years later, George and Molly would retire to England, and George would eventually become honorary secretary to the CAA in London.

Despite the blissful climate, what leisure time we had always seemed to end in a downtown steakhouse, of which there were a number, all very good. It hadn't occurred to me that the climate was temperate enough to raise beef cattle, but I soon learned that the steaks were excellent. Peter Johnson, a thoughtful Australian practitioner and gifted academic, had been to East Africa before and knew that they had excellent steaks but no drinkable wine to go with them, so he had brought with him an extremely good bottle of Penfolds Reserve, which he shared with me one evening. It was a tribute to his knowledge of fine wines that he should have gone to all this trouble to choose a wine that could withstand the rigours of international travel and still seduce the palate.

At the end of the conference, some of us spent the weekend at the Mount Kenya Safari Club before going our separate ways and, having been stuck in a poorly ventilated conference venue for some days, I was anxious to stretch my legs and get some fresh air. The club had a tennis court, but I had some difficulty in finding a partner, until a strange Englishwoman, married to one of the association's officers, said, with a pitying look, that she would take me on if I couldn't find anyone else. Outspoken to the point of truculence on occasions, she wasn't someone you could easily warm to, but it was only a game and hers was the only offer, and in any case, a safety net divided us.

She spun a racquet for service and won. Her permanently red cheeks glowed with satisfaction as she commenced to serve. Everything about her demeanour indicated that playing with me was not only a chore, but a boring one at that. As she was shorter than I was, her delivery was low and relatively easy to return, but the ball did seem to move faster than expected. She quickly won the first game and it was my turn to serve. As I am over six feet tall it was easy for me to get some velocity, and my first service was well in, travelling like a bullet before bouncing clean over the perimeter fencing enclosing the court. My partner's face turned thunderous as I served again and, to my astonishment, the same velocity led to an unplayable bounce within the line that took the ball clean out of the court again. Thirty–love. I then lolloped an easy one over the net which she found so obviously patronising she uncontrollably smashed her return into the net and the ball rolled back lazily to her feet. One of us had to make excuses quickly, so I got in first (for safety's sake), explaining that neither of us was accustomed to the thin air at this altitude which offered little resistance to the ball, completely exaggerating its bounce. I said it was unrealistic to continue, so could I stand her a large gin and tonic? I sounded convincing because it had taken me some time to realise what was happening. I was as breathless as an asthmatic and perhaps shouldn't have suggested a game at all until we were better acclimatised. Predictably, I received no answer as she strode off and I was left to try and find the balls in the thick bougainvillea in fading light.

The following days were my last before returning home, so I gratefully accepted the invitation of a local expatriate to show me more of the country outside the capital. We travelled first to the northernmost slopes of the Aberdare Mountains where, on the edge of the Great Rift Valley's magnificent scarps, stands St Peter's Church, Subukia. Built in 1951, it is a replica of an English medieval parish church, complete with square crenellated tower. I would get used to such architectural anomalies as I travelled the English-speaking world in years to come. After all, I had first encountered a Gothic St Andrew's Cathedral in Singapore some thirty-five years earlier when I accepted that this was the way things were done, in the days before it occurred to anyone to make architectural concessions to local culture and climate.

As it turned out, it was the marvel of *natural* structures that I found most compelling. In Tsavo West National Park I saw termite hills, brick red in colour and standing a storey and a half high. These elaborate and intricate insect-built structures are, in effect, sophisticated community centres containing a labyrinth of passageways served by a natural air-cooling system. Here was organic architecture that stopped me dead in my tracks and, by comparison with the man-made artefacts we were discussing at the conference, it was far more creative and wonderful to behold.

In a country of infinite beauty and myriad lights the eye feasts on countless natural wonders, not least the distinctive form of the trees that occupy the open spaces, whose profiles and silhouettes are the stamp of recollection. The elephant-footed baobab is both clumsy and threatening, whilst the umbrella acacia, with its filament tracery and blow-dry crown, is a vision of Japanese minimalism. No landscape on earth is more imaginatively punctuated.

Such timeless beauty can easily send a Westerner home with a distorted and incomplete picture of Africa as a continent of travel-brochure sunsets, handsome wildlife and vivacious schoolchildren. The reality is different and has every prospect of staying different unless some cataclysmic political intervention takes place affecting the entire continent. Our appointed Kenyan hosts made sure we remained ignorant of the shanty town on the edge of Nairobi. If it was alluded to at all, we were told it housed the criminal element that was the root of all Nairobi's troubles. The gulf between a small, prosperous commercial and professional elite and the remainder of the huge population was only too noticeable, as was the indifference of the haves towards the have-nots, and it was impossible to believe that tribal differences had nothing to do with the situation. No one could have guessed that in a generation's time this particular shanty town would have grown out of all proportion, to merge with the largest and most hellish refuse dump in Africa, where children and stray dogs forage for redeemable scraps in a cloud of flies.

Kenya was not alone in being ruled by a government whose members were largely obsessed with power and money and who would do anything to obtain it, and even more, however reprehensible, to retain it; therein lie the origins of so much unnecessary suffering. Opposition politicians, aid organisations and civil-rights activists show enormous courage in telling the outside world what is going on in the face of often violent repression, although many are inaccurately accused of post-colonial interference and, at best, ignored.

In my more depressing moments I wondered whether the fifty-four countries of the Commonwealth could ever hold together when a number of them were punishing their own people through widespread corruption and maladministration. I was an unpaid volunteer, sometimes giving up part of my holiday entitlement to take part in 'technology-transfer' programmes, and I wasn't surprised to find myself asking such questions – or, worse, wondering what on earth I was doing spending precious time in such places.

But it only needed a single instance, of which there were many, to restore a sense of perspective. I met ordinary people, full of goodness, living in dire circumstances, who retained a dignity, even a nobility, in the face of indescribable hardship. They would greet me with a welcoming smile and invite me to share their evangelical joy at the existence of divine love and the promise of a better future. In that light, how could anyone continue to harbour reservations about what I and some others were doing?

Chapter 35

The Shackleton Legacy

Fascination with faraway lands is prominent in the annals of nineteenth- and twentieth-century history. In an age of imperial adventure and conquest, expeditions of great daring (not all of which were realistically planned) kept an expectant nation on its toes awaiting news of their outcome. Heroes blazed trails across unexplored and inhospitable territory and discoveries, geographical, botanical and anthropological, added to the rapidly growing sum of human knowledge. Original exploration was still possible in a world that hadn't yet begun to shrink and men of historic stature emerged whose example attracted a grateful nation's admiration and served as role models for its children. Such a figure was Sir Ernest Shackleton, the Antarctic explorer, who had attended Dulwich College.

As we had just been appointed architects at Dulwich following successful work at Lancing College in Sussex, I took an interest in its illustrious sons, among whom Shackleton was prominent, not just for the almost unbelievable feat of courage, determination and loyalty for which he is universally known, but as an example to schoolboys whose sense of values were being nurtured by the college.

The narrative is as epic as any Scandinavian saga or Greek myth. Shackleton led an expedition to the Antarctic in the winter of 1914–1915 financed by Sir James Caird, a Dundee jute manufacturer and philanthropist. The vessel in which they sailed, the *Endurance*, had reached a point short of their planned destination when pack ice made further progress impossible.

The expedition members and their dogs were forced to disembark onto the ice of Elephant Island to plan their next move, only to see the pack ice gradually close in around the vessel and eventually crush it to pieces. There was no communication with the outside world and it became obvious that, if they were not all to perish, some rescue plan had to be devised straight away. By this time only one of the *Endurance*'s lifeboats was seaworthy. This was the *James Caird*, named after the benefactor, and it was lowered onto the ice. It was what was known as a whaler, was double-ended, and measured only 22 feet in length. It was rigged with a jib and standing lugsails and offered little protection for its occupants.

After much discussion, it was decided that a rescue party comprising Shackleton and five companions should try and sail it to South Georgia on an 800-mile journey to seek help, leaving the other twenty-two members of the expedition on Elephant Island to fend for themselves as best they could in the meantime. The *James Caird* weighed over one ton and had to be hauled over the ice on sledges at about sixty yards at a time, a task of 'utmost difficulty and misery', but eventually they were able to launch it in clear water. An epic voyage through the Southern Ocean followed and, despite huge seas and much hardship, they made landfall and found help. Meantime, the stranded survivors had to grapple with devastating doubt over the outcome of the rescue mission and seriously wondered whether they would ever live to see their companions again. It was a tribute to their grit and resourcefulness that they managed to keep their spirits up and, according to the expedition diary, each Saturday 'they toasted the Boss and crew of the *James Caird* in melted ice, methylated spirits and ginger from the medical chest'. After what must have seemed an eternity, Shackleton finally appeared with help and eventually brought all his men home safe and sound, an achievement unique in the history of exploration.

Little wonder that many years later Dulwich College decided that the *James Caird*, then on permanent loan to the National Maritime Museum at Greenwich, should be brought back once more to the college as a visible inspiration for the boys. Apparently, it had earlier been stored at the school during World War II and escaped damage when the adjacent science block was destroyed by a bomb, and only then was it agreed to send it to Greenwich. In the following years space in the museum became scarce, resulting in it being moved to another part of the establishment which was small and dark with a low ceiling, so that, to cram it in, it had to be displayed shorn of masts, sails and rigging.

This was how I first saw it when I visited Greenwich at the suggestion of the college, as they had asked me to design an appropriate setting for it in the north cloister of the school, where it would be seen in a fully restored and rigged state by countless pupils when they moved from one part of the school to another. At a time when most boys were absorbed by space travel, Concorde and hands-on Science Museum learning, I couldn't visualise how the sight, however frequent, of an ageing wooden whaler with sagging, faded sails was going to induce the hoped-for inspiration and sense of wonder. I felt that the whole idea had probably resonated far more forcibly amongst members of the college's governing body and an older generation to whom memories of Shackleton's historic venture were fresher and who still subscribed unswervingly to the set of values that had carried them and their families in turn through two world wars.

With the boys in mind, I therefore produced a fairly high-tech display with dramatic lighting behind a plate-glass screen to give maximum effect. Unfortunately, when costed, this was found to involve a five-figure outlay which was thought to be excessive in view of competing demands on the budget for main-line educational purposes. The final setting agreed by the college was fairly basic and did not involve our help, but I could well understand why they chose that option. I've never asked a passing boy what the *James Caird* 'does' for him, but I feel that the impact may be similar to that of peering through the gloom of a Gothic chancel at long-forgotten faded regimental colours honouring bravery on a foreign field in battles long ago.

Despite this, I didn't regard the visit to the National Maritime Museum and its nearby temporary annexe as time wasted. Since it had been established in 1934, increasing pressure on space meant that the contents had spilled out into a row of wartime Nissen huts a mile or so away whose contents were quite wonderful to behold. Here was a maritime Aladdin's cave to bewitch the everlasting schoolboy in all of us and it was difficult for me to keep up with the custodian, such was the fascination of the exhibits I was surrounded with. Each object was neatly labelled with a handwritten, buff card attached by string, giving details of the origin and use, and I couldn't recall ever having seen such an abundance of riches secured only, I noticed, by a garden-shed padlock at the end of each hut.

Passing endlessly fascinating models of ships, brass sextants, manuscripts and tide charts, we finally reached the rescued items from the Shackleton expedition which included a couple of sledges, a sweater, a Bible inscribed by Queen Alexandra, a banjo and, most valuable of all, the logbook. Here was the raw material of legend laid out before me, but I felt ill equipped, humbled by men's bravery and unable to pay them the respect they deserved.

The part of Dulwich College known as 'New College' was designed by Charles Barry, Junior and erected between 1866 and 1870. Barry was the son of the great Charles Barry, architect of the Palace of Westminster, the Reform Club and, incidentally, the Church of St Peter's, Brighton for which I became inspecting architect a hundred years later. The college has a Palladian ground plan but is of eclectic appearance. Barry called it 'North Italian 13th Century', and the walls are constructed in brick and decorated terracotta, reflecting the influence upon him of such places as 'Milan, Florence, Verona, Vicenza, Pavia, Siena and other such towns when I resolved that, if ever opportunity should offer, I would endeavour to use the material in England with as much of the old spirit as my powers would enable me to realise'. Well, he didn't lack spirit, and the resulting confection, a group of now listed buildings, even caught the eye of Camille Pissarro, who painted the scene in 1870.

I was preoccupied by their appearance simply because we had been asked to design a new science teaching block to replace a poorly constructed substitute for the original science building destroyed by wartime bombing. In terms of satisfying the functional brief, the design was relatively easy, but the conspicuous site, seen in front of the main set of buildings, meant that particular attention had to be paid to its external appearance. As no one ever agrees on how architectural contextualism should be interpreted, I fell back on what Lord Holford, a former president of the Royal Institute of British Architects and sometime Brighton resident, had suggested in a conversation we had. He maintained that one should design honestly in a twentieth-century idiom, but at the same time pay special regard to scale, proportion and materials. So this is what I did at Dulwich.

Significantly, Lord Shackleton, son of the explorer, was invited in 1989 to formally open the new science building which was to bear his name. Its siting was not as arbitrary as may first appear, because it soon became obvious that, over the years, new buildings at the college had been added around the periphery with the result that lines of communication from the centre were being extended and journey times from one class to another for staff and students increased. In addition, bad weather made such transfers very inconvenient.

Schools, hospitals, universities, sports centres and the like seem to grow organically – that is to say, haphazardly – to meet a particular need at a particular time, often without a great deal of thought about the cumulative effect. In times of plenty new school buildings pop up to satisfy a current requirement – a swimming pool here, a drama centre there, a chaplain's house somewhere else, usually on the nearest available piece of spare ground. It followed that if we were to design new buildings for Dulwich College, some overall long-term development plan would be necessary as a first step. Although we hadn't specifically been asked to prepare one, when I put the idea to the college, they readily agreed that it made sense if long-term growth and renewal was to be conducted in an orderly manner.

I suggested that before I could start I needed a clear picture of how the school thought it might develop in the longer term. I knew there would be varying views, not to say a bit of axe-grinding and special pleading from certain quarters (there always is), so I suggested that I should talk to everyone on my own as a detached outsider and listen to what emphasis they placed on the future pattern of learning. I did this during the winter months, interviewing well over one hundred staff separately for an hour each, and allocating equal time to all of them. This meant that the assistant groundsman had the same opportunity as the Master (the head), and I asked each of them to tell me in what direction, in their opinion, the school might go in the next ten years and what change in priorities would emerge. I stressed to the college that this wasn't just a piece of democratic tokenism, but an opportunity for ideas to be aired openly outside the hothouse of the common room ('He would say that, wouldn't he?' etc.). My idea was warmly welcomed by the Master, Anthony Verity, whom I came to know as a born leader who could always see a more distant horizon. Everyone seemed happy with the arrangement, so I sat every Friday afternoon, like some friendly uncle, listening to people's visions, ambitions and hang-ups, gradually assembling a picture of what the future might hold. It was an almost ideal way of evolving a master plan and, not surprisingly, when I presented the final version it was easy to reach agreement. For once I was fully satisfied that the new Shackleton science block I was meant to be designing was going to be in the right place to serve its purpose now and enable future development.

Before construction starts, it is customary to dig 'trial holes' to enable the structural engineer to determine the nature of the substratum and its bearing capacity for foundations. It is usual to peg out the 'footprint' of the proposed building and then arrange for two or three excavations to ensure that the geological conditions are consistent before design calculations are made. As luck would have it, they showed that in one corner the substratum was different (changes have to happen somewhere, so there was nothing particularly strange about this), and we patted ourselves on the back for a job well done. Drawings and calculations were completed, a tender price agreed and a contractor appointed, who immediately went to work on the foundation trenches.

This meant that I could think of something else for a few days, and it was a relief to know that, after all these months of preparatory work, the Shackleton science block would soon be rising out of the ground. But it was not to be. Murphy's Law (e.g. the slice of bread from the table always falls butter side down) made its appearance. An anguished contractor came on the phone early one morning to say that, notwithstanding the information derived from the trial holes, the groundwork crew had struck a large area of completely unstable subsoil ('it practically runs through yer fingers, guv'), and because of it, the entire foundations would have to be redesigned, incurring substantial delay and expense. We were totally mystified by this and hurried to the site to see for ourselves. No one we consulted locally could offer any reason for this, but many weeks later when the gossip had done the rounds, we heard from a retired groundsman that on the night the college was hit during an air raid an additional bomb had landed on open ground very near and made a large crater which he and his mate had filled in a few days later with barrow-loads of disturbed soil 'to tidy the place up a bit'. Grass soon grew over it, and as it was beyond the edge of the sports field, no one thought any more about it or the incident. The explosion had damaged nothing and hurt no one so the crater was quickly forgotten. Fifty years later it turned up on our site, and not for the first time was I to hear grumbles about a building project running behind schedule and, worse still, over budget.

Of all the tasks Shackleton had to face, the one he found most distasteful was asking for additional money for his expedition as, though it had been carefully planned, he could not reasonably have anticipated the unforeseen contingencies it would encounter. I knew how he felt.

Chapter 36

London Life Leaves the Capital

The London Life Association's chief surveyor who, on a day-to-day basis, was effectively our client was Derek Brightwell, a larger-than-life figure who would have been equally at home among nineteenth-century merchant adventurers. He was both admired and feared among the City's property fraternity. His employers had the wit to give him a relatively free hand, so successful was he in managing their property portfolio. For instance, they never questioned his lunch-time expenses which, even in the early 1980s, ran to about £20,000 a year. Derek would arrive promptly in the office from his home in Kent, work until mid-morning at the latest, and then leave for lunch, which was usually preceded by a number of barside negotiations with his counterparts sustained by a succession of fortifying pink gins that appeared to sharpen rather than dull his wits. Lunch at the Café Royal, Quaglino's, Sheekey's or somewhere of equal repute would never finish before 4 p.m., but this still allowed him to return to the office 'to sign his letters' before leaving for home or, more likely, heading for Shepherds Market for a 'quick drink' before catching his train. As a lunch host he was both generous and impossible – providing everything to make the occasion memorable, but a nightmare for the maître d', whose lunchtime staff were still bringing extra bottles of claret to the table while most of London was having its tea. He would insist on ordering me a Montecristo cigar and a large Rémy Martin to go with it, and staying sober was almost impossible.

The new Bristol project, where Patrick Caulfield had been commissioned to paint a large mural, was commissioned by the London Life Association, a traditional, highly respected life assurance company. It had outgrown it headquarters in King William Street in the City and, like many comparable organisations, decided to decentralise. This entailed selecting a suitable location, coaxing the entire workforce to move house, and agreeing how information technology could transform working methods to keep the association competitive and at the same time provide a more up-to-date working environment.

Derek Brightwell was, without doubt, the best client I have ever had, rumbustious lifestyle and all, which, I imagine, I half envied. He paid professional fees promptly and fully, and in return demanded 110% service, which he got. On inviting my practice to design what was to become one of our largest and most successful projects, he told me who the co-consultants were going to be, covering site acquisition, structural engineering, quantity surveying and mechanical and electrical engineering. I knew little about the firms he had mentioned but quickly realised that he had assembled a 'dream team'. Within my practice by this time I had a near-perfect team myself, and I was anxious to try it on a sufficiently demanding job that matched its potential.

Adam Suppel, the ex-Polish fighter pilot from my student days nearly forty years earlier, had returned from Canada with his family and had, by now, become my partner. His thoroughness and attention to detail in every aspect of construction had no equal. Cedric Ellis, a flaxen-haired, blue-eyed Yorkshireman of intense interest to the opposite sex, was a gifted designer and quite superlative draughtsman and the easiest possible person to work with. 'You do the silver-tongue bit and I'll draw the lines,' he would say to me. Lastly, I was very fortunate to have as contract administrator Charles Hanks, who had the unenviable task of ensuring the project ran on time and was completed within budget. Charles had been headhunted from the construction industry in the late 1960s, when it was uncommon to include non-architects in the practice, but I had never been convinced that architects showed as much interest or aptitude in running contracts as they did in designing them, so Charles's appointment was the result. There were no gaps in our team and this gave us the confidence we needed to rise to the challenge of designing a 'national' job.

We planned the London Life offices on three floors above a computer suite and included a staff restaurant at roof level with splendid views over the city in general and St Mary Redcliffe Church in particular, the latter once described by Queen Elizabeth I on a visit in 1574 as 'the fairest, goodliest and most famous parish church in England'. A pair of squash courts were planned on one side, but were never used to the extent that they might have been and I guessed that they were included to mollify one or two key squash-playing senior executives who were still in two minds about upping sticks and moving to Bristol. It wasn't just a question of them swapping metropolitan life for a provincial city in the sleepy West Country; their wives had to be persuaded and new schools found and, with a middle-aged management, the proposition may have been too equally balanced for comfort.

'Democratisation' in the office – no single rooms for senior staff and no separate dining room of their own in future – wasn't an easy concept to sell as it meant abolishing time-honoured symbols of status. It also introduced a new (and foreign) word into their vocabulary – *Bürolandschaft*, which means 'open landscaped office'. In such an arrangement everyone worked in a large open space, divided only by low screens to delineate different departments, and the only concession to seniority was the allocation of rather more space around a desk, but it was still in full view of everyone else. Acoustic ceilings absorbed unwanted noise from neighbours and the whole area was fully air-conditioned and permanently illuminated. Windows were triple-glazed to keep out traffic noise and the lighting system was so good that heat recovered from it made a conventional heating installation unnecessary.

Management consultants, systems analysts and architects alike enthusiasti-cally agreed that this was the way forward in the future, but so far few build-ings had been built along these lines. I suggested that, as it was a German innovation in the first place and not an American one for once, we should visit a *Bürolandschaft* building already in use. We went to Hamburg to see the BP European headquarters, a cluster of polygonal buildings designed on this principle. This was something of a revelation and we quickly saw how times had changed. The staff worked 'flexi-time' according to their choice, as long as a core time of 10 a.m. to 4 p.m. was observed. The staff restaurant served breakfast to a surprising number of people who, it appeared, could either make an early start or make breakfast, but not do both together. There were no coffee breaks, but there were areas set aside for beverages to be had when-ever wanted and this was satisfactorily self-regulating because the area was within the open office space and observable by everyone.

We brought back many ideas for application in the Bristol project and, after further reference to one or two other sources, all of whom corrobo-rated our views, we began to finalise our design proposals. A large-scale model and a watercolour perspective were prepared, the last of which was included in that year's Royal Academy Summer Exhibition, and I embarked on a series of staff consultation sessions explaining the benefits of the new way of working. I was not sure that 'consultation' was an appropriate word because it was more a matter of explaining what had already been decided upon, but I tried to answer questions as fairly as I could. In practical terms, there was probably no other way of proceeding as we were only too aware of the apoc-ryphal definition of a camel – 'a horse designed by a committee' – and we had seen such processes fail too often in the past. Nonetheless, one forthright manager was still concerned because, although he worked conscien-tiously, he felt it wasn't always obvious to others. 'Sometimes, when I'm trying to think through a problem I might stand up, yawn, scratch my balls and look out of the window. What the hell will they all think if I do that in full view?'

'They'll think you're human after all and won't bat an eye,' I said.

We completed the designs, which incorporated red engineering brick on the façades to echo neighbouring bonded warehouses and other dockside buildings in Bristol, together with natural stone-aggregate facing panels like those used on the much more recent Roman Catholic cathedral in the city. We were pleased that the tender recommended for acceptance had been submitted by John Laing, a long-established company that had become a household name since it constructed the new Coventry Cathedral and that had a reputation for reliable craftsmanship.

Derek Brightwell chaired monthly progress meetings in Bristol, and these soon settled into a regular pattern and started with most of us joining him for a full English breakfast on the *Bristolian,* which left Paddington around 9 o'clock and reached Temple Meads station an hour and a half later. All the consultants would be asked to report on their progress and the effectiveness of their cooperation with each other (not always a smooth process when art and science are having to work together). Once that was done, the general contractor was invited to join the meeting and was asked, very deliberately, if any of the consultants round the table were holding up progress through lack of documentation. He always said 'no' because, during the previous forty-eight hours, there had always been a series of frantic telephone calls, and reassurances, as well as copious amounts of midnight oil spent to ensure that he said 'no' confidently. Derek knew full well that his question was only a formality, but equally understood that it would always have the desired effect.

Lunch for the team would finish late in the afternoon, by which time some of us could barely stand. All the latest anecdotes culled from livery company dinners, Jockey Club lunches and less orthodox venues had been exchanged, everyone trying to remember them but forgetting them immediately. On one occasion I returned to Paddington with Derek and the final challenge of the day awaited me. After we had settled into our compartment, he bellowed at a passing steward and ordered drinks. These were served in miniatures, which meant that they were taken off the trolley in handfuls 'to make a decent drink'. Having had stomach surgery some years before, I had a very limited capacity for alcohol, but the more I declined the more it sounded like a wimpish excuse, so my protestations were promptly ignored. As he was my client, it would have been foolish to annoy him unnecessarily, particularly as I thought our professional performance was up to scratch, so I resorted to subterfuge. Every time a new whisky miniature slid across the table towards me I waited until Derek was distracted for a moment and then slid the bottle into my nearest pocket. After a few miles I developed the skill of an illusionist and could do it without seeming to move a muscle, but on eventually leaving the train at Paddington I jangled like a milkman at every step and was grateful for every hiss, bang and scrape that platform life could offer. 'No, I'm afraid I can't join you for some refreshment at Shepherds Market, Derek, not on this occasion.' This brought a scowl to his flushed face, but I reckoned that the loss of just one brownie point would be forgotten by the morning.

Difficult though it was, it was all good-natured fun and underneath it Derek had a heart of gold and, indeed, was never above telling a story against himself. He had a very soft spot for his mother, whom he often visited. On one occasion he couldn't wait to tell her how successful he had been in that very morning's property dealings. On his company's behalf, he had just sold a site near St Clement Danes in the City for a handsome profit and felt like a cat with two tails. He had to tell someone, so he told Mum, and to demonstrate the veracity of his story, he retrieved a seven-figure cheque from his wallet for her to see. After glancing at it she said, 'Yes dear, but you do need a haircut.'

Derek was a born raconteur, and although he occasionally fumbled with a Lloyds Bank chequebook cover to remind himself of a recent punchline he had jotted down, he had an exquisite sense of timing. He and another male bon viveur in the property world were going to Cheshire to look at a redevelopment proposal that demanded a prompt decision and, knowing that they couldn't easily do it in a day, decided to stay somewhere pleasant on the Friday night. Neither of them had been to Portmeirion on the North Wales coast, so they thought they'd satisfy their curiosity. Portmeirion is an artful reproduction of an Italianate hill village cleverly designed by Clough Williams-Ellis and has a hotel much used by couples, not to mention Merseyside bosses and their secretaries, seeking a 'romantic' weekend. At breakfast the following morning Derek looked around him at the adjoining tables and, waiting for a lull in the conversation, leant across the table to his companion and said rather loudly, 'It looks as though you and I are the only properly married couple staying here.'

His tastes had an Anglo-Saxon simplicity and he was never happier than when we invited him to a summer show at the Chichester Festival Theatre. One year they were doing a recreation of the Crazy Gang, complete with all the timeless gags and starring Roy Hudd. Well into the show the audience all linked hands and sang 'Underneath the Arches' and Derek, still clutching a balloon given to him by a pretty attendant during the interval, was beyond himself with glee. I didn't think he could ever be happier, until a few minutes later they repeated the old Flanagan and Allen joke about the age of their respective bosses. It ended with, 'That's nothing, my boss is so old that when he takes a girl out for the evening he takes along a younger man and pair of jump leads.'

Looking at Derek, tears of laughter running down his face, one hand clutching his belly and the other still holding his balloon, I knew that, however difficult he could sometimes be, we would all have eaten out of his hand.

The London Life Association headquarters was finished on time, complete with its Patrick Caulfield mural, and was handed over within budget. It looked good, the staff liked it and a leading architectural critic of the day likened its treatment, particularly around the main entrance, to the work of Alvar Aalto, the great Finnish modernist who had introduced an element of humanity into the prevailing machine aesthetic the architectural world still espoused.

The dream team had worked, and we looked forward eagerly to another job on that scale. We were not to know that the late 1980s were to bring the deepest recession in the construction industry since the war, and it would never happen.

Chapter 37

God and Mammon

Selling a new Porsche is a sophisticated task. Whether you are trying to attract a young fund manager in receipt of an unbelievably large bonus or a deep-pocketed, ageing playboy having one last fling is immaterial: they both require careful wooing if they are to disregard the other expensive toys on the market.

I had been asked by Tommy Sopwith whether we would like to design a new showroom and regional office for Porsche, in which one of his companies had taken an interest. He already owned a Mercedes dealership in the Home Counties, and Porsche would add further lustre to his organisation. He hardly expected me to refuse, and I didn't. I immediately set about thinking myself into the rarefied world of glamorous, high-performance automobiles and everything that went with them. Putting aside the all-too-conspicuous, high-gloss features, there remained one aspect that captured my attention – engineering excellence. Porsche obtained this the hard way by only accepting ultimate performance in engine power, control and appearance and, for once in my architectural career, the client wanted a building to match – unmistakable to identify, beautifully engineered and unique in performance. Previous experience had taught me that the commercial sector usually went for maximum floor area for minimum financial outlay, so I was quite unprepared to hear phrases like 'design excellence' and 'top of the market' entering the vocabulary. I couldn't believe my ears. In short, the building had to be as good as the car and speak eloquently of perfection.

I was shown new luxury models which oozed mechanical sophistication and manufacturing finesse and pondered on how an appropriate architectural response could be devised. My building would have to echo the Porsche characteristics – accuracy down to a fraction of a millimetre and unquestionable reliability in all conditions. In short, the medium was to share equal importance with the message. Automobiles go through numerous prototypes to identify problems before going into production, but buildings don't enjoy such luxury. You've got to get everything right first time. In addition, cars are assembled in specialised factories, whereas buildings are erected outside in all weathers and quality control is much harder to manage.

As the site was irregular in shape and tapered sharply at one end, we devised a near-circular plan form made up of twenty delicately faceted sides, all immaculately detailed so that the exterior aluminium panels fitted like a glove. The fully glazed showroom took up much of the ground floor, leaving a mezzanine above for offices and dedicated interview space for intending purchasers. This last requirement took on enhanced significance because I was told that Porsche customers seldom made an impulse buy and always telephoned for an appointment to see an individual sales manager. The atmosphere had to be right, so it was necessary to have smoked salmon and champagne on ice to reinforce the dream after their test drive. The customer expected to be pampered and the motor company needed to sustain the heady illusion for as long as was necessary to clinch a sale. The pile of the carpet had to be luxurious, the canned music soft enough to talk over but virile enough to keep the Bond allusion alive, and the car wax not so strong as to overwhelm the perfume of the disarmingly attractive woman leaning over the customer to pour drinks. This was probably my first awareness of the role in architecture of sensory perception, which many years later was to figure in a totally different context when designing 'healing environments' for hospitals.

When the project was completed everyone was delighted with it and it was only later that we began to realise that it had been delivered just at the point when the vicious recession in the late 1980s had begun to bite. Obviously, the first enterprises to feel the pinch were those at the top end of the market, so within a short time, bowing to the inevitable, the Porsche franchise was discontinued and the building converted for selling Nissan family cars to the multitude. Thereafter, everyone began referring to the building as the 'Nissan hut'; the bargain basement had come out on top after all. The medium and the message had vanished simultaneously, both blowing away like a giant puffball.

As I embarked on another project, the contrast could not have been more vivid. It is probably as necessary as it is salutary to be involved also in designing a building which, in the end, isn't meant to 'matter' particularly to anyone. Our work at the Methodists' West London Mission illustrated the time-honoured God-versus-Mammon stand-off to perfection, although this wasn't universally appreciated by the design team who worked long and hard on this technically complex project.

Some time before, the Methodists had decided to close their centre at Kingsway Hall, best known as the venue of Donald Soper's celebrated sermons, and they moved the West London Mission to Thayer Street, just off Marylebone High Street. It continued to thrive there and, to enable it to work even better, I was asked to enlarge and refurbish the premises adjacent to the existing church to provide for a wider range of church, social and pastoral activities.

Much of the construction work was below pavement level and involved substantial structural engineering. Furthermore, the large extension at the back was complicated by the existence of the neighbours' ad hoc extensions which, because they were there first, had established light or party-wall rights and therefore made designing even more difficult. Technical skill, knowledge of property law and diplomacy were needed in equal measure and, as a result, the design team was larger than usual.

Donald Soper, by then a life peer, was our client and although we dealt with others on a day-to-day basis, his influence was evident throughout. His parents had been devout Methodists from south London and it was no surprise that their son became a probationer minister in that area. Despite, or perhaps because of, his doctorate from the London School of Economics, he fiercely attacked capitalism and was appalled by the poverty he witnessed around him at the time. He was soon attracted to socialism, and his new-found political beliefs coloured his preaching. As long ago as 1926 he began his well-known soapbox oratory which drew large crowds to Hyde Park Corner on a Sunday and later at Tower Hill on a Wednesday and, over a period of years, he became one of the best-known churchmen in Britain. Religion and politics fused effortlessly in his mind. For nearly fifty years he worked – and wrote – tirelessly on behalf of the homeless, single parents and the victims of alcohol abuse.

When our architectural proposals were finally completed, I thought it would be a good idea to mark the occasion by taking the entire team – architects, quantity surveyors, civil and structural engineers, mechanical and electrical engineers and property surveyors – with me to see the plans formally presented to a specially convened meeting. We were all going out for a good meal afterwards, so the team was in relaxed mood and looked forward to meeting a national figure they had heard on radio or television. Following my presentation, Lord Soper was introduced by a church elder and walked towards the lectern, behind and around which all our drawings and perspectives had been carefully hung. Without looking at them he began in a self-deprecating way by alluding to his peerage, the first to be awarded to a Methodist minister – and observed that the House of Lords was 'proof of the reality of life after death'. He then went on to describe the growth

261

of the Methodist church in London and to remind everyone of its aims and mission, stressing the importance of helping the underprivileged and concentrating our attention on non-materialistic objectives in life. He was known as a naturally gifted speaker, never needed a note and was quick with a good-natured riposte if anyone disagreed with him. After twenty minutes or more, which passed very quickly, this slight figure (he was nearing 80) sat down to warm applause and I saw the chairman smile, lean over and say something in his ear, which must have been to the effect that the main purpose of this special meeting was to comment on and, hopefully, formally approve our designs. He rose to his feet again and explained that he had overlooked this and, turning to the audience, said how much he valued their interest and support over the years, how good it was to see so many familiar faces once more and, 'Oh yes – the plans are quite nice,' and then sat down.

'Five words for eight months' bloody slog on a pig of a building?' muttered one of the engineers all too audibly. It was as if the host of a glittering Parisian fashion show had summarised the event by thanking all the designers for arriving so punctually.

It was only later, after we'd seen off ten bottles of good Barolo in a nearby Italian restaurant, that I persuaded the design team that, for Lord Soper in particular and Methodism in general, the five words were both fair and apt and, after all, for everything that the congregation now planned to do, the buildings were only a means to a end and, unlike Porsche, didn't need to be an end in themselves. In the late-evening fug of Bertorelli's restaurant, the engineers simply blinked at me.

Many years earlier, one of the first chaplains at Sussex University, Duncan Forrester, described how he had recently returned from India, and had passed through a very new Charles de Gaulle Airport in Paris on his way home. Hours before, he had witnessed the despair of street dwellers and crippled beggars in the teeming slums of Bombay and now he was being effortlessly wafted from one air-conditioned flight to another in a transparent, perfumed capsule that glided through the airport's space-age interior without him having to stir a muscle, sweeping past shops full of every conceivable indulgence with which to impress a girlfriend or pamper an ego. 'How dare we sleep at night?'

Chapter 38

Extra-Mural Activities

I had been persuaded to stand for election to the council of the Royal Institute of British Architects (RIBA). Together with other newcomers, I thought I would find a national, or, indeed, international forum discussing architecture, which would have been an attractive prospect, but hadn't realised the extent to which professional housekeeping necessarily dominated each agenda. Once there, I found myself looking at papers that touched on every current issue in practice, education and finance but seldom seemed concerned with architecture itself. After a while I made a specific request that at least one agenda item at each meeting should be devoted to an honest and informed debate about some aspect of architecture, and this wish was granted, but not quite in the way I expected.

As students, we were told that professions of all kinds were there to 'serve the public'. While there were practitioners who, because of their business acumen, seemed to serve themselves first, there were also, at the other end of the spectrum, poorly managed idealists on permanently bad terms with their bank manager. The worker-priest movement in South America had received a lot of media attention at the time. Spurning Catholic pomp, left-of-centre idealists thought they would get closer to their pastoral flock by sharing their harsh lifestyle. Some of the more romantic souls in architecture found this vision attractive. They slept with a clear conscience and discontented wives who disliked having to go out to work to keep the ideal afloat. Into all of this came the Community Architecture movement, which was an attempt to change the emphasis of a professional elitism whereby architects thought they knew what the public wanted and gave it to them for a fee with the hope that, in the process, they would be noticed by the trendy architectural press obsessed with innovation and glitz. It wasn't difficult to see how such an attitude alienated the very public the profession was meant

263

to serve. Expensive ego trips for up-and-coming practitioners did nothing for someone on a housing waiting list. What was needed was a grass-roots approach. It was time to think again, question purely prestigious projects and concentrate on the unglamorous task of reviving existing communities without wholesale demolition, thereby retaining some repairable terraced housing, for instance, and with it some of the social cohesion that would otherwise be shattered by 'comprehensive redevelopment'.

Under the leadership of a northern architect, Rod Hackney, Community Architecture took off and we re-examined how we could purposefully consult local people about what they really wanted and then, having achieved local financial support, work alongside them to achieve a shared community objective.

This was a new way of going about things, but having no knowledge of social science, I felt ill equipped to deal with any suitable projects in this way, Eventually it occurred to me that my preoccupation with architecture and building a successful practice had left me with little time to do anything else or indeed think about anything else, so I had to remedy this – and quickly. Opportunities come in various forms, some more curious than others, but it seemed the right time to do it, and my first introduction to the world outside architecture came at the time of a general election, when I was approached by a generous-hearted Liberal activist Frances Hix and asked whether I would offer to take voters to the polls in my car. I wasn't a Liberal, at least not consciously so, but I was interested to meet a group of local people I would otherwise never come across and get closer to the community in the process,

The procedure was simple. I would be given a list of known Liberal supporters who, by early evening, had not voted on the day, and I would offer them a lift to the polling station before it closed at 9 p.m. Last-minute amendments to the list were made by earnest party volunteers with a dying Biro and I was told I had about twenty calls to make. The first house was easy to find but difficult to access, such was the overgrown front garden. The door had a broken knocker and no bell, so I tapped loudly with my knuckles. There was no response. Out of the corner of my eye I glimpsed the glow of a television set behind heavy, faded curtains so I knocked harder. The door remained unanswered, so I trod gingerly into what many years ago would have been the flower bed surrounding the bay window and knocked on the glass before returning to the front door.

"Oo are you? Woger want?' crackled an elderly voice. It was difficult to tell her age – it could have been anything between 60 and 80 – but she moved very slowly and seemed very resentful of my intrusion. I began my well-rehearsed introduction explaining that I understood she was a Liberal party supporter and as she hadn't yet found the opportunity to cast her vote I'd be delighted to offer her a lift to the polling station. She narrowed her eyes at me and said, 'No, I'm watching telly,' and began to close the peeling door. 'I'll wait until your programme is finished if you like,' I added foolishly. She still shut the door and I noticed through the dirty window that she had returned to the television. Fortunately I saw the credits roll across the screen a few moments later so, with what I hoped was a winning smile, I tapped again on the window.

After a long pause, she reappeared at the door and muttered, 'Orrite then. I'll 'ave to put my things on; you wait there.' After five minutes she appeared in a felt hat, faded scarf and long woollen overcoat.

'I can't leave 'im behind,' she said.

'Who?' I asked.

'Me dog, 'e gets lonely.'

'Why not bring him along. I'll wait while you call him.'

''e can't walk,' she stated flatly.

'Do you have to carry him, then?' I enquired.

'Me back's bad. You carry 'im.'

'Where is he then?' I asked nervously.

'On the couch, whereja think? And don't forget 'is blanket.'

I entered the dingy parlour and in the gloom saw and smelled an old, arthritic dog on a tattered cushion. He was huge; no wonder she couldn't lift him. I also became aware of suppurating sores on his flank. Taking a deep breath, which I was determined to hold for as long as possible, I carried the creature out of the room and into the car. 'Next to me; 'e doesn't like cars,' she directed. I eased them both into position and set off at funereal pace because she told me that fast cars are dangerous. To lighten the occasion, I enquired what television programme she had been watching. '*Dysentery*,' she growled. 'I think you mean *Dynasty*,' I suggested. 'Yes, *Dysentery*.'

Unloading them both at the polling station, I waited endlessly while she fumbled with her glasses (she'd brought the wrong ones, apparently) and pondered who she was going to vote for, she took even longer than I feared. Then the whole process had to be performed in reverse, and by the time we reached her house I was appalled to see that my first lift had taken one and a half hours, and there were nineteen more people on my list.

I sat in the car with all the doors wide open examining a road map for my next address, and by the time I thought the car was fit enough to carry another well-intentioned Liberal, set off at speed. A bright, clean-faced facade greeted me this time, and my spirits rose. The door was answered promptly by a youngish man in spectacles carrying a Walkman and I issued my customary invitation to take him to the polling station. 'No thanks. I've just had double glazing fixed,' he said, smiling as he closed the door. I found the answer seriously disconcerting and for weeks afterwards searched my mind for something I might have said or omitted to say that prompted such a breezily surreal response, but still. I couldn't rationalise the short exchange. At this stage I toyed with the idea of chucking it all in and admitting defeat before I damaged the Liberal party's prospect still further, but, after a moment' reflection, I thought I'd have just one more go.

The next address, Alexandra Villas, was known to me, as I had lived in the street as a small child before the war. Since then many of the larger houses had been converted into flatlets, so I wasn't surprised to see 'Flat C' added to the postal number on my list. Having partly regained my confidence I rang the bell and didn't have to wait long before I heard someone on the staircase lalala-ing a number from the American musical *Oklahoma!* I waited while latches were unfastened and security chains released and the door swung open to reveal a heavily perfumed woman of uncertain age wearing a loose silk shift clutching a bottle of sherry in one hand and steadying herself on the door frame with the other.

'I believe you're Liberal and I would like to take you to the vote in my car,' I began.

Still humming, she raised her eyebrows, looked at me thoughtfully and said, 'Darling, *you* can take me anywhere.'

I glanced at my watch: it was five minutes to nine, so I made my apologies for being so late and disturbing her unnecessarily. I wished her well and departed.

One additional vote for three hours' effort, and even then the old woman with the dog may have voted for the wrong candidate – I could have scored nil. By the time I got back to the Liberal HQ they were in the middle of clearing up and preparing to go to the Corn Exchange for the count where, some time after midnight, they would hear the returning officer declare the successful candidate. There was a lot of noise and excitement and I was hardly noticed as I handed in my impoverished list. 'Thank you for trying, dear,' said some kind matron sporting a large orange rosette.

My brush with humanity was over; perhaps there were other ways of discovering one's own community.

Whereas I had expected a degree of uncertainty in the unfamiliar world of local politics, I though I was on fairly predictable ground when I accepted an invitation from the senior partner of an old-fashioned structural engineering practice to accompany him to look at a recently announced development scheme in southern France.

A national initiative to attract commerce, industry and leisure development to what was called Le Grand Delta, a triangle straddling the lower reaches of the Rhône, and stretching from Marseille in the east to Montpellier in the west, had been announced to the media with typical Gallic panache.

Being low-lying and marshy and including wide tracts of the Camargue, the area had remained underdeveloped, but it was now thought that employment opportunities and faster economic growth would flow from the implementation of an ambitious master plan for the entire zone, deserving a national initiative which would put it unmistakably on the map. As a result of an expensive international advertisement campaign using the latest techniques in visual presentation, a special trip had been arranged to attract outside investment from Britain and other adjacent European countries to complement the decision by Renault to site a new assembly plant there. My engineering host had agreed to examine the development potential on behalf of one of his major industrial clients, and as I used his practice on a number of current jobs, he thought that I might find it interesting.

On arrival at Lyon airport we took a reserved train all the way down the Rhône Valley to Marseille, where we were transferred in a sleek white tender to a cruise ship lying offshore which had been specially commissioned for the occasion. The individual cabins resembled small state apartments and the air-conditioning was set at just the right humidity to suit the freshly plucked roses on the bedside table; the temperature was then adjusted for the champagne which had been placed in the ice bucket before we arrived. We felt parched after our journey.

A sumptuous dinner was arranged in a waterside restaurant nearby, and when finally we were back on board we fell asleep in just the right (malleable, I suppose) frame of mind the organisers had hoped for. After breakfast the following day we were whisked away to a congress centre where (there had to be a downside) we listened to a seemingly unending succession of voluble politicians and project managers who lauded the new enterprise and tried to convince us that we would have difficulty in imagining a more noble, creative and epoch-making scheme anywhere else in the world. Superlatives tripped off the tongue with such polished ease that I was at a loss to know what would come next. I should have guessed – a formal luncheon at the Hotel de Ville hosted by the mayor, the stepped approach to which was lined by a ceremonially uniformed, sword-bearing, brass-helmeted detachment of the Garde du Corps. A subtly balanced menu encouraged us to consume more than was prudent until, rather reluctantly, we departed in waiting luxury coaches which would take us to carefully selected sites in the region, one of which had already been developed – a sailing and leisure centre with the strange title of La Grande Motte.

Having disembarked from our coaches, we viewed it across a narrow inlet and saw an abstract composition in glistening white cement looking as futuristic, with its sweeping curves and daring cantilevers, as any of Mitterand's Parisian *Grands Projets* would do twenty years later. It was all a bit flash.

When I looked around, I saw that our party included industrialists, property advisers and investment bankers in addition to civil and structural engineers, but I turned out to be the only architect.

Not surprisingly in the circumstances, a television crew awaited us and, following descriptive remarks by the development area chief executive, the TV producer turned to our party and said how much he would like to hear our response to witnessing such an innovative, post-Corbusian concept. We were unprepared for this and looked at each other sheepishly. My engineering host, I'm sure as an act of courtesy and generosity, said that his guest was an architect and might be able to contribute. I protested that I wasn't an *urbaniste*, I was only an architect, but to no avail: there wasn't an *urbaniste* present, and an architect would be the next best thing.

In the meantime I had discovered that the TV crew had come direct from the wild beauty of the Camargue where they had been filming little-known insect life for a major natural history channel, and they were still accompanied by their entomologists, who had come on here for the ride.

My protests were fruitless and, feeling very uncomfortable with the situation, I asked for a few minutes to gather my thoughts as I gazed across the water to the avant-garde spectacle laid out before me. The camera crew were getting restless, so I thought I must start, if only to show willing. My head spun with platitudes and generalisations and I had to consciously avoid repeating my limited vocabulary of *magnifique, sensationnel, remarquable* and (I chanced it once) *coup de théâtre*. After a while observations came to me in a more ordered fashion and I continued to express them as intelligibly as I could. The cameras were swivelling from my head to the architecture and back again as I spoke and I was beginning to get into my stride when I became aware that the cameras were slowly and surely descending down my body. Visions of sweaty armpits, undone flies or some other horror ran across my screen as I droned on about La Grande Motte until, drawing breath, I happened to glance down and a few inches away from my feet was the largest dung beetle the entomological scientists and their camera crew had ever seen. The sound equipment was promptly turned off and La Grande Motte forgotten, and the entire crew crowded in to record a remote species that had eluded them during their entire stay in the Camargue earlier in the week. The enthusiasm and sense of relief was palpable; immediate kinship abounded, and everyone was wreathed in smiles as they began to hug each other tearfully. For some very French reason I got a big hug as well, so I took it that the whole excursion that afternoon had been an unqualified success. I had successfully made the transition from the surreal to the theatre of the absurd.

Chapter 39

More Extra-Mural Activities

The geographical boundary of the Diocese of Chichester follows that of the county of Sussex. Neither make much demographic sense in today's terms, and the siting of the diocesan cathedral is particularly perverse, situated as it is near the Hampshire border. Having been persuaded to become a Trustee of the Chichester Cathedral Development Fund, set up to provide a reliable source of income for ongoing restoration, I was once asked to visit Winchelsea and Rye at the furthest point from the cathedral but just within the Diocese to encourage parishioners to contribute towards the upkeep of 'their' cathedral. I was courteously received and the audience showed polite interest in my slides illustrating decaying gargoyles, laminating glass and subsiding buttresses. My prepared notes reminded me to stress the ownership of this great building by *all* congregations within the diocese, which prompted the meeting's chairman to observe drily that, from where they were, four other cathedrals were a lot nearer to them, and one of these was in France.

On the long wet drive home that late-November evening I seriously wondered if I was being asked to flog a dead horse, but after a good night's sleep concluded that, wherever it was, the cathedral was of such architectural and historic importance that we just had to persevere with the fundraising campaign. After all, the sight of its great spire in a wintry sun had unexpectedly moved me as a young Army recruit in Chichester over thirty years earlier, and I wasn't alone in wanting it to remain for others who would follow. And in any case, had it not been the seat of Bishop George Bell, who had gone to so much trouble commenting on my student dissertation? As Ian Nairn wrote in Pevsner's *Sussex* in the *Buildings of England* series, 'It is a well-worn, well-loved, comfortable fireside chair of a building − St Francis, not St Bernard; St Augustine of Hippo, not St Augustine of Canterbury.'

As a special event, it was decided to hold an auction of donated objects in aid of the Chichester Cathedral Trust, and Sotheby's kindly offered to arrange it and also forgo their usual commission. Those more conversant than I knew the best way to elicit appropriate gifts, and once Her Majesty the Queen had offered to donate a silver George III vase-shaped mustard pot, and the Queen Mother an equally fine piece, the marquesses, lords and honourables soon fell into place and everyone else followed suit. Altogether some six hundred lots were assembled. Among the donors was John Piper, the internationally known artist who had recently designed tapestries for the cathedral reredos. Before the war he had experimented with abstraction and later developed an enviable reputation as an official war artist, as did Henry Moore. After the war he collaborated with the composer Benjamin Britten, designing sets for some of his recently composed operas, and also showed himself to be a gifted photographer and a well-matched artist for John Betjeman's books of verse. Perhaps his greatest achievement was the design of the great baptistery window in Basil Spence's new Coventry Cathedral.

John Piper had donated a large gouache entitled *Romanesque Variations* which was illustrated in the Sotheby's catalogue for the event. The moment I saw it I was tempted. I had bought nothing at auction before and I knew I couldn't afford it (the usual dispiriting litany of mortgage, school fees and bank overdraft never seemed to leave me), but such was Piper's compelling influence when I was an architectural student that I always yearned to own one of his paintings and it struck me that this opportunity might never be repeated. Many of Piper's paintings had a dramatically dark sky which made the subject matter, usually a building or a ruin, stand out conspicuously. This technique intrigued us as students and, when drawing perspectives, we never lost an opportunity to set what was often an indifferent design against a threatening sky to make it look more convincing. Whilst this never fooled the shrewd eye of our tutor, we nonetheless enjoyed doing it. We were all amused and encouraged to read a contemporary account of John Piper's commission by King George VI to prepare a series of paintings of Windsor Castle, where the artist stayed for a while. These were executed in his characteristic, vigorous style complete with dark skies which threw the bleached stone walls of the castle into prominence. Upon showing the finished articles to the King, whose taste could never be described as avant garde, the only response the artist received was '. . . and what a pity you had such bad weather while you were staying here, Mr Piper'.

The Sotheby's auction took place locally at a small, rural branch in Pulborough near Chichester, and this turned out to be to my advantage. Most people attending were local residents who wished to support the Cathedral and, by definition, did not share the modern tastes of their counterparts in London. In short, John Piper wasn't to their taste and the bidding for Lot 2051 *Romanesque Variations* was sluggish. I found myself up against telephone bidders, presumably London galleries, whose huge markups meant that they were probably unprepared to go beyond the point I thought I could match and, eventually, after a few anxious and sweaty minutes, the picture was mine. Elated at the prospect of taking it home, I had little idea how much pleasure it would give me over the years.

As its title gave no clue to the place of origin, I wondered how best to find out and concluded that the only way to do this was to write direct to John Piper. I felt diffident about doing this as here was someone with an international reputation who was getting on a bit and probably didn't bother with letters from total strangers. I wrote nonetheless. By return of post I received a disarmingly modest, friendly, handwritten letter which read:

Nov 23 1982

Dear Mr Wells-Thorpe

Many thanks for your letter – I spend a lot of winter evenings making drawings from old note-book sketches of mine, or from photographs. One of my favourite sources for the latter is books on Romanesque architecture and sculpture in Germany and France. The drawing you have is one of these. I find it makes me look much more closely at carvings to draw them – and it seems a legitimate use of photographs (half of which are by me, anyway). I cannot tell you where the carving is that I did 'variations' on. It would mean looking through dozens of books to find it.* The date is the winter of 1979 into 1980. I hope the picture will continue to give pleasure.

Good wishes

Yours sincerely

John Piper

* It is not from one of my own notes or photographs. I think it may be a carving in the museum (a splendid museum) at Toulouse.

In an age of celebrity, when agents, middlemen, media commentators, unauthorised biographers and others make direct access to creative minds almost impossible, it was reassuring to be reminded that those blessed with universally recognised talent are often very natural in their dealings with others but, alas, are so often prevented from doing so by the predatory, self-aggrandising coterie of sycophants who surround them.

273

Equally surprising, when considering the openness and modesty displayed by the genuinely famous, was the response to a question I put recently to a celebrated yachtswoman. It came about like this. Continuing my search for a fuller understanding of the community my profession was meant to be serving, I accepted an invitation to join, and later chair, the BBC Advisory Council in the south. Its terms of reference were to comment on the media output to ensure that, as far as possible, the 'public interest' (whatever that was) was adequately protected and that the BBC's founding principles were being upheld. Such lofty ideals are easy to recite but difficult to reconcile with day-to-day decisions taken by producers so, from to time to time, a special event is planned to enable the corporation's managers and broadcasters to meet members of the public.

Such a meeting was arranged at a large Southampton theatre. Here, short presentations were to be given by regional directors and programme makers, to be followed by questions from the public, which I would chair. On such occasions I had always found it difficult to raise the level of questioning from pernickety detail to the broader issue and I recalled the early pioneering days of BBC Radio Brighton when, irrespective of what was on the agenda, the meeting of its advisory committee would always end by arguing about whether or not we should use the 24 hour clock and why there was never enough money to air-condition the basement studios. Try as we might, we were seldom able to rescue the agenda from persistent moans about each of these perennial issues, and this rendered the meeting useless for the hard-pressed manager trying to run the station.

The Southampton meeting was not particularly different: it was freely open to anyone and had been widely advertised on television, radio and public billboards. Perhaps if we had charged a fiver each and made them queue in the rain beforehand, the more informed and focused viewer might have been attracted by the serious intent of the event, but as it was we got an average 'studio audience' who came along with their comfortable prejudices and sometimes their knitting. It was a long grind which started with an insistent member of audience who demanded that I took her question first as she needed to leave promptly 'to be home in time for the BBC Nine O'Clock News'. My colleagues weren't sure whether to be gratified or frustrated by such a pronouncement, but answered her question in good part.

The panel, some of whom had travelled down from London specially for the session, and all of whom were sacrificing an evening to attend, were partly rewarded by a private dinner afterwards at a nearby hotel when pent-up irritation could be safely released over drinks. It was customary to invite a local 'personality' to join us on such occasions, and this time the yachtswoman

Clare Francis was much in the news for her participation in a singlehanded transatlantic race. I seated her on my right, and not knowing a great deal about sailing put a seasoned Cowes Regatta hand on her other side. They both got on very well and it was some time before all the technical experiences had been exchanged and she turned to me. Having read about her exploits, I was intrigued to know about how she coped with the loneliness and sense of desolation on another occasion when she was becalmed for so long. She didn't look a bit like a hardened sea-farer; her high cheekbones, delicate face and small frame made her look far too vulnerable. 'What did you do in such despairing circumstances?' I asked. She looked at me thoughtfully for a moment and said disarmingly 'I cried; and then when I'd finished I got on with what I was meant to be doing.'

Here was another instance of openness and modesty by someone as well-known, in her own way, as John Piper, and who gave an equally simple, pragmatic answer to a question, causing her to rise even further in my estimation as a result of it.

During the last of my forays into the wider community I had joined the Institute of Directors. This may sound strange, but it came at a time when the council of the Royal Institute of British Architects was grappling with a redefinition of 'professionalism' to suit the late twentieth century, and was asking itself whether architects should be allowed to advertise, practice with limited liability and even become directors of their own firms. It was a straight fight between the courteous, gentleman amateurs who still espoused nineteenth-century ethical (but not very commercial) values and the younger turks who could see their inherited territory being eroded by other organisations that were bound by no such constitutional constraints. This debate became worldwide and eventually extended well beyond the bounds of architecture. When 'pro-directorships' won the day, I converted my practice into a limited liability company and became a director.

The Institute of Directors divided its membership into county groups, and after a while I was asked to chair the Environment Committee at the London Headquarters and take over the chair in Sussex where my practice was still based. We held an annual luncheon to which we customarily invited a local 'personality' who, hopefully, would share with us the secret of his or her success. This particular year I had arranged for it to take place in Brighton's oldest and best-known hotel, the Old Ship, where, history records, King Charles II spent his last night before fleeing to France following defeat at Worchester. In directorial terms the figure of the moment was unmistakably Anita Roddick, who, with her husband, had opened the first Body Shop in

Brighton, defying conventional wisdom and probably perplexing her bank manager. Her worldwide success had turned her into the patron saint of small enterprises and, more particularly, environmentalists, so I felt happy with our choice of speaker – one of us, in more ways than one.

So happy was I at the thought of hosting such an event that I spoke to the manager, John Richards, who kept a surprisingly good cellar, some of which he reserved 'for special occasions'. He gave us the Paganini Room, where the great violinist had once placed, the event recorded on a plaque below the surprisingly small balcony from which he had performed. I also arranged for a rather good claret to accompany our main course, and John made a point of keeping our table topped up. Everyone seemed to be enjoying themselves, and as I congratulated myself by emptying a third glass, I became aware of the need to get my introductory remarks in the right order. 'Our speaker is a well-known Brightonian Anita Roddick, co-founder of the Body Shop, who has just received the Veuve Clicquot Business Woman of the Year Award in London.' Simple enough, I thought, so I continued talking and drinking until I glanced at the clock and remembered that some of our members had to return to their offices that afternoon, so I then rose and heard myself say:

'I have great pleasure in welcoming Anita Roddick who, you will all know, has just received the Veuve Clicquot Body of the Year Award.'

Chapter 40

George Cross Island

When I was invited to Malta by David Pace, representing its Chamber of Architects and Civil Engineers, I realised how little I knew about the island. One has random preconceptions about places unvisited, usually drawn from a collection of loosely recalled facts. From the back of my mind (from a cardboard box marked 'miscellaneous') I retrieved one or two leads, inconsequential but useful as a starting point. Hadn't St Paul suffered shipwreck on the island on his way to Rome as a captive? And didn't Caravaggio, the Italian artist, escape justice for his colourful misdemeanours in Italy by fleeing to Malta where, through painterly skill and artful insinuation, he was not only welcomed by the Church but had himself installed as a Knight of the Order of St John?

In World War II, and this I could recall personally, the entire island was awarded the George Cross for Gallantry to sustain their morale when they were being besieged by the Axis powers, constantly bombarded by the Italian air force and incurring huge loss of life. At the outbreak of hostilities the only cover the RAF could muster comprised three elderly but serviceable biplanes nicknamed *Faith, Hope* and *Charity*, who repeatedly saw off much more modern Italian squadrons. As a schoolboy, I possessed three Dinky Toy model Gloster Gladiators of identical mark and followed every wireless bulletin intensely in the hope of hearing news of their latest exploits, so that I could replicate their gallant manoeuvres in hand-held combat in my own private theatre of war.

Later on in life, I discovered that former leisured classes, characterised by the Oswald Sitwell circle and others like it, would escape to either the French or the Italian Riviera to avoid the rigours and pea-soup fogs of a London winter. I assumed, therefore, that at that time of the year the Mediterranean around Malta would be pleasingly warm during the day and immune from the gales and pounding seas of the north. During my first visit, which only lasted a week, I was surprised to find myself forced into my old British Warm with the collar turned up against the biting wind and driving rain.

Following my introduction to the Commonwealth Association of Architects in Hong Kong, I had been asked to accept the oversight of what was rather grandly called the Europe Region of the association. The CAA (which covered architecture in over fifty countries) served its members through five regional organisations – Africa, Asia, Australasia, the Americas (Canada and the West Indies) and Europe, and mine was, by far, the smallest. Apart from the UK, it comprised Cyprus, Malta and Gibraltar. The object of my visit was to find out which areas of practice or technical education were of particular concern to them locally, how they were getting on with their government, and whether there was anything we could do centrally that might help. Coincidentally, the CAA had been founded at a conference in Malta in 1965 and had elected a British chairman, Sir Robert Matthew, so my visit took on added significance. I was also reminded that Dom Mintoff, twice the island's Prime Minister, had read architecture in Britain before entering politics.

I was very aware that although many codes of practice and contract law in Commonwealth countries were based on original British models, the UK must not now be seen as *primus inter pares* (first among equals) in its dealings, when compared with other member states. This wasn't always easy to reconcile, as we were expected to take initiatives and 'lead from the front', and at the same time, not pretend that *our* way was the only one.

Malta is only about 120 square miles in area and supports a population of a little over a third of a million, most of whom are Roman Catholic. The language is of Semitic origin and is thought to derive from Carthaginian and Phoenician tongues, which accounts for visitors' difficulties in spelling and pronouncing place names such as Marsaxlokk, Ta' Cenc and Birzebbuga. However, the English language is widely understood, and this probably stems from when the Maltese requested the protection of the British Crown in 1802, after they had successfully risen against the French garrison installed by Napoleon.

Malta is popular with British tourists, particularly those who have served in the armed services and been stationed there. Instantly recognisable red English telephone boxes (designed by the celebrated architect Sir Giles Gilbert Scott, known for Liverpool Cathedral and also for what would become Tate Modern), equally famous red pillar boxes, a King George VI bar and even a Brighton Store offered reassurance to tourists shy about a foreign tongue and worried about not being able to find fish and chips or familiar brands of beer.

Tourism was beginning to assume primary importance, and with it came the emergence of casinos. On one occasion, after a particularly fruitless day when it never stopped raining and my room stank of paraffin-stove fumes, I was determined to get a bit of fresh air even if night had already fallen. The Dragonara Hotel was situated at the end of a short, rocky promontory outside the principal city of Valletta, and from where I was staying, it looked like a brisk twenty-minute walk in each direction. I needed a drink and a change of scenery so, despite the awful weather, I set off into the wind and salt spray. On this journey I soon discovered that most of the island's coastline is rocky, and yet another illusion – that of warm, sandy Mediterranean beaches – was quickly dispelled. On arrival at the hotel it was clear that most activity was not in the bar but in the adjacent casino, so, after a couple of drinks, I sauntered in to watch the proceedings. The scene would have been familiar to anyone socially conversant with Monaco or Cannes: small groups seated intently around tables and quietly attired in evening dress. Not knowing the first thing about professional gambling, I was curious to watch a table playing blackjack, where participants were being observed by equally well-dressed guests who had wandered through from the bar. I edged my way slowly into a nearby group and looked at the immaculate, brightly lit baize on which the game was being played. Only after I had attempted to discover how the game was conducted did I glance at the players' faces, whose expressions ranged from the casually supercilious to the professionally confident. Where were they all from, I wondered – local or visitors; straight or bent; amateur or doing it for a living? And then, at least from the back, I thought I recognised a familiar head among the seated spectators, but just as quickly discounted what I saw. After all, this was hundreds of miles away, and his calling was as far removed from the world of green eyeshades and minders as could possibly be imagined. But curiosity made me look again. Unable to get a closer view, I edged my way round the group and got much nearer. Despite my conviction that it couldn't possibly be, I realised that it had to be the Venerable Archdeacon of Lewes, Peter Booth. I'd never seen any clergy, let alone an archdeacon, in a black tie at a gaming table, so I gave way to an irresistible urge to move even closer and whisper into his ear, 'Peter, does your bishop know you're here?' He spun round and, with equal surprise but no hint of embarrassment, exclaimed, 'John, what are *you* doing here? How lovely to see you! Come and have a drink.' As archdeacon, Peter Booth had been a generous and supportive patron, having recommended me as architect for a number of new 'daughter' churches being planned in expanding parishes in the diocese, the best known of which is the Church of St Edward in Burgess

Hill, Sussex. He had been in the navy during the war and actively involved with the heavily resisted Allied landings in Italy. On demobilisation, he had been appointed to a run-down east London parish where his energetic and dedicated work in the community had raised levels of social awareness and had deservedly earned him an MBE. He had then come to the parish church of St Peter in Brighton before becoming the youngest of the three archdeacons in the diocese, and it was in that last capacity that I first met him. (It had been the oldest of the three, the frock-coated Archdeacon of Chichester, who had given me such a rough time over the 'relocatable church' project some years earlier.)

Clergy at any level are poorly paid and can seldom afford a decent holiday. This had been recognised by an understanding parishioner who kept a holiday home on Malta and, out of season, made it available to friends. Recalling Peter's Royal Navy links with the island, he persuaded him and his wife Diana to take it for a week. And what better way of spending an inexpensive and entertaining evening than being a spectator at the tables? I reassured myself that the bishop would have been heartened by his archdeacon's initiative in escaping the cloister and the committee room to discover how the rest of the world lived.

I admired Peter unreservedly and it was only because of Diana's serious illness in later years that he later ruled himself out of accepting further preferment as suffragan bishop.

Some years later, in 1988, I found myself back in Malta with a very different remit. At the behest of the Chamber of Architects and Civil Engineers again, the Commonwealth Foundation had agreed to fund a preliminary study which would lead to the preparation of a structure plan for the Maltese Islands, which included Gozo and other adjoining islets. A structure plan is essentially a proposal describing a development strategy, as distinct from an old-style development plan, which was site-specific and proved to be too detailed and too rigid in practice.

Jeffery Switzer, a leading land economist from Cambridge, had already been approached by the Commonwealth Foundation as he possessed a considerable fund of knowledge through having worked in Malta in the 1960s and was very conversant with earlier policies and legislation. As the scope of the study was to cover the design and provision of housing and also include a section on architectural history and the 'heritage' aspect of the survey, I was invited to be the co-consultant. This was probably because they wanted a distinct 'outsider' (in Malta, everyone seems to be related in one form or another, and most certainly, everyone seems to know everyone else's business), and also because my Commonwealth link carried the name of the funding body and suggested a wider European context.

J. F. Q. Switzer was a courteous, quietly spoken man of considerable erudition whose diplomacy and thoroughness made him an ideal appointment. He was a joy to work with. The terms of our assignment were 'to establish the political, economic, social and physical planning objectives which the Structure Plan is intended to achieve' in the first place, and then go on to: ascertain what basic data were required for the task; advise on how the plan should be prepared; identify what disciplines and skills were available to do this; suggest legislative and administrative means necessary for the plan's implementation; and, finally, draft terms of reference for the preparation of the plan.

My first reaction was that all this would take months and push us well beyond our allocated budget and timetable, but Jeffery's calm reassurance persuaded me that, with discipline, we might just be able to do it. What neither of us knew at that stage was that everyone we would speak to in the following weeks would emphasise the pressing urgency of our study because unplanned and often unauthorised developments were taking place by the day and each one would make the final recommendations of any structure plan harder to implement.

We did not know until after our arrival in Malta that the Commonwealth team had been expected to arrive the previous year; that an application had been made a year earlier for EEC funding for the preparation of the structure plan, setting out in great detail what it should contain; that the political and other objectives of the structure plan had already been agreed and were just about to be approved by Parliament; and that a large number of consultants had been appointed and many of them were already at work on sectoral plans or proposals for specific areas, including Valletta. Thus the Commonwealth Foundation assignment which we had been asked to undertake had been largely overtaken by events, especially as it had been drawn up the previous year without knowledge of the work being done by the planning section of the Department of Works.

We were there, we'd unpacked and set up our office, introduced ourselves, met some eager people and already been paid (and in my case spent) a mobilisation fee to get us started, so we could hardly storm off the stage in a huff, not least because no single authority could be blamed for this Gilbertian state of affairs. I noticed that Jeffery's mouth tightened a bit for a few hours when we learned all this, but by next morning he was his usual considerate and reasonable self, so we started work.

Although a selection of assorted maps had been supplied to us, I felt that

I needed an early overview of the islands which would be impossible to obtain by driving around looking out of a car window. The island was pitted with huge stone quarries, some still being worked, and the road system around them had evolved on a seemingly ad hoc basis, so there was no methodical way of my progressing from one area to another sufficiently to give a comprehensive picture.

In the circumstances, and in view of the urgency impressed upon us, I asked if government permission could possibly obtained for the use of a helicopter for a couple of days as this would, in any case, progress our work by at least two weeks. Rather to my surprise, this request was granted, and early one morning we were told to report to a small building on the edge of the airport which housed an air-sea rescue unit funded by the Italians who, we were to discover, were conspicuously generous with their aid to Malta. This was presumably in the hope that, in years to come, such influence would persuade the inhabitants that it would be a lot more sensible to be part of Italy. Anyway, the Maltese had an air-sea rescue service for nothing, so no one was going to grumble.

As we entered the building, I could hear a noisy conversation in the upstairs personnel room and smelled a rich mix of fresh coffee and tobacco with more than a hint of, hopefully, *last night*'s alcohol. There we met the helicopter crew, already in flying gear, who had been told we were coming, but seemed disinclined to turn down the radio and show any sign of wanting to work. We were given coffee, shown the latest centrefold from a girlie magazine that had to be seen to be believed, and asked where we came from, how many children we had and, if they were boys, whether they were old enough to play football.

The Aeronautica Militare helicopter had a crew of three: a pilot, a navigator and a winch-man. The pilot was very well groomed, never removed his dark glasses, wore Milanese, pearl grey handmade boots and looked every part the brooding B-movie lead he probably aspired to be. When I attempted to take a photograph of him wearing a glistening white hi-tech helmet just before he boarded, he carefully moved me a couple of paces to the left so that I could capture the perfection of his 'good' side. The navigator, who, I noticed, walked none too steadily to the aircraft (oh please, may it be a war injury), fiddled with a bundle of folded maps on his lap once he was seated and on one occasion had to rely on the pilot to show him which way up to hold them. I gave him the benefit of the doubt.

I was notably ill equipped for aerial photography, but as we weren't undertaking an accurate, plottable survey but only wanted to gain an overall impression of land mass, approximate contours, cultivated areas and built-up zones, total accuracy was not necessary. I decided to use my small 35-mm camera to take a sequence of shots as we travelled north–south and then south–north, as if mowing a lawn, and piece them together afterwards. The fuselage had a large sliding door on each side, and the only way I could operate was to sit on the open sill and, secured by a double webbing harness clipped to the roof frame, let my legs dangle freely over the side so that, pointing directly downwards, I could take shots between my knees. I was readily assisted in this difficult and vaguely absurd-looking operation by the heavily perfumed, all-enveloping winch-man who, despite the security of my double harness, hugged me tightly to him for the entire trip. Every now and then he would murmur into my ear something reassuring in Italian and seemed puzzled by my unintentional, rather-too-British responses. Perhaps I was being unfair: it may have been in the air-sea rescue training manual for all I knew, but I rather doubted it.

The trip yielded a huge amount of valuable information very quickly: the Grand Harbour of Valletta with its Piranesi-like fortifications; the hilltop citadel of Mdina with its baroque cathedral; the almost tree-less hinterland criss-crossed with protective stone walls against the frequent gales; the high cliffs of the west coast and, to the north, the isolated serenity of Gozo sometimes referred to as the 'Ireland of Malta'. At last I had a feel for the place and could see how the mosaic came together.

As Jeffery Switzer and I progressed with the study, the more fascinating it became and we soon forgot our irritation over the confused terms of reference. Malta was a place of vivid contrasts. Architecturally, the island spanned four millennia, from the prehistoric temples at Tarxien to the exuberant baroque of its churches and cathedral, with not a lot in between. And political expediency had produced another contrast. Libya, the pariah state for so long, was openly given succour by Malta as it simultaneously sought approval of, and ultimately integration with, the West, a sentiment even echoed at street level by windscreen stickers extolling 'Manchester United'. Having your cake and eating it would be demonstrated even more boldly later when Malta Enterprise (a government trade agency) placed large coloured advertisements in British newspapers asking, without a blush, 'What do Britain and Libya have in common?' Answer: 'Strong links with Malta'.

The church in Maltese life was omnipresent. Public holidays are granted on feast days to honour St Joseph, Our Lady, and the Immaculate Conception, in addition to Easter and Christmas. The sound of church bells fills towns and villages frequently through the day, and recognition of the church's life seems to appear even in the most secular settings, once typified by a notice I passed at the splendid entrance arch to the harbour. Immediately under the sign saying 'Malta Drydocks' was a carefully lettered poster adding 'Last Supper display. One hundred yards'.

But perhaps my most puzzling experience took place in the square at the centre of the beautiful citadel of Mdina. I was anxious that Jeffery Switzer should see the dignified baroque cathedral dedicated to St Paul. It occupies the site of a villa where St Paul converted Publius, chieftain of the island, after curing his father of a fever. The interior has splendid frescoes, paintings and mosaics, and is a well-known centre of devotion, usually thronged by tourists. The best time to see and appreciate any building is when it is in use, so I checked the time of Solemn High Mass on Sunday and we set off in good time to park our car nearby. Being early, we waited in the car for quarter of an hour, but shortly before eleven we walked towards the cathedral. Surprisingly, there seemed to be few people about and we were uncertain which door was open. It turned out that none were. When we returned to the great front we saw an old notice pinned to the door which read: 'Closed on Sunday'.

By the time our assignment was nearing completion, I had learned enough about how things worked in Malta to realise that, as the government hadn't paid for our report and as it probably contained recommendations that might threaten jealously guarded local interests, it may not be acted upon as enthusiastically as its Commonwealth sponsors would like. Nothing was said, but by the time we were invited to a small but pleasant dinner party at a local restaurant to mark our departure, I had the distinct impression that our work would be politely noted and then shelved, so as not to upset the delicate balance between political and personal interests that we would never understand unless we had been born and raised on the island. Although we never heard the eventual outcome, my memories of Malta remained positive. We met plenty of genuine, hard-working and generous people at all levels who wanted Malta to prosper, and not just on their own terms.

Architecturally and, more particularly, visually, the island was almost unique for the brilliance and clarity of its natural light. Sharp sunlight contrasts with deep, penetrating shadow, and in between, even on the humblest façade, suffused light animates every feature. No wonder Caravaggio, whose name is so closely associated with chiaroscuro (the contrasts between light and shade in painting), found his chosen place of exile so visually satisfying. It is hard not to.

Chapter 41

Crossing the Green Line

Having become acquainted with Malta, I moved on to a larger part of my CAA 'parish' at an early opportunity and was intrigued to find how many similarities were to be found in Cyprus, and these weren't confined to superficialities like pillar boxes and police uniforms. British colonial influence and being occupied by foreign powers figured as conspicuously in the island's history as they had in Malta. Like that smaller island, I knew little about Cyprus before I arrived other than the fact that it had been under British rule for a long time and that, in 1974, the Turks were provoked to invade the island and occupy its northern territory. This had become international news and was fresh in everyone's mind.

I found a useful introduction by reading Lawrence Durrell's *Bitter Lemons*. For some years he had lived in a restored cottage near Bellapais, not far from the north coast, where he entertained inveterate travellers like Rose Macaulay and Freya Stark. He had an easy capacity for describing the spirit of a place, which he maintained was 'the important determinant of any culture', and I suspect he would like to have stayed there. But eventually he reached a point of restrained anger when that spirit was needlessly shattered by the violent transformations which the conflict between Greek and Turk brought about. And as I got to know the place, I realised how much turmoil, just like in Malta, figured in the island's long history.

Cyprus enjoys a blissfully long summer which often runs from April through to the end of October, and it doesn't seem to experience an autumn, as such. This endless summer stops abruptly with a flash flood and then winter begins. As it snows in the Troodos mountains in the centre of the island between January and March it is possible to ski and, for those anxious to make an impression, it is both possible and comfortable to enjoy this sport on a March morning and then drive to the coast for some early water-skiing in the afternoon, such is the temperature variation.

Such contrasts were not confined to the climate. Pano Platres is a central mountain resort with winding roads lined with scented pines and timber chalets, and is more reminiscent of an Alpine ski resort than anywhere in the Levant. It became popular as an escape from Nicosia at the height of summer, and in the late nineteenth century was a place for convalescence of British troops, becoming known as the 'Simla of Cyprus'.

I had been formally invited by the Cyprus Civil Engineers and Architects Association to act as intermediary between the Greek architects and the Turkish architects who suddenly found their profession split down the middle following the Turkish invasion. The association was represented by Nakos Protopapas, their president, a warm, hospitable engineer who wore his Marxist sympathies lightly, and by Stavros Economou, a short, stout, heavily bespectacled architect whose son had trained to follow his father's profession in London. It took me some time to memorise and pronounce their names, and by the time I had added Lellos Demetriades (the mayor), Alexis Theodossiadis (another architect), and Constantinos Ioannides (a planner), I set about practising these in front of the shaving mirror every morning. Unlike Maltese names they can be pronounced as they are spelled, which made it a lot easier. As I had been weaned on Gilbert and Sullivan and later warmed by the endearing absurdity of Flanders and Swann, what began as a daily elocution lesson became a secret bathroom obsession. The resonance of a fully tiled bathroom leant spurious gravitas to my Levantine litany and I enjoyed it so much that I actually 'collected' equally melodious names of people I would never meet just for the fun of getting my tongue around polysyllables. One day, after I had collected about twenty and my performance had become longer, my Bertie Wooster behaviour was discovered by a dour Liverpudlian commercial traveller in the next room, who asked if I'd turn down the local radio first thing in the morning.

Stavros Economou had been employed in the London County Council Architects' Department after World War II and had, in fact, worked for Sir Robert Matthew, who later became the CAA's first president. All of this made my introduction to the capital, Nicosia, a lot simpler, and everyone's advice on sites of artistic and architectural interest enabled me to use my spare time enjoyably.

Some sites, like Paphos on the south-west coast, had an archaeological history extending back to Neolithic periods spanning between 6,800 and 3,900 BC and were still being worked over, but for sheer visual wonder it was the Roman period which left such an exceptional and indelible mark, principally through mosaics. These had been laid on the floors not of great public buildings, but of large private houses, often built in favourable positions close to the sea and its breezes, and were usually occupied by wealthy citizens of the time. One such was the House of Dionysos, which had been discovered accidentally only in 1962 and is distinguished by its size and its superb mosaic decoration. It covers more than 2,000 square yards and occupies an entire block on the original street layout of Paphos. The plan form is typical of the Roman house, which has all its rooms grouped around a peristyle atrium with an open garden pool in the centre. All the living rooms overlooking the main atrium are lavishly decorated with magnificent mosaic floors, many of which depict hunting scenes or subjects from popular mythology. Peacocks and minotaurs compete for one's interest and the remarkable state of preservation makes their impact all the more vivid and immediate. Further wonders were evident at the adjacent houses of Theseus and of Heracles. Experts argue that the quality of the mosaic ateliers must have been as good as any to be found in the entire Empire. I'd never seen anything like it and would happily have travelled to Cyprus only to see them.

Visual wonders of an entirely different and later order awaited me in the shape of abundant churches and monasteries on the island. The churches, many from the tenth century, looked to me like abstract compositions in solid geometry: clusters of shallow-domed drums intersecting rectangular volumes with apsidal protrusions. They are almost windowless, but where a small number of apertures do occur, they still give light internally, so strong is the sun. There is no intention to flood the interior with light as Gothic builders would do later, but such suffusion of light lends that air of mystery necessary to convey the impression of the transcendence of God in Orthodox worship. What better way to provide a muted setting for the painted glory of an iconostasis (the screen which shuts off the sanctuary on which icons are placed)? The Church of Saints Barnabas and Hilarion at Peristerona is a rewarding example of this design approach.

During other interludes in my work I enjoyed the compelling simplicity of the superbly sited Roman theatre at Kourion overlooking the sea, and later, venturing to the north of the island, the remains of the fourteenth-century Gothic Cathedral of St Nicholas in Famagusta, much of which is still standing despite being severely damaged in the siege of 1571 and subsequently converted into a mosque.

The 'British period' began in 1878, when the government assumed administration of the island; and although it formally remained part of the Ottoman Empire, the first British High Commissioner was appointed. This period ended in 1960 when Cyprus became an independent republic; its very last governor was Sir Hugh Foot, who later, as Lord Caradon, I was to meet in London.

A recurring theme in nineteenth-century British foreign policy was the strategic need for a '*place d'armes*' to protect our interests in the eastern Mediterranean. At this time Malta was thought to be too remote, and the government needed a convenient location where troops could be assembled if they were needed anywhere in the Levant. History repeated itself in 1956 during the fateful invasion of Suez under the Eden government, shortly before the island's independence. As long ago as the 1800s, Hegel, the greatest idealist philosopher, observed that the only thing to be learned from history was that nobody did learn from history, and at no time was this more painfully brought home to a British government.

History demonstrates that there is no single 'Cyprus problem', but the latest problem, and certainly one of the most intractable, stems from the 1974 Turkish invasion. This was triggered by a coup in Cyprus instigated by the regime of the colonels in Greece which overthrew the government of Archbishop Makarios with the objective of uniting Cyprus with Greece. Five days later, Turkish forces invaded the island and occupied the north, ostensibly to rescue a fifth of the populace that were ethnic Turks. By the time I arrived some ten years later, the UN had set up the Attila Line, which separated Turkish Cypriots from Greek Cypriots and the military forces of their mainland neighbours.

In his semi-retirement, Lord Caradon had set up an all-party group involving both Houses and Parliament, and called 'Friends of Cyprus', which aimed to bridge the political and physical gap caused by the establishment of the Attila Line which effectively prevented any personal contact between the two sides. Many Cypriots, irrespective of ethnic origins generations ago, still saw themselves first as Cypriots and only as Greeks or Turks after, and had become accustomed to living and working successfully alongside each other, sharing one small island and a single economy. Whilst they were aware of differing family kinships, this didn't prevent them practising medicine, law, architecture or anything else that served the entire community. The Attila Line put an immediate stop to all that, as Greeks from the north were repatriated south and Turks from the south went north and were thereafter encouraged to posture and jibe at each other by Athens and Ankara, respectively.

Lord Caradon's initiative was pragmatic and full of common sense. It was taken up readily by both sides on the island, who were dismayed by the overnight fragmentation of their trades and professions and were grateful for this slender token of ongoing unity. Lord Caradon (still referred to by expatriates as the 'right Foot', to distinguish him from his left-wing relative Michael Foot, who was leader of the Labour party at Westminster) had already set up two exchanges across the Attila Line involving, first, teachers, and then journalists, to assess the usefulness of such an arrangement. It had obviously worked at a modest level, so he now wanted to try something more ambitious and chose architects as the next group. As I was going to be in Cyprus at the time in any case, his office contacted me and asked if I would be prepared to help. Probably out of curiosity, I agreed.

The arrangement was simple. I would take a brief from the Greek architects one day, involving issues they would hitherto have discussed directly with their Turkish colleagues, and then on the following day I would take their questions and observations to the Turks, elicit their response and bring back their messages and questions for the Greeks to ponder. It was a poor man's version of shuttle diplomacy, but it worked surprisingly well once I got used to the cumbersome political formalities. I would present myself with some seemingly ad hoc documentation early in the morning at the Greek checkpoint, which was unmistakingly emblazoned in the blue and white national colours, where they would check my name on their security list for the day. Once the militia were satisfied who I was they scratched out my name on their list with an old Biro, and the blue and white pole was lifted to let me through; in stepping over the border, as far as the Greeks were concerned, I no longer legally existed. I had then to walk, unaccompanied, straight down the narrow concrete path past the now empty and forlorn Ledra Palace Hotel, its shutters still banging in the wind, and which had the misfortune to be in the wrong place when the political line was drawn and was now in no-man's-land. Both sides of the path had been mined and the corridor was protected by thick coils of barbed wire. About 150 yards away was the Turkish border post, equally unmistakable in national red and white stripes, and, as I approached, it would lift hesitantly. A Turkish infantryman would ask my name and then, painfully slowly, write it as best he could. Legally, I would exist once more and be allowed to proceed on my way. It sometimes occurred to me that if I ever had the misfortune to suffer a seizure in no-man's-land, not only would my very existence be difficult to establish with the authorities, but neither party would be inclined to take any interest in my plight as I wasn't on their particular territory.

On my first visit the Turkish reception party was delighted to welcome me. I was unlikely to solve their problems in one go and had to learn a lot more about the political background first. This didn't seem to worry them; they were engaging, surprisingly cheerful, and just anxious to talk to another architect who had no political axe to grind. They fell on the messages from the south and were anxious to hear how their erstwhile professional colleagues were faring. Understandably, at the end of the day their overenthusiastic hospitality often led to my ear being bent about the villainy and duplicity of the Greeks and how unjustly the Turks had been victimised. I soon heard the other side though, when being similarly entertained by the Greek architects later. In their view, everything I had heard was totally unfounded and it was political opportunists in Ankara who were completely to blame for the deliberate vandalism of Greek churches in the north and the impossible conditions they now found themselves trying to practise in. And so it went on, and in some ways the protestations cancelled each other out. I reminded myself that enmity between Greek and Turk went back centuries and if I took too much notice of these passionate outbursts or, worse still, took sides, then I would achieve nothing. So I stuck to architecture and fortunately had sufficient in my knapsack to keep both sides engaged in trying to maintain technical and legal standards in their common profession and prevent it slipping into complete disarray during what could well become a long political impasse.

From time to time I was asked why I was making these Commonwealth trips, bearing in mind that I wasn't paid and derived no material benefit from them. The answer was simple. Before I left I would have to update myself on every aspect of professional practice and impending change in order to dispense such information to others, and I doubt if I would have bothered if I didn't have to stand up and sound word-perfect. This helped me run my practice at home more effortlessly. But the real bonus was both intangible and unpredictable, and stemmed from chance encounters with people I would otherwise never meet and wouldn't have known existed.

One day, I was far away from any town, having decided to explore some of the monastery sites in the mountains, and I was staying in the only village offering some sort of accommodation when I succumbed to a dental emergency. I found a loose crown in my mouth which left its metal pin exposed against my cheek, so I sought urgent advice as to whom I could go from the owner of the small inn I was staying in. He explained that the village had no medical services, but on two evenings a week a dentist came from a nearby town on his two-stroke motorbike and set up a makeshift surgery in a rented room. Where he lived was two villages away and difficult to find, so it was arranged for me to take a taxi there. This tiny place didn't seem the sort of village to run a taxi service, but I took his word that he could organise it. He made a telephone call while I waited and it was arranged for me to be collected later that evening.

In a lean-to corrugated-iron shed at the end of the village a Greek mechanic ran a one-man business repairing farm vehicles and servicing the miscellany of old cars that occasionally spluttered past. Leaving his work, still in greasy overalls and driving with even greasier hands, he followed the owner's instructions and took me to the dentist. It was a wordless journey; he was obviously not a big talker and I was happy to remain mute as the metal pin chafed my cheek every time I spoke. After twenty minutes or so we climbed another hill, turned a corner and saw the outline of a farm cottage and in it one room illuminated by a bare bulb just visible behind the old shutters. My driver indicated that we had arrived and led the way into the cottage past the still-warm two-stroke propped against the wall. The two exchanged a few words in Greek and, to my surprise, the young dentist, obviously a probationer allocated to rural work while he gained experience, turned and spoke to me in English. He explained that he had completed his formal training in Birmingham and this was his first assignment at home. I gave him the loose crown so all that was necessary was for him to refix it in position. However, this appeared to give him some difficulty, which wasn't helped by critical grunts from the mechanic, who was keeping me in close view as I hadn't yet paid him. The dentist turned the crown first this way and then that, but obviously felt uncertain which way it was intended to go. Having watched this with increasing impatience for ten minutes or so, the mechanic suddenly stood up, pushed the dentist aside and plunged his Castrol-flavoured hands into my mouth. He got it right immediately and shrugged his shoulders as he returned to an old chair in the corner. With the crown now securely fixed I felt the comfort immediately and rose to thank the dentist and enquire how much I owed.

'Oh please, I'm not asking for a fee,' he said. 'You see, you're British, and my father was always grateful to the English authorities for the way they helped us get justice following an incident many years ago and we always remember their fairness. Please accept my services gratis.'

I was stunned. 'But I would like to offer you something to show my appreciation,' I protested.

He paused for a moment and then said rather diffidently, 'Well, perhaps there *is* something. Would you do me the honour of signing my visitors' book?'

Another equally unique encounter involved a backstreet shoemaker. Cyprus is renowned for its leather goods so, taking local advice, I asked if shoes could be purpose-made. As I take size twelve and most multiple retailers stock nothing over eleven, I was always interested in finding a pair that fitted comfortably. The address I'd been given was very hard to find, well up the hill behind a medium-sized town, and in a fairly nondescript area. Directions had been scribbled on the back of an old bar bill in pidgin English but without any street name or number. 'You won't need these, you can't possibly miss it,' they said. I spent over an hour in the searing midday heat missing it and had to resort to gestures and hand signs to passers-by. This antic amused a steadily growing band of small children, one of whom appeared to be attached by a string to a menacing dog which may have been attracted by the smell of my feet. At least they had got the message, and I was led to a doorway, squeezed between two shops and covered by a plastic tape blind behind which sat a small, monastic-looking figure working at a last. I looked again at my directions. Could it possibly be the right address? Could this be the man I was told was the best shoemaker in Cyprus and who had an order book running a year ahead? It transpired that he was and he had, so I sat down on the old van Gogh-like chair he offered me and started to explain what I needed. Very courteously, he interrupted to say, in good English, 'You need a size twelve and, with that narrow foot, a D fitting, don't you?' It was more of an assertion than a question and I nodded vaguely, my attention now having been distracted by a wall covered with faded letters of recommendation and, in some cases, signed photographs from satisfied customers. As I looked more closely these were no ordinary customers, not even Cyprus dignitaries, but international politicians, archbishops, concert soloists and well-known film stars who had obviously been customers for years and returned as regularly as their professional commitments would allow. A grateful Cary Grant looked down from one photo and the opposite wall contained row upon row of carefully measured templates of distinguished feet, so that the shoemaker could respond to a telephone call from Hollywood or some distant caliphate and make the caller yet another pair (or pair of pairs in the case of the Americans).

Upon finding I was British, he showed me some work in progress on his latest order.

'This is another pair for the Speaker of your House of Commons.'

'Not George Thomas?' I replied.

'Of course; he tells me that he's going to become Lord Tonypandy and he'll wear this pair for his installation in the Upper House, whatever that is.'

Could he be making this up – some leg-pull patter for tourists just to amuse his family? I thought for a moment, but yes, George Thomas was slight in build and almost dapper. His natural theatricality, nurtured by many years on Labour platforms and in chapel pulpits, brought out the lurking thespian in him and I could now well imagine his predilection for a beautifully crafted pair of handmade shoes. Lord Hailsham had called him 'a national institution', and he was going to live up to the appellation.

At about this time, the Mediterranean countries were beginning to feel the effect of cheap air travel for the first time and it didn't take local landowners long to cash in on the bonanza. This led to a rash of ill-considered developments which ignored environmental pollution, jeopardised priceless historic destinations and put intolerable strains on rudimentary infrastructure. However small the landholding, it was considered the owner's unalienable right to build on his land if he wanted to, irrespective of the damage it might do to the landscape or the community at large.

It was understandable that a family toiling on unproductive soil for centuries should want to grasp the opportunity to better themselves and build an eight-bedroom taverna instead, especially if it was near the sea, but when this happened on an unprecedented scale, often cutting off stretches of public foreshore in the process, then they were sowing the seeds of their own destruction.

On one occasion when it was discovered that I had environmental interests, I was invited to speak to a group of businessmen and landowners to try and persuade them to take a longer view before it was too late. My premise was simple. The Mediterranean basin contains some of the most valuable historic sites which are the envy of the world and which attract discerning visitors with money to spend. Indiscriminate and ill-considered new developments in their vicinity will jeopardise them and discriminating (and heavier-spending) tourists will begin to turn their backs on the area and seek out cultural destinations elsewhere. In short, for the sake of a quick buck now, future generations of travellers will be alienated and go further afield, so that centuries of tradition, cultural interest and investment will be thrown to the winds. I had seen first-hand at Mycenae on the Greek mainland, the site of the Treasury of Atreus and the world-renowned Lion Gate, how cut-price mass tourism was quickly eradicating the very qualities of the place which had attracted the tourists in the first place. The area was choked with an acrid layer of diesel fumes from countless coach engines left running so that the air conditioning remained on for the benefit of their returning passengers. It was the same again at the Minoan Palace at Knossos in Crete, which was grossly overcrowded because no limits were placed on numbers: here I was moved around almost forcibly, apparently pinned between the shoulders of my equally hapless neighbours, so that stopping to admire a particular feature was quite impossible. Who in their right mind would ever go back there? And is this what the tourist authorities really wanted? In addition, there was mounting evidence of increasing pollution from untreated sewage emanating from huge coastal hotel developments, which meant that one could no longer enjoy swimming in the crystal-clear water of the Mediterranean and, very noticeably, every new resort project included a large, land-based swimming pool even if it was only a hundred yards from the sea.

I was thanked for an 'interesting and thought-provoking' talk, asked some polite questions and interviewed by the editor of the *Cyprus Weekly*, grateful for a scary headline, and that was that – and presumably remained that for as long as the money rolled in.

Greek Orthodox theology must presumably embrace the words attributed to St Augustine: 'Make me chaste and continent, but not just yet.'

Chapter 42

South of the Equator

'Jambo boss, tafadhali cable come. Tutaonana.' [Hello boss; please, a cable has arrived. See you soon.] My perspiring messenger, having thrust the telegram into my hand, disappeared as quickly as he had arrived. When I opened the crumpled envelope it read simply, 'Two one Cantab. Love Flossie.' That was all I wanted to hear. My daughter Frances, always known by her schoolgirl nickname, had just read the degree results posted on her college noticeboard and was as anxious to share the good news as I was to read it. Such information usually arrives in a dull, buff envelope on a suburban doormat, but my unfamiliar surroundings heightened the sense of occasion and, at the same time, made me realise how far away I was.

I had been in Tanzania just over a week, following an invitation from Preece, Cardew & Rider, with whom I had worked previously in Saudi Arabia. They wanted help in designing a technical institute in which to train students to become skilled technicians capable of maintaining the country's electricity distribution system. The Tanzanian Electricity Supply Company (Tanesco) had just adequate generation capacity, but it kept going wrong; what was missing was an efficient cadre of engineering technicians who could diagnose problems and then remedy them in the field. This is a very common problem in developing countries where a very small number of young people from more prosperous families obtain a degree at a European university and then, when they return, because of their scarcity, are given quite senior jobs early on in their careers, leaving a large gap between them and the semi-literate manual labourers who do the heavy and dirty work.

Preece, Cardew & Rider were to advise on an appropriate curriculum which would be recognised by the government's Education Minister, and were also to describe how such a technical institute should be staffed and run. I was to plan and design the buildings to house these activities.

295

Apart from my glimpse of the Sudan and British Somaliland when taking on cargo during my troopship voyage to the Far East, the continent of Africa was still much of a closed book to me and, in those days, Tanganyika and Zanzibar had not yet merged to form the territory of Tanzania.

When I was a schoolboy, much of my popular learning came from collecting cigarette cards. There was one in each packet and my long-suffering father, who usually smoked Player's cigarettes, was persuaded by me to buy four packets of five each time instead of one packet of twenty, as this accelerated the growth of my collection before the manufacturers, usually with no notice, changed to a different subject. A set on wild flowers would be succeeded by another devoted to popular sportsmen, Empire military uniforms or flags of the nations and, for the price of one old penny, I could buy an album to stick them in. No one knew how long a series would run, so, after a while, a hot trade in swaps built up in an effort to complete the total of fifty before the issue changed. On a wet afternoon I would pore over my incomplete collection in order to be word-perfect on gaps before next Monday's school. There were full descriptions on the back of each card which were so inherently interesting, it never struck me that I was actually learning. 'Flags and badges of the British Empire' was a favourite and, together with my burgeoning stamp collection, introduced me effortlessly to the wider world. Tanganyika was represented by the head of a giraffe and Zanzibar by a dhow in full sail. I still remembered them on my arrival in Dar es Salaam fifty years later, despite the country now having an entirely new national flag. Who on earth originally thought up anything as banal as a giraffe's head and shoulders as the appropriate symbol for a proud nation drawn from Bantu tribesmen with a colourful history behind them? It wasn't difficult to imagine the post-prandial scene in a club in St James's. Settled deep in leather armchairs and sustained by a glass of crusted port in one hand and a Havana in the other, a Permanent Under-Secretary might have said:

'Something I meant to tell you. We've got this new place in East Africa, y'know, called Tanganyika, and on the agenda this afternoon we've got to think of a symbol for their new flag. Never been there: disease-ridden probably. Can't readily think of a motif we haven't already used elsewhere. Mind's gone blank, dammit.'

'What about a wild animal?'

'Well, Kenya's got the lion on its flag, Uganda bagged the ostrich, Somaliland's got the impala, so the best ones have already gone.'

Having only yesterday given his new godson a trip to the zoo, his colleague might have suggested brightly, 'Could a giraffe do, perhaps?'

The Under-Secretary would slowly draw on his cigar. 'Capital idea. I knew you'd come up with something, Carruthers. Let me refresh your glass.'

By comparison, Tanzania's flag today is rigorously geometrical, contains a politically correct area of black and, on balance, is not a great deal better than the old one. Clearly it isn't the age for picturesque gestures. And I was to learn quickly that neither was it the age when technical cooperation could take place without political interference. Our engineering counterparts at Tanesco knew what was needed and, as long as money was going to be made available, were easy to collaborate with. But despite their seniority, they were seldom allowed the last word. Throughout the organisation, non-technical party officials were appointed as managers and were allocated slightly larger and better furnished offices immediately next to each engineer, and they presented themselves at every meeting. It was hard to gauge whether their obduracy was due to party discipline and the need to toe the line or whether they just resented not following a technical conversation and pushed their weight about just to show who was boss.

I soon realised that annoyances of this sort had to be seen in a realistic perspective and allowances made in a country which was only fifteen years old. Tanzania had been immensely fortunate in having Julius Nyerere as its first prime minister and later president. Originally a secondary-school teacher, he was the first of his countrymen to study at a British university, where he read economics and history and, in the process, encountered Fabian thinking. In 1977 he became chairman of Chama Cha Mapinduzi, the Revolutionary State Party of Tanzania, and he soon began to develop his own version of socialism which sought to connect with African communal living and its values. He was first and foremost an African and second a Socialist. He was also a devout Catholic and, despite the relative poverty of his country, became a highly respected and honoured figure throughout the entire continent.

Our team had to take the political background into consideration, but this did make our work a lot harder, compounded by the (understandable) fact that there were large gaps in the architectural and planning personnel for me to work alongside, so I had to make more assumptions than I felt comfortable with. In the absence of local technical advice, I often had to rely on an informed guess.

Having selected a site for the new institute, it was necessary to survey it to obtain accurate dimensions, record physical characteristics and plot contours. This process, using a theodolite, could not be undertaken alone, so I asked Tanesco for another pair of hands. In due course I was allocated an assistant who had the largest and most engaging grin I had ever seen, but he only spoke Swahili. As I wasn't known for a lot of grinning and only spoke English; the stage looked set for an expensive farce. My new associate wasn't going to mind either way because the beaming smile never left his face and he was determined to be friendly whatever we got up to. I and my theodolite were obviously a novelty to tell his family about when he got home.

As we began to realise that the spoken word was redundant, he was the first to start drawing in the dust with his huge index finger. My hand had been bitten by a strange insect the day before so he quickly found me a twig to use instead. Wordlessly, we drew and gesticulated and, stage by stage, agreed who should do what next. A nod here, a raised eyebrow there enabled us to build our technical vocabulary and within half a hour we had set to work. He often had to stand some way off holding the measuring staff while I operated the theodolite, but whenever I looked up there were the flashing white teeth of his enthusiastic grin. Together, we proved that not only could it be done, but we managed to do it.

I often drew up my proposals on a makeshift drawing board in the evening when it was quieter and cooler. But one seemingly simple thing caused me untold difficulty and made the whole planning process (which should have been easy – I'd designed far more difficult buildings) a challenge that slowed down all my intuitive decision making. I realised that, for the first time in my life, I was in the southern hemisphere, and therefore the sun's arc would be 180 degrees different from what I had been accustomed to for the last thirty years. It shouldn't have been difficult to adjust, but, in design terms, it was like the sudden distortion of a sense and was disproportionately disturbing. The established drawing convention is that north is towards the top of the sheet of paper you're drawing on and everything else relates to this. But this dramatic change was so fundamental it completely unnerved me and I reluctantly and naively switched from 'automatic' to 'manual' in order to make any progress at all on the design. I even resorted to drawing everything upside down to begin with, but that was plainly ludicrous, so in the end I recast my mind in the mode of kindergarten 'painting by numbers' until I had adapted my intuitive responses. Looking back, it was strange to think that such a simple thing had undone me, but I supposed that, whatever we do for a living, if you suddenly knock away a cornerstone, the whole edifice will wobble.

While the remainder of the PCR team were still in Dar es Salaam, I had been asked to go ahead to Morogoro, about 100 miles upcountry, and look at the proposed site for the new institute. The town, situated some 3,500 feet above sea level, was growing in importance and now possessed improved rail links due to the Chinese, who were diligently cultivating emerging Socialist states at the time. I was told that Tanesco had booked me into the Savoy Hotel in Morogoro, which sounded all right, so I sat back to enjoy as best I could the long and dirty truck journey from Dar es Salaam. We stopped once or twice to pick up goods or, more often, to enable the driver and his companion to go off for a smoke or a drink with a relative from the village we were passing through. When we eventually reached Morogoro it was late afternoon and there were not many people about. The driver had to ask where the hotel was and, after he was misinformed twice, I joined him in trying to find the place. All the buildings looked about the same size, so nothing stood out to make the search any easier. After we turned several further corners I saw the word 'Savoy' hand-painted on the corrugated iron roof of a flattish structure. It was difficult to read at first as some of the letters were badly worn and covered with bird droppings, but it turned out to be my destination.

I was shown to a fairly bare ground-floor room that overlooked the street outside. It had an iron bedstead, a chair and a small table, and although everything was very old and had been repaired many times, it looked as if an attempt had been made to clean it after the last visitor. A nominal bedside mat was provided, which I had previously learned never to move for fear of disturbing unknown insects. In any case, this one must have been there many years and looked fairly immovable. In a recess of my room was a metal shower head fixed to the ceiling, and beneath it a floor gulley for the water to drain into. I was glad of an opportunity to get clean and delighted when the wall tap supplied ample water, albeit slightly orange. Not realising how tired I was, I lay down on the bed afterwards but didn't intend to sleep. Despite the unfamiliar noises and smells outside my window I must have dozed off, only to wake later with a start. There was something moving in the room. The evening light was fading fast and I couldn't quite see what it was. Prudence told me not to move on the bed, so I swivelled my eyes slowly towards the door. It took me a while to discover what was happening. With disbelief, I saw that my bedside mat was moving, making its way towards the window. Schoolboy thrillers about voodoo in darkest Africa filled my mind, but eventually I summoned up enough courage to lift myself up on my elbows and look around. I soon saw a wide pool of dusty water advancing from the shower area which, upon reaching my mat, had borne it away towards the other side of the room. The gulley must have been blocked and it was all easily explainable, but having pondered the phenomenon for a while, I preferred to think that the sound of approaching water had alerted the legions of centipedes who had comfortably colonised the mat's woven underbelly and, as one, they had straightened their shoulders, taken a deep breath and moved off in closed ranks towards safety. I didn't go anywhere near it for the rest of my stay.

As our clients explained the planning brief to us, the overall design began to suggest itself. The site was generous and was given interest by a gentle crossfall. The prevailing winds were fairly constant and therefore natural cross ventilation of the buildings was easy to accomplish; temperature variations were manageable, so the resulting block layout became obvious. All of this, together with consideration of the smooth relationship of the institute's constituent parts, led to a comparatively simple plan. This was essential in any case, as the budget wouldn't stretch to a sophisticated design, nor would local building methods be suited to complicated construction. The campus also had to be inexpensive to maintain. This was certainly not an opportunity for the architect to show off with a flashy design in the hope that it would attract the attention of an international editor looking for an eye-catching cover for his magazine's next issue. Such things occur far too often, and displays of Western cleverness leave a legacy of disillusion in their wake.

The issue of easy maintenance was borne out time and time again during my visit to Tanzania, where the absence of a technician class able to repair things was felt everywhere, and nowhere more than at the harbour at Dar es Salaam. The country exports coffee, cotton and cashew nuts and imports capital equivalent, oil and oil derivatives. The whole operation depends on dockside efficiency. To help facilitate this, an international aid agency visits each year to see what is required. On one occasion I asked the port manager why there was a heap of discarded forklift trucks abandoned behind a shed at the harbour. They looked quite new to me and appeared to suffer from relatively minor faults involving a missing component here or a damaged unit there, but they had been consigned to the scrap heap as a matter of course. The manager explained that there were no trained technicians to repair them and once the forklifts failed they had to be totally replaced. At a recent aid-agency visit they had been asked 'what they'd like for Christmas' and replied, 'Ten forklift trucks, please.' These were promptly requisitioned by the earnest, anxious-to-please, Third World do-gooder representing the agency, thus effectively stifling any local initiative to try and repair the broken ones themselves.

After a while I had grown accustomed to sitting at my hotel window at the end of a working day cleaning my equipment while watching local comings and goings, and I knew by sight all the street vendors, the fruit sellers and the all-too-many cripples, often young children with congenital deformities attempting to get on with their seemingly hopeless lives. The cripples had no purpose-made aids to help them along and usually relied on a roughly fashioned piece of scrap wood to lean on. I also suspect that many had no parents to lean on either and would die an early and unnoticed death. And there was I fussing about keeping the theodolite clean.

Towards the end of my visit to Morogoro I was moved to the Tanesco rest house at Kidatu. I had been told that preparations would be made for my arrival, so I bade farewell to the Savoy.

After a long, demanding day on site I returned to my new quarters and put my feet up, only to fall asleep again. On this occasion I was woken by a high-pitched, protesting yelping from the concrete courtyard just outside my new room. This went on for so long that I leapt to my feet and, pulling the faded curtains aside, witnessed the final stages of a goat being slaughtered for tonight's dinner – in honour of my arrival, I was later told.

That evening I was duly served a generous portion of stewed goat at the table and all eyes watched anxiously to see if it met with my approval. Lost for a truthful response, I muttered something about it being 'an entirely new experience,' which seemed to satisfy them. It was a bit chewy and fibrous and its flavour was neither one thing nor another, but it filled a gap. There must have been a lot left over because we had it again the next night and it was only upon its third appearance the following evening that I realised it was the dish of the week. A few days into this culinary routine I was passing through the back room of the rest house to collect some equipment when I looked through the kitchen window and saw, suspended from a hook, half a goat which, kebab style, had already had part of its flank excised, leaving the other half, or as much as the blowflies would be prepared to leave us, for our delectation during the remainder of the week. As the days went by the meat went off and its flavour took on a characteristic unfamiliar in the West. I began to dread the next meal of the day, although my local colleagues seemed to savour it. Not for the first time did I have doubts about the capacity of my digestive tract to cope with the novel experiences to which my journeys introduced it, but, to my intense relief, they were unfounded. I saw my hitherto taken-for-granted antibodies in a new light.

On the night before my departure a party was arranged for our team. The local personnel appeared in their company uniforms for the occasion and the evening began with a lot of local beer and chatter on the makeshift terrace. After an hour or so about a dozen of the Tanesco team broke away from their friends and lined up in front of us where, to carefully punctuated whistle blasts, they jumped rhythmically on the spot. I had seen the same dance in Kenya with the Samburu tribe. Presumably the tradition had travelled south to what is now Tanzania when tribal boundaries were a lot more fluid. Many of the dancers had their own whistles and, after the beer had loosened tongues and limbs, the performance took on a self-sustaining momentum that looked incapable of stopping, not because they'd forgotten how to, but more because they all appeared to be enjoying it. Rather than ending, it petered out as, one by one, they sloped off to finish bottles at the nearest table. A round of applause from us seemed pretty inadequate so I stepped inside and picked up a box of fifty cheroots I'd bought at the airport and always took on tropical travels, mainly to keep insects off if I wanted to sit outside after supper and admire the night sky, but also because I enjoyed them. I took the box over to where the exhausted dancers were sitting and started to offer them round. The first man needed no encouragement and took a handful, and was only stopped from plunging his other hand into the box by a much bigger colleague who leaned heavily on him and promptly took an even larger handful. As a third man completely emptied the box I suddenly found myself apologising that I hadn't got enough for everyone. The others drifted back to their tables without too much muttering, picked up their conversations and got on with drinking. The whole episode had lasted less than a minute and, in a continent where for centuries only the fittest survived, it was easy to understand. The have-nots seemed unperturbed by their misfortune because that is how life is; it never hands out consolation prizes, so no one feels let down, unless, of course, you are diseased or crippled, and even then you only pin your hopes on getting through the rest of the day. All this makes our 'school of hard knocks' in the West look pretty feeble.

After a while, the hand drums stopped and one or two of the performers came across with the last crate of beer to share it with us. There was a spontaneity in the way they did this and we were very glad to have their company as we watched the last strands of dusk-light fade from the horizon. There was a particularly clear moon, and for the first time that night I was aware of the looming presence of a huge monkey bread tree silhouetted against the silver light. It could have been an opening shot from *Out of Africa*, and so spectacular was it that I hurried inside to fetch my sketch pad and charcoal. I had about five minutes before the light moved and lost its intensity, but if the drawing was to look fresh and unlaboured, that would be enough. As I drew I became aware of an unnecessarily respectful silence around me and, but for the heavy smell of ingested beer, I could have been alone in a distant idyll anywhere on earth.

When I finished I removed the page from the pad, got up, made my excuses and left the sketch on the table. Not immediately realising that they could keep it, nothing happened, but when I looked over my shoulder for the last time I was amused and relieved to see that they were not, on this occasion, going to grab a piece each but had carefully pinned it up on the wall.

Chapter 43

Rum Jamaica

In breaks from day-to-day practice in Britain, my mind often wandered back to the Commonwealth. In the same way that my Army experience in Ceylon and Malaya had given me sufficiently itchy feet to accept design commissions in Saudi Arabia, Malaysia and Tanzania, so those experiences, in turn, fed my interest in the even wider world. The Commonwealth involved all five continents, so it was the ideal vehicle for more exploration. Visits to Malta and Cyprus had only been toes in the water.

At about the same time I realised that I enjoyed being more of a generalist than a specialist: I wouldn't have got involved in projects as diverse as 'relocatable churches' or the 'ecology of the mangrove swamp' if I'd just wanted to design houses for the rich and famous in SW3 – it would probably have been more lucrative, but not nearly so much fun. I also recalled a timely observation by one of the twentieth century's best-known communicators, Jacob Bronowski, who, as a mathematician, poet and humanist, was the quintessential generalist. In referring to specialists, he reminded us that as they progress they so often 'know more and more about less and less', and that held little appeal.

Having taken more than a passing interest in the Commonwealth since my first foray to Hong Kong in 1979, I now began spending more of my scarce leisure time undertaking work for the CAA and, as a result, attended its annual conference and General Assembly in Ocho Rios, Jamaica.

One part of the CAA region was grandly called 'the Americas', and this included both Canada and the Caribbean, and it was the turn of the West Indies to host the event. Jamaica is the largest island of the group and was thought to be sufficiently attractive a venue to guarantee a good attendance. In this it succeeded.

Jamaica became an independent state in 1962. It had been an English

303

colony for nearly three hundred years following victory over the Spanish who had held it since its discovery by Columbus in 1494. Its 2.5 million population, most of whom speak English, live in three 'counties', unbelievably called Surrey, Middlesex and Cornwall, which sounds as if they were named by John Betjeman rather than by some distant, conquering commodore.

Despite the fact that Jamaica exports alumina, bananas, bauxite and sugar, the economy faces many problems, including interest payments on debt, low market prices for export and interest rates of around thirty per cent. Unemployment is high and urban unrest persist. Local records from 1703 record that the present capital, Kingston, was first recognised as a 'town' despite being 'an unhealthy area of weak defences and low morals'. Three hundred years later, the country's first female prime minister would still be trying to reassure a restless electorate that her first priority upon taking office would be to 'plan to reduce general lawlessness'.

And yet all this sits beside an unstoppably creative and colourful culture personified by one of the island's most famous sons, Bob Marley, who introduced reggae to the world and had the pride and conviction to compose songs in his own dialect, which until then had been seen by promoters as a marketing liability. It seems that years of laughing at adversity had brought exuberance and vitality to a country with not much to laugh about, although sometimes one senses an underlying hopelessness beneath the brittle veneer of fun.

The CAA conference programme, which, without strong chairmanship, could quickly be eclipsed by internal political and ethnic squabbles, included some very good papers highly relevant to the local scene that gave Jamaican architects a higher profile among the government ministers and commercial leaders present. Everyone seemed to agree on what was needed, but too many people looked at their feet when we discussed how to achieve it.

After one such occasion I left the conference centre, which was only a short walk from our hotel, with a well-respected partner of a British architectural practice specialising in university design. His firm, Norman & Dawbarn, had successfully undertaken work in many parts of the world, including Tanzania and the West Indies, and had some talented and thoughtful people in its top echelons. As we both strolled back to our hotel the conversation reverted to the unresolved issues of the day and I listened to my companion's views, not just because he was a good deal older, wiser and more experienced in tropical architecture, but also because he was mild mannered, rational and approachable. To the outside world he looked almost professorial with his white hair, clear blue eyes and pink cheeks, for all the world an authority on medieval theology at some ancient university. No sooner had we begun walking then we were surrounded and followed by the customary swarm of young street vendors who appeared from nowhere, offering to sell us ganja (cannabis) or, just as likely, an hour with their pretty sister. This sort of thing happened so frequently that I though we could ignore it and walk on unimpeded, but our obvious disregard for their suggestions reinforced their determination, and they became noisier and more persistent than ever. Quite suddenly, my thoughtful and gentle colleague reached breaking point and turned on them with a vehemence which surprised even them, and yelled, 'Piss off!' to which, after a moment's stunned silence, one of them replied 'Cool it, doc,' and they drifted away.

At the end of the General Assembly which dealt with the business of running the CAA, elections to office for the forthcoming term were held. It was an unspoken rule that the presidency should rotate through the five regions of the Commonwealth, and it was Europe's turn next. Professor Peter Johnson from Australasia had filled the post superbly during the previous period, succeeding the avuncular Canadian Fred Rounthwaite, whom I had met in Nairobi. As, other than the United Kingdom, the Europe Region included only Gibraltar, Malta and Cyprus, it was more than likely that a British candidate would be nominated for election. In the event I was asked to stand, as there had been no British president since its founding father, Sir Robert Matthew, held office in 1964. Such elections, especially in international organisations, are never simple to get through. National groupings are capable of demonstrating either laudable impartiality or Machiavellian guile; it was not easy to see which way the nominations would go. In the event I was elected and on the last evening of the gathering formally appointed.

Every morning since my arrival at the hotel a tall, languid and utterly charming waiter had served me at the breakfast table. Having ascertained how I took my coffee, on each day I appeared he would be there leaning against a nearby pillar, his head tilted a little, smiling a smile of glazed politeness; then he and would raise an eyebrow and say, 'Good morning, sir. Coffee with sugar?' 'Yes, please.' This small ritual took place every morning but what I didn't realise was that on the evening of my election he had been working overtime and had watched the installation ceremony from the back of the hall. I suppose I shouldn't have been surprised when, as I came down to breakfast the next morning, he greeted me with 'Good morning, my lord. Coffee with gold dust?'

Jamaica had been chosen by Noël Coward as the ideal retreat just after World War II and I imagine the locals in those days would have shown the same cheeky charm. Perhaps that was part of the attraction. In April 1948, shortly after arriving for the first time, Coward wrote in his diary, 'This is the island of Jamaica and it seems to me to be a good place to start writing a book' (which he was entitle *Future Indefinite*, and which was the sequel to his first volume of autobiography written nearly twenty years earlier called *Present Indicative*). Although his life has been well recorded by both him and others, there are always extra insights to be gleaned. His old villa, Firefly Hill, superbly sited on a slope with magnificent views, was still being looked after by his old housekeeper when I was taken there by a friend. Understandably protective and not readily forthcoming, she nonetheless explained that, despite the debonair gaiety and elegant froth of his legendary hospitality, he invariably dined alone in the evening and much preferred his own company at the end of the day.

My next visit to Jamaica a few years later when, together with an engaging New York architect called Max Bond, I was invited back. Max had, in fact, been baptised James Bond many years before Ian Fleming's hero became a worldwide phenomenon and his passport still carried his correct name, which had made him the butt of heavy-handed humour every time he passed through Immigration. We had both been asked to judge the Governor General's Award for architecture, the island's most prestigious prize for the built environment. Understandably, Jamaica being a relatively small place, the authorities wanted as judges complete outsiders who, it was thought, would have no particular axe to grind.

The entries for the award were varied and ranged from the regional office of an oil company, through a number of ostentatious private houses, to small, self-build enterprises in poor areas of the island. After examining drawings and photographs, Max Bond and I visited each building to gain a fuller impression of their work and speak to the people there.

The luxury houses were extravagant displays of new wealth and would not have been out of keeping on the outskirts of Las Vegas. Billiard rooms, gun rooms, libraries, and terrace jacuzzis jostled for attention, and nothing less than mosaic and marble finishes seemed acceptable to their owners. To make doubly sure there was no mistake in indentifying them, the entries were entitled 'the Murphy Residence', 'the Franklin Residence' and so on, and their occupants were always delighted to receive us and show us around. One particular entry caught my eye; it was called simply and rather strangely 'a Residence for eight Persons' and was sited high in the hills well above the coastline. Late one afternoon I sat next to our driver who had been hired to take us to this destination. While Max and I checked that we had all the papers, letters of introduction and suitable camera equipment, our driver examined the road map and then opened a small compartment separating the two front seats to make sure he'd packed his gun. My eyes widened, but he was very matter-of-fact about it and explained that no one would go into the mountains without one. Once it was fully loaded and the safety catch applied we began our long, winding ascent during which I occasionally caught a glimpse of the glittering sea below through the dark, heavily wooded slopes.

His map reading was good, and after half an hour or so we arrived at a set of black-painted metal gates. It was almost dark now and the security lighting went on immediately. Somewhere behind the gates the Dobermann pinschers began barking. We waited while a surly-looking individual with a long scar under his left ear asked who we were and what we had come for. It was beginning to look as if our introduction would take some time, but it was interrupted by a shrill female voice from the veranda instructing her nightwatchman to let us in. As Max and I walked up the drive the elegantly dressed and heavily perfumed wife of the owner came to meet us. She welcomed us warmly, saying we would enjoy a Campari after our long climb, and that she had been expecting us and would be delighted to conduct us round the house. We declined the drink as graciously as we could, pleading lack of time as we still had other buildings to visit. She smiled sweetly and made a point of saying how much her husband would have liked to meet us and take us round himself but, alas, he had been detained and sent his apologies.

It was much like the other houses we had already seen and no doubt similar to those we still had to visit, so there was not a lot Max and I had to note particularly. After twenty minutes or so we thanked our hostess, took our leave and returned to our driver who had remained in the car with the windows up and the air-conditioning and radio going full blast. He asked how we'd got on and I explained that the house was broadly what we'd seen already, although we didn't meet the owner, as he had been detained. Our driver pulled a wry face, paused for a moment and then replied, 'You bet he has – he's currently doing eight years for running a drug cartel.' It was as well that we were not thinking of including any of the flashy houses in our recommendations for the top award, distressing though this would be for their pushy owners.

The 'commercial' buildings were no more than adequate, notwithstanding or perhaps because of their bravado. In the end, Max and I selected for the main award a remarkable self-build clinic in Port Antonio which served a poor community and had been achieved against impossible odds, both financial and political. Glitz was conspicuous by its absence and the clinic's honesty of expression and social worth made it stand out head and shoulders above the others.

Our unanimous recommendation remained confidential until the black-tie award dinner, where architects and their expectant clients clustered round decorated tables laden with celebratory alcohol to mark the successful conclusion of a construction contract, if not the receipt of the coveted award. Max and I were at the centre of much bonhomie and total strangers came up to say how much they appreciated the amount of time we had devoted to the judging. We were showered with invitations to dinner, golf or offshore fishing, but had to decline as we had other commitments on the island before returning home.

Rather like a Miss World contest, the awards were announced in reverse order, leaving the Governor General's Award until last. While Max and I spoke briefly about each recipient's entry there was an audible buzz of excitement, particularly as one or two of the less brash residences were included on the shortlist, but the hall then fell silent in anticipation of 'the big one'. It fell to me to explain the criteria the judges were guided by and I could see one or two faces in the audience tighten as I finally announced that the ultimate accolade went to the small clinic in Port Antonio. And that was it. Was it all over? Hadn't something been left out? And wasn't anyone going to clap? After an awkward moment which seemed to go on for ever, one of the competition organisers thought he should clap and succeeded in encouraging a dribble of applause from the audience. Furrowed brows registered total disbelief and other entrants did what anyone there would do in the circumstances – they leant across the table and opened another bottle. Meanwhile, at the back of the hall, the news had just reached a large group of architectural students who had been watching the ceremony through the open windows. They couldn't believe what they'd heard and let out a triumphant whoop of joy, accompanied by much hand clapping, high fives, and a trumpet.

Max and I were shown back to our table which, fortunately, had been reserved for local dignitaries and the organisers, so we didn't have to spend the rest of the evening trying to justify our decisions. By the time the last course of the evening was served everyone had regathered their wits and set to enjoying what they had paid for so expensively. For a community that has long learnt to pick up the pieces after a hurricane and get on with life, this was obviously par for the course. Apart from my immediate neighbours at the table, no one spoke to us for the rest of the evening and it was as if we weren't there. Although offers to be collected from the hotel to go to the dinner had abounded, Max and I found that our return journey at the end of the evening took place in a noisy old banger crammed with exuberant students who would have carried us shoulder high into the hotel if they had had their way.

Over the years I found that time spent with architectural students in various parts of the world was rewarding and enjoyable. Although this experience didn't start in Jamaica, what I found there was typical: students bring energy, freshness and idealism (qualities easily lost later in professional life), and are sharp and demanding enough to keep a practitioner on his toes.

Professor Ivor Smith had been co-designer of the groundbreaking and monumental post-war housing scheme at Park Hill, Sheffield and more recently had led a course at Bristol University, when he was asked to advise on an architectural curriculum at Kingston. I met him in Jamaica. He was in the process of devising a course for young architectural technicians who, in later years, would work as assistants, or perhaps, in suitable cases, go on and fully qualify as architects.

For the first time Ivor was faced with material rawer and younger than would be acceptable to read architecture at university level. On Day One, students would be taught to call a ruler a 'scale' and a rubber an 'eraser', and that it was the head of the drawing pin that held down the paper, not the spike. Simple practicalities to start with; more difficult would be stirring their imagination, striking the first creative spark and getting them to visualise the intangible, especially as many of them came from very limiting backgrounds. To measure their response, he would drop them into the deep end in a fascinating way. He realised that you can't ease people into believing in the parity of the subjective and the objective, or the divergent and the convergent; it had to be experienced directly.

Thus, the first-year students were asked to produce either a sketch, a rough model or a layout to represent 'A Place to Play', and after that, 'A Place to Stay', and finally, 'A Place to Pray'. For young teenagers whose functional skills probably evolved from mending a bike or helping their father repair plantation machinery, such seemingly abstract concepts came as a shock. They were deliberately left unaided to puzzle their way through this unfamiliar territory but usually, after an awkward start, and encouraged by what their peers next to them might be achieving, they would express their ideas in new ways, utterly vital for developing future architectural awareness. I found this method of teaching a revelation and saw it as an excellent tool for fashioning the young mind, especially in developing countries.

Over the years, I had become increasingly aware of the Commonwealth being 'a small place', despite its geographical diversity. This was brought home to me a few days later when I discovered that Lord Caradon, who had recently invited me to visit Cyprus on his behalf, had, earlier in his career, been the last but one Governor of Jamaica and had steered the new constitution through its difficult introduction towards eventual independence. The next day I found it even stranger to learn that the last incumbent of that post was Sir Kenneth Blackburne, who had exercised such tact and diplomacy in handling the volatile Archdeacon of Chichester all those years ago when I presented my proposals for a 'relocatable' church in the diocese. No wonder he had been so adroit on that occasion. Future generations will think it quaint that, at this time, in the absence of Google and other search devices, most of us stumbled on people's backgrounds long after we met them for the first time.

The Governor General at the time of my visit, the Most Honourable Sir Florizel Augustus Glasspole, was only the second Jamaican-born holder of the office. He had a generous figure and comfortable demeanour to match the impressive title and was regarded as a Great Son of Jamaica, whose presence at every public ceremonial event lent lustre to the occasion. The son of a country-bred Methodist minister, he had applied himself diligently to his early studies and eventually came to Ruskin College, Oxford before taking up accountancy. He was soon drawn to trade unionism in the 1930s through witnessing the plight of the ordinary working man at home, and joined the People's National Party, later to become a highly successful MP for the East Kingston and Port Royal constituency.

When I met him he was an old man and it was evident that a lifetime sticking to his last had taken its toll, but even now no important decisions were contemplated, still less taken, without his advice. His avuncular presence still conveyed authority and trust. In conversation he didn't have a great deal to say, but amiably asked a few questions when I explained what I was attempting to do on the island. When our meeting was drawing to a close and I rose to go, he looked at me directly and said quite suddenly, 'And you have an interesting son, don't you?' Presumably my family name sticks in the mind longer for not being called Smith, but his sharp observation brought me up short. How did he know about Peter? Very gradually it became clear. Peter, who worked in the music industry, had earlier taken over the management of a unique Jamaican music group in London comprising players who performed reggae on classical orchestral instruments. At a time when the music industry was searching harder than ever for 'new sounds' this eclectic enterprise caught the attention of promoters as far away as Japan, so, encouraged by their success, the group thought it was time to show the old folk back home what all the fuss was about. In London they had called themselves the RPO, to the passing annoyance of the Royal Philharmonic Orchestra, who had to be persuaded the Reggae Philharmonic Orchestra was just as entitled to use the initials as anyone else. The Governor General had recently heard the RPO play in Kingston, so the only white non-Jamaican to be introduced to him afterwards was going to be fairly easy to remember. He didn't, however, go as far as expressing an opinion on reggae played on violins and clarinets; he was much too wise an old bird for that.

The capital had grown rapidly and haphazardly since the war and I was aware that there still existed one or two vernacular timber buildings that had survived hurricanes or been rebuilt after them. I was anxious to photograph one in particular which was situated in a bustling area of downtown Kingston. Experience had taught me prudence when shooting in areas such as this: look as though you've slept in your clothes; wear a cheap Swatch; use a plastic pen; don't carry conspicuously expensive camera equipment around your neck and never point it directly at people. I was advised that Kingston suffered high levels of street crime, so to make doubly sure, I chose a well-lit vantage point with plenty of people around me, and had also accepted the offer of being accompanied by a tall, muscular member of the hotel staff. Reasonably reassured, I began the pleasing task of framing the best shot of this lovely façade, but it wasn't as easy as I thought. A battered old truck full of vegetables arrived in front just as I was about to click the shutter, and then one or two annoying clouds shaded the part where I wanted to record the shadows of the veranda balustrade. I shifted my position slightly, and when the sun shone again, immediately raised the camera to my eye. Almost simultaneously, I felt a sharp pain in my right calf and looked down to see it bleeding inside my torn trouser leg. My minder gave chase to a young, bearded derelict who had apparently thrown a large stone at me. Probably still fuelled by the alcohol and drugs which had prompted his action, he leapt over an empty barrow and disappeared down an alleyway. My burly chaperone was no match for his youthful speed and gave up the chase, spluttering apologies for what had happened.

I reluctantly abandoned the photography and limped off with him to get some medical help and then purchase another pair of trousers. After I was patched up he insisted on buying me a large beer and repeated his abject apologies. He was vociferous about my assailant but, after I had drained my glass, I began to see the incident differently. I explained to him why I had become less upset than he was, although I think he remained unconvinced of my argument. It was really quite simple. The vagrant had the same priority every day – survival – and that meant finding something to eat and drink and a place to get some sleep where the stray dogs wouldn't find you, whereas in his eyes, I would never suffer these privations. My air-conditioned aircraft had transported and fed me until I had arrived safely in Jamaica. Like all Westerners, I could afford a comfortable hotel and a decent camera, so *my* priority for the day was only waiting for a vegetable truck to move so that I could record yet another beautifully composed image for my middle-class

311

audience at home and glow in the warmth of their quiet admiration. Bloody pathetic, he would think; life was not only meaningless, it was grossly unfair, so, unable to contain his boiling indignation any longer, he hurled a brick at me. To him, I represented wealth and an oppressive past and I should never have gone photographing in such a place.

The following day, a Sunday, I took it easy as my leg still hurt, but after tea I went for short walk to stop it stiffening up. On my way I passed a Methodist church. I had heard the congregational singing from three streets away; the sound was not only loud, but full of joy and the open windows enabled them all to share their exuberance with the whole neighbourhood. It wasn't a salubrious area, and there were no polished cars on the street, but nothing was going to stop them reassuring themselves and everyone around that present misfortune will eventually be overcome. Their belief in salvation was palpable. The West lost this simple faith long ago.

When my work was complete I prepared for the flight home. I had been routed through Donald Sangster International Airport, Montego Bay, at the other end of the island from Kingston, which was served by Norman Manley International Airport, so I needed to book a taxi in good time. The hotel arranged this and I presented myself, my bags and my cherished supply of Blue Mountain coffee in the foyer punctually, as I wasn't sure how long the journey would take. After a quarter of an hour I asked at reception whether my taxi was coming and received the universal reply: 'On its way, sir,' without the bellboy so much as looking up from yesterday's cricket results. I waited another twenty minutes, and just as I was about to enquire again, in strolled a dreamy figure who looked around him slowly and then approached me with, 'Manley, man?' I replied, 'No, Sangster, Montego Bay please.' 'OK, hop in,' and with that he went back to the taxi and lit a cigarette while I trundled my own luggage.

I then repeated to him which airport I wanted and the check-in time. He gave the smallest of nods and we set off. The journey was very picturesque as we passed through parts of the country quite unknown to me, so time went quickly. Despite everything, I was beginning to feel regretful at having to leave Jamaica. Every now and then the driver stopped for a drink or to buy cigarettes, and as I realised this might rest him and hopefully improve his driving, I didn't get bothered. His behaviour at the wheel was no more erratic than anyone else's, but it still gave me the impression that he believed he had a charmed life. After another stop I glanced at my watch and was alarmed to see how little time we had left. 'No problem, man,' he said, with the first grin of the day. On we progressed until once more, without warning, we screeched to a halt and he leapt out to embrace a friend he hadn't seen for some time. His companion must have suggested a quick drink to celebrate the occasion, and off they sauntered to a nearby bar without so much as a glance back at the taxi. By the time he eventually returned my ex-colonial wrath had reached boiling point, but I managed to bite my tongue and just point angrily at my watch. 'No problem man, no problem,' and he put the car into a wheel-spinning start, less, I thought, to reach our destination more promptly than because he loved doing this and the taxi didn't belong to him in any case. I now moved conspicuously to the edge of my seat so that I was close to his ear, but my sudden gesture didn't translate itself into more positive action. As we approached the outskirts of Montego Bay we stopped in a queue of trucks strung out behind a broken-down vehicle which already had its wheel removed and was being closely examined by passers-by offering opinions on what needed to be done. Without further prodding from me, my driver reversed, sought a diversion through some narrow back streets and then got completely lost.

I had now reached the point where stick and carrot were equally useless, so I slumped in my seat and let my sweat glands speak for me. And then, after countless turns and twists, the longed-for moment of revelation arrived. We emerged from a dingy street and suddenly caught sight of the airport control tower in the distance with a row of parked planes nearby. 'Oh,' he said, unable to conceal his surprise. Conscious at last of his irascible passenger, he put his foot down hard and, as we drew nearer the perimeter fence, I looked anxiously for the British Airways tailplane (it was the only London flight of the day) and, to my joy, spotted it in the distance. Unbelievably, it was still there. Or was it? Under the shimmering sunlight it seemed to be moving, but was this an illusion? No, it wasn't. It was actually moving. 'NOW look what you've done,' I exploded. He narrowed his eyes and looked carefully at what he had done, paused, and then said brightly, 'No problem, man. My brother's got a hotel near the airport and we'll get you in, promise. He'll give you special discount, 'cos you're my friend.'

Chapter 44

The Old Dominion

A short, dishevelled figure in sandals and carrying a rough linen tote bag bearing the words 'Capitalist's Tool Kit' passed me, accompanied by a taller, elegant woman. I watched as they made their way to reserved seats at the front of the congress hall. When they turned round briefly I could see that they were Sir Hugh and Lady Casson; they were here at the University of Toronto for an international conference organised by the Heritage Trust, of which he was deputy chairman. It was a typical Casson entrance. Following school in Eastbourne he went to London to read architecture, and after the war his big opportunity came at the tender age of 38 when he was appointed as Director of Architecture for the Festival of Britain Exhibition on the south bank of the Thames. After this huge success he never looked back. His wit, charm, superb draughtsmanship and ferocious energy took him even higher and his career was crowned in 1976 by his election as President of the Royal Academy. On the one occasion we worked together on a project in Hove I found him unstuffy, amusing and hugely encouraging. He was also a spontaneous raconteur and could always be relied upon to prick pomposity, to everyone's delight.

The Heritage Trust was chaired by Lord Duncan-Sandys, for whom I had taken the Civic Trust film to Saudi Arabia in such bizarre circumstances all those years ago. As he was unable to attend on this occasion, Hugh Casson was officiating. Since my early work with the Civic Trust (of which the Heritage Trust had become an international arm), I had taken an interest in how to assimilate new architecture into historic settings without compromising either, an aspect of design that would come to be known, rather inelegantly, as 'contextualism'. Undeterred by my earlier failure to convince the Cypriot hotel owners of the threats to their history posed by uncontrolled tourist development, I was anxious to hear what experiences other countries had to offer.

315

I was happy to be invited to this event, which seemed to be attracting greater international kudos every time it took place. This was the first occasion it had convened in the New World, and its theme was particularly relevant to the well-publicised work of UNESCO, which had been trying to raise levels of awareness of contextualism globally.

At the end of the conference a small group of us were to meet under the chairmanship of the Dean of Trinity College to discuss where the next conference should be held two years hence. It was very evident that the purposely strong Chinese delegation wanted to host it and it was agreed that they be invited to a short post-conference meeting to present their bid. Later that evening, after I left the convivial farewell party, I returned to my hotel to find that every TV and radio channel was overwhelmed by breaking news of the Tiananmen Square massacre in Beijing. Extra editions of evening papers were being rushed out and the atmosphere was electric. Faces around me expressed disbelief and horror. Student demonstrators had occupied Tiananmen Square for nearly two months, refusing to move until their demands for democratic reform had been met. It was the greatest challenge to the Communist State in China since the revolution of 1949 and had been care- fully arranged to coincide with the visit to Beijing by the relatively new Soviet leader, Mikhail Gorbachev. The military response erupted after several failed attempts to clear the square in time, but its appalling ferocity attracted imme- diate worldwide condemnation. Several hundred students and innocent bystanders were shot dead and hundreds more wounded or beaten up. The TV picture of a single white-shirted student defying a column of approaching tanks became one of those indelible images that would take its place in world history alongside Princess Diana's shattered Mercedes in the Parisian under- pass or the conflagration of the Twin Towers.

As we gathered to consider the Chinese bid next morning the atmosphere was tense, but our courteous and thoughtful chairman ensured that we heard what the Beijing delegation had to say. Five expressionless faces in well- rehearsed turn began to describe the 'very modern' conference venue, its convenient distance from modern hotels, 'no much walking', and the itin- erary of 'very interesting' post-conference tours 'which would all be accom- panied', and, above all, Beijing's traditional reputation for hospitality. Our group deliberately avoided looking at each other as one expressionless (and increasingly meaningless) delivery followed another, and it was only because the meeting was in danger of descending into farce that our patient academic chairman interrupted them to ask, as gently as he could, whether they were aware of what the entire world had witnessed in the last twenty-four hours. As they all spoke and read English it was inconceivable that the media storm had gone unnoticed by any of them. Following the chairman's interjection, they resumed their presentation as though the question hadn't been put. They were on the point of reaching the last of their long list of blandishments when he stopped them more deliberately, asking whether they had understood our concern. After the shortest of pauses their leader said that by the time of the next conference, any 'unfortunate trouble' would be forgotten and the Beijing authorities could be relied upon to ensure that our visit would be a safe and happy one. Our chairman's face clouded, not because of the obtuseness of their answer, which irritated us all, but probably because he understood something of their dilemma. They had obviously been rigorously selected for the privilege of representing their country, and the fact that they had been given passports to visit Canada was an almost impossible honour even for senior party officers, for whom foreign travel at this time was only the stuff of dreams. They had been instructed to make a successful bid on behalf of the largest emerging country in the world, and as it was probably Asia's turn anyway, Beijing assumed that selection should be well within their grasp. Their delegation was presentable, deferential and statistically word-perfect: they couldn't possibly go wrong. Their further career preferment would obviously depend on their success, and everything had been triple-checked. It seemed that our Chinese delegates either were pretending the massacre hadn't happened or hoped no one had noticed. There was no Plan B, and they knew they had no authority to depart from their approved script. It was hopeless. The dean, with a hint of a caring smile, explained that in all the circumstances their bid could be considered no further, but he hoped that on some future and more appropriate occasion, they may consider reapplying. And with that we all went our separate ways.

It was in Hong Kong some years earlier that I first met Tom Howarth, a born-and-bred northener who had taught at Manchester University before emigrating to Canada, where he eventually held a chair in architecture at Toronto. He was universally known for the earliest, and still probably the best, comprehensive study of the architect, designer and watercolourist Charles Rennie Mackintosh, who established a style of architectural art nouveau. Some acclaimed Mackintosh as the father of the modern movement and the greatest Scottish architect since Robert Adam, but others had dismissed him out of hand as little more than an eclectic decorator. As so often happens, he became a cult figure of international importance only long after his death. As a relatively young academic, Tom Howarth had taken a particular interest in Mackintosh at a time when little was known about him. During many years of patient research, he obtained or was given drawings of designs for a wide variety of his work. As his modest purse allowed, Tom had purchased items of his furniture which no one else seemed to value at the time and slowly assembled a formidable collection which would give particular focus to much of Tom's life in Toronto. He owned a large apartment in Bloor Street, in the centre of the huge city, that overlooked the landscaped grounds of the university. Here he kept on display his most precious pieces – so precious, in fact, that each chair had a length of furnishing cord across it, so finding somewhere to sit down wasn't easy. As the collection grew and the cordon sanitaire around each piece increased in line with its rising value, so moving around what was meant to be his home became ever more difficult and I had to sidle crabwise, following a serpentine path from one piece to another. In the end I imagine even Tom realised it was no longer an easy place in which to entertain, so he would often take friends out for a meal. He was a generous host, and on one such occasion he invited me to the Royal Canadian Yacht Club which had been built on a nearby island on Lake Ontario and was reached by a small, open ferry. The setting was almost colonial and enjoyed views of the dramatic Toronto waterfront on one side and the infinity of the lake on the other. Like most old-established clubs, its atmosphere was genial and it had the reassuring air of a past era, emphasised by its southern-style architecture. It cherished its unquestioned traditions and hierarchies in defiance of the intensive modernity that faced it across the harbour. Tom must have been a non-sailing member – he was not a sporty type – but took quiet satisfaction in having been elected to membership. We talked about Mackintosh, and about the CAA, of which Tom had been a regional vice-president, and we spent an enjoyable evening together, much of it on the veranda until it got too chilly. Looking around me, I had a sense of what it meant to be Canadian in a place like Toronto, but what was to happen next morning would show me it was illusory and was being rapidly consigned to the past. Tom walked me down to the ferry and I sailed off to my hotel. The lake was much larger than many inland seas and was prone to sudden changes in weather. As we pulled away the temperature on deck dropped quickly and, only clad in a lightweight suit, I was happy that the journey was short.

After an uncomfortable night, I woke the next day with what felt like a chill on the bladder and it felt sufficiently uncomfortable for me to ask the hotel where I could get some medical advice. They supplied me with the address of the private clinic to whom they referred visitors, which was only two blocks away, so I walked there immediately after breakfast. The clinic was a small but very efficient operation staffed by alert young clinicians who didn't hang about, so I was soon ushered into an examination room where a female doctor who still looked in her late teens took me briskly through a diagnostic checklist. Once I had explained my condition to her, she began with the preliminary details, following her tick-box format:

'Name?'

'Gender?'

'Visa card number?, Expiry date?'

'Temporary address?'

And this led directly into the clinical questions.

'Sexually active?'

'Men or women?'

I couldn't believe this was happening to me. Here was I, not that far off retirement, being grilled by a complete stranger younger than my daughter. She approached her task as factually as a street-side pollster, but without the smiles. Her face expressed nothing as she concentrated on her diagnosis with a speed that would have impressed her recent tutors. She finally looked up and said that my own diagnosis was probably correct, 'so here are some pills and may I have your credit card?' I was out of the door before I knew it, eighty-five dollars lighter and aware, for the first time that, in the New World time is money, which didn't allow for personal niceties. The studied politeness of old Canada that I had observed the evening before was rapidly being replaced by the businesslike approach of North America.

Now in retirement, Tom had embarked on a commercial enterprise which capitalised on the newly awakened interest in art nouveau in general and in Charles Rennie Mackintosh in particular. Having assured himself that there were no residual copyright restrictions, he had decided to make scrupulously accurate reproductions of Mackintosh dining tables and tall, high-backed chairs, marketing them as an authenticated 'limited edition'. He had discovered nearby a talented cabinetmaker of Austrian extraction who could undertake the technically demanding task of assembling the pieces from original design drawings in Tom's possession. One morning I was taken down to a small workshop in a run-down area of the city to see the craftsman at work and witness the imprint of the Howarth/Mackintosh copyright brand burnt into the underside rim of each completed piece. He obviously enjoyed the process of examining each joint and the direction of the grain, and verifying the overall symmetry of the piece. Only when he was completely satisfied would Tom give instructions for the immaculate little brand to be heated. A glossy illustrated pamphlet advertising the product had been circulated widely among his friends and colleagues, and by this time he had already received enquiries from as far away as Malaysia.

Due to declining health (and lack of space, I imagine), there came a time in the early 1990s when Tom decided he would dispose of part of his collection, so he invited representatives of Sotheby's, Christie's and Phillips to visit him in Toronto and bid for the privilege of holding an auction in London. Christie's won the bid, and I attended the event, which finally took place in 1994. I recorded the occasion for a national journal with the following account:

Revaluing an Icon

When Charles Rennie Mackintosh died, 'the entire contents of the two studios were practically of no value – and were estimated to be worth £88. 16s. 3d.' (*Charles Rennie Mackintosh and the Modern Movement*, Thomas Howarth, 1952).

Even from the comfort of a front row seat in the celestial grandstand, Mackintosh would have been unprepared for the scene at Christie's last week, when the Thomas Howarth Collection of his and related work came under the hammer and realised well over £2 million.

The red walled octagonal auction space of the Great Room proved insufficient as dealers, curators, architects and the professionally curious overflowed into adjacent rooms early in the afternoon.

At '2.30 p.m. precisely', as the effortlessly impressive £10 catalogue had it, the house lights went up, the overseas currency converters flickered into life and the first of 143 lots comprising sketches, designs, artefacts and furniture was offered. An array of silver-tongued, sharp-eyed Christie's staff scanned the room from beside the auctioneer, while Middlemarch below-stairs porters adjusted their white gloves before carefully displaying each exhibit.

Telephone bidders vied with the regulars, who in turn had to put up with the irregulars, some of whom had come with the intention of buying only one small drawing at £1,000 to find it going for more than twice that figure. Throughout the proceedings, buyers came and went like figures in a Roman church during a long mass, either thankful in success or humble in failure.

And what of the vendor? Thomas Howarth's interest in Mackintosh started more than fifty years ago, and the result of a life's work of scholarly diligence and painstaking acquisition was bearing fruit before a spell-bound audience.

Tom Howarth says he is not bereft at the loss of such a substantial part of his collection, and has wisely retained a representative group of artefacts and drawings, not just because they are particularly dear to him, but also because they are a reminder of a quite extraordinary day in the life of a British architect.

Notwithstanding the depredations of the taxman, one hopes that a way will be found to perpetuate the memory of a consummate talent born out of his time before Mackintosh, like all the others, goes out of fashion again and into relative oblivion.

Apart from the Great Lakes, Canada has countless smaller lakes scattered widely over its territory, some in northern latitudes of permafrost, some more agreeably situated further south in the hinterland of great conurbations like Toronto. Muskoka Lakes is one such area and lies on the edge of the Algonquin Provincial Park. I found the term 'provincial park' misleading as, coming from a small island, to me it suggested municipal greenery provided by benef-icent Victorians to alleviate the scourge of urban tuberculosis. In fact, the Algonquin is about the size of Wales.

The well heeled of Toronto discovered the remoteness and beauty of the Muskoka Lakes (of which there are some 1,500) at the end of the nineteenth century and began erecting cottage retreats there. Fred Rounthwaite, the Torontarian I'd first met in Hong Kong in 1979 when he was honorary treas-urer of the CAA, had inherited such a cottage from his forebears and would doubtless pass it on to his children in due course. 'Cottage' was equally a misnomer, as it comprised a group of stoutly built and well-equipped timber structures complete with a separate guest suite, all with screens to exclude blackfly. It sat on the steep bank of a lake with a wooden stairway linking it to a private jetty and boathouse in which was stored a beautifully maintained motorboat of 1920s' vintage – all brass and marine-varnished hardwood – and an Indian canoe.

When Fred became president, he would invite the CAA secretary and me to this idyllic retreat for what today would be called 'blue sky thinking'. Sustained by a constant supply of fresh coffee (and, later in the day, serious alcohol), the three of us would sit on the wooden balcony and have to concentrate really hard in this distracting setting. Our talk was mostly of the 'what if' or 'if only' variety, but the physical distance from petty ethnic argu-ments and special pleading gave us a detachment which undoubtedly helped. We worked hard to make some sense of Commonwealth intentions and their architectural and social implications, so Fred was always anxious that we should spend some leisure time at the end of the day, either swimming or on his magnificent launch. Despite it being summer, I found the water too cold for swimming, but loved the Mr Toad experience of taking the wheel of the boat from time to time. It was relatively easy to operate, probably because it had been designed and built at a time when superfluous electronic gadgetry and planned obsolescence had not been included in the specification.

The Indian canoe was quite another thing. Having thought I'd mastered the boat, I imagined this would be even easier, but Fred insisted on a short lesson. He would teach me to paddle as noiselessly as a Mohican tribesman approaching prey or enemy. It involved mastering the J stroke. If you sit in the back of the canoe and paddled from one side only, the canoe will gradually go round in a circle, so this has to be corrected by twisting the paddle at the end of the downstroke (which propels the craft) and finishing with a curl (which corrects the direction) in order to maintain a straight course. The J stroke began with the thin edge of the paddle entering the water noiselessly and ended with an equally quiet withdrawal. Clever but obvious, I thought, so I had a go and completely failed. I tried again – and again – but still couldn't do it, so Fred gave me another faultless demonstration. When I tried – and inevitably tried too hard – the result was equally shameful. My frustration was compounded by anger at discovering a profound and probably congenital lack of coordination I never knew I suffered from. I'd never found it difficult to ski, double-declutch or lead the line in 'Strip the Willow' if I had to. And I wasn't dyslexic. Was the fact that Ramanath told me I bowled off the 'wrong foot' at cricket a hint that genetic predisposition had dealt me a wild card?

Fred knew a lot about the Algonquin tribe and its customs, but he wasn't sure how much was myth. And I could readily recall my unquestioning schoolboy attraction to the legendary Red Indian princess Pocahontas, which evaporated years later when I discovered that she hadn't after all defied her tribe and saved the life of one John Smith, as legend had it, but had become a Christian, married an Englishman and died in a lodging house in Gravesend.

The Canadians I met were remarkably loyal to the Crown, and those of Fred's generation who fought in World War II were stalwart supporters of Britain; some of them, like him, visited London every year to watch the Trooping the Colour ceremony before the Queen on Horse Guards Parade. I found it hard to visualise what it would feel like to be asked to join in a war being fought by another country over three thousand miles away, and pondered over whether the characteristic of 'Canadianness' could be described.

Some years later, I had the opportunity of asking one of Canada's best-known living writers Margaret Atwood, a native of Toronto, how she saw the national quality. She answered by quoting from a winning entry in a recent literary journal competition asking how 'Canadianness' could be defined. The journal had given by way of example 'As American as apple pie' and invited readers to complete the phrase beginning 'As Canadian as . . .' The winning answer was 'As Canadian as can reasonably be expected, given the circumstances.'

Chapter 45

Travels with an Edwardian

Sharing expertise and encouraging technology transfer were tasks central to the work of the CAA. From time to time funds were made available by the Commonwealth Foundation to organise seminars in developing countries. Africa and Asia had strong moral claims on our time and the CAA was invited to respond to their requests. Whilst in other fields aid was easy to deliver, in architecture this was not always so, partly because its half art/half science characteristic didn't make the subject easy to package.

Having recently chaired the Practice Committee at the Royal Institute of British Architects (RIBA), I was asked to help in what was a non-remunerated assignment, presumably because I had some previous knowledge of Africa and Asia and didn't mind giving up some holiday time. I was told my co-lecturer would be Stanley Cox, a respected academic from Cardiff who specialised in the legal aspects of professional practice. It was this aspect of architecture that often got neglected, as it wasn't glamorous and didn't figure predominantly on the pages of the international glossies. But it was still essential and was a sufficiently self-contained topic to fill the two-day seminars we had in mind. We decided on Africa as I had existing contacts there, and planned an initial trip to Nairobi as the city was developing very quickly.

I had never met Stanley Cox before but was aware of his reputation as an authority on Contract. I suggested that we could give three papers each, as alternating speakers, which meant that I opened and followed with talks three and five. Stanley readily agreed and I asked him for his titles early on, mainly to avoid repeating an experience I once had when speaking at a conference on colour in architecture in the early days of the Institute of Advanced Architectural Studies at York. The programme of speakers had been prepared by the time I was invited and I was the last to forward a title to the organisers. On the day of the conference I looked at the printed programme to find that my talk, entitled 'Application of Principles', immediately followed one from an industrial chemist specialising in pigmentation which he had called 'Principles of Application'.

My topics in Africa were very wide ranging, probably because I wasn't a specialist in the sense that Stanley was. My talk 'Future Directions in the Profession' included the need for diversity; 'Environmental Impact Assessment' was based on my Malaysian experience; another talk was entitled 'Internationalisation of Practice', and the one I enjoyed giving most but was clearly not a 'hard' subject was 'Regional Identity in a World Context', which I usually introduced over dinner when everyone was more relaxed and didn't need a notebook.

Stanley Cox's lectures were really hard-edged and included 'Building Procurement Methods', 'Contract Administration' and 'Managing Risk'. These were followed intently by every audience, not only because he was a good communicator but also because, in the days of Empire, all the countries we were to visit had adopted the RIBA form of building contract and its ancillary documentation. This would have been applied by an expatriate trained in the UK who was now running the Public Works Department in his new assignment. It was the same in the fields of health, education, law and government administration, so updating a British system was always much easier than starting from scratch with a totally unfamiliar model.

Stanley came across as the authority he clearly was; he even looked the part – balding, with a tuft of white hair on either side, pink complexion, a little portly, and very courteous. What I didn't know was that he had seldom been out of Britain, let alone to a tropical country, and that he would rely on me unhesitatingly for all the introductions and organisational arrangements. His newness to the experience became increasingly clear when he stood up to speak before a crowded and eager audience of Kenyan architects in a Nairobi hotel one Monday morning. Trying to disguise his discomfort in a starched shirt, tightly knotted tie and traditional English suit, he smiled broadly and said, 'I bring you greetings from the University of Wales.' Rows of intent eyes registered surprise. He welcomed them as if he were opening a garden fete. As his first topic was about dispute resolution, he began immediately with a detailed description of a recent court case involving accidental damage to a pipe organ in a remote Nonconformist chapel caused by rainwater penetration during repairs to a Welsh-slated roof. This boxful of novelties completely intrigued the audience. Pipe organs, Ebenezer chapels and Welsh slates didn't figure prominently in Kenyan life and I wondered what they would make of this glimpse of a faraway country from which this foreign figure had come. I was very concerned that we might have lost the audience on the morning of Day One, but the reverse happened. They were so fascinated by the unique content of Stanley's examples that they digested the difficult part of his talk about liability for consequential damage with comparative ease.

As I got to know Stanley, it was clear that he should have been born in a gentler age. He was a perfect gentleman at all times, punctual, always well prepared and unfailingly considerate. A Bristolian by birth, he disliked long-distance travel and, unbelievably, had never visited say Paris or Rome, but, on his own admission, preferred trips to Liverpool or Bradford, where he was extremely knowledgeable on nineteenth-century municipal architecture. We were to share accommodation in future seminars all over Africa during the next few years and I grew fond of his immaculately folded flannel pyjamas and the portable radio he kept tuned to the BBC World Service. It helped him to go to sleep and he always used a discreet earpiece so that if the heat or the mosquitoes did wake him during the night, the reassuring voices from Bush House, London would soon soothe him back to sleep without waking me.

A visit with him to Ghana the following year repeated much the same format, although by now he had seen enough of African building construction to offer less esoteric examples to illustrate his talks. The seminars became successful, and as the word got round (I assumed through Commonwealth channels, but more likely through social and tribal links), our audiences got bigger. I imagine it wasn't because we were particularly good, it was more that nothing else of this sort was on offer. When glancing at the delegate list on one occasion in Accra, I was astonished to find a number of Nigerian names and later learnt that they had crossed two adjacent countries, Benin and Togo, to reach us.

After a respectable period back in Britain to justify my existence to the long-suffering colleagues who had been minding the shop, Stanley and I planned one last series of visits the following year. By this time, the Commonwealth Foundation probably thought we'd had enough funding and it was the turn of another non-governmental organisation (NGO) on their books, of which there were nearly thirty, covering most professions.

The itinerary for our final visit was to include Zimbabwe, Namibia, Botswana and two centres in South Africa. If Stanley's introduction to the continent had, until then, been incomplete, this next trip would fully immerse him. In Zimbabwe we visited Livingstone, a town east of the Victoria Falls, and while in the area I just had to take a photograph of Stanley beneath the huge bronze statue of David Livingstone, whose likeness was as determined as Stanley's was self-conscious. The everlasting schoolboy in me had triumphed.

In 1855 the great missionary and explorer Livingstone had discovered the place where the Zambesi cascades over four hundred feet into the boiling cauldron below, and named the magnificent falls after Queen Victoria. His reputation was made, but the epic contribution to history of Henry Morton Stanley, the thirty-year-old American journalist, would have to wait many years before it was fully acknowledged. Stanley had solved Africa's most important geographical riddle by establishing that Lake Victoria was the main source of the River Nile, thus completing Livingstone's uncompleted exploration. When the doctor went missing, the English establishment, principally through the Royal Geographic Society, had manifestly failed to locate him. They gave Stanley little recognition and, in any case, regarded him as only a pushy American journalist, not a 'real' explorer.

My Stanley, on the other hand, could not have been more different from this intrepid journalist, though he was probably more like the image of Stanley that had passed into the common imagination. If places had been changed, my Stanley probably *would* have said, with his customary courtesy, 'Dr Livingstone, I presume?' whereas history concludes that the American probably said nothing of the sort, but only later embellished his account to make it more memorable for his editor.

By this time there were four of us travelling together, as the CAA secretary George Wilson, whom I first met ten years earlier in Nairobi, had joined us, together with the Nigerian who was currently CAA Vice President for the Africa Region, Dr Wale Odeleye. A lot of our internal travel was undertaken by air. High-wing monoplanes are well adapted for short flights in this climate, and we could have never kept to our tight schedule had we attempted to travel overland all the time. On one occasion, following a fairly intensive week, we accepted an invitation to fly from the Zimbabwean capital Harare to see Lake Kariba, about two hundred miles to the west. The construction of the massive dam on the border of Zimbabwe and Zambia downstream from the Victoria Falls, to supply power to both countries, produced a huge reservoir that ultimately became Lake Kariba. The expanse of water is absolutely vast even when seen from the air, and our destination was a phenomenon called Fothergill Island. Planned flooding took a decade to fill the surrounding area while wildlife progressively retreated to higher ground, and as the pace of the operation was relatively slow, animals and birds had time to adapt to their changing habitat. A prior extensive survey had predicted that a small plateau of higher ground would remain above the final water level, and over the years the wildlife migrated there and established itself on what eventually became on island. This created an artificial game reserve where the flora and fauna of the whole region could be easily observed in one visit.

There was just enough space for a rudimentary airstrip, and our young Afrikaner pilot, clad in sleeveless shirt, shorts and deck shoes, brought us down with consummate ease. He accompanied us, and we were given the choice of joining one of the small safari groups, the first travelling in comfort and safety on the back of a three-ton truck, the other on foot. I'd been in such vehicles before in Kenya and, for obvious reasons, they seldom got near enough their quarry, so it felt more like a Sunday school outing. The other three weren't discouraged by my opinions and opted for the truck. I chose a foot safari because you can get much nearer to where you want to be, and also – and this was probably just nostalgia – I knew I would be issued with a .303 Lee-Enfield rifle with live ammunition. As I hadn't had that experience for over forty years; I couldn't resist it. The intention was not, of course, to fire at any wildlife but only to take a firearm as a precaution. I loosened the webbing sling so that I could carry it comfortably over my shoulder and then withdrew the bolt to insert a clip of five rounds into the magazine, closed the bolt and applied the safety catch as if I'd done it every day of my life. It felt good. Only then did I realise that my small-arms training had been so efficient that I could do things in my sleep if I had to, despite the torrent of verbal abuse which invariably accompanied the tuition. We set off to explore, stopping every time we heard a twig snap or the grass rustle, but came across very little. My safari ranger was also a botanist, and after a while he began to concentrate on discovering flora, presumably to compensate for the conspicuous lack of fauna. I trotted along behind him, hoping still for a bit of excitement, when I saw him suddenly drop to his knees. I did the same and heard him give a long, low whistle of surprise. Looking around me, I could see and hear nothing. He beckoned me forward, his face near the ground – examining a plant not much bigger than a scarlet pimpernel. I watched his hand approach the delicate flower, and as his index finger got closer to the petals, it closed up of its own accord; after he moved away, it reopened. 'Bet you've never hunted one of those down before,' he said. 'Not with a fully loaded rifle,' I replied. We rejoined the others as they clambered off the truck. They were buzzing with excitement and reeled off the names of all the animals they had spotted.

By the time we returned to our small plane to depart, it had become unbearably hot as the pilot had been obliged to park well away from any tree cover. A blanket of heat hit us as we climbed aboard, and because I thought he'd like it, I arranged for Stanley to sit next to the pilot. Leaving the door open to cool the aircraft before take-off didn't work – it merely admitted more heat – so the pilot said we'd have to get used to it, but there was one thing we might do. Turning to Stanley, he said that as we increased speed to get airborne he would like him to open the outside door next to him so that it would act as an air scoop and cool us for a minute or two. *So that's why John put me here*, he must have thought, but I insisted, unconvincingly, that that was not so.

'And just how wide would you like it, skipper?' asked Stanley helpfully.

'Until it pulls ya hand off,' came the thick Afrikaans reply.

'I hope I don't damage the lock,' Stanley mumbled to no one in particular.

Shortly before arriving in Botswana for our next seminar in the capital, Gaborone, we had one more night in a game reserve in even more primitive accommodation made of reed and straw. Botswana is famed for its wildlife and I was particularly anxious to see cheetahs and Cape buffalo if I could. Stanley was my overnight companion, as usual. I think neither of us knew how hot and humid it was going to be at night, and no sooner had we had a rudimentary wash in the canvas 'basin' than we broke out into a heavy sweat again. This brought back memories of military life in Singapore that were definitely not nostalgic. We would just have to cope. As the noises of the night closed in around us, becoming shriller as early darkness descended, we found it hard to identify the separate parts of the cacophony of growls, yelps, ticks and buzzes that engulfed us. Noticing Stanley sitting nervously on the edge of his bed, I said airily, 'Well, we're here and this is what we've come for.' 'Sort of,' he replied, knowing full well that this wasn't at all what he'd come for. The mosquito nets provided were of the old, rectangular-box type and I showed Stanley how to slide in like a sloth without leaving space for any insects to enter at the same time. He did it (sort of) first time, but after a few minutes found it suffocatingly airless as it excluded any cross ventilation – not that there was any, but there was always the hope that it might appear later in the night. My observation that it would be safer under the net even if he had to lie in his own sweat all night did not find favour, so he carefully rolled up his net, thanked me for my consideration and dozed off. The next morning Stanley was up and washed before me, presumably because he'd slept badly, and when it was my turn for the ablutions he casually asked if I could identify a number of elongated weals that were appearing on his forearm and neck. I couldn't, but offered him some Dettol from my kitbag. We ate an early (and silent) breakfast as we had to travel into Gaborone to prepare for our first seminar. We didn't need much time for this as we were by now word-perfect with our individual scripts, so after we'd booked in and changed at our next stop, we went straight on to meet the organisers, who greeted us warmly. Stanley was much quieter than usual, and although he did his best during the introductory pleasantries, he didn't seem to engage with his customary warmth. He still looked sweaty, but I thought this might wear off in the air-conditioned corner of the room. I asked him if he felt all right and he said he didn't. I suggested that, to give him time, I should give all three of my talks in succession to allow him to rest before he spoke, but he didn't think that would be necessary. I blanched at the thought that I might have to give his paper because, while I usually nodded sagely from time to time during his immaculate deliveries, I would have been completely out of my depth over the detail and an embarrassment to everyone if I had to field questions. I got up and started nervously on 'Future Directions for the Profession', not listening to a word I said, but glancing every now and then at Stanley to see if he was still with us sufficiently to perform. By the time his first talk was due he rose quite slowly and stood bolt upright for a few moments, breathing rhythmically, before starting his lecture which, mercifully, he must have known by heart. All the facts were there, in the right order, and nothing was noticeably missing; half an hour later he sat down heavily to take questions. His shirt was soaked. He leant over and asked me anxiously, 'Have I just given this talk?' I knew something was seriously wrong and we needed help from our hosts to get some quick medical advice. After hastily rearranging our lecture sequence to bring forward a discussion period which could look after itself, a very helpful expatriate quantity surveyor made immediate telephone arrangements to get Stanley to a nearby hospital.

Luck was on our side and he was seen promptly by a white female doctor well versed in tropical diseases whose first suggestion was that he might be suffering from tick-bird fever, although she was concerned that the elongated weals on his arm didn't support this diagnosis. She then conducted a number of simple tests and within a couple of hours her conclusion was that he had been stung during the night by a swamp spider. She immediately wrote out a prescription for a quick-acting antidote that would put Stanley back on his feet in forty-eight hours, and it did. Mosquito nets were never mentioned, but I recalled in later years that Stanley never went anywhere near Africa again, or indeed ever left Britain.

Due to an excess of zeal on the part of our conscientious secretary to whom I had stressed the need for strict economy in our travel arrangements, Stanley and I found ourselves being put up not in a hotel (of which there wasn't a wide choice in Gaborone in any case), but in a recommended bed-and-breakfast house run by a jolly woman who turned out to be more enterprising than I could have imagined. The place was adequate for our needs as we spent most of our time away running the seminar or with new friends in the evenings, but it was clear that the little establishment had a fairly rapid turnover. While I was unpacking, Stanley, who had his own room for once, walked into my room to enquire if I was ready to leave for the seminar and I asked him what his room was like. He said it was all right but a bit untidy and was mystified by the number of discarded little 'envelopes' littering the wardrobe shelves. I was too distracted by changing the film in my camera to take much notice, but the mystery still troubled his very orderly mind, so on our way out I went to see his room. It didn't take long for me to realise that the income derived from commercial salesmen and others staying during the working week was supplemented at weekends by simply arranging for the place to be used as a knocking shop. It was conveniently close to a number of bars and must have been a little gold mine, particularly as the enterprising proprietor was able to show the police properly receipted records for her Monday-to-Friday 'day job'. Although he wouldn't have dreamed of saying so, it was clear that Stanley thought my interpretation was unduly cynical.

Our seminars ended in Durban and Johannesburg, where the mainly white practitioners were still undertaking most of the architectural work and were anxious to maintain 'Western' standards of practice. It was a revelation to see how little South Africa, at least among this group, had been affected by international sanctions. I had expected to see privations and conspicuous shortages, but soon realised that the imposition of sanctions had, at least on this level, stimulated innovation and enterprise, and taught people to be more self-sufficient and adventurous than they had been before the sanctions. At the same time, it was obvious that the white population anticipated profound political change and, indeed, a number of the white academics were very left wing and courageously espoused the black cause.

My team's arrival in early 1995 was less than a year after the first democratic elections in South Africa and the abolition of apartheid. Everyone, white, Cape-coloured and black alike, was very aware that wholesale bloodshed had been avoided since the end of World War II and therefore willed the new government of national unity to succeed. Of course there would be huge problems along the way, but everyone I spoke to nurtured the hope that it would come right in the end, even if it didn't all happen in their lifetimes. This was borne out to me when I read the inscription by our host, the President of the Transvaal Institute of Architects, in a handsome volume she presented to me as a memento of our visit, and which was also an admission that, despite the superficial luxury of the splendid houses and the brand new four-by-fours I saw around me, they had sorely missed the hand of international professional friendship:

Johannesburg, January 1995
    Dear John
    In celebration of the dawn of a new era from where the dialogue
left off!
    With grateful thanks.
    Mira Fassler Kamstra

Stanley was equally touched by the response of our hosts, but I gained the
impression that the political maelstrom of the last half century didn't figure
conspicuously in his thinking. He had been invited to help the CAA by talking
about 'his' subject, but international politics wasn't his natural territory.
Although he knew that South Africa had had a terrible time, it probably
hadn't touched him, as it was outside the field of specialism he had laboured
so hard to perfect. It was not that he lacked feeling – far from it – it was
just that his life was complete without another extraneous factor.

Chapter 46

Mitzi

The 1960s saw the arrival of unexpected freedoms. Flower power came over from the States and it advocated universal love in place of materialism. Following the collapse of the *Lady Chatterley* obscenity trial, the poet Philip Larkin wrote the memorable lines 'Sexual intercourse began in nineteen sixty three (which was rather late for me).' But a few years later, student action was to become a lot more volatile as anti-Vietnam demonstrations took place in Grosvenor Square, London and, following the shooting of a West German student leader, riots broke out at universities throughout Europe.

The University of Sussex was founded at the beginning of that decade and was the first centre of higher education to be built since World War II. Six more were to follow elsewhere. In both educational and architectural terms it broke the conventional mode and became a focus for innovation. For instance, at curriculum level, the traditional single-subject Department was replaced by the multi-subject School, thus combining subjects that would normally be kept apart. The School of European Studies was one of these, and American Studies was to follow.

Equally innovative was its architecture, which owed nothing to Oxbridge or red-brick precedent. Sir Basil Spence, designer of the recently consecrated Coventry Cathedral, had been selected as architect, and, following a master plan for an initial phase of the campus, designed its first building, Falmer House, which was to be used jointly for faculty and students. Its architectural vocabulary, in specially made Sussex brick and wood-grained concrete, was unique, although the influence of Le Corbusier's Maisons Jaoul of 1954 was not hard to recognise. One of Spence's early decisions, which was universally supported, was to site the main buildings in the fold of the surrounding hills and limit their height to that of the mature trees which gave the site its special character. His design was highly sculptural and, with deft use of water

335

to give carefully arranged reflections, he produced a design that was unashamedly romantic and a long way from the machine aesthetic that had so dominated the early days of the modern movement.

The novel atmosphere of the campus appealed to Mitzi Solomon Cunliffe, the sculptor-wife of the first Professor of American Studies, Marcus Cunliffe. By temperament, she was a child of her time and enjoyed the buzz of the place, making a point of meeting many of the architects who flocked to see its emerging architecture. I decided to invite her to give a talk to my fellow professionals about her approach to artistic collaboration and she suggested that we meet first to discuss the idea at her Kemp Town apartment in Regency Brighton. It was in one of those 'highly sought-after' Grade I listed, stucco-fronted houses that look superb from the front but, when viewed from the back, are a grey jumble of ad hoc excrescences that, in their heyday, would have formed servants' quarters and stabling; unquestionably a case of 'Queen Anne front, Mary-Anne behind'.

The Cunliffes had an upper-floor flat, and Marcus joined Mitzi and me for coffee. She apologised for the sugar still being in a packet and got up to fetch a bowl. 'Don't be so bourgeois,' he muttered tersely and plunged his wet spoon into the packet. She raised her eyebrows at me and tried to continue what she was saying. He interrupted to say that he couldn't stay long. Mitzi's sigh seemed one of obvious relief. He explained that he was trying to finish writing a book and had to 'go underground' for a couple of weeks. Apparently, he was also preparing papers on 'The American Response to Industrialisation' and 'George Washington: Man and Monument', and made no attempt to conceal his opinion that Mitzi's flirtation with architects was really rather trivial. After he left she let out an extravagant groan and re-jangled all her loose jewellery like an Afghan hound emerging from water. 'Now we can *really* talk, John. Where's the lecture? How long can I speak for? Are ninety-five slides too many? Will you promise to pick me up?' And then, after pausing for breath, 'What about this necklace then? Didn't you notice it the moment you came in? It took me three weeks to make and . . . and . . .'

Six of one and half a dozen of the other.

In later years Mitzi became famous for her design of the golden Jason mask presented to the winners of the BAFTA (British Academy of Film and TV Arts) Award, but it was her early work in marble, stone, wood and bronze that originally attracted attention, including that of Le Corbusier.

My generation of architectural students first came across her work at the 1951 Festival of Britain site on the South Bank, where she designed the instantly acclaimed bronze door handles for the Regatta Restaurant. They were both representational of the human hand and eminently functional. A gently curved female hand was fixed horizontally to the plate-glass doors so that the graceful knuckle side suggested that you push it, whilst the inward curled fingers on the other side were for pulling. Beautiful to look at, sensual to touch and faultless in use; no wonder everyone was talking about them.

As years passed, she moved on to larger-scale work, often decorating buildings with what she cheerfully called 'sculpture by the yard'. Her final architectural commission came in 1971 when she carved four large stone panels for Scottish Life House in the City of London.

A year or so after this I met her for the last time. I was early for an appointment in Knightsbridge, and as it was a beautiful, fresh day, I decided to walk across Hyde Park from Marble Arch tube station. Drinking in the unexpected luxury of my detour, I was miles away in thought and failed to hear staccato footsteps behind me. As they got closer I was also aware of jangling accoutrements, but my thoughts were still elsewhere. 'John, are you *completely* deaf?' It couldn't possibly be anyone else. I turned and smiled at Mitzi. 'Got something to give you,' she said breathlessly and began rummaging in her voluminous and highly decorated handbag. She couldn't immediately find what she wanted so she dropped it on the path impatiently. 'Must be here – don't go.' I didn't. Eventually, with a flourish of success, she thrust an envelope into my hand. 'What it is?' I asked. 'You've got to come, everyone will be there, so no excuses.' 'Any particular occasion?' I enquired naively. 'You *must* have heard. It's my divorce party.'

Chapter 47

Cameroon and the Bomb

'And where are you going, sir?' enquired the policeman who'd waved me down.

'Heathrow, and I'm late.' I was only half awake.

'You seem to be in a great hurry.'

'I'm trying to catch a plane,' I answered flatly.

'Pull over, please.'

'I hope this won't take long, Sergeant.'

'It'll take as long as it takes, sir. Open your boot, please.'

'It's only my luggage.'

'Open the boot.'

I was completely mystified. It was only 5 a.m. No one else was on the road. I hadn't been drinking. As I looked around I became aware in the early dawn light of other police officers, some of whom were preoccupied with their radios and others with lengthening the barricade. It had all the appearances of a hastily arranged roadblock and presumably had been set up on the Brighton boundary to check any vehicle leaving the town. The air crackled with tension and there seemed a lot of uncertainty among them over who should do what next. Another police Land Rover suddenly appeared from nowhere and the occupants hastily exchanged messages.

'Can you tell me what's happening, Officer?' I asked.

'Where do you live, sir?'

'Brighton.'

'Are you telling me you didn't hear the explosion?'

'What explosion, Sergeant?'

'*The* explosion.'

I had heard nothing and, before finally waving me on my way as presumably I didn't smell of cordite, slowly I gathered what had happened. Mrs

339

Thatcher and her entire Cabinet were staying at the Grand Hotel, Brighton for the Conservative party conference. In the early hours of the eve of the conference a huge IRA bomb had exploded. It was difficult to take in. In Brighton? At the Grand, of all places? The Prime Minister? Fatalities? I left very unnerved. As I drove past them I vividly remember the early sunlight brushing the top of the stone pylons which mark the town's northern boundary. In later years I always had this vision when anyone mentioned the event. I suppose we all carry some idea of where we were when we heard that President Kennedy had been assassinated or when Princess Diana was killed in a motor accident.

Brighton, along with Bournemouth and Blackpool, were favourite venues for party conferences and in 1984 it was Brighton's turn. The formula didn't vary very much, and although its citizens were reminded that such events bring a lot of money to the town many felt, particularly in view of renewed IRA activity on the mainland, that a lot of visitors were put off by the security measures and general disruption they caused.

The night preceding the conference opening was always very convivial. Everyone had unpacked and, bumped into old friends (or political enemies) and, knowing they were going to be stuck in a windowless conference hall for three days, were determined to relax before the highly stage-managed conference started. There were two main events on offer that evening. One was a formal ball where Mrs Thatcher and her immediate entourage would make a splendid appearance; tickets were in high demand by those anxious to meet the Iron Lady or at least touch the hem of her ballgown. The counter-attraction was an evening of political satire at the nearby Dome concert hall fronted by the well-known TV satirist John Wells which attracted a very different sort of audience, and to which I found myself invited because someone had dropped out at the last minute. Political satire had come a long way since its early days on television and now had a sharper bite. The audience either hoped or feared it would overstep the mark and word would get back, and this gave the show an extra frisson. The entertainment was over all too quickly, but this was to allow the stage personalities to catch the last train back to London. This meant that those of us in Brighton were all in our beds shortly after eleven, unlike the conference ball-goers. After the last waltz, some tagged on to the inner circle and retired to the Grand Hotel for a nightcap, perhaps hoping for one last chance of a brief exchange with the leader. How tragic for them such a decision proved to be.

By the time I reached Heathrow, news-stands were awash with late editions spilling onto the floor and it was evident that the world's media had lost a complete night's sleep. During my flight to Cameroon, where I was representing the CAA at a pan-African conference, the flight-deck kept passengers fully acquainted with breaking news and slowly the full significance of the catastrophe became clear. Neither did the tension lower when I changed planes at Douala for the internal flight to the capital, Yaoundé.

Upon landing, I was pleased to see that I was being collected by car, but the glow wore off when, shortly afterwards, at a military post on the road, they examined my passport in great detail and, concluding I was English, the brighter one in the posse decided that I was an escaping fugitive and may just have something to do with the international news which had reached even them. I was ordered out of the car at gunpoint by a surly young man wearing ill-fitting fatigues and a back-to-front beret who told me in broken French to unload my case from the car and open it at his feet by the roadside. The heat was intense – we weren't that far from the equator – and it took me some time to get everything unfastened. He kicked the case a bit nearer to the area of shade he wanted to stand in and then, with the muzzle of his rifle, disdainfully turned over the entire contents as if he were moving a dried turd from his front path. Carefully ordered files, photographs and pieces of underclothing became entangled as I stood sweating through the fine layer of dust thrown up by passing vehicles. After a look at the soldiers' faces, I decided against trying to explain, in inadequate French, that I was here as a guest of their government and let them just get on with it, guessing that this would be quicker than confrontation. So it was. My very savvy driver waited until they showed signs of flagging and then offered them cigarettes, which they eagerly snatched from his hand before drifting back to their hut. I picked my clothing off the boiling tarmac, each item now embellished with an abstract pattern of ginger dust like some Indonesian batik. Too tired and dishevelled to get angry, I concentrated on reaching the conference centre as there was no longer any time to call at the hotel first. I looked, and felt, remarkably unpresidential but was determined to make the opening ceremony.

Following insurrection against French rule, Cameroon had become independent in 1960 and Yaoundé was its capital. It is not a particularly large town, so the conference hall was easy to find. I only had five minutes in hand. Hopefully I would need nothing from my ailing luggage and would be given a conference pack on the way in. So, running a dirty hand through my hair, I entered to see the entire company assembled and a vacant chair awaiting me on the platform, and I picked my way past the others, many of whom were in full national dress, as unobtrusively as I could. Halfway through this awkward manoeuvre I was spotted by the chairman who, with a wondrous smile, immediately grasped the microphone to say that the President of the

Commonwealth Association of Architects had managed to reach here from Brighton, UK, 'straight from the disaster area'. I certainly looked the part, but was disconcerted to hear the warm and spontaneous applause that greeted me. I knew immediately that I'd missed a trick. In Danny Kaye's film *The Secret Life of Walter Mitty*, the nobody he plays adopts different guises to attract attention. In one such sequence he appears as an RAF flight lieutenant with his arm heavily bandaged in a sling and is asked by a sympathetic bystander how badly he was wounded. Raising his chin and putting a determined look on his face, he brushes the enquiry aside and says nonchalantly, 'Just a scratch.' If I'd put on a bit of grubby Elastoplast in the foyer and walked in with a pronounced limp it would have been so easy to have had my moment as the heroic survivor.

The conference, bringing together architects from the whole continent of Africa, was held under the auspices of UNESCO and was obviously well funded – the unnecessarily personalised document folders and other freebies bore testimony to that. I was puzzled by the sheer lack of realism on the part of the senior UN bureaucrats who presumably thought that a pan-African event could achieve something. What, for instance, have Morocco and Tanzania to say to each other? And what about those numerous states at odds with warring neighbours? I vividly remember the dismissive answer when I asked a wealthy delegation from oil-rich Nigeria if their country had ever considered a little financial aid to other poorer African countries. They looked at me disdainfully and I never asked again. So where was this sudden African unity going to spring from? One of UNESCO's self-appointed tasks is 'to build peace in the minds of men'. Well, the expensive jamboree in Cameroon probably built some sort of peace in the conscience of UNESCO's programme planners, but did they really think that a prestigious event for wealthy professionals from richer African countries, gathering to agree a manifesto about the values of prosperity and concord (with a bit of glitzy architecture thrown in), would make a scrap of difference in this vast conti-nent affected so conspicuously by famine, poverty and corruption? Perhaps it was just Cameroon's turn to hold a junket.

The conference concluded with conspicuous agreement on what everyone would like to see happen, but with not one suggestion as to how to achieve it. It was like being back at the party conference: a lot of cleverly worded resolutions delivered to a receptive audience, but no indication how or when such objectives could be achieved..

Chapter 48

Ghana

Gordon Mattey took over the secretaryship of the CAA in 1981 following a successful career in the RAF and later at the Royal Institute of British Architects. It was at short notice and he only expected to fill this post until a permanent replacement was found. This took far longer than anyone expected, and in the meantime he found himself quite enjoying the job, miserably paid though it was. Gordon was my real introduction to Ghana and, more particularly, its politics, although I had been there before on my own.

As a senior RAF officer, he had taught a Ghanaian officer, one Flight Lieutenant Jerry Rawlings, to fly aircraft, little knowing that his pupil would one day lead a successful coup against the short-lived civilian government in Ghana and would chair the Armed Forces Revolutionary Council. Although civilian rule was later restored, another coup had brought Rawlings back to power. All this meant that Gordon Mattey was not only *persona grata*, he also had a good understanding of the Ghanaian psyche. To me, they came across as a warmer, sunnier people than those from some neighbouring West African states and they seemed to bear their many privations stoically. Perhaps this was because of their almost-universal Christian belief, which shows itself everywhere. Not untypical was a sign at the front of a passing lorry pushed into service as a bus which proudly proclaimed, 'God's Time is the Best'. I recall one Sunday when I was walking through Sodom and Gomorrah (the name given by residents to the stinking, sprawling shanty town on the edge of the capital Accra), when I heard joyous singing coming from a tin-roofed shack used for Pentecostal worship. Picking my way round pools of stagnant green filth, I looked through the open door to see a dozen or so women in bright headscarves circling the small interior in swaying file, rhythmically waving white kerchiefs above their heads as they sang a hymn. I had seen that same beatific smile before in Jamaica in equally abject surroundings and knew that their unquestioning faith enabled them to rise above their circumstances and even pass on their radiant hope to their slum-mired children. If faith is 'the substance of things hoped for, the evidence of things not seen', I was looking at a faith now scarcely seen in the West. Maybe this had been born out of generations of sadness. What was originally the Gold Coast had been the centre of the slave trade serving the cotton and sugar plantations in America, and perhaps what I was witnessing was a nobility of spirit able to bear life's bleakest misfortunes.

In 1957 Ghana was the first British colony in Africa to gain independence, and at that time it had abundant supplies of gold and cocoa, and efficient civil service and more than £250 million in foreign reserves with which to get started. Independence was a significant occasion attended by many world leaders, including American Vice President Richard Nixon. President Eisenhower's health had been failing for some time, but the United States was anxious to have a visible presence as it watched the 'winds of change' sweep over Africa. Nixon was supported by a large entourage and by an even larger media corps covering the event nationwide, with journalists and cameramen attending from as far away as Washington, DC and the Deep South. When at midnight the Union flag came down and the new Ghanaian flag was hoisted to mark the first seconds of independence to the accompaniment of a glittering firework display, the American cameras swung across to Richard Nixon, who was clearly expected to say something extempore. Quick-thinking as ever, he looked around him and asked the nearest black face, 'And what does it feel like to be free?' The very audible reply came back, 'Dunno, I'm from Alabama.'

In the years following independence the economy faltered badly and, like many other African states going through the same process, Ghanaians witnessed civil war, tribal conflict and inept dictatorship. Only neighbouring Nigeria, which wasted its oil wealth, has suffered more coups. The road to recovery was bound to be hard, and at the time of my visit there were some hopeful signs, but also a reluctant awareness that it was going to take much longer than anyone thought.

The Ghana Institute of Architects had been founded at the time of independence in 1957 and mostly comprised practitioners or academics trained in the United Kingdom. Martin Adu Badu, with whom I stayed in Accra, was one such architect, and, by Ghanaian standards, he enjoyed a good standard of living. He and his wife Grace (who cooked the finest pineapple sponge I've ever eaten) lived in a generous house he had designed just outside the city. Driving a Mercedes and wearing a well-cut lightweight suit, he epitomised success and was well connected with banking and commercial figures in the capital. He also appeared to be involved (quite legitimately) in a number

344

of other investment enterprises outside architecture, an arrangement forbidden in Britain by our institute's code of conduct at that time.

He was an easy host and liked to reminisce about his time in the UK. After dark, we would sometimes go up to the flat roof and have a drink while we wondered at the unclouded heavens, as I had so enjoyed doing in Saudi Arabia, and Martin became quite proprietorial when, for instance, he drew my attention to a moving speck of light which he identified for me as a satellite. From this vantage point you could usually hear the distant hubbub of the teeming city, but on one particular night during the football World Cup when Ghana was still in contention long after stronger nations had been eliminated, Accra went completely silent. It was as though plague had struck. There was no one about. Traffic stopped and the city held its breath as everyone crowded around the nearest transistor radio or rare TV set during what was a very tense game. Every now and then when there was a near miss or, less frequently, a goal, a collective roar of support would echo across the city and dissolve into the humid night. This momentary distraction for shanty-town dwellers must have been heaven.

One morning when I came down to breakfast I was surprised to see Martin not in his usual immaculate tropical suit but clad only in a coarse-textured tribal garment thrown over one shoulder. It was in burnt sienna with a number of symbolic motifs superimposed in white. He was also wearing sturdy sandals. He made no attempt to explain his new appearance but I gained the impression that he expected me to ask him. Apparently the paramount chief of his tribe had died some weeks earlier and, as was the custom, a durbar was to be held in the village in the Ashanti region, from where Martin hailed. The event was to honour the memory of their late leader and to give the opportunity to pay respects personally to his bereaved wife. Since his death a similar act had taken place in a number of small townships in his territory and this was to be the last such ceremony before he was finally interred. It was never explained to me how his body was preserved during this period in such a climate.

I asked Martin how long he would be away but, to my surprise, he said I would be made very welcome if I went with him. I couldn't begin to visualise how I would fit in on such an occasion and disliked the idea of my intrusion being seen as a tourist's 'photo opportunity'. My reservation was quickly brushed aside and he assured me that, if I could spare the time, he would like to present me to the paramount chief's widow. I still felt rather uncertain, but such was Martin's matter-of-factness that I eventually accepted, although this was probably out of a sense of curiosity.

I went as I was, as I didn't have a selection of clothing with me and, in any case, would have had difficulty attempting to anglicise tribal wear. It didn't seem to matter, so we set off on what was to be a dusty drive north which took longer than even Martin had expected. Upon arrival a good three hours later than planned, we left the car and made our way slowly up a small wooded incline which led to a wide open valley, upon the slopes of which were already gathered several hundred tribesmen, many of whom had travelled, some on foot, for several days. Without exception they were all attired like Martin and he introduced me to those he knew personally. A bank manager stood next to a toothless goatherd, sharing reminiscences. They were brothers for the occasion, and not for the first time did I realise that tribal affinity would always be more important than national identity. Empire builders had successfully brought education, health care and administrative skill, but their political masters were often naively boneheaded when drawing national boundaries.

The paramount chief's widow sat on some sort of improvised throne and received her supplicants as her husband would have done. In a voluminous garment covering her generous frame, she sat quite immobile with half-closed eyes, either because she was, understandably, tired or perhaps even because she was bored: it was impossible to tell. In due course I was pushed forward to offer my condolences. I mumbled something about loss and undying legacy and she didn't blink an eyelid, but it was clear when my time was up, and I made way for others.

Apparently these occasions are not totally solemn and a good deal of drinking and dancing accompanies the formalities, such activities spreading into the side streets and occasionally manifesting themselves in spontaneous unions to ensure the numerical strength of the tribe. After all, the durbar was celebrating a long and fruitful life, and hereabouts life expectancy was very low.

My remit in Ghana included a visit to the Faculty of Architecture at the University of Science and Technology at Kumasi to give a paper on 'Regional Identity' and also to meet its head, Professor John Owusu-Addo, a good friend of Gordon Mattey. They had been pals for many years. Every time Gordon visited, he brought a bottle of East Coast malt, and they would sit down to laugh, talk and drink it. John easily brushed off the innumerable difficulties faced in trying to run higher education in Africa and had learned, through long experience, the art of survival by not taking life too seriously. He was larger than life, quick to laugh and got things done or, more often, through sheer force of personality, got others to do them. A lesser man would never have survived in this place.

Kumasi lies on high ground about 150 miles northwest of Accra, and getting there and back involved another long and unpredictable journey, so I was given a driver for the occasion. On our return journey we were no longer driving against the clock and I had time to look around me for a change. We kept up as reasonable a speed as road conditions allowed, but had to slow down to a snail's pace as we passed through villages. Small children, stray chickens and abandoned handcarts and fruit stalls reclaimed the territory after each occasional vehicle had passed through. At a point where we had almost drawn to a halt stood a group of enterprising boys, who couldn't have been more than eight or nine. They were all holding live rats by their tails for sale to travellers. Fresh bush meat. Before the days of refrigeration in the West we all kept our food live in dovecots, ponds and pastures, so what could be more sensible? I nervously asked my driver if he ever ate rat, but he told me he preferred eating grasscutter (whatever that was), as it offered a better cut for the family on a Sunday. 'It's difficult to describe,' he said. 'Come and try some with us on Sunday; the kids love it.' As it was probably a herbivore and couldn't possibly be blamed for spreading plague, it was difficult to refuse but, alas, refuse I did, though I added a couple of quid for the tip.

Having been delayed by all this, my driver put his foot down and we climbed out of the village at some speed. He wanted to get back to his family and I wanted a shower and a change of clothing. Just as I was musing on the very traditional, almost pastoral scene we had just witnessed, a uniformed figure stepped out into the road ahead of us and waved us down with his hand-held speed indicator. A radar trap. And only a hundred yards away from a live-rat takeaway. This was Africa.

The following day I attended a meeting in Accra at the request of local architects engaged on government projects who had not had their fees paid for a long time and were experiencing cash-flow problems. Could I help them? They were diffident about making too much fuss themselves for fear of incurring disfavour and having their names removed from the government list of external consultants. I found out the name of the minister responsible and, flying the flag of the Commonwealth, sought an early meeting. Military governments, in my experience, don't quite know how to 'read' the Commonwealth, but probably know that its headquarters are in London and therefore tend to err on the safe side and avoid dismissing its requests too readily. A date was arranged for my meeting, and I arrived a few minutes early at the nondescript building that acted as the ministry's centre. After half an hour of waiting, I asked how long the minister might be, without disclosing the fact that I'd already seen his car arrive. The secretary said that he was expecting me but I had to appreciate that 'the minister is always very busy' and he would see me as soon as possible. I let a further hour pass and then enquired again. I was aware that my enforced wait would deliberately be drawn out so that I might reflect on the importance of his ministerial status.

347

An hour and three-quarters after the appointed time I was called in and found the minister, dressed in well-pressed fatigues, perched on the corner of a table with his back to me, nonchalantly swinging a leg to and fro as he studied a file. Without turning around he asked me what I wanted, and I explained the architects' dilemma as diplomatically as I could. He showed no sign of listening and it was clear that the file in his hand was on a totally different subject. I ploughed on as patiently as I could, but was brought to an abrupt halt by him calling his assistant to fetch another file. I hadn't been offered a seat and was apparently speaking to myself. This annoyed me so I began to extemporise. Fortunately, I had read in that morning's paper that his government had made a bid for substantial financial aid from Britain to start a much-needed hydroelectric scheme in an underdeveloped part of the country. Changing my persona to something far brisker, I indicated my personal interest in and knowledge of the aid package and implied that its success would depend on the informed view of UK technical experts who would need to check the veracity of the details supplied by his department.

The effect of my charade was as instantaneous as it was magical. He swung round to face me, expressed surprise that I hadn't been offered a chair, grimaced a smile, ordered tea and turned an attentive ear in my direction. He was probably in his early forties and had reached his present post through conspicuous involvement in the latest military coup. In sub-Saharan Africa I was meeting the model for T. S. Eliot's character about whom he observed, 'the trowel in hand, and the gun rather loose in the holster'.

As a result of this meeting, all the architects received their outstanding fees within two days and everyone was touchingly grateful. It was ridiculously easy. I didn't work there, I had a return air ticket in my pocket, I might never come back, so it didn't matter if I over-egged the Commonwealth involvement and embroidered the extent of my own influence in London. Everyone was happy and my conscience didn't trouble me.

Before I left to return home I was presented with a ceremonial hardwood stool with the words 'God the omnipotent' carved beneath the elaborately fashioned seat. I was relieved to know that this had nothing to do with my having practised white magic on the minister, grateful though everyone was, but was more an enduring expression of their deep-rooted Christian belief. I learned much later that in former times when a king was appointed among the Ashanti, his intricately carved stool was carried in procession before he was 'enstooled' rather than enthroned, and since that time a stool has been regarded as a more superior mark of status.

I was only just beginning to understand the land I was visiting, but little knew I was to return in stranger circumstances in years to come.

Chapter 49

Africa West and East

Much has been written about the arbitrary nature and ethnic irrelevance of the political boundaries imposed under colonial rule. Nigeria, which achieved its independence in 1960, is no exception. It houses 373 ethnic groups speaking over 500 different languages and occupying a land mass of three hundred and fifty thousand square miles that varies in character from tropical rainforest to semi-desert in the extreme north. Half the population owe allegiance to Islam and half to Christianity and there have been many clashes between Muslim Hausa people and Christian Yoruba groups, usually over the ongoing ambition to introduce Shari'ah law. But one country it now is, and it is arguable whether any self-imposed political boundaries would have been any more successful in the long run.

The Nigerian Institute of Architects was formed in the same year that the country attained independence and many of its members had been trained in Britain, so it was not all together surprising that, as President of the CAA, I was invited, together with Owen Luder, President of the Royal Institute of British Architects, to join their 25th Anniversary Conference in the then-capital Lagos in 1985. In addition, Oluwole Olumuyiwa, a well-known Nigerian architect, had been CAA president when the association met in Hong Kong in 1979, and we knew each other well.

Throughout the Commonwealth, customs and procedures originally imported from Britain still abounded, whether it was rubber stamps and forms in triplicate or Rotarian and regimental formalities at institutional gatherings. Commemorative lunches and celebratory dinners in Nigeria were heavy with precedence, speeches, toasts and so on, and I could understand why the institute's celebrations were going to occupy a full week.

In the post-war years in Britain, when building materials were scarce and only obtainable on licence, a number of more adventurous architectural practices opened offices in developing countries, among them those of Raglan Squire, Maxwell Fry and Jane Drew, and Ronald Ward, the last of whom had an office in Lagos run by Edward Moore and Peter Whitehouse. Ted and Peter shared a very modern house which I assumed they had designed themselves, full of carefully detailed luxury. It was serviced by indigenous employees, the most engaging of whom was 'Joshua', who was delegated to Owen Luder and me. Owen had been allocated a beautifully equipped lodge beyond the pool at the end of the luxuriant garden, whilst I was given a fine room on the first floor of the main house. Although both Ted and Peter were accustomed to West African life, they had planned for their retirement by acquiring property in Rabat and on the Isle of Wight. They were thoughtful and accomplished hosts. Making guests comfortable in a hot, humid climate isn't easy and I could see their running battle with condensation made evident on the extensive plate-glass windows of the main house.

In the mornings Owen and I were left to breakfast on our own so that we could confer about the daily conference in which our hosts were not involved, but they made sure Joshua looked after us well. Joshua was boyish and good-looking and had worked happily with his employers for a long time. He wore a well-cut apron which stretched from his chest to his knees, and only when he turned round did I notice that it stopped well before his back and all that he wore otherwise was an elegantly minimal pair of shorts which did full justice to his pert bottom. His culinary tour de force was the breakfast melon which, with consummate skill, he hand-sculpted to make a carrying basket containing perfectly even slices, all carved from a single fruit. Maxim's in Paris would have been proud of this offering and I guessed that either Ted or Peter would have taught him how to serve such delicacies as part of his probationship when he first became houseboy.

On the first night we were given a reception at the British High Commission, where we met many expatriates. On most subsequent evenings, we visited or were visited by friends of our hosts for drinks and, apart from the now mandatory question, 'I suppose you don't, by any chance, have any English newspapers you've finished with?' conversation reverted to more local issues. After a while, guests' faces began to look familiar and I realised that they were the same ones I'd seen at our first reception at the British High Commission and the next day at the British Council. Haphazard though it seemed, this social round had a form of logic about it because, in the end, all the various guests took their turns as hosts and this not only kept a lively rumour mill going, but provided some mutual support in what was, by any standards, a very volatile city.

Every large detached villa had its high walls and patrolling nightwatchman, and although social arrangements looked relaxed, there were certain things you didn't do. This was brought home to me on reading the invitation from the British High Commission on my arrival. It stated that the event would start at about 5 p.m. and be over by 7.30 p.m., which seemed quite brisk for an evening meal. It was explained to me that the police had suffered so badly at the hands of the lawless that they had been ordered to retreat to the safety of their barracks by nine o'clock each night and to stay there until seven the following morning, thus handing over the entire city to unfettered crime and violence. It was therefore incumbent on every host to ensure that guests reached 'home' safely before the mayhem started.

As with so many countries I had visited, the violence was not directed exclusively at expatriates, least of all at those like Ted and Peter who had been there long enough to become part of the community, but more particularly it was aimed at anyone in possession of a valuable commodity that could be turned quickly into cash. Improvised roadblocks would suddenly appear and anyone foolish enough to be driving a private car late in the evening could expect to lose a wallet or Rolex or even the car itself. Wholesale corruption in both the police force and the army made it doubly difficult to improve a desperate situation, despite half-hearted efforts by the authorities. It seemed as if the city had come to accept things as they were and had learnt to work and live around them. I had seen the same happen in other parts of the Commonwealth where everyone knew they could not do much about them: annual floods in Bangladesh; drought and bush fires in Australia; hurricanes in the Caribbean and earthquakes in Pakistan. Such events breed a flat, dispiriting acceptance that saps the will.

Nigeria has always suffered from endemic corruption despite the promises made by a procession of military coup leaders in the years following independence, and the situation would worsen still more under General Sani Abacha. Similarly, violence was never far beneath the surface and, apart from ethnic clashes, it would persist for years as a result of oil wealth falling into the hands of the few while those who toiled in its production in the Niger delta were left conspicuously under-rewarded and suppressed. Future church historians would be baffled by the aggressive stance that would be taken by Nigerian Anglican bishops choosing to concentrate their invective upon homosexuality whilst appearing to turn a blind eye to widespread denial of human rights and wholesale corruption on their own doorstep. Did they pretend that St Matthew didn't write, 'Why beholdest the mote that is in thy brother's eye, but considerest not the beam that is in thine own eye?'

Against this fraught background some good architecture had managed to emerge, albeit with a heavy modern-movement flavour, modified only slightly to respond to a profoundly different climate. Expatriate architects arrived, better-off Nigerian students were sent to train in Britain and before long all-Nigerian practices began to appear. It followed that one or two schools of architecture were established in the country so that architects could be trained at home, and strenuous efforts were made to include the subject in burgeoning centres of higher education.

I had been invited to visit and speak to students at the new university at Enugu, and before leaving the UK I had prepared a fully illustrated lecture entitled 'Regional Identity'. The topic had interested me since my earlier days in Saudi Arabia, where access to unlimited money had led the Saudis to go from goatskin tents to air-conditioned Manhattan-style buildings without the slightest consideration about whether their new architecture in any way reflected their culture, climate or religion. Some of us hoped that, in places like Nigeria, once new construction technology had been fully assimilated, the international style they had started with might be modified and developed so that their buildings could reflect their location without having to resort to cliché. This might have happened, though the subsequent rate of globalisation was going to make it increasingly unlikely.

The flight from Lagos to Enugu took me to a higher and cooler region where the atmosphere seemed less oppressive and more conducive to study. I remembered that Enugu had been the capital of Biafra, the short-lived secessionist state in southern Nigeria which existed from 1967 to 1977. The war extinguishing this small country ended in a humanitarian catastrophe because Nigerian blockades prevented supplies from entering the region and hundreds of thousands of people died in the resulting famine. Within three years the Republic had been incorporated into Nigeria. Arriving only fifteen years after this atrocity, I half expected to see some evidence of those awful times, but instead here was a fully fledged university contributing to the nation's development and its occupants gave every appearance of having got over it all. Communities seem to recover from cataclysmic events far more quickly than we imagine possible and the poorer the country the more resistant its people seem to be, perhaps because turmoil has figured so frequently in their lives. Young people in particular seem very resilient and here they were, toddlers at the time of the Biafran war, now calm and focused students.

I was met at the small airport and driven to the university where, to my surprise, I was greeted at the entrance by the vice chancellor, who had been patiently awaiting my arrival and wanted to accompany me to the assembly hall. I had checked my slides on the plane and felt reasonably sure that they fully illustrated the main points of what is a fairly wide-ranging subject. As we walked up the drive discussing the role of the Commonwealth we came in sight of a largish structure, and as we drew closer I recognised its very African form. It comprised an extensive pitched roof covered in a natural forest material which was supported on all four sides by stout wooden poles, the wide spaces between them being completely open to the elements. Seated in orderly rows and wearing immaculate white shirts or blouses were a hundred or so architectural students who must have been in place for some time, patiently awaiting my appearance. I asked anxiously, 'Is this where I'm giving my talk?' and was told that it was and the students were looking forward to it. I looked around even harder as we entered the building. It had no walls and light streamed in all round. Not only were there no surfaces on which to project images, there was no means of blacking out the searing light and, in any case, there was no sign of a projector or screen.

We've all had anxiety dreams where perhaps we arrive at an airport and discover we've forgotten our passport or are walking onto Centre Court and find we don't have a tennis racquet. This was much worse. It was real. It was happening to me now. Had I come from a more extrovert family I could have offered extempore extracts from Gilbert and Sullivan instead or – and this was a greater temptation – I could have swamped them with the modish psychobabble so beloved of faculty in second-division schools of architecture; but I didn't have the vocabulary. No, there was nothing for it but to press on. In the three minutes of my host's introduction I had to turn a carefully prepared, fully illustrated lecture on a highly visual subject into a lecture on a highly visual subject with no illustrations whatsoever.

Gradually recalling the sequence of my slides, I resorted to describing each image in my mind as vividly as I could probably in the manner of a trainee teacher explaining parables to a Bible class – and it seemed to work. Perhaps traditions of storytelling in tribal homelands enabled this audience to visualise and anticipate better than Western students would have done but, for whatever reason, they seemed satisfied with my stilted performance. Such reassurance, however, didn't stop me from thinking that they would have been just as polite had I read out the first ten pages of the Lagos telephone directory.

It was a mercy to not know that far worse would befall me one day in Pakistan.

I had an equally unnerving and very different experience in Harare the capital of Zimbabwe, not long after. Like most people, I value a few hours 'off duty' before a lecture or speech, particularly after travelling, not just to have a shower and change, but more to try and gain some equilibrium before an event which often could contain unforeseen political or technical difficulties. Recitalists will tell you they must not be disturbed for twenty minutes before walking on stage, and clergy need a period of quiet to still themselves before administering the sacrament. I thought the process was almost universal until one day I visited the surgeons' changing room in a large British hospital where I was planning an extension. In every respect it looked like a rugby football locker room – shoes kicked off upside down on the floor, concertinaed trousers just stepped out of, half-knotted neckties hanging off the bench and the BMW engine still warm outside – all only yards away from the theatre where the most delicate surgical interventions were being performed. I am sure they regard themselves as an exception.

In the late 1980s and early 1990s Zimbabwe was still relatively prosperous and Harare an orderly place to visit. Having a long and fairly formal evening ahead of me, I decided to first relax by having a look at some of the new buildings, as I wanted to have some idea of what had been accomplished so far. I took my camera and happily strolled about, unwinding in a blissful climate that had all the characteristics of an English June morning. A number of large projects had been completed and one of these was quite near the hotel. It was a sixteen-storey, light-coloured concrete structure that looked surprisingly well maintained in a country where this seldom happened. Like some of its neighbours it had been designed conscientiously, if somewhat unimaginatively, so I thought I'd take a photograph as a record. I wanted it to be seen within its urban setting, so I did not have to get too close and shot the view from a number of angles as the sun wasn't coming from a particularly helpful direction. By the time I'd finished I slowly realised I was being closely watched by two men a short distance away. Not wishing to be relieved of my camera, I turned to walk back to the hotel and, in so doing, caught my shoe in a large crack on the side of the road. I was wearing an extremely comfortable but old pair of suede shoes which I took everywhere as they were ideal for hot climates. As I extricated my foot I saw that the worn sole had almost detached itself and I bent down to stamp it back on as well as I could. My action wasn't very effective and I had to limp rather conspicuously to keep it on. Before I knew what was happening I became aware of first one and then two hands on my shoulders, accompanied by a quiet but firm voice asking what I was doing photographing the headquarters of the ruling ZANU-PF party and demanding to know whose authority I had obtained. I said I had no idea what the building was and I hadn't been particularly close to it anyway. I realised, though, that Harare was not the sort of place where local people engaged in architectural photography and I could presumably be taken for some unwanted alien agent. They required me to accompany them to the police station for further questioning and each of them held me firmly by the upper arm as I was escorted away.

We entered a small, sparsely furnished room at the back of the station with one high, barred window which bore an uncomfortable likeness to every KGB interrogation room I had ever seen on screen, complete with bare light bulb. It was very close and stuffy and smelled of stale cigarette smoke. My all-too-visible sweat could easily have been interpreted as fear rather than me being too hot and I felt this impression was not going to help my situation which, by now, had all the appearances of becoming a long, drawn-out affair. I gave a detailed account of who I was, why I was there and my professional interest in architecture, laying particular emphasis on my role as an unpaid volunteer trying to impart the latest know-how to their countrymen and wishing to use local architectural design as a comparison. It was all so different from stolen goats, illicit drugs and petty market-stall theft that mine must have sounded like a complete cock-and-bull story. The questioning continued and it was clear that my explanations were making no impression at all. The interrogators then demanded my camera, which had a part-exposed film in it. Refusing my offer to open it myself and, if necessary, sacrifice the spool, they handed it from one to another and said something in a local dialect that I couldn't follow. As they were doing this I explained weakly that I was due shortly to be entertained as guest of honour at a dinner given by the Institute of Architects of Zimbabwe and had a limited amount of time available. And then, suddenly, as I looked nervously from one unimpressed face to another, I caught sight of a coloured football calendar on the wall behind them. It contained a large picture of (yet again) Manchester United, whose fans, it seemed, cover the face of the earth.

What happened next was entirely unpremeditated. I very loudly exclaimed, 'Manchester United,' beaming at them both. They were so taken aback at my enthusiastic outburst that they turned to look over their shoulders at the best team in the world. 'And do you know what they did in Madrid last night?' I asked before they could resume questioning. The one nearest me said, involuntarily, I imagine, 'No, did they win?'

'Wonderful. 3–1. Terrific game. Pity you missed it.'

From that moment on it was plain sailing. An instant bond had been formed. There was mutual recognition. I had stumbled on a shared interest (one so much more appealing to them than civic architecture). They then asked who had scored and, as I had no idea, I had to fend off a line of questioning by going into elaborate detail about a new stadium, the redesigned strip, and talent scouts coming as far as Africa in search of top players. I thought I had better not overdo it, so slowed down before I completely lost touch with reality. The interview then began to break up, my stickily-fingered camera was returned complete with a now prematurely exposed film, and they left me to wander back to the entrance and return to my hotel as their attention focused on something else that looked rather more fruitful.

I looked at my watch and saw that I had only half an hour before making a formal entrance and meeting all the other invited guests. There was a limit to what I could do in the time and I had to prioritise. Getting my shoes repaired was out of the question, so I brushed them and concentrated on a shower and a clean shirt before donning a suit. It was one of those occasions when you were expected to wear your chain of office, so I pulled it out of the bottom of my suitcase and gave it a cursory rub on my sleeve before putting it on. It looked ridiculously old-fashioned, but that wasn't my fault; it was just one of those occasions when you had to appear like this.

To make matters worse, the platform party which I was to lead had to make its entrance from a mezzanine above the grandly named ballroom floor and this involved descending a short flight of stairs when the proceedings began. At the required moment I stepped forward to the top stair and paused while the rest of the party lined up behind me. In so doing, my foot partly overhung the first step and, to my astonishment, my errant sole came away completely and slowly made its independent descent before me. I could only proceed as though nothing untoward had happened, so I made my way, less magisterially than planned, down the wide staircase in slow pursuit of a frozen kipper, all the while smiling beatifically at the reception committee awaiting us at the bottom. Seeing what had happened, they were equally flummoxed and, in an attempt to be both helpful and courteous, one of them carefully picked up the sole and handed it to me discreetly as I walked past. I slipped it quickly into the programme folder I was carrying. I remember saying something like, 'Thank you. An extra bookmark's always handy.'

Chapter 50

North of Lahore

As early as 1940 Muhammad Ali Jinnah, the leader of the All-India Muslim League, had publicly proposed the Two Nation Theory, and a clearer historical assessment now acknowledges that the debacle of partition was not just the fault of the British. Wherever one attributes blame, the event caused untold bloodshed and widespread destruction as enraged mobs took to the streets to purge their newly defined territory of their religious opponents. Looking back at the partition of India into separate Hindu and Muslim states in 1947, Nayantara Sahgal, the niece of Pandit Nehru, observed that it was based on the 'fantastic notion that religion constitutes nationality' and it was therefore destined to fail.

Many historic buildings of Lahore, for instance, were seriously damaged during the conflict and it was some years before a reconstruction programme could be undertaken, largely with financial help from the United Nations. As the capital of the Punjab Lahore is the second largest city in Pakistan after Karachi. There the comparison stops, as the latter is heavily commercialised, accommodates much industry and has a flourishing port. Conversely, Lahore is the cultural, political and educational centre of the country and contains some of the loveliest city gardens, some dating back to the Mogul Empire.

I had been invited to take part in the fifth Asia Congress of Architects, to be held at the Lahore University of Engineering and Technology, whose Department of Architecture was based there. The theme of the congress was 'Towards a New Direction in Architecture', which was one of those catch-all titles chosen to accommodate the widest range of opinions, and which optimistically presupposed that a new direction was necessarily a good thing, and that we would be capable of finding it. The programme stated that I would speak on the first morning, following a paper entitled 'Urban Space as an Expression of Power' to be given by a curiously named Professor

Vandal. Fortunately, I was not required by the programme makers to respond to this in any way, so I didn't need to identify myself as either a hawk or a dove, but spoke instead on Environmental Impact Assessment, to be illustrated with a selection of worldwide slides I had carefully cleaned of fingerprints before leaving the UK.

I handed these to the projectionist in the newly built lecture theatre, a windowless building completely dependent on air conditioning. I then embarked on a five-minute verbal introduction, and just as I asked for the auditorium lights to be dimmed, there was a power cut and everything went off. No one seemed particularly perturbed as it was a common occurrence here, but as the minutes went by, it became oppressively hot and the darkness prevented any movement or chatter by my audience. After twenty minutes, to a weary cheer, power was restored and I nodded to the technician to install my carousel. I saw him bend down to take it out of its box as, almost immediately, all the lights went out again. Over a collective groan I then heard him drop the carousel. There was a clatter as the entire sequence of slides spilled at his feet. Then there was silence. No one, least of all me, knew what to do, so we just sat in the dark and waited. Obviously embarrassed by the mishap and anxious to do something constructive, the technician began scraping the floor with his foot in an effort to retrieve as many as he could reach before the lights went on again, hoping to reduce any further delay. In my own puddle of darkness I knew exactly what was happening, but felt powerless to do anything about it. I only too clearly visualised a sticky thumbprint on each slide. By now someone had found a cigarette lighter to illuminate the floor at the projectionist's feet, so he triumphantly scooped up each one and dropped them into the carousel. After an age the lights went up and we were off again. I pressed the lectern button for the first slide, knowing its appearance would probably appal me. Slide number 14 appeared first so, thumbprint apart, I called to the technician, explaining that I was hoping for slide number 1. There was a delay and then slide number 8 came up. At least we were getting nearer. I repeated my request, only to be faced next with the penultimate slide of the entire lecture. A quick decision was needed: either take an early coffee break or plough on defiantly. I ploughed on with a jaunty instruction to the projectionist that he could put the pictures through in any order he found convenient and I would try hard to think of something interesting to say about each one. It was rather like using a child's 'painting by numbers' kit to describe Da Vinci's Last Supper, but it seemed to keep everyone entertained. I was never invited to speak there again.

As I had also found in India, Victorian domination had produced an eclectic array of public buildings in every possible style; occasionally they acknowledged local culture but only, I felt, out of a sense of novelty. Western influence in Pakistan has not always been a good thing and one of the succeeding speakers at the congress observed that the designs of some of Karachi's newest hotels and commercial centres were over-influenced by fashionable Western architects used to practising in a cold climate, thus imposing a huge burden on air conditioning, and maintenance costs that was entirely unnecessary. But passing fashion is always seductive, particularly among young practitioners.

I played truant in the afternoon, principally to get some fresh air but also to enjoy seeing some of Lahore's justly famed architectural heritage. Many buildings are of Mogul origin, such as the Badshahi Mosque and the Lahore Fort, while some were only built during colonial times, such as the High Court and the General Post Office, all of them impressive. Justifiably, English fascination with the city goes back a long way; in 1670, for instance, John Milton even referred to 'Agra and Lahore, the seat of Great Mogul'.

When seen from a vantage point, the city unfolds like a huge cubist painting, a panorama of square or rectangular buildings punctuated dramatically by striking minarets and domes, the surfaces of which glint in the sharp sunlight. Washing fluttered playfully from many flat roofs and it was easy to imagine them crowded with excited groups of kite-flying enthusiasts engaged in the competitions held every year during Basant, the Punjabi festival marking the coming of spring. The festival attracts participants from all over the country as well as abroad and involves huge skill in both constructing and operating the kites. It is aggressively competitive as, if one is to win, any competing kites have to be grounded first. This is often accomplished by an opponent gluing ground glass onto his own kite string and then manoeuvring the kite downwind to cross with that of his nearest competitor, whose line he can then sever with a quick tugging movement. The grounded kite is then his to retrieve. It is a surprisingly dangerous occupation, as people are often killed by celebratory gunfire, sharpened kite strings or electrocution due to fouling power cables, all of which adds to the macho thrill of competing and draws in more participants by the year.

Some of Lahore's finest monuments include the seventeenth-century Wazir Khan Mosque – a building sumptuously covered with tile mosaic forming complex geometric patterns and arabesques, and with exquisite calligraphy – and the Badshahi Masjid of fifty years later, with its massive entrance portal framing the view of the triple-domed prayer hall beyond. Having lived in Brighton for much of my life in Britain, I am visually word-perfect on the design and decoration of the Prince Regent's fun palace, the Royal Pavilion, a unique confection which is strangely Chinese on the inside and Mogul on

359

the exterior. When the architect John Nash 'Indianised' it (it was originally a much smaller and simpler building) he must have had access to travellers' sketchbooks in addition to his own studies, because here in downtown Lahore I saw again the domes, arches, decorative stone fretwork and carved parapets whose detail I knew like the back of my hand. Every corner I turned in the noisy, dusty, teeming city seemed to offer another recollection of home. Here was architectural influence travelling in the other direction, but only for a folly. Although Queen Mary, wife of George V, would have had the whole place pulled down, she found it so disagreeable.

Before I left Lahore, my hosts were determined to entertain me and thoughtfully made arrangements for a group of us to be collected by horse-drawn tonga and driven in the balmy evening air through one of the city gardens to a performance by one of Pakistan's most celebrated dancers, Naheed Siddique. As well as being a consummate exponent of her art, she had achieved some notoriety because of the supposed sensuous nature of her skilfully choreographed movements, which by Western standards wouldn't have raised an eyebrow, but the Islamic fundamentalist faction put pressure on the police from time to time to ban her performances. The largely male audience was transfixed by her dexterity and the subtle interpretation of her dance routine. Implication and nuance replaced the banal pelvis thrusting of the West and demonstrated gracefully how a traditional art form could be made perfect. She distilled years of practice into perfect expression through allusion alone. Two hours later we were still begging for more.

One of the attractions of visiting Pakistan was the opportunity it gave to travel much further upcountry. Other than Delhi, my recent destinations had mostly been on the coast – Bombay, Madras and Colombo – so I was curious to go further inland. I hoped to see something of Kashmir (always referred to, tellingly, as 'Disputed Territory' on official maps) and also reach the Afghanistan border. Quite responsibly, the Foreign and Commonwealth Office said it was not something they would necessarily encourage, but it was up to me to make my own decision. The problem was, how to get there. Travel agencies showed no enthusiasm for the venture, so I decided to make my own arrangements by going down to one of the busier bazaars to see if I could hire a driver. The Anarkali Bazaar, named after the famous courtesan of the Mogul emperor Akbar, looked the most likely. It was full of stalls selling traditional articles, including leatherwork, beaten gold and silver jewellery, and embroidered silk. It was obviously a place where everyone knew everyone else, and after a few false starts I was introduced to a painfully thin English-speaking driver called Wahid, who appeared to have worked for a military support company some years earlier and had picked up sufficient English to get him through. He seemed willing to help, but he had no car. But he knew someone who did. Eventually an arrangement was made for Wahid and a car to present themselves at my hotel the following day for an indeterminate trip north. He needed cash up front for the car and petrol and I advanced him half of the agreed fee, the remainder of which was to be paid on the satisfactory (whatever that meant) completion of the journey.

The Indus River runs roughly north–south up the centre of Pakistan, emerging into the Arabian Sea at Karachi. It has numerous tributaries, some of them extending through wide, flat terrain to the north of Lahore. On our journey up the Grand Trunk Road from Lahore to Islamabad, the new capital, we passed through irrigated fields of the Punjab plains which produce a large proportion of the country's crops of wheat, rice, sugar cane and cotton. We soon reached Jhelum, where we stopped to find food. I got out of the car to look around and stretch my legs. It was not long before, to my surprise, I came across an Anglican church. It had been closed the previous year because of devastating floods in the area and had just been reopened. A group of volunteers from Yorkshire had been there for the past three weeks distributing clothing and bedding to parishioners whose homes had been ravaged by flood water. Winter was approaching, so their intervention was very timely and they went about their work with typical matter-of-factness, laced with down-to-earth humour, as if they were doing a weekend stint at an Ilkley Moor scout camp. They found my sudden presence as unexpected as I did theirs. When I explained that I came from Brighton, the group's favourite mum piped up, 'Tha's a bit lost then.' When they stopped laughing I said that maybe, but I had a resolute driver. She glanced in his direction, shook her bouncy hair and observed, 'Tha'd better fatten him up a bit or he won't last the journey.'

A long time later Wahid and I reached Islamabad, a large modern city laid out by the currently fashionable Greek architect Constantinos Doxiadis. The capital is triangular in plan form with a rigorous grid of tree-lined streets, impressive public buildings and well-organised bazaars. Its architectural claim to fame is undoubtedly the enormous Shah Faisal Masjid, reputedly the largest mosque in the world, capable of accommodating 15,000 people, with space for another 85,000 in the courtyard. Designed by the Turkish architect Vedat Dalokay, it was largely financed by Saudi Arabia, and takes its form from an eight-faceted desert 'tent' supported on four giant piers, surrounded by a quartet of three-hundred-feet-high minarets. The mosque is faced with white marble and decorated internally with elaborate mosaics and a spectacular central chandelier. It is undoubtedly impressive, but I wondered whether one could go on enlarging mainstream Islamic architectural forms ad infinitum without needing to find a fundamentally different expression for buildings of that magnitude. I recalled that at the time of the Festival of Britain in 1951, the architects of the Royal Festival Hall in London were faced with the same problem. At that time, the country had few buildings in the modernist style and they were only of modest size, so there was no stylistic precedent for a metropolitan edifice designed on a necessarily monumental scale. An appropriate architectural expression had to be found: they couldn't just 'inflate' the style of smaller contemporary buildings and hope that it would look right. In the event, they accomplished something quite unique. Here in Pakistan, however, I didn't have sufficient time on my hands to try and figure this one out in a Muslim context as we were due to push on north into the hills to reach our final destination, Murree, not far from the north-west frontier.

Murree sits 7,500 feet above sea level; it enjoys a cool climate in summer and is crisply cold in winter. This made it a favourite hill station after the British annexed the Punjab in 1849 and many officials and their families would retreat there from the plains during the hottest months of the year. The climate permits the cultivation of cherries, strawberries and raspberries and this adds to the feeling of little England. The town boasts an Anglican church in the tin-roofed, pared-down, Gothic Revival style of the type seen throughout the Empire. I began to feel that, wherever I went in the world, I was entering the same building, as if they had been made available by mail order from Lambeth Palace during one of the evangelising campaigns of the nineteenth century. Occasionally the Church's enthusiasm got the better of it, as I was once informed, with great solemnity, that Murree was so called after the Virgin Mary, which is ridiculous, as the original name, Marhi, simply means 'high place' in the local dialect. In British times it had a mall or promenade, parks, clubs, schools and cafés and was easily accessible from nearby military garrison of Rawalpindi. It even snowed in winter, which made the entire community feel particularly at home.

One morning I climbed the steep hill to Kashmir Point. The weather was good enough to obtain magnificent views across the Jhelum river valley into Kashmir. This is what I had come for, and I marvelled at just how easy my journey had been, recalling the flat reluctance of any tour company to help me arrange it. Apart from the splendour of the views I experienced for the first time what the relatively uncharted regions of parts of Central Asia must feel like. It seemed that all my life I had skirted the great land mass of Asia, with most of my destinations being on or near the sea. From Singapore to Hong Kong the maritime character had prevailed, but here at last I was somewhere entirely different.

Despite the locally made fur hat I bought at the bazaar on my first day, I must have been very conspicuous, if only because everyone else looked so similar to one another, particularly the men, all of whom had long black beards and swarthy, lined faces, crowned with typical local headgear, which resembled two large superimposed pancakes. Most of them carried old, convention firearms and some even wore a bandolier of .303 cartridges slung over their shoulder. Their penetrating brown eyes never looked threatening and, despite me standing out, they got on with what they were doing without a second glance.

Wahid had a distant relative living in Murree, so he quickly arranged for me to stay in a small converted rest house in the middle of town. It was clean and simple, and offered the essentials for an overnight stay. As the proprietor spoke no English and I couldn't recognise his particular dialect, Pashtu, still less speak it, Wahid arranged terms right down to the number of fried eggs for breakfast, so all I had to do was nod and smile at appropriate moments.

After a good night's sleep I washed and began the next day with a just recognisable version of an 'English Breakfast', which they were determined to serve, and I was ready to leave by 8.30 a.m. when Wahid appeared to collect me. He asked for the bill on my behalf and then passed it to me. It was the equivalent of one pound sterling, so I handed it back and said there must be some mistake. Wahid explained to the proprietor that I was querying the account and the two of them then began a heated conversation about its accuracy. It took me a long time to realise that Wahid had not fully understood me and was apparently remonstrating with the owner because I thought I had been overcharged. Pencil and paper were produced from the manager's draw and every item of my stay was laboriously itemised. I stopped Wahid in the middle of all this, but before I could say anything, he explained that the final bill was only this high because, for an English visitor, they had to send out for drinking water and a toilet roll, which were not normally provided; otherwise the bill would have been less. Blushingly, I doubled the amount asked for in order to get away and was almost carried to the car by an ecstatic manager.

Reluctantly, I accepted the fact that the time had come to return to Lahore and I agreed with Wahid that we'd try and do it in one go. On the way up to Murree we had stopped on a number of occasions, and as I'd spent my time marvelling at the views, I hadn't really taken in the realities of driving the Great Trunk Road. The route had been constructed originally by the Mogul emperors in order to connect Kabul with Calcutta, but unfortunately it had not been upgraded to cater for today's traffic. I knew we were near the Afghan border, but had not noticed how impossibly congested and twisted the road was. Sometimes cut into the side of steep hills with blind corners and often steeply descending halfway to the valley floor before rising again, it was a road better suited to international rally driving, but was now having to cater for scores of huge, highly decorated vehicles, many conveying fresh vegetables and passengers from Afghanistan down to the port at Karachi. Without exception, the trucks were covered with Mogul folk art supplemented by an array of brightly coloured lights fixed to the cab and body. Each vehicle carried a large slogan to identify it, saying such things as 'Carrying dreams', 'People across the country' or 'Passion for journeying'. Wahid explained that the decoration and embellishment of these lumbering vehicles told you their place of origin and even the social standing of their owner, so that every motif conveyed information and was much more than artistic exuberance. Interesting though all this was, I was becoming very apprehensive about the dense clouds of black smoke each lorry emitted and the extent to which it obliterated the view at a concealed bend. As if that wasn't hazardous enough, drivers in both directions hogged the middle of the road to avoid potholes at its edge, but principally, I thought, to engage in a game of chicken with whoever was coming in the opposite direction, to see who would give way first. I am not easily frightened, but in the space of one day, after passing no less than six vehicles flipped on their side, one with the rear wheel still spinning (quite apart from breakdowns and burst tyres), I began to experience genuine fear and pleaded with Wahid to slow down and take more care. I had made the mistake of paying him off before we left Murree, so I imagined that he no longer felt bound to please his master, and instead just concentrated on getting home as quickly as possible, even if it meant driving like a maniac. He sat grim-faced at the wheel pretending he didn't understand, and determined to show me how skilled he was. I sat next to him, equally grim-faced, with my fists clenched and my eyes closed. As the miles passed the simmering tension between us seemed only to increase his flow of adrenalin. At one point, I even found myself trying to remember which drawer in my study filing cabinet contained my will.

When we eventually arrived in Lahore, the fact that we hadn't been killed or killed anyone else led Wahid to feel fully vindicated and he took no pains to disguise it. After I got out we said our farewells and shook hands grudgingly. No one had really won, but nothing on earth would have persuaded me that he deserved a tip, so he didn't get one. But I felt bad about it the next day.

Chapter 51

Ceylon Had Become Sri Lanka

Alan Bennett isn't the first person to explore what 'forty years on' feels like. On returning to Sri Lanka for the CAA rather than with the Armed Forces this time, I knew that I wasn't going to hear the flip-flop of the rickshaw wallah's feet on the warm tarmac again, nor would I find the Peiping Chinese Restaurant ready to serve two consecutive full meals to the same customers without raising an eyebrow. However, the climate felt the same, the smells were still there (if now laced with diesel), the kerosene lamps still hissed on the street vendors' stalls, and the child beggars and pimps still jostled for a place on busy corners. The old expatriate rendezvous, the Galle Face Hotel, had apparently moved downmarket but stubbornly retained a degree of the colonial gravitas that, in years past, had put it on a par with the Raffles in Singapore and the Peninsula in Hong Kong.

The country's history is similar in many ways to that of other Commonwealth lands in Africa and Asia, in that a succession of European adventurers arrived first, only to concede their interests to Britain in the early nineteenth century, but this was no longer Ceylon, as it had been renamed Sri Lanka (meaning Resplendent Island) in 1972, when it was declared a republic.

It is tragic that so beautiful an island and so warm-natured a people have had to suffer a sporadic but bloody civil war ever since 1983 which, despite strenuous efforts by willing and impartial countries to mediate, still persists. The issue is a familiar one and is played out in countless countries around the world – namely, the wish to establish a dedicated homeland for an ethnic minority, who in this case are the Tamils in the north and east of the island. The Liberation Tigers of Tamil Eelam guerrilla group is engaged in almost constant conflict with the Sri Lankan forces, and what could be a prosperous island growing rich on a tourist economy has become impoverished by the ongoing strife.

My visit took place at a time of relative calm, but I was still advised not to attempt to travel north towards the Jaffna peninsula, as some of the jeep tracks had been mined. It is easy to forget how life goes on – it has to – in all the world's hot spots. In Sri Lanka I found that people worked hard and still knew how to laugh and relax, religious rituals were still rigorously observed, fragile governments made modest progress in spite of it all, and amid the turmoil, architecture was still being taught and practised.

Having spoken to the students in the university and run the by-now-customary seminars for the Sri Lankan Institute of Architects, I wanted to revisit Kandy, the capital of the Central Province which, because of its historical significance as a sacred city, had now become a UNESCO World Heritage Site.

Kandy was founded in the fourteenth century and is sited 1,500 feet above sea level in the hilly centre of the island. It lies about sixty miles inland from the commercial capital of Colombo. Because of its remote and easily defended position it remained a small independent kingdom long after the coastal regions had been conquered by the Portuguese and Dutch and it wasn't until 1815 that it finally fell to the British, together with the rest of the island.

Kandy's lasting significance is due to its being the sanctuary of Buddha's tooth. Since the fourth century, the custodian and protector of the only relic was recognised as an appropriate ruler of the land. Over the years the Royal Palace and the Temple of the Tooth became associated with the administrative and religious activities of the city, and even after the British took over, Kandy preserved its function as the religious capital of the Sinhalese and a place of pilgrimage for Buddhists. The Temple of the Tooth is what confers upon the city its uniqueness and the relic became a focus of wide interest in later years following the decision by a succeeding king to openly display it for the populace to venerate in a ceremonial procession every year. The festival in which this takes place is known as the Perahera.

The colourful procession is elaborate and full of symbolism. The relic casket is placed on a *ransivige* – an elaborately decorated dome-like structure – which is secured to the largest and grandest elephant in the ceremony, a royal tusker. As its stately appearance heralds the climax of the event, it is preceded by bare-chested whip-crackers who you can hear approaching in nearby streets. It is a strange and unnerving sound, like clustered pistol shots, and it adds tension to everyone's anticipation. Following them are fireball acrobats who clear the path for Buddhist flag-bearers who precede the *Peramuna Rala*, the master of ceremonies, riding on the first of many elephants. Then come the elaborately dressed Kandyan drummers and dancers to further enthral the throng, who by now are pinned, good-naturedly, shoulder to shoulder and sweating profusely. Countless elephants now appear, each differently dressed and painted, to be followed by other groups of musicians, dancers in elaborately embroidered tunics, conical hats and swirling white skirts, and provincial flag-bearers, all of whom show great dexterity in avoiding the occasional volley of compact cannonballs passed by the elephants. To conclude the spectacle, and to gasps of wonder, comes the Maligawa tusker, carrying the Sacred Tooth Relic.

Since the sixteenth century the ceremony has seen many changes and elaborations. These days it is also witnessed by an increasing number of tourists, for whom this is probably no more than a highlight from the glossy brochure and, like the Changing of the Guard at Buckingham Palace, its original significance has become eroded.

I was not particularly surprised, therefore, to see the temple drummers reappear at the opening ceremony of the Sri Lankan Institute of Architects' 'Sessions', their annual conference, to which I had been invited. The drummers heralded the arrival of the minister responsible for the infrastructure who had a family name as long as his speech, and when he finally ended each of us in the group was given a taper with which to light one of the little oil lamps which branched delicately from a central moulded standard. The sequence of lamp lighting had been very carefully worked out so as to recognise professional and political sensitivities, and after the minister lit the last remaining lamp he formally declared the sessions open, nodded to the institute's president and left promptly by car. He must have done it many times before, and it rather looked like it.

Sri Lanka is as well known for its elephants as it is for its lush tea plantations. The beasts are an integral part of local culture, cherished to the extent that one of the most popular institutions is an elephant orphanage where abandoned offspring are protected and nurtured until they are able to fend for themselves.

Naturally, elephants feature prominently at the local zoo and I was once asked by my hosts if I had ever seen an elephant play a mouth organ. My blank expression was all that was needed for him to arrange a visit to witness the phenomenon. Upon arrival, I saw a semicircular arc of seating, like a miniature ancient Greek theatre, focusing on a flat performance area in which stood the presumably musical elephant, accompanied by his young keeper. There was an obvious bond between them and I gained the impression that whatever trick was about to be performed had been perfected without resort to physical cruelty. The animal and the boy were inseparable and whenever the boy wandered away to fetch a prop necessary for the act the elephant tried to follow him and assist in some way.

I was seated on the concrete steps with a host of young Sinhalese boys who had never seen the act and were full of excitement. The young keeper positioned the elephant so that he could reach its mouth and arranged a stool to stand on, whereupon, to the crowd's delight, he produced the harmonica we'd all been waiting for. It was about two feet long, made of hardwood and had been crafted and tuned to produce a generous octave. The audience, me included, couldn't begin to work out how the lumbering beast was going to play it and a good deal of well-rehearsed showmanship went into building the tension. When, after gauging that our patience was running out, the boy quickly put the harmonica to the elephant's mouth, we waited anxiously for it to breathe out. With great skill, he slid the instrument from side to side phrasing the notes to synchronise with the animal's exhalations. It was a bit like 'Auld Lang Syne' on a clapped-out pub piano, but we loved it and asked for more. I hadn't laughed so much since years earlier when I had seen a cockatoo performing on roller skates in Ibiza.

In view of the fact that the Commonwealth is largely made up of developing countries, the subject of low-cost and self-build housing was always high on the agenda wherever I travelled. At the time of my visit my attention had been drawn to the initiatives of one Commonwealth Prime Minister in particular who had been motivated by the declarations made at a UN conference on human settlements held in Vancouver some years earlier. It was the Sri Lankan Prime Minister, Ranasinghe Premadasa. When his government had first been elected to power in 1977 he had been appointed Minister of Local Government, Housing and Construction and had immediately committed them to building 100,000 new houses during their first term of office. This was a gargantuan task, as both the World Bank and the International Monetary Fund were against the idea: they thought it would absorb scarce resources that could be put to more beneficial use in other areas of the economy and that its impact would therefore be dangerously inflationary. Undeterred, he went ahead and in the event the target was exceeded by about twenty percent, a remarkable achievement by a government housing programme in a developing country.

Ranasinghe Premadasa expanded his message at subsequent world forums, and largely due to his vision and determination the 37th Session of the UN General Assembly formally designated 1987 as the International Year for Shelter for the Homeless (IYSH). Building on this achievement, Sri Lanka had taken the lead among nations by now launching a Million Homes Programme. Religion and politics were very closely intertwined, and on one important public occasion when he announced that one million rupees would be spent on housing for the 'Poorest of the Poor', he acknowledged that this had 'become a reality entirely due to the blessings of the Sacred Tooth Relic'. This was by no means an isolated event, because the inauguration of IYSH had been marked by religious observations in every temple, church and mosque in the land.

All this was grist to the mill of the CAA, as affordable housing was central to its purpose, so I took an early opportunity of contacting the Prime Minister's office, seeking an appointment with one of his senior aides. This was the opportunity I'd been waiting for.

I was courteously received in a rather glum office with a noisy ceiling fan. I explained that a forthcoming combined conference of the CAA and the International Union of Architects (IUA) was to be held in the United Kingdom and that 'Homelessness' was going to be a principal theme. It would be a large international gathering and Mr Premadasa might think it desirable to share his timely message there with others; if the idea was attractive to him, he would be billed as the conference's keynote speaker.

The aide and secretary listened carefully, but I was aware of the fact that nobody there knew me and they could only take my word for it all. Furthermore, my approach was not being made through the normal diplomatic channels (the idea had only just come to me and I didn't have time).

A further meeting was therefore arranged, before which they undoubtedly took the opportunity to check my bona fides and those of the CAA, at the end of which they agreed to ask Mr Premadasa if he would like to be present at the conference. Shortly after my return to the UK I heard that he had accepted, but with the request 'would it be possible for him to pay a visit to No 10 Downing Street and meet Mrs Thatcher whilst he was here?' This was more difficult, so I passed the request on to others with greater influence.

The conference was to be held in Brighton at the centre used frequently by the main political parties and the Trades Union Congress; it had been the venue for the Conservative conference at the time of the IRA attack on the Grand Hotel in 1984. As arrangements developed, the CAA and the IUA were joined by the Royal Institute of British Architects. I hoped that all of us together would provide a worthwhile forum for the visiting Prime Minister.

The congress title agreed by the three organising bodies was 'Shelter and Cities: Building Tomorrow's World'. I felt Mr Premadasa would have preferred more emphasis on *rural* shelter, as such conditions were often worse than their urban counterparts, particularly in Sri Lanka, but it looked as though this was as near a consensus as the three host organisations were going to reach.

Before I introduced him from the platform I decided that I was not going to dwell on the political background against which Ranasinghe Premadasa had had to struggle to be heard. Sri Lanka's civil war had been going on for a long time and anyone in his position was extremely vulnerable, both phys-ically and politically. In fact, only a month after our congress he was injured in the leg during an unsuccessful bomb attack in the Sri Lankan Parliament aimed at killing President Jayewardene, in which six Cabinet members were also injured. The words of their national anthem, *Namo Namo Matha* (We All Stand Together), had become crueller by the day.

Premadasa's address contained a clear challenge for the architectural profes-sion, and the key passage read:

> Those of us in public administration in the Third World look to your profession for four inputs:
>
> - We want you to develop new materials and new ways of building so that we can reduce costs and maintain quality.
> - We want you to create designs that will provide the occupants of low-cost housing with constructions that are culturally and climatically compatible, and meet their needs for improved sani-tation and lifestyles.
> - We want you to give us simple methods of construction that less educated people can use themselves.
> - We want you to show us ways in which older buildings can be inexpensively renovated and all buildings can be inexpensively maintained in inhospitable climates.
>
> These are not very new nor very easy tasks to accomplish. However, they remain central to our purpose. Your profession has planned and supervised the most fantastic of modern buildings. Surely it can solve these very fundamental and basic problems that afflict most of humankind.

Apart from its striking relevance to our chosen theme, his speech was signif-icant for two other reasons. First, like many others, he associated architects with designing 'the most fantastic of modern buildings', which was not neces-sarily the only impression many of us wished to give; and second, although the tasks he set us (like developing low-tech construction methods suitable for self-build communities) sounded easy, few of us had training or experi-ence in this field and a sizeable minority of architects present were not inter-ested in going so far downmarket. However, his address was well received and got a good press, so I had the impression that his delegation were satis-fied that the visit had been worthwhile.

A few days later I received a polished camphor box containing a gold porcelain tea set accompanied by a warm letter of thanks. The gift was inscribed 'from the Honourable Prime Minister and Madam Hema Premadasa in appreciation of your expressions of friendship'.

I was never to see him again. A few years later he was elected president, and at a May Day rally held in Colombo in 1993 he was the victim of a Tamil suicide bomber who had infiltrated his inner circle by befriending his private valet. When I heard the news I was filled with flat despair. Whatever next, for God's sake? Hadn't this man tried hard enough? And the only words that came to me were those of Stanilaus Lec, about whom I know next to nothing, other than he once penned the line, 'Burning stakes do not lighten the darkness.'

Chapter 52

The Great Subcontinent

There is not a great deal to distinguish between booking offices, whether for rail or air, in any part of the Indian subcontinent. They are all overcrowded, noisy and undermanned by harassed staff who do their best to keep the system going. This one was no different. It was so full that I could barely open the door from the street and it took me some time to see where anything was. I filtered through the jostling crowd of hopeful travellers and their fractious offspring, and headed towards the back where I leant against the rear wall while I got my bearings. The hubbub, a mixture of irritation, excitement and exhaustion, made it difficult to see what was going on. There seemed to be an inordinate number of cases, boxes and packages, and those not conspicuously accompanied had been left on the floor, adding to the confusion and providing a unique opportunity for losing small children. Not for the first time did I realise that everything here took longer, a lot longer, so I might just as well get used to it and stop fretting. My sullen introspection was broken by the sight of a uniformed official who, with some difficulty, had emerged from behind the counter and was clambering towards a large bulletin board fixed to the wall. Very slowly and deliberately he began writing what must have been a hastily arranged instruction from his beleaguered manager which read simply 'Refrigerators will no longer be accepted as hand luggage'. No one appeared to take the slightest notice of this, or indeed of any other exhortation, but I still felt guilty about my determinedly Eurocentric impatience. Things didn't improve, but when I was told they could provide me with tickets for a flight two days hence, I felt grateful that my visit hadn't been entirely fruitless.

When travelling from Britain to India I didn't need a visa, and nor would I need one if travelling from Britain to Sri Lanka, but I couldn't fly from Sri Lanka to India without one. Logic didn't come into it, but I knew enough about the rigidity of regulations in these parts to stop myself arguing. This delay meant that I was now going to miss chairing my first CAA executive in Madras, which had been carefully planned to coincide with a convention of the Indian Institute of Architects. Nonetheless, I still needed to reach that city at some point, so I took a phut-phut, a motorised trishaw, to the Colombo booking office of Air India directly I received my visa from a particularly helpful employee at the British High Commission.

I made what amounted to a valedictory appearance in Madras to visit Pondicherry on the coast before leaving. Pondicherry looks and feels French, due to its long history as a French possession which also extended to a larger hinterland of the same name. The town is laid out on a rigid grid plan with streets at right angles to each other. The two sections of the town, known as Ville Blanche and Ville Noire, are blunt reminders of a colonial past, and their architectural features are emphatically different. The first section, the French quarter, contains gracious villas with tall, shuttered windows and mansard roofs which would not look out of place on the Riviera, whilst the Tamil quarter is constructed with verandas and open grilles to acknowledge the climatic conditions seemingly ignored by the Europeans. French street names and speech are commonplace, and the Alliance Française has a credible presence there. When the colonial power eventually left it offered French citizenship to the local population, but few, it seems, availed themselves of the offer.

A little piece of France stuck onto the east coast of this vast subcontinent. How did it happen? One could ask the same of any British, French, Dutch or Portuguese territory along the eighteenth-century trading routes and discover an intriguing history of buccaneering commerce, military conquest or political one-upmanship. Such local adventures are only footnotes in world history and you have to stumble on them to find them. Goa, off the west coast of India, Malacca on the Malaysian coast, and Macau on the Chinese seaboard have equally fascinating histories, and such instances are among the unexpected pleasures of travel.

My next stop was Bombay. Due to the rapid growth of the city's infrastructure, its School of Architecture appeared to be thriving and I was received graciously. The students had made garlands for my arrival and some of the young women had arranged an exquisite floral decoration on the entrance-hall floor to express their welcome. It comprised complex traditional patterns infilled with flowers of exquisite intensity that would only last a few hours, but must have taken days to design and accomplish. Most external examiners in Britain are treated with barely concealed resentment, so it was both surprising and slightly embarrassing to be received like this.

As I was offering design guidance, my task was made no easier by the real-isation that currently in Commonwealth countries, architectural expression was in a state of flux. But the sequence of change from imperial times to present-day independence makes any study fascinating because it shows how architecture reflects the circumstances of the time, be they political, religious or economic.

Pre-colonial indigenous design exists in many surviving Indian Buddhist and Hindu temples which, because of their status, were built of longer-lasting materials than their secular counterparts and are therefore easier to codify. However, following imperial domination, the large public buildings became quintessentially British in appearance and were designed with no thought for local culture or climatic differences. The imperial stamp was imposed, as of divine right, and was visible evidence of the new order. I examined photo-graphs of St Andrew's Presbyterian Church in Madras, which was built in 1821, which show a classical building that could have been lifted neatly out of Trafalgar Square, while Calcutta's robust Gothic Revival–style High Court of 1865 could pass for a well-mannered neighbour to the Victoria and Albert Museum.

Over the years, later expatriate architects had been appointed to central government, all of whom designed in a variety of styles, but no one matched the stylistic synthesis achieved in New Delhi by Sir Edwin Lutyens and his partner, Herbert Baker, in the early 1920s. This scheme marked the dawning of a more sympathetic attitude to local building forms and rather better understanding of climate. Their masterpiece has a genuine Anglo-Indian char-acter achieved by integrating domes, minarets and Renaissance detail into the composition with considerable fluency. It is hard to say whether their design was influenced by any pro-Indian sentiment or whether it was merely because they were so accomplished at synthesising different traditions; it was one more opportunity to demonstrate their skill to an admiring audience.

For the next forty years from the 1930s, the International style took hold, introduced by European architects or their Indian counterparts trained in the West. 'Modern' buildings were now perceived as symbols of success and were sometimes funded by international agencies for whom this was the obvious style in which to build. Again, local decision-makers had often spent long periods in Western countries in education and training programmes. The resulting buildings were not always a complete success, and one senses a whiff of arrogance among one or two internationally known architects who didn't have the wit or humility to seek local advice about key climatic and cultural considerations.

With the emergence of university-standard schools of architecture in recent years, the position has begun to improve and there is clear evidence that culturally and functionally balanced architecture is beginning to appear which looks as though it belongs in India and equally belongs to the twentieth century.

All of this made for an engaging dialogue with the students, many of whom fully expected me to dispense the latest design ideas from the West and were initially puzzled when I dwelt on the importance of local vernacular. They were at first disappointed that I wasn't going to show them how to build their own Pompidou Centre, but very slowly they began to acknowledge the role played by their own culture in the design process.

The Indian Institute of Architects had been through a thin time and had recently become sufficiently insolvent to have to close for a while. Part of the difficult background sprang from the inescapable fact that, traditionally, most people there thought that buildings were designed by 'engineers', not 'architects', and from a position of strength the engineers understandably worked hard to sustain that impression. The institute was therefore fortunate to have a Bombay architect, Rusi Khambatta, as president at a critical stage in its revival and he accomplished a great deal during his term of office, adding credibility to the profession's role in that great subcontinent.

Rusi invited me to spend some time with him during my visit and generously offered to take me to see whatever I wished. He was only mildly surprised when I asked to visit not new building projects, but the Towers of Silence used for exposure of the dead, a time-honoured practice started by Parsi Zoroastrians. Their tradition considered a dead body to be unclean and therefore a potential pollutant, and to protect against this a method had to be devised for disposing of the dead as safely as possible. This was done by placing the body on top of a specially constructed tower to be exposed to the sun and to birds of prey. It is always easy to spot the site of such structures some way off, as numbers of vultures can be seen slowly circling each tower. Once the bones have been bleached by sun and wind they are collected in an ossuary pit in the centre of the tower, where they gradually disintegrate. The remainder of the material is then flushed away by rainwater and passed through coal and sand filters before running out to sea.

From an architectural viewpoint the towers were just as distinct and valid as a separate building type as a crematorium is in the West, but reflect a much longer religious and cultural history. Rusi and I weren't to know that, a generation later, the West would no longer regard the Towers of Silence with such revulsion, but admire them for their 'green' credentials, as they were now seen as models of environmental responsibility. Neither could anyone foresee that their ecological reputation has been just as quickly compromised, because the vultures were beginning to decline in numbers due to increasing city pollution, urban growth destroying their natural habitat, and the widespread used of toxic drugs to protect livestock. Inventive to the end, the Parsi community are currently considering captive breeding of vultures and the use of 'solar concentrators' to accelerate decomposition – not so different from the West's current preoccupation with combating global warming through timely innovation. But vultures – ugh.

Forty years after independence it was revealing to see vestiges of the old Raj creeping back into daily life. Understandably, at the time of partition in 1947, a swell of national pride led to the overnight renaming of streets that hitherto carried British names and the equally prompt removal of statues of Queen Victoria, of which there were plenty. More Hindi was going to be spoken and written instead of English and any institutional reminder of the imperial past was hastily dismantled. It was all the more surprising, therefore, when I visited Bombay to come across an example of this happening in reverse. I had arrived in Bombay straight from the UK and had gone to bed immediately upon arrival to catch up on sleep before meetings arranged for the following day. I knew it would be disorientating – it always is – and before falling asleep, I was vaguely aware of the irritating whine of the hotel's elderly air-conditioning system. But nothing was going to keep me from sleep; I was exhausted and dropped off almost straight away. Awaking after a few hours, I saw that it was dark outside. Looking at my watch, I noticed that it was 6.30 p.m., so I toyed with the idea of getting up, but still felt too drowsy to do much about it. I became aware once more of the seemingly distant whine of the air conditioning. Propping myself up, I realised that the noise didn't originate in my room but came from somewhere outside and, more unnervingly, it was vaguely tuneful. By now I was more awake, and my curiosity got the better of me, so I walked wearily to the window and looked outside. There, in immaculate uniforms, were the serried ranks of the Bombay Police Pipe Band playing Scottish airs from Loch Lomond, watched only by a desultory group of taxi drivers having a quick smoke while waiting for their next fare.

In a land where the poor don't look an opportunity in the face, I watched as groups of homeless people began arriving opposite my hotel to bed down for the night. This happened late in the evening when the pavements became clear. It was very orderly and done without fuss. There were whole families who brought what few possessions they had with them and probably occupied the same spot every night, one next to a lamp post, another conveniently next to a drain, until the entire pavement disappeared. The rains hadn't quite arrived and I wondered what they would do when they did. I found it impossible to visualise how they existed and wondered at the fact that they all looked reasonably clothed and must have had access to water daily. Before turning my hotel light out, I opened the curtain once more to observe this pathetic scene, and by now even more street dwellers had arrived who, seeing the pavements full, began to occupy space on the edge of the road itself as soon as traffic thinned nearer midnight. The process still hadn't finished, and in the next half hour I saw more and more of the tarmac covered by bedding rolls and pots, leaving only a vestigial gap on the crown of the road for any remaining drivers foolish enough to try and get through. I woke early next day just as dawn had broken. Looking out, I saw that many of the street dwellers had been up for some time, not just because of impatient car drivers. The womenfolk were first to stir: they had to fetch water before their families packed up and once more were absorbed into the teeming throng. The women rose, carefully adjusted and straightened their saris, brushed their thick hair and effortlessly placed a water pot on their head. With a natural grace and poise, they walked silently towards the nearest standpipe, which was probably a couple of streets away. Before me was a human strand who countered 'despair with elegance; emptiness with grace'. The next day the monsoon arrived with Wagnerian ferocity and they all disappeared to God knows where.

My last destination was Bhubaneswar, in one of the poorest and most neglected states in the country, Orissa. It sits on the north-east coast overlooking the Bay of Bengal. For reasons that were difficult to fathom it had been decided to establish a new school of architecture there, and I had been invited to meet the staff and speak to students. There was no question of travelling there direct from Bombay, but I was heartened to see that I could get there by air, which would obviate a sequence of lengthy, if scenically fascinating, journeys by rail. I would have to change flights in Delhi, which doubled the distance, but was much quicker.

It was a Sunday and I reached the capital in good time for my onward-scheduled journey to the coast, only to discover that the flight had been summarily cancelled. No reasons were given and I didn't waste my time asking why, as I knew I would be given the first answer that came into an official's head. I concentrated instead on trying to contact my Bhubaneswar hosts to explain that I'd be on the same plane the following day. I now had to find overnight accommodation, so I telephoned an old friend, who regretfully couldn't put me up (he had a sick wife), but instead arranged for me to have temporary membership of the oldest club in Delhi, founded in the days of the British Raj.

As I entered I felt as if I had wandered into an abandoned filmset from

The Jewel in the Crown. Silver polo cups in polished mahogany cases jostled for space with stuffed hunting trophies and endless sepia photographs of Commissioners in plumed hats or topees. Ceiling fans reluctantly pushed humid air around the Tiffin Room, which led to a generous veranda where the sound of ice being dropped into generous glasses beckoned. My elderly host had arrived to introduce me to the club secretary, who in turn invited me to meet members standing or sitting nearby, all of whom, without exception, were Indian. I had expected that, post-independence, the club atmosphere would be markedly different and a new cultural identity would have been firmly stamped on the place and its occupants. But no, here were the club's members standing about casually in smart navy blue, gold-buttoned blazers, cravats and immaculately pressed grey trousers greeting each other with, 'Hello, old boy. So glad to see you. Do tell me, how's your wife? Fancy a drink?'

This surreal scene made complete sense. It is generally accepted that, in modern India, English is the mark of affluence and education. Much of the power in the country rests with those who speak English and are involved in the global economy, so it isn't surprising that the British way of life has been retained and nurtured.

One particular club member intrigued me when he came over to speak. He was well built, handsome and authoritative and had a certain military bearing. He was very obviously accompanied by a much younger, lithe man who never let him out of his sight and followed his every word, now and then looking nervously over his shoulder at the immediate surroundings. He wore very tight trousers with flared bottoms which were very fashionable among young men at that time. We weren't introduced. After a while, a club steward came up to the older member to say that there was a telephone call for him in the office, so he excused himself, saying that he may be away for a short while and hoped we'd understand. As the young man turned to get up as well I saw just how tight his trousers were and how bulging was one of his ill-tailored pockets. He walked with his 'friend', holding him gently by the arm, all the while looking intently into his face. After the waft of cheap male perfume cleared I hoped that someone was going to change the subject and allay my suspicion. However, for once in my life, the old one-liner attributed to Mae West, 'Are you carrying a revolver or are you just pleased to see me?' turned out to be true. It was explained that the well-respected member was the brother of a senior Punjabi police chief who had recently and very publicly arrested a much-wanted gang of dissidents on the north-west border. The remainder of them, still at large in Delhi, had vowed immediate and bloody revenge. It had therefore been decided to allocate a personal armed bodyguard to his brother, who enjoyed a prominent public profile in the city and was a natural target. My 24-hour stopover was rapidly turning into farce.

Orissa has a long, exposed coastline and is subject to tropical cyclones which, from time to time, cause severe damage and thousands of deaths. It is conspicuously underdeveloped and this has led to most roads remaining unsurfaced and to over half of the population being without safe drinking water. Orissa receives the lowest per capita investment from central government of all twenty-eight states and this has led to widespread discontent. At one time its rich forest cover provided a natural habitat for an infinite variety of wildlife, but it has now been denuded. There remain, though – admittedly only for the archeologically minded – hundreds of magnificent temples, many abandoned and overgrown, for which Bhubaneswar is justly famous, and these would fully justify an extended visit, which, alas, was not what I was there for. By way of compensation I was presented with an illustrated booklet on Orissan temple architecture prepared by Rashmi and Nishitha, both second-year students at the College of Engineering and Technology at Bhubaneswar. Their publication was a real achievement in such an obviously under-resourced institute, and even contained illustrations in colour.

Even in such a remote situation as Bhubaneswar, old Western educational influences still lingered. These two students devoted a whole page of their book to identifying and codifying no less than seventeen separate architectural or decorative features appearing on the façade of a typical Hindu temple. This was undertaken with such thoroughness that they *must* have seen a similar analysis applied to classical Greek temples on a well-thumbed page of the universally known English architects' 'bible', *A History of Architecture on the Comparative Method,* by Sir Banister Fletcher, which was first published in London in 1896, and over the years has run to well over twenty editions. (I can still quote bits from memory.)

The primitive standard of my hotel in the town was to be expected. What I hadn't anticipated was that one day when I went down to breakfast I found that it wasn't only the residents who were discontented and looking forward to leaving – the staff had beaten them to it and had all left the hotel in the night, never to be seen again. We so sympathised that we didn't grumble too much about dragging our suitcases somewhere else. At least there was a somewhere else. The sheer frustration of nothing appearing to work anywhere was illustrated by an Independence Day procession I saw from my new hotel window. It was led by noisy demonstrators carrying a huge banner bearing the fruitless slogan 'Ban Power Cuts'.

This was the setting in which I had to provide encouragement and instil optimism in students who, fortunately, were both eager to learn and idealistic, and whose parents had probably made huge sacrifices to get them there. I did my best and dwelt on universal values which could be applied anywhere. It was the antithesis of fashionable 'hi-tech' and I concentrated on what was, for them, achievable.

The rapport between us all was very natural and spontaneous and when the heat of the day became too unbearable, they'd all leave and tumble onto a ramshackle bus, always insisting that I should join them for an hour on the long, sandy shoreline down the road. When we arrived they ran across the damp sand to the exquisite water's edge, the girls in vivid saris, shrieking with excitement and urging me to join them. How could they possibly behave as if they hadn't a care in the world?

Chapter 53

The Antipodes

That year the monsoon moved north across India with familiar and often dire results. Admittedly, the deluge delivered much-needed water and gave relief from searing temperatures, but it also brought havoc and misery – and not only for the street-dwelling multitudes. Drains and sewers couldn't cope and, particularly by the shoulder-shrugging echelons of the city's Sanitation Department, weren't expected to. Water-borne infections multiplied overnight and those without indigenous antibodies were the first to fall. It took me three and a half hours to reach Bombay airport from my hotel because of the floods, and my arrival coincided with the first symptoms of a virulent stomach disorder.

The airport facilities were nothing to write home about, but I soon ceased to care as my temperature and pulse rate rose. Instead, I was preoccupied with how I was going to reach my first destination in Australia without becoming an embarrassment to myself and to others; this was a long flight. On board, the cabin crew were considerate and helpful, and as I resigned myself to remaining pale and wan and feeling, as a former colleague used to say, 'like a scooped-out avocado pear', the entire journey blurred. I comforted myself with the thought that I would probably be over the worst in forty-eight hours and turned my mind to my first formal lunch meeting in Sydney, where I would have to speak to assembled members of the Royal Australian Institute of Architects (RAIA).

I arrived relatively intact and was met by a bluff, bouncy New South Wales member who looked as if his natural home was the rugby field. He welcomed me with a finger-crushing handshake, and in the car to the hotel explained who would be attending the slap-up lunch they had arranged to mark my arrival. I smiled bleakly; I couldn't think of anything worse than an hour's hard drinking and a hearty five-course meal. I explained my dilemma and he

383

assured me it would soon pass. I told him it had, one way or the other, but I still felt very fragile.

Upon arrival, I asked a waiter if I could have a glass of still water and a dry biscuit to nibble on while the rest were having lunch, although I hadn't realised how difficult it would be to exude enthusiasm and bonhomie among colleagues already on their third glass of Hunter Valley Semillon. I fixed a smile on my face as best I could and went through the motions of being 'one of the crowd'. The next challenge was to make a Bath Oliver last five courses and look as though I was enjoying it. I was expected to speak for about twenty minutes – nothing new, but I'd never done so in the role of hollow man. Fortunately, I knew my piece fairly well as I'd planned to repeat it at subsequent destinations, so getting through wasn't too difficult. I was all too aware of my false gaiety, but my audience, by now on their fourth or fifth glass, would have laughed at anything, and they let me off very lightly.

Afterwards, having explained more fully to my jolly host how unwell I continued to feel, he took me to a nearby hospital where a doctor friend of his worked, and waited until I had been through a couple of tests and given prescription medicine. They said the results of the tests wouldn't be known for forty-eight hours at the earliest and asked me if I could call back, but as I was due in Brisbane the following day they arranged to telephone the hospital there with the diagnosis.

Upon arrival in Brisbane and still feeling very below par, I called at the hospital where they told me the tests were inconclusive so I'd have to have some more. This I did, and during the following days when I travelled on to Melbourne and then Adelaide, I had to report at each respective outpatients' department to find out whether the suspected amoebic dysentery had been confirmed. It was an unfamiliar way of conducting a lecture tour, but eventually, with the help of metronidazole, my affliction petered out. I had at least perfected the art of public speaking without a shot of alcohol.

The RAIA convention was to be held in Adelaide, a quiet, tidy and pleasant enough city. The gathering had been arranged in two parts, the first in Adelaide itself and the second at the recently completed Yulara tourist resort at Ayers Rock. The South Australians were well organised and generous hosts and there was only one minor hitch, when it was discovered that the Boeing 737 chartered to fly the conference delegates north could not accommodate the last four participants. It was therefore agreed that the visiting President of the American Institute of Architects and his wife, together with me as current President of the Commonwealth Association of Architects, should travel separately, accompanied by one of our hosts. It was explained that a separate light aircraft had been booked for our use, but this would take rather longer (very much longer, it transpired) as it had to refuel frequently, and they hoped we wouldn't mind this too much. In the event, the only thing we minded was having to check in before dawn at a small outbuilding reserved for such aircraft adjacent to the main airport. It was quite difficult to find by the taxi's headlights, but eventually we located it, although it showed little sign of activity. Fortunately, the entrance door was unlocked and we were pleased to get inside to escape the chill night air. After a few minutes of searching we located a uniformed official to whom we showed the tickets we had been given the day before. They had been issued by 'Opal Airways – a Gem of an Airline' and looked much like any other airline tickets. He showed us to a departure lounge where we waited for other personnel to appear. After an immigrant cleaner strolled past carrying a bucket and squeegee and disappeared through a distant door, everything went quiet again. The silence was eventually shattered by the clatter of a security shutter being opened to reveal a small counter where refreshments were sold. While we had been waiting, for want of something to do I had been studying the ticket pages, where I came across a notice reminding passengers that, as there were no catering facilities on board the small aircraft, travellers were advised to consume sufficient food and drink beforehand for the long flight. As we had eaten no breakfast, we all fell on what was offered at the counter, practically clearing its stock. A tea urn and fridge produced a range of drinks, and by the time we were met by the pilot, we were full to the gunnels. Leading the way to the plane in the first light of day, he told us the route he would be taking and the height at which we would be flying – 'Low enough to spot a dingo, cobber.' As we boarded, far too late, he added casually, 'Of course, we have no dunny aboard, so I hope you're all comfortable.'

The eight-hundred-mile flight took us north-west over the Flinders Ranges on a route that included stops at Coober Pedy, Olympic Dam and other outstations. We were over territory famed for its opal mines, and about to become even more important for its huge uranium and copper reserves. The short airstrips the pilot used were often very rudimentary and comprised no more than a flattened dirt surface, a windsock and a tin shed. While the passengers made a dash for the nearest eucalyptus, the pilot would hand over mail and newspapers and refill the tank from a handpump. News was exchanged and nothing was hurried (there was no point), and occasionally a spare seat was occupied by a mining manager or geophysicist heading for the next stop north. We were always welcomed by 'ground staff', even if they seldom looked the part, and found ourselves sharing in the delivery of letters and papers and even refuelling the aircraft if we wanted to take a turn. An opal-mine prospector sat next to me for part of the journey. We chatted about our working lives, our families, and our way of looking at things, and marvelled at how little similarity there was between us. Our lives could not have been more different.

Hours later, we were finally greeted by our architectural hosts, who'd arrived much earlier at Alice Springs. They apologised once more for having to send us separately and expressed genuine disbelief when we said we wouldn't have missed the experience for the world; we had enjoyed every second.

Alice Springs started as a tiny settlement supporting a telegraph repeater station on the original line linking Adelaide in the south with Darwin in the far north. In later years it became the destination for travellers wishing to see, or climb, nearby Ayers Rock, the world's largest monolith. More recently still, with the advent of cheap air travel, even greater numbers of tourists began to arrive and unauthorised accommodation sprang up in a sprawl of cheaply constructed buildings which disfigured the epic setting. Eventually, the authorities decided that these structures should be swept away in favour of a properly designed replacement worthy of the site. In the early 1980s Philip Cox, a well-known Sydney architect, was commissioned to design a brand-new tourist resort at Yulara, sufficiently distant not to distract from the great natural wonder.

The commission posed a unique design problem for the architect. What would be the appropriate expression for such a building in such a location? To suggest a design that reflected the massing and texture of Ayers Rock could have produced a travesty of a solution, looking like a styrofoam stage set for a pantomime. Equally unsuitable would have been a design based on the timber-and-corrugated-iron vernacular of the outback, so Philip Cox took the decision to start afresh without any contextual reference and rely on responding to the challenge of the climate to determine its ultimate appearance. On the edge of the vast desert that covers much of Australia's hinterland, the temperatures are severe and the rainfall almost non-existent. Solar control therefore becomes a prominent consideration so, by deft use of sail-like canvas canopies suspended over freely arranged single-storey accommodation, the architect managed to provide an entirely apt and workable design without resort to whimsy or pastiche.

We stayed there overnight and the next morning a small group of us decided to climb to the top of the Rock before breakfast while it was still cool. Having longer legs than most, I was the first to descend and, knowing that our rendezvous with the truck to take us back was not for another hour, began wandering around the long base of the Rock. There are occasional indentations in its side down which any scarce rainfall will run, and because they provide shade, they allow one or two hardy trees to exist. I heard, and later saw, sitting on a gnarled branch, a solitary bird which gave out a very unfamiliar call, more distinctive than a cockatoo, and like nothing I'd heard before. It was the size of a large parrot and was black and white. Fascinated to know what it was called, I looked around to see if there was anyone I could ask. In the distance, near a couple of pickup trucks, I saw a tall Aborigine who was selling carved wooden replicas of long, lizard-like creatures that were decorated with indented lines resembling scales. Although it was over two feet long and I didn't know if I would be able to get it home, I bought one and took the opportunity of asking the vendor about the bird. I carefully explained that, in the middle of this vast desert, I had seen a largish black-and-white bird with a distinctive call and was interested to know what it was called. The Aborigine was an impressive figure, tall, with a deeply lined and pitted face and receding curly hair. He paused and looked at me hard but said nothing, so I repeated the question slowly and deliberately in case he hadn't fully understood me, whereupon he waved his hand impatiently, indicating that he fully knew what I was saying. He paused once more before saying, with an air of complete authority, 'A penguin.'

Some years later when I was giving a talk in London attended by the Australian High Commissioner, I quite innocently showed a slide of an elegant new bridge in Canberra, on the side of which I noticed had been hand-sprayed 'Land Rights' by a local activist. I saw the High Commissioner colour up and mutter something indignantly to his colleague. He obviously thought I was being deliberately provocative and it reminded me how sensitive their government still is about the whole Aboriginal question, so maybe my Aborigine was equally sensitive and determined for a put-down.

After the convention, I decided to visit Canberra, the centre of the Australian Capital Territory. The appeal of Canberra lay not in the creation of an entirely new and therefore artificial city (cities grow organically – you can't just go out and make one; Brasilia tried and failed), but in the design of its recently completed Parliament House. An international competition had been held in 1979 and it was won by the architectural firm Mitchell/ Giurgola & Thorp. The building stands on Capital Hill at the hub of Walter Burley Griffin's master plan of 1912. Although quintessentially of our own time, the new Parliament House is a classical composition which draws its inspiration from the topography of the site and the axiality established by the earlier plan. But one feature in particular gives it an unmistakably Australian characteristic. The whole composition is set *into* the hill in such a way that it doesn't dominate it or the surrounding conurbation. Before its construction you could walk over the hilltop – it was *your* hilltop – and now the new Parliament building is there, you still can, because much of the accommodation, both administrative and legislative, is tucked into the hill with windows looking out only on one or two sides. In Robert Hughes' book *The Art of Australia,* he asserts that 'Australian painting is very self-conscious – it is obsessed with the problem of what its identity ought to be.' It is much the same with its architecture, and the designers of Parliament House probably won the competition by understanding the attitude of the average Australian towards a Member of Parliament. 'Just remember who put you there, mate. We're not 'aving it look down on us from a great height.' And they don't. The green sward continues over the top of the formal composition for everyone's ongoing enjoyment, and the local inhabitants taking their dog for a walk can look down on the assembly – a feature, incidentally, that would be successfully incorporated in another context a generation later when Norman Foster designed the new Reichstag building in Berlin.

The entire composition of Canberra's major civic building was completed with the addition of the new High Court of Australia and, nearby, the Australian National Gallery, again both commissions won in competition. They are monumentally abstract and capture the architectural idiom of the time – and will probably 'date' accordingly.

Increasingly aware that Australia had more to offer than architectural experiences, I decided to head next for the remote coastline of North Queensland which contained as rich a history as many better-known places. I flew to Cairns, a small coastal town about 800 miles north of Brisbane where pelicans and parrots roost in trees, and then on in an Air Queensland 16-seat Otter to go further north to Cooktown, named after Captain James Cook, the English navigator, who stopped there in 1770 to repair his ship *Endeavour,* which had been damaged on a nearby coral reef. The work took much longer than expected and many of the crew died of malaria and other diseases during their time ashore. For many years the town remained a backwater until, in the nineteenth century, alluvial gold was discovered. But after reserves ran out, and following both a cyclone and a fire, the population fell back to a few hundred. Only with the recent advent of tourism have numbers increased again. Some 120 years after the shipwreck an impressive memorial to Captain Cook was raised, only to be outdone recently by a more prominent notice nearby saying, with typical Australian practicality, 'Caution, there are crocodiles in this river'.

The only other feature of any significance in the town is a memorial to a Mrs Watson, originally from Cornwall, who emigrated with her parents at the age of 17 and opened a small school to help the family finances. She later met her husband, a Captain Robert Watson, who ran a small fishing business on Lizard Island, two days' sailing from Cooktown, and to which they moved. While Watson was away on an extended fishing expedition, Aborigines from the mainland arrived unexpectedly and killed Mrs Watson's Chinese gardener and wounded her cook. Fearing for her life and that of her young baby, she tried to flee and take the injured cook with her, but couldn't find a boat; all that was available was a square empty tank that was used to boil the *bêches-de-mer* (sea cucumbers) which her husband sold to the mainland. The three of them clambered in and the two adults managed to paddle for a few days, hoping that a passing vessel would spot them, but none did and they died of thirst. Months later, the washed-up tank was discovered on nearby Howick Island with their bodies still inside it.

I came across an equally sad story on Deliverance Island, offshore from Cape York, which would have remained untold had not Somerset Maugham been travelling in Queensland waters collecting material for his novels in the early part of the twentieth century. The writer met an individual known as 'German Harry' who, in the 1880s, arrived on an adjacent island with two companions to purchase a lugger and go fishing for *bêches-de-mer* to sell to the Chinese, who used them for soup-making. One day his partners absconded with the lugger and abandoned him. As a result, German Harry never again trusted his fellow men and left for Deliverance Island, where he spent the rest of his life as a hermit. There Somerset Maugham met him thirty years later, and when he heard of his lonely sojourn, regaled him with the latest news from Sydney and Europe in which, sadly, the hermit showed no interest, so Maugham left, but not before he made a sufficient entry in his notebook for a sketch he subsequently published in 1924. Had this not happened, this bleak little tragedy would have remained unrecorded, like millions of other personal stories around the world.

I was looking forward to reacquainting myself with Sydney, which would be my last destination. The city's architectural phenomenon is, of course, the opera house, which has attracted as much praise as it has criticism and is probably the first structure to attract the grossly overworked epithet, *iconic*. I had been invited to the city by my immediate predecessor in the CAA, Professor Peter Johnson, who taught at Sydney University and whom I first met in Hong Kong years earlier, when I recalled his gentle admonition that my attitude to Commonwealth affairs was much too Eurocentric: it probably was. We had become good friends and we enjoyed each other's company. He was one of those rare architects who managed to balance being a good practitioner with being a respected academic, and he was highly regarded by the government. Being on the spot, he was word-perfect on the saga which led to the opera house becoming a political cause célèbre.

The commission had been won in competition in 1957 by a little-known Danish architect, Jørn Utzon, whose design drawings had been seductively ethereal and, some say, were no more than a poetic allusion. Notwithstanding the lack of detail, they provided the imaginative gesture that appealed to the international award jury, who gave the design first prize. After the initial euphoria had subsided, the first of many problems began to emerge, not least of which was how to construct such a novel design whose appearance owed more to the billowing sails of harbour yachts than to architectural precedents. It was thought to be unbuildable and rancour set in early between architect and structural engineer, soon to be exacerbated by ever-increasing estimates of construction cost. The latter reached a level where political intervention was inevitable, which put the entire project in jeopardy. Many others have described the almost melodramatic progress of events that followed, involving the resignation of the architect, the dismissal or resignation of other members of the construction consultant team and the political shenanigans that surrounded them. Only one firm stood its ground and persisted in trying to make sense of it all, and that was Ove Arup, the structural engineers, who spent many months and a lot of their own money grappling with the mathematical modelling necessary to evolve a design and erection system capable of delivering the desired shapes. In many ways Ove Arup are the heroes of this entire epic. When, in 1973, it was all over and the opera house opened, opinions were still divided over its performance and capability.

Returning from a performance there of Donizetti's tragic masterpiece *Lucia di Lammermoor* one evening, I walked in a leisurely way back to the nearby Regent Hotel where I was staying. It was a balmy, cloudless night made perfect by a full moon, and before entering the lobby I turned and looked back at the opera house now bathed in clear light, its cluster of soaring roofs penetrating the night sky with exquisite precision and beauty. If I needed a Pauline conversion, here it was. It was now that I understood why a tradition-breaking artefact, one which had been labelled a disaster, now appeared on every T-shirt, travel brochure and postage stamp you could lay your hands on and would for ever be associated around the world with Sydney's success as the host of bicentennial celebrations and, later, the hugely successful Olympic Games.

Perhaps there is a place for this sort of building in any era. In India, when Shah Jahan's beloved wife Mumtaz Mahal died in 1631, he commissioned one of the finest buildings on earth. It took twenty-one years to build and involved the sacrifice of many lives among the workforce. In practical terms, it was only a tomb and was built to express the grief of a single individual, but nonetheless it managed to become a cherished gift to any soul who sets eyes on it. Schiller maintained that the arts provide us with a sense of freedom unfettered by practical concerns; most certainly, Jørn Utzon didn't feel constrained by them.

Chapter 54

The Windy City

When I arrived in Australia straight from India, it presented a very different picture, and I was struck by the simple geographic realisation that, as I was nearly halfway round the world, I might consider circumnavigating, particularly if I could break my journey in the States and visit every architect's Mecca, Chicago.

With this inducement in mind, I further justified the decision by travelling via New Zealand, not just because that would really put me halfway round the world, but also because it gave me an opportunity to visit a couple of old friends, one of whom was Professor Allan Wild, head of the School of Architecture at Auckland University. We had worked together in the CAA at Nairobi, Kuala Lumpur and other places, and his particular diplomacy had seen us through some difficult educational moments. He was, in any case, very agreeable company.

It was only when I arrived in Auckland that I realised the clothes I had with me had been chosen for the Indian subcontinent. On this trip I wasn't properly equipped for New Zealand temperatures. As Allan had a previous commitment on the first day of my visit, he suggested I might enjoy a walk round the city at my own pace to explore new surroundings until he was free. For architects this is always the preferred way to see a city, so I agreed readily, but asked if I could borrow a warm outer garment. Allan thought for a moment; he was already wearing his own coat, but then he suggested, 'Of course, you can borrow my father's, if that's all right with you?' 'But is that all right with him?' I enquired. 'Oh perfectly,' Allan said. 'He's been dead for years.' Adequately, if not elegantly, attired (the old overcoat nearly came down to my ankles), I shuffled my way into the city, not realising that every store, restaurant and place of entertainment closed at midday on a Saturday. I felt more like a displaced person, loitering in shop doorways out of the wind and probably looking, in the eyes of others, as if I'd escaped from a Russian circus. The population seemed to be somewhere else, but there was a certain charm about shop blinds being lowered promptly at 12.30 p.m. – it could have been Folkestone or Tunbridge Wells in the 1930s. It reminded me of a line from an early Ealing comedy film when two characters enter a deserted town and one observes, 'Bit like Aberdeen on a flag day.'

While there, I happened to say that I'd never seen a kiwi and, despite the fact that the New Zealand temperament is less ebullient than its Australian counterpart, I wasn't clear why it had been chosen as a national symbol. It is probably the least interesting creature I have ever set eyes on. It is a nocturnal, flightless bird – two major disadvantages, to which are added its dull plumage and the functional difficulty of producing eggs that are larger in relation to its size than those of any other bird. But it still goes on postage stamps and everyone likes it.

Three days later, flying via Honolulu and San Francisco, the journey to Chicago was easier than I imagined, although I recall that crossing the entire width of the Pacific seemed interminable.

Chicago is unique in architectural history and it effortlessly displays another dimension that sets it apart from any other city on earth. By the 1700s the town had become a centre of activity for furriers and traders, but it was much later, when the Illinois and Michigan Canal was dug, that the entire state began to prosper. Further progress was achieved by the completion of the Illinois Central Railroad, which turned Chicago into a national transport hub that could move lumber from Michigan, coal from the south, ore from Minnesota and wheat and cattle from the prairie. The city probably thought it would never have to look back, but in 1871 the Great Chicago Fire swept unabated through the city for two days, destroying much of it, particularly its wooden buildings, and claiming hundreds of lives in the process. Fortunately, the Union Stock Yard was untouched and much trade continued unaffected, with massive insurance payouts speeding the city's recovery. Rebuilding began quickly, but the city forbade any form of timber construction and significantly this embargo led to the architectural innovation for which Chicago would become world-famous. In 1885, the city's architectural leadership was established by the construction of the world's first skyscraper, the nine-storey Home Insurance Company building. The aftermath of the fire saw architects arriving from everywhere to help create a style that is still known as the Chicago School. A cast-iron skeleton of columns and beams was developed and a quantum leap in architectural design took place which influenced the rest of the world.

Chicago, I was told by locals, is known as the 'windy city' not because of its exposed position on the shore of mighty Lake Michigan, but because of the windy rhetoric of its political fathers. However, one day during my stay I was walking to the end of Navy Pier to try and take in the immensity of the lake – more like an inland sea, with no vestige of an opposite shore in view – when I watched the sky fill quickly with menacing clouds which grew blacker and thicker as they approached. The breeze became a wind and the wind became a gale in a matter of minutes. The rigging of the yachts in Monroe Harbor pinged against the aluminium masts in a gathering cacophony and every flag in sight was stretched into a shuddering rectangle, rattling its cords to the accompaniment of plastic chairs flung from their café terraces. And then, quite suddenly, there was a bolt of lightning, a deafening thunderclap and a heavenly waterfall. The sudden force of the storm was as frightening as it was exhilarating and very soon all the skyscrapers disappeared from sight, enveloped in blinding rain. In another half an hour it was all over; the sun came out, the sidewalks steamed, the plastic chairs were retrieved and the children reappeared to continue playing in the promenade fountains. Yet they still persist with this heresy about windy politicians. Perhaps both interpretations hold good.

Years ago, when BBC Television's first 'cultural' programme, *Monitor*, appeared on the black-and-white screen, I asked its editor and presenter, Huw Wheldon, why he didn't sometimes include architecture alongside the staple diet of art, music and drama. 'It isn't sufficiently visual,' he replied flatly. At that time architecture wasn't much talked about; it was thought to be rather technical, so wouldn't hold an audience. Whether later architecture caught the British public's imagination or whether they just loathed it is debatable, but for one reason or another it did get talked about a lot more, although we would have to wait a long time before it would be classified as 'cultural'.

Chicago had no such difficulty. It knew it was good; it was supremely confident about its buildings and it responded to not only public but also international interest by setting up the excellently run Chicago Architecture Foundation, whose mission is described thus: 'The Chicago Architecture Foundation advances public interest and education in architecture and design through a comprehensive program of tours, exhibitions, lectures, special events, and youth education programs.' And so it does.

The foundation arranges a choice of over sixty-five tours by bus, boat or bicycle or on foot, conducted by well-informed guides. They succeed in dispensing detailed knowledge in a relaxed way – an American gift – and manage to attract the average tourist as well as the discriminating expert with tours like 'Frank Lloyd Wright on Thursdays'. Whether the National Trust would be more successful in Britain if it rebranded its trips with titles like 'Lutyens by Lamplight' without trivialising the subject is debatable.

There is so much on offer in Chicago, and as the famous buildings unfold before you, you learn much about the social and commercial history of the city at the same time. Figures as various as Al Capone, Michael Jordan and Oprah Winfrey are indelibly linked with the place. A two-month visit felt like a minimum requirement, but as that was impossible, I had to make an arbitrary selection of buildings to visit, which I promptly did.

I started with the Sears Tower which, when completed in 1974, was the world's tallest building, to be overtaken in 1996 by the Petronas Towers in Kuala Lumpur. I was clear in my own mind that the attraction had nothing to do with tallness or any of the measurable characteristics that qualified it for entry in the record books: it was just a very good building. I've never understood why tallness, length or any other measurable feature matters, because that alone doesn't automatically confer distinction. Yet politicians and captains of industry are constantly attracted to a unique statistic, never asking themselves whether it is any more mature than a grown-up version of the pubescent exchanges in the school shower room – or any more meaningful. But the magic remains for them, even if its expression is as puerile as personalised car number plates.

At the Sears Tower, Skidmore, Owings and Merrill, post-war giants on the architectural stage, produced a disciplined cubist composition with absolute conviction, 110 storeys high, and sheathed in black aluminium and bronze-tinted glass. So unique is the resulting design that no architect since has attempted to go one better using the same idiom. It is hard to believe that it has 10,000 daily occupants until someone explains that some of its elevators travel at 1,600 feet a minute.

The Illinois Institute of Technology, designed by the German exile Mies van der Rohe, was my next choice. Known for his philosophy 'less is more', he distilled the elements of architectural construction to the point where everything arbitrary had been excluded. His work exemplifies the machine aesthetic and it possesses a distinctive, spare elegance, much envied and copied, often poorly, elsewhere. I've yet to meet an architect who didn't admire its clarity. Such an aesthetic demands immaculate maintenance, and that involves a serious ongoing investment that only wealthy institutions can provide. Upon my arrival at the campus I was faced with a scene impossible to imagine. Many of the buildings, as fastidiously designed as a Swiss watch, were now covered with ivy that had grown in the last half century. It was like lifting the bonnet of a new Aston Martin and seeing the pristine engine encased in damp moss. Had there been a titanic battle of two cultures in the senior common room, eventually won by traditionalists? Or had the high-tech research activities there been so focused on breaking yet another scientific barrier that they left the estate to look after itself? Or, best of all, was this just a metaphor for the transience of human achievement?

Perhaps the answer had something to do with the overbearing attitude of Mies van der Rohe, who had deliberately imposed an aesthetic of his own choice without much thought about the visual sterility this would inflict on owners, occupiers and neighbours alike. He was known to have fallen out with some of his clients, not least the feisty and independently minded Edith Farnsworth, who had commissioned him to design her weekend retreat sixty miles away in Plano, Illinois in 1945. The finished project, albeit the last word in minimalism and spatial continuity, cost much more than she had allowed for, was impractical to live in, and was tremendously expensive to run. Mies was obviously determined to deliver elegant reductionalism, whether his client liked it or not. The colourful history of this commission is as much French farce as it is Greek tragedy.

Arrogance of that order was to be replicated in other well-known projects around the world in the ensuing half century, where a knowingly ego-preening architect delivered 'inhabited sculpture' using somebody else's money and land. It would be easy to dismiss this by saying that artistic arrogance has always been with us because, in part, it has (exhibited by Pablo Picasso, Maria Callas and others in our own time, though often masquerading as 'temperament'). But we also need to remember the lives of other great figures. It is not unknown for one man of genius to defer to another, as Schubert did when he first heard Beethoven's String Quartet, Opus 131, the apotheosis of that composer's work, and declared, 'After this, what is left for us to write?'

As my time was running out, I deliberately left until last what I regarded as the 'best', because it was regarded universally as a seminal work, even if its architect was not known for his modesty. The design of Robie House had captivated me as a student and I could still recall spending three full weeks toiling over a drawing board with pencil, Indian ink and watercolour to reproduce an accurate impression of Frank Lloyd Wright's masterpiece, reconstructing it from old photographs, press articles and reviews published upon its completion in 1909. One of Eliot's 'footfalls in the memory', I suppose. Fortunately, the Chicago Architecture Foundation ran a tour starting from the Santa Fe Building called 'Architecture Highlights by Bus', which covered thirty miles of varying districts, residential and educational as well as commercial, and was scheduled to end with the climax of Robie House. The home had been originally built for a successful young businessman, Frederick C. Robie, and today is classified as a National Historic Landmark. It stands on the corner of Woodlawn and 58th Street and is the best-known example of Wright's 'Prairie style', characterised by an emphatic, horizontal emphasis and low sweeping roofs, which make an oblique reference to the flat Illinois prairie which surrounds it. The site is quite narrow, and this led the architect to design the house on a single axis, arranging a sequence of rooms of differing volumes around a great hearth, all adding to the spatial excitement. Viewed externally, the vertical supports are so subtly incorporated as to seem non-existent and the building appears to float in tiers above the ground. Even in the terse language of the magisterial *A History of Architecture* by Sir Banister Fletcher, his description of it ends with the admission that 'the effect is transcendent'. Snatching up my camera on arrival, I couldn't wait to get off the bus, but was prevented from doing so by the formidable matriarch acting as guide who, having consulted her watch, announced that if we were going to keep to the advertised schedule, there would not be enough time to go inside, but we could look at it from the bus for a few moments. On hearing this, indignation welled up within me and, to my surprise, I burst out with, 'I've travelled six thousand miles, waited fifty years to visit this masterpiece and that is what I intend to do, so bugger the timetable!' The coach fell silent. Maybe they had never heard an Anglo-Saxon outburst of this nature and didn't know what to do. After an awkward pause the matriarch recovered herself and, between pursed lips, brought herself to say, 'OK sir, but no more than twenty minutes, please.'

Chapter 55

Lion City

'Cannery Row in Monterey in California is a poem, a stink, a grating noise, a quality of light, a tone, a habit, a nostalgia, a dream.'

Returning to the sardine-processing community of Monterey after a long absence, John Steinbeck begins his book *Cannery Row* thus, reflecting how he first knew the place and musing how it affects him now he has returned. Here I was, wondering, less expertly, how a location I knew well would have changed in my absence.

Forty years had passed since I was in Singapore as a young gunner serving with the 1st Malay Coast Battery. Over the years I heard that much in the city had altered, but I was unprepared for the extent and depth of change. Gone was the smell of rotting vegetation, banished were the mosquitoes and muted was the clatter of Chinatown. Under the political leadership of Lee Kuan Yew, the city had survived separation from a now independent Malaysia, turning itself into a confident city-state and, in the process, undergoing an unbelievable transformation.

Singapore had become a spreadsheet, a sauna, a disciplined hum, a seriousness, a sanitised attainer, an investment.

Nowadays, if you eat a durian (a foul-smelling but fine-flavoured Malayan tree fruit) in your hotel room as a late-night delicacy you'll be promptly escorted to the front door. On the other hand, a woman on her own can walk down Orchard Road (Singapore's equivalent of Oxford Street) at midnight on a Saturday and feel perfectly safe. The Singapore of my schoolboy adventure stories had completely disappeared. The place where sampans and opium schooners surrounded the *Cutty Sark* on her first voyage, the place where the last tiger was shot under the billiard table of the Raffles Hotel, the place where the guns faced the wrong way when the invading Japanese arrived from the other direction in 1942 is no more.

The transformation had started in 1949 when the young Labour-leading lawyer Lee Kuan Yew and his People's Action Party assumed government from the Crown. Most of the new ministers were English-educated Chinese who promoted moderate socialism and the dissolution of remaining ties binding them to Britain. The decades which followed were to mark the ascendance of Singapore to a point where it would emerge as an economically powerful city-state without parallel, and by the turn of the century the Government of Singapore Investment Corporation would be regarded by the entire world as the sovereign fund which every new sovereign fund would seek to emulate. It was not surprising that I found the new generation of Singaporeans focused, serious and bent on conspicuous achievement.

In the race to look like Manhattan, Singapore had demolished large swathes of the historic city, destroying the essence of the place in the name of profit and hygiene. Hong Kong had done the same. History was subservient to the dollar, which brushed aside the handful of conservation enthusiasts. Irreplaceable historic buildings were lost in the two decades following independence and the seemingly unstoppable urban-renewal programme only slackened when the government woke up to the fact that the tourists they were anxious to attract wouldn't bother to get off the cruise liner if there was no historic quarter left to visit. Tokenistically, a few streets were repaired and gentrified, but they looked very artificial against the backdrop of a modern city, and as none of the traditional activities of the old shophouses could generate the rents now being asked, the luxury trade had moved in to serve tourists and the fast-growing nouveaux riches: hand-crafted, high-fashion leather belts now hung on the rails originally used for dried fish.

Whilst the quality of the city's modern architecture was good, the juxtaposition of new and old looked surreal. The restored shophouses appeared Lilliputian beside the fifty-storey megaliths that had sprung up all around them, but few people locally seemed to find this strange. At the time of my visit in the late 1980s, I was assured that this contradiction was now being recognised and that the city understood the value of its genuine past, but I received the impression that the volte-face was due more to concern about potential tourist revenue than to genuine acceptance of the cultural value of history.

The question of cultural identity cropped up in a different context later when the Minister for Trade and Industry reminded citizens that Chinese culture and social values were at risk of being eroded through English becoming the dominant language and that aspects of their heritage were now under real threat. If there was a Chinese expression for not being able to have your cake and eat it, then I didn't hear it.

Looking really hard, I discovered remnants of my time there as a soldier: the Victoria Hall, the Post Office and Anderson Bridge, all tucked away in the shadows of Manhattan, and it was only when I came across the Padang, the large open space that provides a noble setting for the government buildings and the old supreme court, that I experienced the reality of being back. The King's Birthday Parade used to take place here every year; it was part of the military calendar. I remember the preparations well. Reveille would be sounded at 4.30 a.m. on the adjacent island of Blakang Mati where I was stationed, to allow us time to give a final polish to our boots and brasswork before marching to the cookhouse for an unrecognisable breakfast. We would then make our way to the jetty where motorised wooden whalers would take us past the sampans and the intermediate island of Palau Brani to Singapore island itself. Awaiting us would be three-ton trucks which would transport us to the Padang, where we would be reunited with the battery of 25-pounder field guns which had been sent on ahead: they would fire the 21-gun salute at a given signal. It seemed to me that the entire event had been scheduled ridiculously early in the day for one perverse reason only: we had to be particularly smart for the inspection, and it had been decided at high-ranking level that the moment sweat appeared between the shoulder blades of our freshly pressed olive green uniforms we ceased to be smart and we therefore needed to be removed from the pageant as promptly as possible. As the sun came up quickly, this would happen early. The adjutant, I imagine, had been charged with devising a minute-by-minute programme backwards from the perspiration point to reveille. Not being blessed with a military mind, I never understood the reasoning. Soldiers are paid (very badly) to sweat, particularly in the tropics, and even more particularly when a heavy gun has to be prepared for action near the equator. I felt that there was nothing ignoble in all that, but obviously the sight of Tommy perspiring was thought to offend the genteel sensibilities of those expatriate members of the fairer sex privileged enough to watch the parade from under their parasols before leaving for lunch at Government House.

Wandering around the city, I found that, despite all the modernisation, Raffles Hotel, that timeless reminder of an imperial past, not only still stood, but was soon to have a massive amount spent on it to add a new wing of suites (a sure affirmation of financial confidence), while the remainder was being completely refurbished.

Named after Sir Stamford Raffles, founder of the former British colony, the hotel was established in the 1880s by two Armenian brothers and it soon became the centre of social life in the tropics. Rubber planters from up-country spent their leisure hours there, convivialising in the Long Bar and the luxury dining and billiard rooms. It was probably a blessed relief from the monotony of their lonely existence on the peninsula. Following the First World War a period of escapist gaiety set in and the Raffles attracted personalities from all walks of life – statesmen, royalty, celebrities of stage and screen, and particularly writers, among whom Somerset Maugham and Noël Coward were prominent. On this return visit, when staying there for a couple of nights, I was given a room named after a writer from an earlier generation, Joseph Conrad. Beds in all the 'famous' rooms were wide enough for four occupants at least, but I could find no one on the staff who could tell me why. Perhaps the management had trained them to extol the virtues of the present, like effective air-conditioning and international cuisine, rather than dwell on the Pompeian diversions of earlier days. The late 1920s and the 1930s had seen a wave of frivolous superficiality throughout the Western world among those who could afford it, but this was particularly marked among expatriate communities, whether they were coffee planters living in the White Highlands of Kenya or rubber estate owners from the Malayan heartland. The carefree euphoria in which they lived seemed to rob them of any awareness of external military threat. By 1942 the complacency of the colony's defenders led to the successful occupation by the Japanese, whose senior officers requisitioned Raffles for their own quarters, but not before a loyal Chinese chef had hastily buried the hotel's valuable silverware in the garden, where it remained undetected until the Japanese capitulation. The account of this chef, who had gone into hiding during the occupation, returning to his old employer's premises with a shovel strapped to his bicycle to recover the famous silver has passed into local folklore.

The hotel's double-height Tiffin Room is world-famous, but it had lost much of its authenticity as it now attracted coachloads of passengers from passing cruise liners, all of whom queued meekly for a pale imitation of a Singapore Sling in the Long Bar as part of the packaged 'Singapore Experience'.

My main reason for being in Singapore this time was to act as visiting tutor to students at the university, which was a welcome change from running professional practice seminars for practitioners, which hitherto had been my Commonwealth remit. Without exception, the students were a delight to work with. The second years had already come to terms with fundamentals and were now beginning to find their creativity and express their idealism. At the same time they were hungry for hard knowledge and sought approbation at every turn. Male and female students alike were polite and very open to persuasion, to the extent that I occasionally wished for more aggravation and dissension. Year Two was a comfortable year, as they didn't face the prospect of their degree examination until the end of the following year, so could enjoy the prospect of developing their creativity a little longer. One of the design exercises given took the form of a bit of fun, albeit with a practical purpose. Under the direction of their tutor, Ong Boon Lay, there was to be a cardboard boat race across the Singapore River in craft designed and built by the students. Each one had to be capable of transporting a single occupant safely to the other side. Scrap cardboard was collected from alleys behind the godowns (warehouses) and shophouses, where it was abundant, and, with the minimum of guidance from tutors, the students set about their task, which had to be accomplished to a strict timetable, but could take any shape as inspiration struck. One took the form of a military tank, another a banana (which grew locally and whose geometry was well understood), whilst a third tried a space-age variation of a sampan. The students worked in small teams during the design and construction process, but the boats had to be navigated singly, simply because they could barely take the weight of one person. They were launched in turn amid confused last-minute instructions and yelps of excitement from collaborators and howls of derision from competitors awaiting their turn. Not unexpectedly, one after another, elegant and innovative though they were, they sank within seconds of hitting the water. The task I had been given was to act as judge and declare a winner. When approached about this earlier in the day I thought it might be difficult, but the moment the event began it was clear that the winner would be the boat that managed to merely survive the crossing or, if none did, the award would go to the craft which went furthest before sinking. Completely absorbed, I watched a fairly ramshackle assembly of second-hand packaging zigzag its way across the tidal water, each one propelled by a web-footed student who looked as though he was strong enough to support the floating jetsam above his head until he ran out of breath. I thought I had my winner until moments later his creative assembly disappeared from sight. I turned my attention once more to the shore when, seconds later, with porpoise-like agility, the student who had just sunk erupted from the water to shrieks of delight from his supporters gathered on the far side. I reflected that all this might be good training for trying to get planning permission in Britain with all the odds stacked against you.

This was imaginative teaching. Had the students been told that the day was to be devoted to an analysis of 'The Properties of Materials', everyone would have groaned inwardly and dragged themselves reluctantly to the lecture theatre, but done this way it was worth a dozen textbooks and each participant would remember it for the rest of their career. An architect has to understand the limitations and potential of each material specified, whether it is steel, glass, metal, concrete, timber, stone, plastic or any one of countless

403

other types. So perhaps if you get soaked and swallow something revolting in the process of learning, you never forget.

The fourth year was similar to the second, in that although they now had their degree behind them, they were not yet in their last year concentrating on finals. Their design programmes became a lot more advanced as they tackled local problems like high-density, low-cost housing; a multicultural centre, and a shopping centre for the minority Indian community. They had to obtain a real insight into the different traditions of the Chinese, Malay and Indian parts of Singapore's diverse population before putting pencil to paper, and undertook well-structured fieldwork in the weeks leading up to the design process.

The fourth-year curriculum introduced conflicts of ideology and caused students to question orthodoxy in ways which the all-controlling government may not have wished to encourage. But this is what universities are for. I wasn't there long enough to see whether this was anything more than a safety valve strategically placed in the course, but the limited vision that stems from political and technical ideologies was illustrated by one lecturer, Fong Hoo Cheong, by reference to an old Chinese adage called 'Frogs in Wells'. It tells of frogs who, trapped all their lives in wells, would describe 'sky' simply as a blue disc occasionally with white patches crossing it. Planners, whose blink-ered approach was thought to limit the broader ecological and moral remit of architects, were exhorted 'to climb out of the well and see the entire picture'. The students loved it.

Although Westerners are told that all Chinese look alike, it should come as no surprise that in reality individuals obviously differ from each other as widely as they do in any other race. Lee Soon Chye was no exception. 'Don't worry, all Englishmen look the same, as well.' This gentle but pointed reminder from him followed my slowness in recognising him on his own territory, as we had only met once before, briefly, in London. After a while, I realised that he had spent a lifetime perfecting the edgy put-down of the Brits through being in the happy position of not having to conform. He was very comfort-ably off and enjoyed demonstrating it. He was also a bachelor and kept count-less pedigree hounds at the avant-garde house he had designed for himself. I believe it was his membership of Crufts, not love of the British architec-tural establishment, that brought him to London from time to time. He took a particular interest in architectural education, which was probably how we first met. On one occasion Lee Soon Chye had arrived in London with a shopping list of projects and initiatives that were going to cost much more to fund than was available and I was asked to explain this to him. This didn't go down too well and he emphasised the vital importance of each of his proposals if his complete task was to be executed properly. The RIBA received his requests 'with interest' but made it clear that *all* of us, without exception, had to live within our income. Lee Soon Chye thought that the RIBA was too patrician in its attitude and that I had not supported his cause vigorously enough, so we parted on cool terms.

He got on much better with an engaging British practitioner and educationalist, David Horsfall, and on one occasion he invited David to visit him in Singapore. The occasion was made memorable by two incidents in particular, which go a long way to describing the extent that Lee Soon Chye was different from most of his Chinese professional counterparts.

He asked David if he would enjoy an afternoon's kite-flying (a very different activity from that practised in Pakistan). Kites here were very traditional, handcrafted and lacquered, beautiful in both elegance and symmetry, and altogether made for a civilised diversion. His wartime service in the Fleet Air Arm and his general sense of curiosity encouraged David to accept the invitation, so he duly presented himself at Lee Soon Chye's house, ready to rediscover a schoolboy enthusiasm. A houseboy led David to a large expanse of well-manicured garden, where his host awaited him at a table laden with cool alcoholic drinks, either side of which was the type of canopied Bermuda deckchair that could have graced an Onassis Mediterranean yacht. Soon Chye beckoned him to sit down, and together they chatted amiably while successive cocktails were served. Feeling a bit light-headed, David thought he'd better pause a while if he was going to handle a kite, but his host brushed aside his reservations and went on talking. Eventually, Soon Chye said the entertainment should begin, so he leaned forward in his chair, clapped his hands, and two boys attired in freshly laundered sarongs appeared, each with an armful of beautiful kites, which they proceeded to launch one by one while the audience lay still further back in their luxurious chairs, trying harder and harder to focus before succumbing to the heat and drink and drifting into blissful, kaleidoscopic sleep.

So successful was the event that Soon Chye invited David to visit again and take advantage of the splendidly appointed swimming pool. It stood conveniently near the house, and from the changing cubicles David could hear the snuffles and fidgeting of well-groomed hounds in adjacent kennels. The appealing thought of an idyllic pool all to himself quickened David's step as he left the changing room, and all his cares, behind. He had been in the pool for a couple of minutes when Soon Chye arrived to see how he was getting on. 'Would you like some company?' he asked, and out of politeness David said, 'Yes, of course.' Whereupon his host clapped his hands once more and an unseen houseboy unlocked the kennel gate and out poured the entire pack of hounds who, lemming-like, threw themselves into the water. One by one they sought David's reassuring hand, competing for his attention. All refreshingly un-English.

If the change I saw in Singapore City had been dramatic, then the transformation of the little offshore island of Blakang Mati, my military base for two years in the late 1940s, was even more marked. This was not a case of *plus ça change* . . . , this change was profound and irrevocable. Neither was it a case of 'change and decay in all I see', as an English hymnal describes our shifting world: decay had been effectively obliterated by diktat. The shreds of the past that remained served a new purpose – 'my' guns were no more than a tourist attraction along with the new coral museum and the nine-hole golf course. Blakang Mati had had its Malay name altered (it meant 'behind death', a reference to an old burial site) and was now called Sentosa, 'place of tranquillity', as a very necessary precursor to the development of the island as a tourist destination.

From my side, I was no longer the young, wide-eyed, somewhat mystified soldier teaching gunnery just because the Army couldn't think of anything else for me and my compatriots to do now that the Pacific war was over: I was now a generously paid visiting 'academic' brought in, with others, to try and widen the perspective of university students who shared the international aspirations of their faculty and were hungry for new ideas. Perhaps the only common factor spanning the many years was the row of expectant brown faces (although it occurred to me that one or two of them could be some of my old squad's grandchildren).

I didn't consciously revive the vivid memories of my past on Blakang Mati; but they were just too deeply etched to ignore. Back then, the island was studded with 6-inch and 9.2-inch coastal defence gun emplacements, all of which had proved useless during the war, and by the time I was stationed there they were abandoned and overgrown, the centre of weekend exploration by a small handful of inquisitive teenagers like myself who found the experience one step up from Cowboys and Indians. We photographed each other with an old Brownie box camera standing on top of the gun casings and sent the snaps home so that our families could share in our adventures.

Come Monday, we were jolted back to solid reality as we absorbed more advanced training on our new 3.7-inch ack-ack (anti-aircraft) guns. An IG, which stood for Inspector of Gunnery, but more colloquially 'I'm God', with the authority that suggested he had spent his civilian life in a shire manor house, would explain that the practice of heavy ack-ack artillery was a *science* and we were privileged to be chosen to learn about it, whereas light ack-ack (using smaller and more mobile gunnery pieces) was an *art* 'just like duck-shooting', and on our return to civilian life participation in this activity would mark our social acceptance. We had no idea what he was talking about, but enjoyed listening to him, particularly on other occasions when he had difficulty in explaining the details of personal discipline. Venereal disease was on the increase in the regiment and much of this due to the ready availability of *binte* in Singapore itself, so it fell to the IG to warn us of the dangers of infection and the rigours of military sanction if any soldier was discovered with the condition. He found the disciplinary measures easy to describe (they were all set out in a military manual), but not the sexual congress that caused all the bother, so as the monthly finger-wagging sessions took place, we relished watching the IG look vaguely at the ceiling before opening his homily with, 'If some of you insist on going into Singapore for your ... your greens, you must fully understand the consequences.' I have gone through life ever since feeling nervous about asking for more greens.

The other big medical risk was malaria, and the Army employed local labour to cut back the ever-growing grass and scrub that flourished in the hot, humid climate and led to pools forming in which mosquitoes bred unseen. There was a lot of this spare, wild acreage and the method the contractors employed was to line up a dozen or so labourers side by side to cut a wide swathe through the coarse, broadleaved growth, rather like a combine harvester. The coolie labourers wore a loincloth, an old vest, and a sweatband around their heads, but remained barefoot. They advanced, swinging their sickles in a continuous circular motion, and if they disturbed one of the venomous snakes, silver krait or pit viper, they would pick it up in a flash, cut it in half in mid-air and discard the pieces without missing their rhythm. And there were we, in ankle-height boots and webbing gaiters, hesitant about taking short cuts through the grass. Where was that elusive *Boy's Own* sense of adventure?

Although the grass-cutting operations were reliable in minimising the pools, the contracting companies themselves were notoriously unreliable and had to be changed frequently. On one occasion when I was instructed to interview yet another applicant for the contract, he stepped forward and announced his name – Goh Ho Soon. I lacked the iron will to prevent myself saying, 'About one week at the present rate.' The IG, who was standing behind me, told me to grow up or he would find someone else to do the job.

Due to the nature of our uniform and particularly the thick socks we had to wear under our ammunition boots, we suffered constantly from prickly heat, for which there was no available treatment, other than standing (as minimally clad as possible) in a torrential downpour, of which there was at least one a day. This was bliss, but if the rain didn't arrive as we came off duty, we resorted to stripping off and diving into the sea, which had much the same beneficial effect. Our new-found salvation turned out to be short-lived after the commanding officer's wife complained that, from her distant balcony, naked servicemen could be seen and this would diminish the respect in which the regiment was held. We possessed none of today's psychological insights that would have told us she was a screwed-up bitch, so we just thought she was a spoilsport.

Everyone looked forward to Saturday evening, when an old black-and-white film would be shown in the 'cinema', an abandoned ammunition shed. It had hard wooden benches to sit on, unless one were to share the floor with domestic animals and small local children who wandered in and out all the time. To add to the enjoyment, a few cents would buy roasted water-melon seeds sold in a twist of old newspaper, which we would scour afterwards to see if the harbour news recorded the arrival of known troopships. None of us knew how long our posting was going to last and it gave us hope if we saw reference to a familiar name.

After the film I enjoyed walking back to my quarters along an unlit road past the clanking generator that just managed to keep us supplied with electricity; there was no refrigeration or air conditioning, so its load wasn't heavy, but it was our only link with normality and we were ever-grateful to our colleagues in the Royal Engineers who were stationed nearby. The walk from the cinema would take about twenty minutes and the moment I had left behind the main regimental buildings, the noises of the rainforest increased in both volume and variety. The sound of frogs in the monsoon drains adjoining the road would be magnified a hundredfold by the echo their habitat provided, and it was always a surprise to find how small these creatures were; a bit like singing in the bathroom; they must have enjoyed their Walter Mitty existence. Orang-utans, monitor lizards and parrots joined in the cacophony, which increased with every step. One particular bird emitted a single sound, like a low, double-bass string being mournfully plucked, and it did so incessantly about every ten seconds. Was this the 'brainfever bird' often talked about in Africa and India? I never knew, but if I couldn't sleep because of the heat or humidity, it was particularly unnerving. Despite the darkness that surrounded me on my walk, often near-continuous sheet lightning lit my path. It also illuminated banks of sharply silhouetted 'cauliflower' cloud separating each layer, like a stage set. It was mesmerising and every bit as fascinating as a five-star *son et lumière*.

On my present visit I was surprised how total was my recall, bearing in mind that only a few scraps from the past still existed. The sampan trip from Singapore had given way to a spectacular cable-car ride, and there were plans afoot for a direct monorail link to the mainland. The mangrove swamp had made way for a golf course and the island had been substantially increased in size by importing vast quantities of silt and sand, a technique perfected by civil engineers building one of the world's favourite airports a few miles to the east at Changi. Dutch land-reclamation procedures used to lead the way, but the Singaporeans were now hard on their heels.

When I reached my hotel on Singapore mainland again I received an invitation to go up to Kuala Lumpur in Malaysia to join a few old friends at the annual dinner of Pertubuhan Akitek Malaysia, their equivalent of the Royal Institute of British Architects. A short journey by air, which originally could only be accomplished by overnight train, had me there in no time and my hosts had booked me into the hotel where the dinner was to be held. As with Singapore, I barely recognised the capital, but it was good to meet former Malaysian and expatriate colleagues once more. Knowing that these events can still be very formal, I asked if I could see the list of current office holders who I knew would form the long receiving line. Unlike the situation in the West, Muslim names are relatively few in number and many Malays share similar or identical names. Ahmed, Akib, Hussein, Mohamed, Aziz, Talib, Osman, and Abu Bakar crop up time and time again in various forms so, having read the list, I wasn't at all sure who, if any, I had met before and decided to err on the side of formality in case I made a silly mistake. At the reception I smiled and bowed at the right moments and muttered something harmless to each host until, at the end of the line, I was greeted by their president, who said brightly, 'Don't you remember me?'

I didn't, but found myself mumbling, 'Ah, yes, of course, your face is very familiar, but just where was it we met? Do remind me.'

'You were my external examiner.'

My heart sank. I had seen scores of overseas students at the Architectural Association in London, but seldom for more than a few minutes at a time, and usually with my nose buried in the graduate's examination paper. I paused, hesitatingly asking, 'Did I pass you?'

'Oh yes,' came the reply. 'You awarded me a distinction.'

Quite how I could have eaten their six-course dinner if I had failed him kept me preoccupied for most of the evening, despite my lively neighbours at the table.

The evening was considerably lightened by the welcome and unexpected appearance of Kuala Lumpur's first female architect, Menaha Ramanath, who had started her own practice. She is the daughter of the Malaysian client for whom I undertook the Port Klang Environmental Impact Assessment and who was also a former cricketing friend of mine from student days. Menaha had read architecture in the UK and worked briefly in my office before returning to Malaysia for her first job. The demure, methodical assistant had metamorphosed into a smartly dressed, confident woman who, as she leapt out of her impressive car before the dinner, looked ready to take on the Kuala Lumpur architectural establishment – and all this in a country that was beginning to show leanings towards fundamentalism.

A few years later I was to return again to the Malaysian capital as the guest of the British High Commissioner who, hearing that I was chairing a CAA council meeting there, invited us all to dinner at his newly designed official residence. As a dozen of us sat down to the well-appointed table, I casually asked the steward if I could see the bottle of a very attractive dry white wine that had accompanied our fish course. To my surprise I saw that it had been imported from a small vineyard near Ditchling, about five miles north of my home in Brighton, and I rather naively remarked on the coincidence to the First Secretary. He returned a rather patronising smile and assured me that the High Commissioner always wanted to 'make his guests feel at home'. Of course. Peter Ustinov used to say that he was convinced that there was a small room in the attic of the Foreign Office where diplomats were taught to stutter. They certainly had a room to teach them how to wear a pitying smile.

I would have liked to stay longer in Kuala Lumpur and, among other things, visit the Salangor cricket club pavilion on the Padang to see if my initials carved on the back of a dressing-room lavatory door were still there, but I had to return to Singapore; another, and final, CAA meeting was to be held there before we all dispersed. I found that, for economy, we were all sharing rooms and that my room-mate was the deliciously named Ruskin Punch, who came from Port of Spain, Trinidad. He was one of the nicest people imaginable. Tall, good-looking, quietly spoken and talented, he had trained in London before returning to the West Indies, and after marrying became director of a well-known local practice. We had met before and I was glad to know I would have such a congenial companion. Despite our very different flight schedules, we arrived in the hotel lobby at about the same time and I picked up the plastic room card on our behalf. Ruskin wanted to shower and then ring his wife, for whom he was buying some carpets from Singapore as this was her line of business in Trinidad. I explained that after a flight I liked to get some fresh air and said I would like 'to walk around the block' for an hour or so before turning in. I left him sitting on the edge of his bed telephoning his wife and, on leaving the room, withdrew the plastic key.

I got back after a deliciously cool walk down to the new shoreline: it had rained earlier and the air was full of bougainvillea and spice. On reopening my hotel door with the plastic card, I discovered a sweating, exhausted companion, prostrate on his bed. After I had left there had been a programmed twenty seconds' continuity of supply and then the electricity and everything it served had switched off. I had left Ruskin without light, air conditioning or working shower. When the light came on there was evidence of his abortive attempts to unpack, wash and get organised for the next day, all undertaken in rank darkness. I would have been really touchy if it had happened to me, but Ruskin gave me a nonchalant smile and told me not to fuss. He was one of that rare breed incapable of holding a grudge.

I felt all the more despairing therefore to hear, a few months later, that he had been killed in a car crash in Port of Spain.

Chapter 56

Bouncing Off the Ropes

We walk through life expecting it to follow an accustomed path, only to feel let down when it doesn't. Approaching the end of my working career, I was meant to be easing down before full retirement, my mortgage and school fees behind me. I was looking forward to free wheeling the last furlong, relying more on experience than on energy and feeling reassured that, with the help of the grey pound, my health would be sustained while I enjoyed exotic travel, comfortably gift-wrapped in a warm glow of quiet satisfaction.

So when, after forty years, for reasons completely outside my control, the predicted pattern faded and then totally disappeared, I was left not so much angry as mystified. Although I knew I was a victim of a global phenomenon, that didn't seem to help. Friends trying to be supportive said, 'You've got to be philosophical,' whatever that means, but that only took my mind back to a fusty fourth-form classroom where a tubercular-looking English master would struggle to remind us of Keats's salutary observation that 'philosophy can clip an angel's wings'.

The late 1980s and early 1990s saw the worst recession in Britain since World War II. There had been small (9 to 15-month) blips on the screen before – several of them – but they were containable. This was something much worse, although, when it started, no one had any idea of its gravity or duration. The UK was not alone – the experience was shared by the rest of Western Europe, North America and even Australasia. It all began on Black Monday, when the world stock market crashed, starting in New York on Monday, 19 October 1987, resulting in great falls in the values of stocks and shares in markets worldwide.

The construction and development industries are always vulnerable to a sharp downturn in the economy. People just stop building, and certainly don't build at risk; so if building stops, so does design.

Fifteen years later, when we were once more living in abundant prosperity, academic economists would maintain that the British economy had all the hallmarks of being stuck in a low-growth investment cycle and that it still awaited a convincing diagnosis of its ills; which is another way of saying that we wouldn't know when the next downturn would come until, once more, it would take us by surprise.

The effect of this on architectural practice was little short of cataclysmic. Together with other firms, we hung on until our bank manager's frowns turned into something more severe. We were running up a salary bill well in excess of our fee income. Using old contacts, I placed one or two senior staff on secondment to Singapore, which hadn't yet felt the squeeze (although the Tiger Economies were to suffer similarly a couple of years later), and reluctantly I began to make redundant valued members of the office. It was little comfort to know that all the construction professions (surveyors, structural and civil engineers, town planners and landscape architects) were in the same boat as us.

The situation got so bad that in the early 1990s, the London Region of the Royal Institute of British Architects sought help from the European Social Fund to finance a course in project management for architects who found themselves suddenly unemployed. The aim was to develop specialised skills and thereby increase employment opportunities in fields closely related to architecture. This service was of particular use to architects in the large London practices that were very badly affected at this time. The crisis affected everyone.

As architectural work diminished I was able to participate more fully in Commonwealth affairs as, by now, my links had been considerably strengthened through having served a term as President of the CAA just before the downturn began. But this did not help the practice. To add to our difficulties, some of our clients in the private sector were retiring early and, even had architectural work still been available, their successors, a generation younger than me, were no longer obliged to continue using their predecessors' advisers and usually did not. For me the ensuing 'big stop' was abrupt and uncomfortable. I therefore decided to hand over the practice partly to younger colleagues who still had heavy family-related financial commitments.

At that time Britain itself was an uncomfortable place in which to practise. The year 1990 saw the massive violence in protest against the proposed poll tax, as well as the IRA bomb at the Stock Exchange and, early the following year, their attack on Downing Street. No one quite knew what to expect next. In 1992 the government and British Coal announced the closure of 31 collieries. A few weeks later Windsor Castle went up in flames. To the casual observer the old order was changing, and changing for ever.

My own order changed more profoundly than I could have anticipated when I was formally invited by Virginia Bottomley, Secretary of State for Health, to become chairman of one of the new NHS Trusts being set up by the Conservative government. To improve delivery of service and achieve better financial control of the NHS, it had been decided to split 'purchasers' from 'providers' within the system. New Health Authorities would purchase health care in its many forms from NHS Trusts, who would provide it. South Downs Health was one such Trust; it covered an urban and rural population of about a third of a million, employed over two thousand staff, operated out of 52 separate locations and had an annual budget well in excess of £50 million.

The new Trust was to be run by a board comprising executive directors (the existing heads of medical, nursing, financial and human resource services), together with new non-executive directors, who would be recruited from the local community. With my chief executive, Alan Bedford, I chose a lawyer, a bank manager, a management consultant, a GP, and the widow of a former health minister who had been a local consultant.

Not everyone was particularly happy about the new organisation, least of all the unions, who campaigned vigorously against its establishment. In Brighton the unions went so far as to invite opposition spokesman Robin Cook to speak to a crowded meeting a few days before we launched the Trust. I was aware that he had read English literature at Edinburgh and that he chose his words deliberately, often to devastating effect, and could sell 'misinformation' without it being noticed better than anyone if it suited his political purpose. Mark Lawson in *The Times* had described him as 'the most witheringly destructive, resourcefully scornful despatch box talent in this parliament'. It was therefore an edgy few days for us as we waited to see if our first meeting as a board would take place as scheduled. But despite all the windy rhetoric, we opened for business on the appointed day without interruption.

I had one huge advantage: there was no precedent for the way we worked, no inherited rule book, no weight of history. We could fly by the seat of our pants, and I was made responsible to one person only, the Secretary of State. She could have my head off, but she was the only one who could. This arrangement conferred on me the freedom to be truly innovative and breathe new life into a heavily encrusted system. My fellow architects were known to ask, 'What the hell is an architect doing running the NHS?' And my answer, only half glib, was, 'I come to it untainted by experience.' This turned out to be truer than I thought. As I had no career involvement in the NHS, was not party to its politics and internal tensions, and had no personal allegiances

415

to respect (I knew no one), it was much easier to see it all from the outside and offer a detached view. Being able to stand back from this vast organisation of over 1.2 million employees (only the Red Army and Indian Railways had more), I could be much more objective. Certainly there was a lot to learn, but the generalist in me relished the prospect.

The Trust headquarters were situated at Brighton General Hospital, a former nineteenth-century Poor Law Institution of formidable appearance. The General housed a wide range of clinical and administrative functions that could not be accommodated on the site of the Royal Sussex County, the nearby district general hospital responsible for all acute work, which later had a Trust of its own.

South Downs Health was set up to concentrate on mental health, rehabilitation and community health. At the good suggestion of my chief executive, our offices were housed in the same block as a mental-health day unit, so that we were reminded of our *raison d'être* every time we entered the building. In any organisation it is only too easy for administration to be physically divorced from its core activity, nearly always to its detriment.

The nineteenth-century city fathers who commissioned the workhouse had been at pains to conceal its presence from public gaze and built it on top of steep farmland outside the town, as they would have done any lunatic asylum at that time. This configuration was rather fortunate because in the early twentieth century the municipality had built a racecourse adjacent on the crown of the hill, and my new boardroom window now overlooked part of the course. I was tempted by the thought of manipulating the order and timing of board agenda items to give us an insider's glimpse of the 2.30 Pavilion Handicap or the 3.15 Regency Plate.

The Institute of Directors had taught me the importance of 'walking the talk' in getting to grips with a new organisation, and as the Trust operated its various services out of some 52 different addresses across our catchment area, I planned to visit one each week during my first year to meet staff and find out what they did. South Downs Health was a non-acute Trust and was responsible for many of the less glamorous, less publicised services. Unlike the acute sector, whose work was kept in the public eye through numerous television soaps and current-affairs programmes, we could only offer schizophrenia and leg ulcers, so part of my job was to raise the hitherto Cinderella-like profile of such work and at least give it equal status alongside acute Trusts. Familiarity with what we did was therefore essential, and I set to work accordingly.

My first visit, deliberately unannounced to avoid any artificial arrangements, was to a Victorian property in Wellington Road, Brighton which had been converted to provide community health support in various forms. Shortly after nine one Monday morning I walked in and waited by an unmanned reception counter. Not seeing anyone, I rang a rather old-fashioned bell of the type more often seen in Cotswold tea shops. Nothing happened, so I rang again and then heard anxious footsteps approaching. To make up for the delay the earnest young man in charge obviously decided to demonstrate efficiency and helpfulness by making a quick appraisal the moment he saw me, as neither of us had ever met. He glanced at my greying beard and said cheerfully, 'Have you come for your incontinence pads? How many do you need?' Not knowing what to say, I shifted awkwardly from one foot to the other; I didn't want to mortify him by announcing that, metaphorically, I signed his salary cheque each month. He took my silence as embarrassment over my unfortunate condition, and after too long a pause, I eventually mumbled something about joining the Trust recently and wanting to find out better how it worked. He nodded rather seriously, but I'm not sure he believed me.

I had to do better next time.

As it turned out, next time was Christmas week. As a layman, I had always been aware of how particularly well medical and nursing staff looked after their patients over this period and was acquainted with the tradition of a senior surgeon coming in on Christmas day to carve the turkey. So I thought I should try and honour the custom in some small, albeit less expert, way. I decided to visit the New Sussex Hospital, a mental-health facility near the centre of the town. As it was 25 December, I had agreed with my chief executive that my visit should be as informal as we could make it and that I should dress down accordingly. The meeting would not be prearranged and I would just 'call in as I was passing'. All this sounded easy, so I set off late that morning, left my car at the end of the street and approached the (surprisingly open) front door. Again no one was immediately visible, but I could hear voices and some laughter and could smell coffee and cigarette smoke. I didn't know where it was coming from, but I followed my nose along dark corridors festooned with balloons, some of which were already losing their puff. I became aware of cigar smoke adding another festive layer to the occasion. After turning another corner I came across a contented and animated group of people. They were mostly seated, but one or two were leaning against furniture, all of them glad, I imagined, of a break from the usual routine. I looked hard for a member of staff and then remembered that it was now customary for staff in mental-health centres not to wear uniform lest it create another barrier between them and the patient whose confidence they were trying to win. This was of no help to me, and no one knew, or indeed seemed to care, who I was. After a few moments a chair became vacant and I asked if I could sit there. My misty-eyed neighbour said it was OK and before long someone asked me if I'd like a mug of coffee. It arrived in a cracked Snoopy mug and someone else offered me a biscuit he had just picked off a seat. I wasn't word-perfect on Manchester United's latest form for their Boxing Day match, so I couldn't add much to the general conversation; instead, I sat back and enjoyed my snack. At this point the chair next to me became vacant and someone quickly sat down and began to speak to me very gently. He asked me where I lived and whether had I been there long and if my relatives lived in the area – straight waiting-room or first-time pub talk, and I thought nothing of it. It was only when he reached behind him for a clipboard that I felt something was wrong. When the continuing queries involved the name of my GP and my date of birth, the penny finally dropped. I was being treated as a *self-referral*. Once more I was faced with the dilemma of disclosing my identity without embarrassing a dedicated and caring ward manager who had volunteered to work on Christmas Day and was prepared to offer immediate support to a stranger who'd wandered in off the street. Eventually I had to explain I wasn't a patient, but that as a new 'member of staff' I was interested to know how the system of informal admissions worked. I told him that I hoped I hadn't wasted his time and that I appreciated the chat and coffee. Only a couple of weeks later at a staff meeting would he realise who I was, and by then time would have cushioned the blow.

Both these incidents were revelatory. In each case they showed initiative and a ready willingness to help. Everyone cared and tried to see things from the patient's perspective, revealing an underlying empathy that in previous generations would have been called a sense of vocation. This was all very different from the private sector, and I liked what I saw.

Chapter 57

A New Beginning

The deep recession of the early 1990s which decimated the development and construction industries, together with attendant professions, seemed never-ending. National names in building were never to recover and soon they dropped out of the vocabulary. Redundancy became an ever-increasing concern among architects. I assumed that the remaining links with my profession would be severed. However, through circumstances I could not have visualised, I then found myself involved with a substantial capital programme, but this time not as architect, but as client.

After its identity and geographical boundaries had been established, South Downs Health NHS Trust found it needed new facilities in different locations. The building types required were often innovatory and included a new polyclinic which grouped diagnostic, clinical and physiotherapy activities and some aspects of mental health under one roof. Enthusiastically I read the design brief that had been prepared before my arrival and, no doubt, if a scheme had been designed to its requirements, an acceptable new building would have arisen. However, when I re-read the brief, it didn't make me want to throw my hat in the air with excitement, and nothing in it suggested the innovation that the new situation demanded, so I sat down and completely rewrote the document with the (probably unfair) advantage of knowing how to elicit an imaginative response from an architect, by couching it in language that would hit the G-spot.

In addition to the polyclinic, a sequence of other projects included a neighbourhood clinic, a medium-sized mental-health unit, a hospital for the elderly and physically or mentally frail; and a rehabilitation unit for seriously injured children. They were all to be constructed during my term of office, so, to my surprise and delight, I found myself once more directly involved in a substantial architectural commission. For each project I set up a limited architectural competition to be adjudicated both by clinical and managerial colleagues and by externally appointed architects. Central to my thinking was that we would select architects who had never before designed a health-care building in equal number with those who had, to compete with each other in the hope that new ideas and approaches would emerge, if only to test them against established practice. As the clinicians and managers had been fully involved with the revised design brief and would have equal judging status with the architects, I hoped we would attract entries of high quality and that my NHS colleagues would feel a genuine sense of ownership of every project for which they would be responsible.

Careful to retain impartiality, I invited one local and one nationally recognised architect to act as judges and it was particularly fortunate that, in the latter category, Sir Philip Powell, a hugely admired figure by clients and architects alike, agreed to join the team. Immensely approachable, greatly experienced and completely unpompous, he brought credibility and liveliness to each project and was as happy as I was when three of the competitions were won by architects new to health-care design.

Under his professional leadership I was entirely comfortable with the judging procedure, which involved the entries of all the competitors being pinned on the wall adjacent to each other to allow direct comparison. The six separate schemes, often involving ten or more drawings each, were hung up, and during a long day of adjudication (when I had the greatest difficulty in keeping out of the room), schemes thought to be less good would be taken down one by one and put on the floor, forming an ever-growing pool. By the time only two of them were left on the wall (and here was an act of faith), the architectural judges left the room to allow the 'users' of the new building to make the final choice. With anyone of lesser calibre than Philip Powell I would not have been prepared to take the risk, because an untutored eye finds it difficult to interpret and compare architectural drawings, but I knew he would have left the two strongest schemes on the wall and, however different they were, he knew that either would be capable of being developed into an eminently worthwhile solution. My Trust colleagues would have eaten out of his hand.

The extent of my involvement with health-care design gave me little time for deciding whether to resume practice after my six-year term as Trust chairman was completed. I knew that my Commonwealth work would probably continue, but I'd thought that could likely be accommodated within any return to practice. I was in no particular hurry, as life was still full of interest, and currently I had the pleasure of working with some very talented people in the Health Service. Although it never became a preoccupation, I occasionally toyed with the idea of practising again, until, one memorable day, my mind was made up for me. Not being in the least superstitious by nature, I don't go through life looking for signs, portents and omens, but there comes a time when an event so emphatic occurs it can't be ignored.

One day, nearing St Peter's Church, Brighton, which overlooked my former office, I became increasingly aware of escalating commotion. When I got nearer I was overtaken by a police car and two fire tenders, which screeched to a halt outside my old office in Richmond Place. It was ablaze. Sheets of flame emerged from dormer windows at roof level. Extravagant tongues of fire like those that belch from fantastical serpents embellishing the nearby Royal Pavilion leapt through unexpected gaps as rafters began to collapse. I couldn't believe my eyes. Verdi and Puccini were competing for dramatic impact at my old workplace. Glyndebourne had arrived, complete with effects.

The police quickly established that there was no one to rescue, so the fire-fighters concentrated on preventing the conflagration reaching the adjoining property in Richmond Place where, countless years before, I had taken a bath in my first employer's time as an act of youthful bravado. Later I was told that, during the recent recession, the landlord of my more recent office had sold up, tenants had had to move elsewhere, and this had given an oppor-tunity for squatters to move in and bring their edgy lifestyle with them. In such circumstances, a fire was just waiting to happen, and today was the day. I stood looking at it with utter disbelief, not perhaps because of the spec-tacle, impressive though it was, but more from experiencing a deep feeling that this dramatic scene was being played out for my benefit, indicating in the most vivid way possible that a firm line had been drawn under my days in architectural practice and that forty years was quite enough. Dramatists and scribes have traded in portents ever since Old Testament days, so who was I to question what was happening? I assigned my days as an architect to the past.

Until a year or so later I found myself one step removed through involvement as consultant to Nightingale Associates, the largest architectural health-care practice in the country, who were a pleasure to work with. I had come across them first when they designed the new polyclinic in Hove. I was returning from their London office one day, and as my meeting had finished early and it was a sunny spring day, I decided to walk to my next appointment in the City. Having time in hand, I diverted down Cheapside where, in the shadow of St Paul's Cathedral, a massive redevelopment was being completed. It was replacing a post-war scheme that had sprung up rather too quickly which had comprised a group of faceless rectangular office blocks, best described by John

Betjeman as 'rent-collecting slabs'. In those heady days clean, white modernity spelled progress and the designer's façade vocabulary limited itself to variations of intersecting straight lines, like upended graph paper. Not a single curve was visible. Today's 'contextualism' was an unknown consideration. The usefulness of these buildings of the 1960s had been short-lived as more sophisticated requirements were demanded by the banking and insurance world. By now, the extensive use of computers and air-conditioning was mandatory and this meant that underfloor voids and suspended ceilings were needed for cable management and service ducts, none of which could be fitted into the older buildings. The City took a decision to demolish the whole area and start again, and this time be more mindful of the original historic street pattern; the opportunity of creating a pedestrian-friendly enclave, and the need for a varied architectural expression that did not resort to pastiche. The massive investment needed for the project had taken time to assemble and numerous master plans were prepared to meet the optimum townscape objectives as well as ensuring an attractive return for the developers.

Not being personally involved, I only had a background knowledge of this new scheme's progress through articles in the technical press, often stumbled upon when I was overseas, and only read because I assumed the redevelopment area included the site of the Bank of Boston, on which I and others had laboured long and hard and which had involved me in numerous trips to stone quarries on the Isle of Portland where the adjacent cathedral's stone had come from centuries earlier.

On the day in question I approached the cathedral from one of the new, deliberately narrow pedestrian streets that led into the main piazza and saw in the distance the restored and re-erected Temple Bar which, in addition to its historical significance, is a deft foil to its new neighbours. Looking around me, I realised that there was too much to see in the time available and I made my way back towards Cheapside, promising myself I'd come back again and have a longer look on another day. Suddenly I spotted the Bank of Boston building still standing there. This didn't make sense, because I assumed that the whole site had been comprehensively cleared. But no, there it was. Obviously a clear decision had been taken to retain it. It was the only building on the entire site to be preserved as part of the new redevelopment. Whether the City fathers were attracted by its unique profile or whether its relative 'good neighbourliness' towards Wren's masterpiece swayed opinion I would never know, but I was very happy to see that it had been kept. There was something of the prodigal son about this and I felt a glow of satisfaction to realise that, just occasionally in this life, events turn out as one would wish.

My surprise was both pleasurable and reassuring. How glad the others in my original team would be if they knew, but I had no idea of their whereabouts. My partner Adam Suppel was dead, my co-designer Cedric Ellis had retired to Spain, and others had scattered with the years. I remembered that even the ever-serious Goethe had once said, 'Nothing is worth more than this day,' and I wondered what occasion had prompted that observation from him.

As I walked on I whistled to myself and lengthened my stride, feeling that life had something to commend it, so much so that, in the noisy rush of the passing traffic, I lightened my step. Even the very old briefcase I was carrying felt less burdensome in my hand. It was only when swinging round a corner, I glanced down, and realised that all I held in my hand at this moment was its handle, the case having fallen off unnoticed some streets earlier while I was enjoying my burst of elation. I suppose it may have felt a bit light, but lightness of heart must have made me more carefree than usual. I stopped for a moment and toyed with the idea of not going back for it – after all, it only contained minutes, some scribbled notes and a rail timetable, all of which I could live without or replace. It was with some reluctance that I realised then I might provoke a security scare of some sort if I left it where it was, so I went back. When I saw it I noticed that, in typical metropolitan fashion, people were just walking round it! Once more recalling my aversion to any form of superstition, I could not easily accept this curious event as any sort of 'sign' denoting the final unburdening of my professional responsibilities, yet, perversely, part of me wanted to respond to fate's nudge; so I emptied the contents of the case into the first litter bin I passed. That felt better and I continued on my way clutching the handleless case in the crook of my arm. It had served me well all these years and curiously it felt more as if I was carrying a faithful old dog to the vet.

Church of St. Mark, Derby Road,
Portsmouth © Wells-Thorpe and Partners